# Strategic Human Resource Management and Organisational Development

# STRATEGIC HUMAN RESOURCE MANAGEMENT AND ORGANISATIONAL DEVELOPMENT


**Dr. Ramakanta K. Patra**

*B.A., M.A., LL.B. (Professional).*
Director,
DSMS Business School,
Durgapur, West Bengal.



**First Edition : 2011**

Himalaya Publishing House

MUMBAI • NEW DELHI • NAGPUR • BENGALURU • HYDERABAD • CHENNAI • PUNE • LUCKNOW • AHMEDABAD • ERNAKULAM • BHUBANESWAR • INDORE • KOLKATA • GUWAHATI

**First Edition : 2011**

---

**Published by** : Mrs. Meena Pandey for **Himalaya Publishing House Pvt. Ltd.,**
"Ramdoot", Dr. Bhalerao Marg, Girgaon, **Mumbai - 400 004.**
Phone: 022-23860170/23863863, Fax: 022-23877178
**E-mail: himpub@vsnl.com; Website: www.himpub.com**

**Branch Offices** :

**New Delhi** : "Pooja Apartments", 4-B, Murari Lal Street, Ansari Road, Darya Ganj, New Delhi - 110 002. Phone: 011-23270392, 23278631; Fax: 011-23256286

**Nagpur** : Kundanlal Chandak Industrial Estate, Ghat Road, Nagpur - 440 018. Phone: 0712-2738731, 3296733; Telefax: 0712-2721215

**Bengaluru** : No. 16/1 (Old 12/1), 1st Floor, Next to Hotel Highlands, Madhava Nagar, Race Course Road, Bengaluru - 560 001. Phone: 080-32919385; Telefax: 080-22286611

**Hyderabad** : No. 3-4-184, Lingampally, Besides Raghavendra Swamy Matham, Kachiguda, Hyderabad - 500 027. Phone: 040-27560041, 27550139; Mobile: 09848130433

**Chennai** : No. 85/50, Bazullah Road, T. Nagar, Chennai - 600 017. Phone: 044-28144004/28144005

**Pune** : First Floor, "Laksha" Apartment, No. 527, Mehunpura, Shaniwarpeth (Near Prabhat Theatre), Pune - 411 030. Phone: 020-24496323/24496333

**Lucknow** : Jai Baba Bhavan, Church Road, Near Manas Complex and Dr. Awasthi Clinic, Aliganj, Lucknow - 226 024. Phone: 0522-2339329, 4068914; Mobile: 09305302158, 09415349385, 09389593752

**Ahmedabad** : 114, "SHAIL", 1st Floor, Opp. Madhu Sudan House, C.G. Road, Navrang Pura, Ahmedabad - 380 009. Phone: 079-26560126; Mobile: 09327324149, 09314679413

**Ernakulam** : 39/104 A, Lakshmi Apartment, Karikkamuri Cross Rd., Ernakulam, Cochin - 622011, Kerala. Phone: 0484-2378012, 2378016; Mobile: 09344199799

**Bhubaneswar** : 5 Station Square, Bhubaneswar (Odisha) - 751 001. Mobile: 09861046007

**Indore** : Kesardeep Avenue Extension, 73, Narayan Bagh, Flat No. 302, IIIrd Floor, Near Humpty Dumpty School, Narayan Bagh, Indore - 452 007 (M.P.). Mobile: 09301386468

**Kolkata** : 108/4, Beliaghata Main Road, Near ID Hospital, Opp. SBI Bank, Kolkata - 700 010, Phone: 033-32449649, Mobile: 09910440956

**Guwahati** : House No. 15, Behind Pragjyotish College, Near Sharma Printing Press, P.O. Bharalumukh, Guwahati - 781009. (Assam). Mobile: 09883055590, 09883055536

**DTP by** : HPH, Editorial Office, Bhandup (Priyanka)

**Printed by** : Shri Krishna offset Press Delhi-93

# DEDICATION

**Dedicated to Students, Managers, and My Family Members**

**My Mother**

**Late Smt. Yashoda Patra**

# Perface

Liberalization and privatization have brought about changes in the business environment, resulting in heightened competition and growth of the services sector. Changes in political, economic, social, technological, and employment environments over the past decade have caused organizations to confront several unique challenges to survive and to excel. Human Resource Management (HRM) has been the focus of intensive research recently, and in India too, management of the human resources is slowly moving into a strategic realm. The basic aim of this book is provide a comprehensive knowledge related to the concept of strategic HRM with special reference to Indian context. The book tries to analyze the concept of Strategic HRM from micro and macro perspectives and its effectiveness with respect to organizational performance. The broad plan followed in this book is to look at strategic Human Resources (HR) policies and practices, the various dimensions of strategic HRM and to incorporate the recent researches done on the topic. The book also examines the perception of Indian managers and the role of strategic HRM in Indian as well as global organizations operating in India. The book, further discusses case studies from Indian and foreign global organizations operating in India.

An attempt has been made to deal with the subject matter comprehensively and efforts have been made to concise it. The book is presented in twentyone chapters. In this book, the focus is on the reality of "people management" in large, complex companies considered world class in their management of people. All are among the top five best performing organizations within their sector in India. In their diversity, they represent the kind of large organizations found in the western world and face the challenges of present-day globalization. It is an attempt to reflect on the experiences, concerns and aspirations of people at all levels in these companies in India. This book will be of help to students, teachers, policy makers and practitioners of management in India. This book is intended to be a basic text book for all undergraduate and postgraduate students as a course of study, besides also being useful to practicing HR professional and managers.

**Dr. Ramakanta K. Patra**

# Contents

# Part – I

# 1 Concept of HRM

To understand strategic HRM, it is necessary to have a firsthand knowledge of HRM. This chapter, however, starts with a working definition of HRM and continues with sections describing the origins of the concept and its subsequent development, and next summarizing the reservations expressed about it. The differences, if any, between HRM and Personnel Management, as practiced today and how HRM has been assimilated into personnel management are then explored.

## Definition of HRM

HRM can be defined as a strategic and coherent approach to the management of an organisation's most valued assets – the people working there who individually and collectively contribute to the achievement of its objectives.

### Categories of HRM Theories

Guest (1997) has identified three categories of HRM theory:

- Strategic theory, which identifies key environmental influences on HRM (Hendry and Pettigrew, 1990) or classifies HR strategy in relation to models of corporate strategy such as those produced by Miles and Snow (1978) and Porter (1980).
- Descriptive theory, which sets out to describe HRM in a comprehensive way by classifying the content, as did Beer et al (1984).
- Normative theories, which are more prescriptive in their approach. These include those advanced by Walton (1985) advocating a mutual commitment approach, and the best practice list of Prefer (1994).

## Hard and Soft varieties of HRM

The hard approach to HRM emphasises that people are important resources through which organisations achieve competitive advantage. These resources have therefore to be acquired, developed and deployed in ways that will benefit the organisation. The focus is on the quantitative, calculative and business strategic aspects of managing human resources is as 'rational' a way as for any other economic factor. It regards people as human capital from which a return can be obtained by investing judiciously in their development.

**Soft HRM** – The soft model of HRM traces its roots to the human relations school, and emphasises communication, motivation, and leadership. The soft approach HRM stresses the need to gain the commitment – the 'hearts and minds' – of employees through involvement, communication and other methods of developing a high commitment, high-trust organisation.

## Matching Model of HRM

One of the first explicit statements of the HRM concept was made by Fombrun et al (1984), part of the Michigan school. They held that HR systems and the organisation structure should be managed in a way that is congruent with organisational strategy, and hence, it is favoured by 'matching model'. They further explained that there is a human resource cycle which consists of four generic processes or functions that are performed in all organisations. These are :

- selection – matching available human resource to jobs
- appraisal – assessing performance
- rewards – the reward system is one of the most underutilized and mishandled managerial tools for driving organisational performance. It must reward short as well as long-term achievements, bearing in mind that business must perform in the present to succeed in the future.
- development – developing high quality employees.

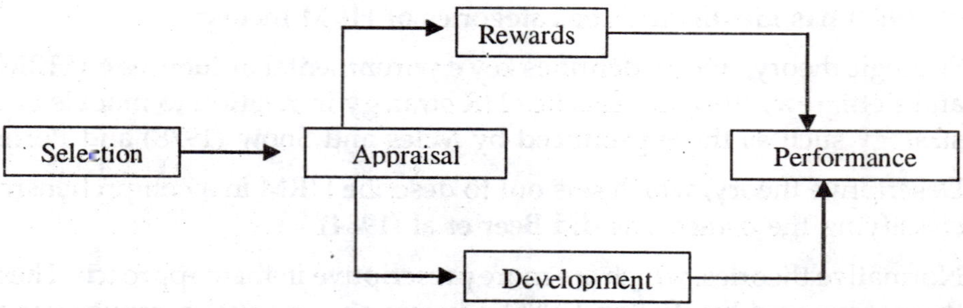


**Fig. HR Cycle**

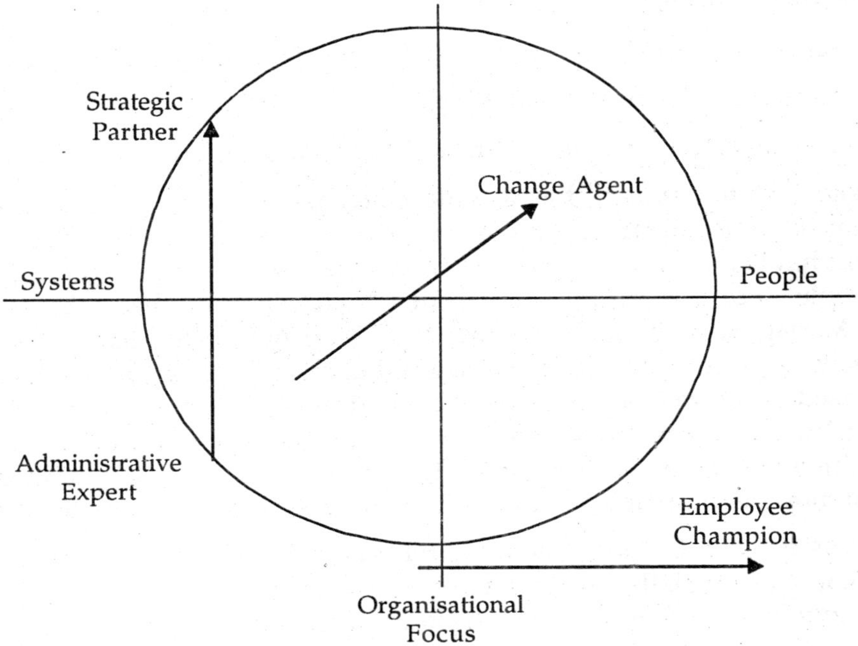


**Fig. HR as Business Partner Strategic Focus**

Human Resource Management encompasses those activities designed to provide for and co-ordinate the human resources of an organisation. The human resources of an organisation represent its largest investment. In fact, government report shows that approximately 73.0 per cent of national income is used to compensate employees. In addition to wages and salaries, organisations often make other sizeable investment in their human resource. Recruiting, hiring and training represent some of the more obvious examples. Human resource management is a modern term for what has traditionally been referred to as personnel administration or personnel management. The meaning of Human and Person can be abbreviated as below:

**HUMAN**

H = Head with the human beings

U = Urges of higher nature

M = Memory (comparatively being lasting)

A = Analytical Mind

N = Norms (Social, Economic, Political and Organisational)

**PERSON**

P = Peculiarities of Labour - Perishability of Colour

E = Emotional

R = Relating (Through McGregar)

S = Sensitive, Superstitious, Supportive (group formation), Suggestive.

O = Objectives (Individual's and group's)

N = Norms (Social, Economic, Political, Organisational, Cultural and Historical).

The form "Management" has a wide concept, and it is pivotal to know what management is before detailed discussion on Human Resource Management (HRM). Management has been defined by Mary Parker Floett as, "The art of getting things done through people". But it is felt that management is much more than what is said in this definition. Management is further defined as "That field of human behaviour which manages them, organise, staff, direct and control human, physical and financial resources in an organised effort, in order to achieve desired individual and group objectives with optimum efficiency and effectiveness". The term, human resources is quite popular in India with the introduction of 'Ministry of Human Resource Development' in the Union Cabinet. But most people may not know what exactly the term 'Human Resources' means.

According to Leon C. Megginson, the term human resources can be thought of as, "The total knowledge, skills, creative abilities, talents and aptitudes and beliefs of the individuals involved". The term human resource can also be explained in the sense that it is resource fix any natural resource. It does mean that the management can get and use the skill, knowledge, ability, etc. Through the development of skills, tapping and utilising them again and again. Thus, it is a long term perspective, whereas personnel is a short term perspective. Human resources are also regarded as human factor, human asset, human capital and the like. The terms labour and manpower had been used widely denoting mostly the physical abilities and capacities of employees. The term personnel had been used widely in the recent past to denote persons employed in any services. Thus, this term denotes the employee as a whole but it does not clearly denote various components of human resources like skill, knowledge, values etc.

## Personnel vs. Human Resources at Various Levels

At the macro level the term human resources stands for the total sum of all the components (like skill, and creative ability) possessed by all the people (employed, sub-employed, unemployed, employers, owners etc.) whereas the form personnel even at the macro level is limited to only employees of all organisations. Human resources even at the organisational level includes all the component resources of all employees from rank and file to top management level, all the employees like managing director, board of directors, persons who work on honorary basis, experts drawn from different organisations, and those people (particularly family members) influencing the human resources of the group. In short, it includes the resource of all the people who contribute their services to the attainment of organisational goals and others who contribute their services inorder to create hurdles in the attainment of organisational goods. Further, human resources include human values, ethos and the like.

Thus, the human resources is much more broader than the term personnel either at the components level or in organisational level or even at the macro level. Hence, human resources management at organisational level (Man, Machine, Money, Materials and Methodology) tasks mean management of the dynamic compounds (resources) of all the people, may it be the owner or employment or directly or indirectly related at all levels in the organisational hierarchy round the clock and throughout the year.

**Personnel vs. Human Resource Management**

| Personnel Management | Human Resource Management |
|---|---|
| Personnel means persons employed. Personnel Management is the management of people employed. | Human Resource Management, is the management of employees skills, knowledge, abilities, talents, aptitudes, creative abilities etc. |
| Employee in personnel management is mostly treated as an economic man as his services are exchanged for wage/salary. | Employee in human resource management is treated not only as economic man but also as social and psychological man. Thus, the complete man is viewed under this approach. |
| Employee is views as a commodity or tool or equipment which can be purchased and used. | Employee is treated as a resource. |
| Employees are treated as cost centre and therefore management controls the cost of labour. | Employees are treated as a profit centre and therefore, invests capital for human resource development and future utility. |
| Employees are used mostly for organisational benefit | Employees are used for the multiple mutual benefit of the organisation, employees and their family members. |
| Personnel function is treated as only an auxiliary. | Human Resource Management is a strategic management function. |

From the above discussion, it has been observed that the traditional concept of Personnel Department has been replaced with Human Resource Management. As a research, the Department of Commerce, Schools of Management Studies, Department of Personnel Management in various universities have begun calling this academic area as Human Resource Management (HRM). Still, this process is in the state of transition.

## Meaning of Human Resource Management

Different scholars have frequently used various terms regarding human resource management, *viz.*, labour management, labour administration, labour management relations, employee-employer relations, industrial relations, personnel administration, personnel management, human capital management, human asset management, human resource management and so on. Though these terms can be differentiated widely, the basic nature of distinction lies in the scope or coverage and evolutionary stage. In simple sense, human resource management means employing people, developing their resources, utilising, maintaining and compensating their services in term with the job and organisational requirements.

Institute of Personnel Management, U.K. as defined and subsequently adopted by Indian Institute of Personnel Management is as below:

"Personnel Management is a responsibility of all those who manage people as well as being a description of the work of those who are employed as specialists. It is that part of management which is concerned with people at work and with their relationships within an enterprise. It applies not only to industry and commerce but to all fields of employment".

The definition given above can be summarised as below:

1. Personnel Management is a responsibility of all line managers in an organisation, *viz.*, general manager, production manager, marketing manager, finance manager, etc., and it is a staff function, i.e., it is the function of personnel manager who is appointed as a specialist. Thus, all managers in the organisations are vitally concerned with personnel management as they must achieve organisational goals through other peoples' efforts.
2. Personnel Management is a part of management. This part is concerned with the people and their relationship within an organisation.
3. This applies to all organisations in the universe, i.e., economic, social, political, religious, etc.

## Evolution of Human Resource Management

The development of personnel management in U.K. and USA was largely voluntary. But in India, it emerged because of governmental interventions and compulsions. In the beginning of 20th Century, various malpractices in the recruitment of workers and payment of wages were prevalent which caused a colossal loss in production due to industrial disputes. The Royal Commission on Labour in India (1931) under the Chairmanship of J.H. Whitley recommended the abolition of the 'Jobber' system and the appointment of labour officers in industrial enterprises to perform the recruitment function as well as to look after the welfare of the employees. After independence, the labour welfare officer was identified with the personnel manager created by legislation under Section 49 of the Factories Act., 1849. Evolving along the years, a new approach the human resource management has emerged.

## Human Resource Management

Concern with the management of manpower or human resources has engaged the attention of social scientists, economists, researchers, executives as well as management thinkers since the early 19th century till the modern times. Robert Owen (1771-1858), who successfully managed one of the largest spinning wills in Scotland, introduced and later on initiated a reformist movement for the improvement of the workers' conditions. He aimed at making the spinning mill, which he managed for more than 25 years, not merely an efficient factory, but a well-governed human community, based on good living. In his mill employees were given all the benefits. It was his duty to ensure them all the means of good living to pay good wages to avoid unreasonably long hours of work, to provide good houses and good food and clothing and reasonable prices, to make the factory village a sanitary and pleasant place and, above all, to ensure to the children, whether employed in the factory or not, the best education that sympathy and knowledge could place at their command. In-spite of the reformist zeal of owner, however, the impact of the workers cause, which he upheld, was not binding except for the enactment of factory legislation for the protection of workers and the trade union movement which were inspired by him.

Although Charles Babbage and Henry Towde, after Robert Owen, contributed towards the formulation of a science of management, and also considered matters relevant to man-management, it was Frederick Taylor who pioneered the introduction of scientific methods in management more consistently than others. The ideas of Taylor and his associates were founded essentially on the principle of specialisation through division of work. Taylor not only proposed that work be divided into simple routine and repetitive tasks so as to utilise minimum skills and abilities of workmen. He was also in favour of specialisation of managerial jobs, along-with standardisation of working conditions, machines and tools. To quote, "each man from the assistant superintendent down shall have as few functions as possible to perform (and) if practicable, the work of each man in the management should be confined to the performance of a single leading function". Taylor also introduced, and his associates (Gantt, Frank and Lillian Gilberth, Cooke and Emerson) refined, the incentive schemes of wage payment to bring about correspondence between efficiency and compensation. Taylor's ideas were widely accepted and practised in the Unites States and Western Europe. However, Taylorism met with strong criticism with the emergence of the Human Relations School and the behavioural approach to the problems of Human Resource Management. "The gravest weakness (of specialisation)", James Worthy observed, "was the failure of recognise and utilize property management's most valuable resources, the complex and multiple capacities of people. On the contrary, the scientific managers deliberately sought to utilise as narrow a band of personality and as narrow a range of ability as ingenuity could devise. The process has been fantastically wasteful for industry and society". It was, thus, contended that the fragmentation and routinisation of work to the point where it loses significance has dire implications. The organisation may suffer because the rewards for submissive compliances produce apathy, indifference, non-involvement, and alienation on the part of workers. They become highly dependent and incapable of solving problems and making decisions. The organisation may become rigid and its members unwilling to accept and adapt to changes necessary for growth and changing socio-economic conditions.

In the work of Taylor's principles of scientific management, other classical writers, including Mooney and Reiby, Max Weber, Gullick and Urwick, emphasised the significance of the structure of organisation and the span of management to be essential for effective supervision, management and control. They also emphasised the importance of the formal organisation, based on grouping of similar activities, followings revealed that the grouping of persons according to similarities in their work may be contrary to the natural development of human organisation for people often tend naturally to organise on a basis other than the technical requirements of work. They may organise in terms of sentiments, social customs, codes of behaviour, status, friendships, cliques. In other words, co-operation may flow more in terms of the natural relationship of informal organisation and not necessarily on groupings based on work arrangements and/or economic incentives. Thus, an organisation may function best and the members highly motivated when people in the organisation hold overlapping group membership. A restricted span of control, postulated by classical management thinkers, has been pointed out as a source of contradiction with the principle that there should be few levels in the managerial hierarchy so as to reduce the administrative distance between the individuals and, thus, to reduce red tape, waste of time and efforts. A narrow span inevitably leads to an increase in the number of levels of management for a growing concern.

The implicit assumption of the classical approach to manpower management was that the ability of the individual corresponds to the formal authority of the function. In other words, it was assumed that authority tends to equal the capacity of the people actually performing organisational function. A rational programme of personnel administration was expected to promote the tendency on a closer examination. This proposition was found to defend upon the sufficiency of administrative information regarding the job content and individual capacities. The neo classical thinking questioned the proposition on two grounds. They feel that the individual capacity could not be assessed easily and it was difficult to bring about a proper match between individual ability and career opportunities in the organisation. Moreover, the logic of formal relationships was not the only logic prevailing in human organisations. The system of power network of influence and the decision making processes were after known to be at variance with the system prescribed by the formal authority structure.

## Case Study

### Kansha Laboratories Ltd, Bhadarpur

Munna Lal was working as an accountant at Kansha Laboratories Ltd. Bhadarpur for nearly three years. When his boss retired in the year 2000, R.K. Tandon, the company's president, asked Munna Lal to take over the charge of the Accounts department, and being head of the accounts department of the company, he has to supervise eight employees working in his department.

After one year of taking over his new job, it has been very easy to work with all the eight employees. All of them have been in their jobs for at least 3 – 4 years. They knew their jobs very well, and they required very little time from Munna Lal for guidance. Because of Munna Lal's personal care and concern, everyone in the department had high regards for him.

Rekha, one of the employees in the department unfortunately become a completely different story just after a year of Mr. Munna Lal's occupying the accounts department. She is the senior most in the department. She is brilliant and very good looking. Though her age and education are not significantly different from her other seven colleagues, she commands a lot of respect from them. When she used to finish her work she was helping others in completing their jobs. Rekha is in her early 30s. She was the university topper in B.Com with accounting honours. But in the last few months she has become headache for Mr. Munna Lal due to her unplanned leave and sudden absence from the office as well as piled up pending works.

Rekha's job is to handle general records of accounts department. She also acts as the accounts department's link to the service department. She provides advice and support to service on anything having to do with credit, cost control, the computer system, and the like. She also looks after the TA and DA account of the complaints from sales department about non-clearance of their traveling bills. Some employees have even sent written complaints to the president about the delay in clearing of their bills.

The first sign of the seriousness of the problem began three weeks ago. Rekha filled in sick on both Friday and Saturday. Including Sunday she was on leave for three consecutive days, but she came to work on Tuesday morning. She was looking like she had not slept in all these days. Mr. Munna Lal called her into his cabin and in an informal manner tried to find out what was going on. She was very open, and admitted that she had not been ill. She reported in sick because she did not have the emotional strength to come to work. She shared her ongoing problem that her present marriage was in trouble. Her husband is a chronic drunkard, and for that reason he has lost his third job in the past couple of months. Total liability of the family was on her shoulder, including her children and other elderly family members. She had one school going son and two younger daughters. Mr. Munna Lal encouraged her to keep her spirits up and assured to help her within the framework of company's existing HR policy.

Munna Lal was keeping a vigil on Rekha's movements in the office, and found minor impact, and she had taken three more days medical leave. But it is visible from her face that in the office that she still is absent minded, and spends inordinate amount of time on the telephone. All the problems are nothing but her personal life situation, and it was found that sometimes Rekha became emotional and wept in the office.

Yesterday was the third working day of the new month. Rekha should have completed the closing of last month's books yesterday, which is an important part of her job. This morning, soon after she arrived in the office, Mr. Munna Lal asked about the progress of her work. She got up and her eyes filled with tears, went to the ladies' room. Munna Lal found that last month's books are still lying on her table. He opened them up, and found them incomplete. She has already failed to complete within the deadline, and Munna Lal failed to understand, how to complete the same and submit to the top management.

## Questions

1. Do you think that Mr. Munna Lal is doing the work of personal management or personnel management?
2. Is it necessary for a manager to manage the personal matters of employees rather than personnel matters in an organisation? If so, why, and if not, why?
3. Mr. Munna Lal should have taken action for failing to meet the deadline by Mrs. Rekha – What do you think?
4. Suppose you are in the position of Mr. Munna Lal, what action would you have taken?

## References


- Dr. Nageshwar Rao, Dr. R.P. Das, *Cases in Human Resource Management*, Himalaya Publishing House, 2002.


***

# 2 Concept of Strategy and Strategic HRM

## The Concept of Strategy

Strategic HRM, though it is based on HRM principles, it incorporates the concept of strategy and we should know the origin and evolution of the concept of strategy.

'Strategy' derived as a military term, and as per Oxford English Dictionary it is :

The art of a Commander-in-Chief, the art of projecting and directing the larger military movements and operations of a campaign.

The basic meaning of strategy is that it is an art, and the ultimate responsibility for it lies with the head of the organisation. A strategy can be defined as a pattern or plan that integrates an organisation's major goals, policies and action sequences into a cohesive whole. A well formulated strategy helps to marshal and allocate an organisation's resources into a unique and viable posture based on its relative internal competencies and shortcomings, anticipated changes in the environment, and contingent moves by intelligent opponents.

Business or corporate strategies consist of statements of what the organisation wants to become, where it wants to go, and broadly, the means to get there. In its crudest form, strategy in a commercial enterprise answers the questions 'what business are we in?' and 'over the longer term, how are we going to make money out of it?' In a public sector or non-profit making organisation, these questions might be phrased as 'what is the purpose of this organisation, and over the longer term how are we going to achieve that purpose?'

The concept of strategy is not a straightforward one. There are many different theories about what it is and how it works. Strategy can have a number of meanings :

- a plan, or something equivalent - a direction, a guide, a course of action.
- a pattern – an organisations fundamental way of doing things.
- a ploy – a specific 'manoeuvre' intended to outwit an opponent or a competitor.

## Fundamentals of Strategy

Fundamentally, strategy is concerned with achieving competitive advantage. Formulating a strategy to do so requires defining intentions (strategic intent) and allocating or matching resources to opportunities (resource based strategy). Thus achieving strategic fit between them. The effective development and implementation of strategy depends on the strategic capability of the organisation, which will include the ability not only to determine strategic goals but also to develop and implement strategic plans through the process of strategic management.

**Competitive advantage** arises when a firm creates value for its customers. To achieve it, firms select markets in which they can excel and present a moving target in front of their competitors by continually improving their position.

### Importance of competitive advantage

- differentiation, which consists of offering a product or service that is perceived industrywise as being unique.
- focus – seeing a particular buyer group or product market more effectively or efficiently than competitors who compete more broadly.

### How to gain competitive advantage?

- innovation – being the unique producer.
- quality – delivering high quality goods and services to customers.
- cost leadership – the planned result of policies aimed at managing away expense.

**Strategic Intent** can be described as an expression of purpose – what the organisation intends to do and how. It can be sequencewise be described as under :

1. a broad vision of what the organisation should be.
2. the organisation's mission.
3. specific goals, which are operationalized as.
4. strategic objectives.

**Strategic fit:** The concept of strategic fit implies that to maximise competitive advantage of firm must match its capabilities and resources to the opportunities available in the external environment. A critical aspect of top managements work today involves matching organisational competeness (internal resources and skills) with the opportunities and risks created by environmental change in ways that will be both effective and efficient over the time such resources will be deployed.

**Resource based strategy:** The resource based view of strategy is that the strategic capability of a firm depends on its resource capability, especially its distinctive resources. The resource based view of the firm emphasises on the distinctive human resource practices that help to create unique competeness which differentiate products and services and in turn, drive competitiveness. Indeed, the whole theory of resource based strategy, with its focus on distinctive capabilities, underpins the concept of strategic HRM by emphasising that the unique and non-imitable resources that create competitive advantage are the human resources of the organisation.

**Strategic capabilities** is a concept that refers to the ability of an organisation to develop and implement strategies that will achieve sustained competitive advantage. It is therefore about the capacity to select the most appropriate vision, to define realistic intentions, to match resources to opportunities, and to prepare and implement strategic plans.

**Formulation of strategy:** The formulation of corporate strategy can be defined as a process for developing and defining a sense of direction. It has often been described as a logical step-by-step affair, the outcome of which is a formed written statement that provides a definitive guide to the organisations long-term intentions. Many people still believe and act as if this were the case but it is a misrepresentation of reality.

## Systematic approach to formulating strategy

In theory, the process of formulating strategy consists of the following steps :

1. Define the mission.
2. Set objectives.
3. Conduct internal and external environmental scans to assess internal strengths and weaknesses and external opportunities and threats (a SWOT analysis) and to analyse political, economic, social, technological, legal and environmental factors (a PESTLE analysis).
4. Analyse existing strategies to determine their relevance in the light of the internal and external appraisal. This may include gap analysis, which will establish the extent to which environmental factors might lead to gaps between what would be achieved if no changes were made and what needs to be achieved. The analysis would also cover resource capability, answering the question 'Have we sufficient human or financial resources available now, or which can readily be made available in the future, to enable us to achieve our objective'.
5. Define in the light of this analysis the distinctive capabilities of the organisation.
6. Define the key strategic issues emerging from the previous analysis. These will focus on such matters as product market scope, enhancing shareholder value, and resource capability.
7. Define corporate and functional strategies for achieving goals and competitive advantage, taking into account the key strategic issues. These may include business strategies for growth or diversification, or broad generic strategies for growth or diversification, or broad generic strategies for innovation, quality or cost leadership, or they could take the form of specific corporate/functional strategies concerned with product market scope, technological development or human resource development.

8. Prepare integrated strategic plans for implementing strategies.
9. Implement the strategies.
10. Monitor implementation and revise existing strategies or develop new strategies that is needed.

## Types of Strategy

- Classical – strategy formulation as a rational process of deliberate calculation, the process of strategy formulation is perceived as being separate from the implementation.
- Evolutionary – strategy formulation as a evolutionary process that is a product of market for us in which the most efficient and productive organisations wade through.
- Processual – strategy formulation as an incremental process which evolves through discussion and disagreement. It may be impossible to specify what the strategy is until after the event.
- Systematic – strategy is shaped by the social system in which it is embedded. Choices are constrained by the cultural and institutional interests of a broader society that by the limitations of those attempting to formulate corporate strategy.

**Strategic Management:** The concepts of strategy management and its main characteristics are operationalized by strategic management. This can be regarded as a continuing process which in theory consists of a sequence of activities – strategy formulation, strategic planning, implementation, review, and updating – but in practice, as noted above, is seldom applied so logically.

Strategic management means that managers are looking ahead at what they need to achieve in the middle or relatively distant future. They are concerned with the broader issues facing the organisation and the general directions in which they must go to deal with these issues and achieve longer term objectives. They do not take a narrow or restricted view.

Strategic management deals with both ends and means. As its ends it describes a vision of what things should look like in a few years time. As a means, it shows how it is expected that the vision will be realized. Strategic management is therefore visionary management concerned with creating and conceptualizing ideas of where the organisation should be going, but it is also empirical management which decides how in practice it is going to get there, bearing in mind that organisations exist in a constant state of change.

Strategic management can be summarised as:

- The full scope of an organisation's activities, including corporate objectives and organisational boundaries.
- Matching the activities of an organisation to the environment in which it operates.

- Ensuring that the internal structures, practices and procedures enable the organisation to achieve its objectives.
- Matching the activities of an organisation to its resource capability, assuring the extent to which sufficient resources can be provided to take advantage of opportunities or to avoid threats in the organisation's environment.
- The acquisition divestment and reallocation of resources.
- Translating the complex and dynamic set of external and internal variables which an organisation faces into a structural set of clear future objectives that can then be implemented on a day-to-day bases.

Beyond above theoretical concepts, the reality of manager's attempting to behave strategically in conditions of uncertainty, change, and turbulence, even chaos, can vary from organisation to organisation. Strategic management is as much. If not more, about managing change during the process of implementation as it is about producing long-term corporate plans. Organisations which successfully manage change are these which have integrated their human resource management policies with their strategies and the strategic change process. Training, employee relations, compensation packages and so on are not merely operational issues for the personal department – they are crucially concerned with the way in which employees relate to the nature and direction of the firm, and as such they can both block strategic change and the significant facilitators of strategic change.

From the above discussion, we can say that human resources of an organisation plays a crucial role in achieving change. Simultaneously, it can be concluded from the analysis of strategic management in this chapter that it is as difficult as it is desirable, and this has to be borne in mind at all times when considering strategic HRM.

## The Concept of Strategic HRM

### What is Strategic HRM?

Strategic HRM is an approach to making decisions on the intentions and plans of the organisation concerning the employment relationship and its recruitment, training, development, performance management, record and employee relations strategies, policies and practices. The key characteristics of strategic HRM is that it is integrated. HR strategies are generally integrated vertically with the business strategy and horizontally with one another. The HR strategies developed by a strategic HRM approach are essential components of the organisation's business strategy.

### The Aims of Strategic HRM

Strategic HRM is concerned with the relationship between human resource management and strategic management in the firm. Strategic HRM refers to the overall direction of the organisation's wishes to pursue in order to achieve its goals through people. Because intellectual capital is a major source of competitive advantages and it is people who implement the strategic plan, top management must take these key considerations fully into account in developing its corporate strategies. Strategic HRM is an integral part of those strategies.

Strategic HRM addresses broad organisational issues relating to organisational effectiveness and performance, changes in structure and culture, matching resources to future requirements, the development of distinctive capabilities, knowledge management and the management of change. It is concerned with both meeting human capital requirements and the development of process capabilities, that is, the ability to get things done effectively. Overall, it will consider any major people issues that affect or are affected by the strategic plan of the organisation.

## The Rationale for Strategic HRM

The rationale for strategic HRM is the perceived advantage of having an agreed and understood basis for developing approaches to people management in the longer term. The rationale accepts the fact that the degree to which the concept of strategic HRM can be applied within organisations and its form and content will vary widely. It is understood that organisations may be so pre-occupied with survival and managing the here-and-now that perhaps unwisely — they do not have an articulated corporate or business strategy.

## The meaning of Strategic HRM

According to Hendry and Pettigrew (1986) strategic HRM has four implications as under:

- the use of planning
- a coherent approach to the design and management of personnel systems based on an employment policy and manpower strategy, and after underpinned by a 'philosophy'.
- matching HRM activities and policies to some explicit business strategy.
- seeing the people of the organisation as a 'strategic resource' for the achievement of 'competitive advantage'.

## Resource Based Strategic HRM

The concept of resource-based strategic HRM is based on the ideas of Penrose (1959), who wrote that "the firm is an administrative organisation and a collection of productive resources". The benefit arising from competitive advantage based on the effective management of people is that such an advantage is hard to imitate. An organisation's HR strategies, policies and practices are a unique blend of processes, procedures, personalities, styles, capabilities and organisational culture. One of the keys to competitive advantage is the ability to differentiate what the business supplies to its customers from what is supplied by its competitors. Such differentiation can be achieved by having HR strategies and policies which ensure that (1) the firm has higher quality people than its competitors, (2) the unique intellectual capital possessed by the business is developed and nurtured, (2) organisational learning is encouraged; (4) organisation–specific values and a culture exist that find the organisation together and give it focus.

The aim of a resource bases approach is to improve resource capability – achieving strategic fit between resource and opportunities, and obtaining added value from the effective deployment of resources. In line with intellectual capital theory, resource based theory emphasises that investment in people adds to their value to the firm. Hence, a definition of a business in terms of what it is capable of doing may offer a more durable basis for strategy than a definition based upon the needs (e.g., markets) which the business seeks to satisfy.

**The Formulation Strategy:** The formulation of corporate strategy can be defined as a process for developing and defining a sense of direction. It has often been described as a logical step-by-step affair, the outcome of which is a formal written statement that provides a definitive guide to the organisations long-term intentions.

The two basic approaches to the formulation of HR strategies described below are the classical sequential approach and the empirical needs-based approach. In using these approaches, consideration has to be given to achieving strategic fit, and to be choice between the various models that describe different ways in which HRM can be applied in any organisation.

## The Classical Sequential Approach

This approach generally follows the traditional belief that strategy formulation is a formal, logical, systematic and sequential process:

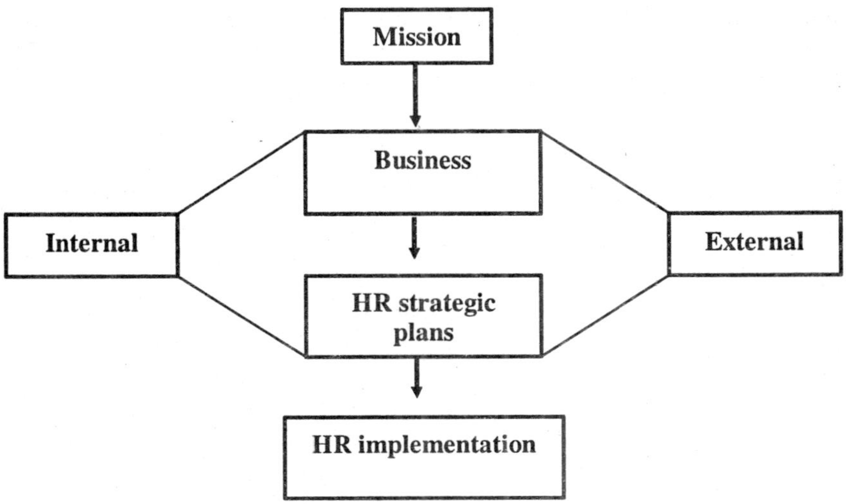


If the required information is available, and mission and business strategies have been articulated, a systematic approach to formulating HR strategies which considers all the relevant business plans and environmental issues has much to commend it such as:

1. **Assess feasibility:** From HR perspective, feasibility depends on whether the numbers and types of key people required to make the proposal succeed can be obtained on a timely basis and at a reasonable cost, and whether the behavioural expectations assumed by the strategy are realistic.
2. **Determine desirability:** Examine the implications of strategy in terms of sacrosanct HR policies (e.g., a strategy of rapid retrenchment would have to be called into question by a company with a no redundancy policy).
3. **Determine goals:** These indicate the main issues to be worked on, and are derived primarily from the content of the business strategy. For example, a strategy to become a lower cost producer would require the reduction of labour costs. This in turn translates into two types of HR goals : higher performance standards (contribution), and reduced headcounts (composition).
4. **Decide means of achieving goals:** The general rule is that the closer the external and internal fit, the better the strategy, consistent with the need to adapt flexibility to change. External fit refers to the degree of consistency between HR goals on the one hand, and the exigencies of the underlying business strategy and relevant environmental conditions on the other. Internal fit measures the extent to which HR means follow the HR goals and other relevant environmental conditions, as well as the degree of coherency or synergy among the various HR means.

## The Empirical needs-based approach

Although systematic approaches such as those mentioned above appear to be desirable, an empirical approach to strategic HRM based on an understanding of the realities of organisation life is more realistic. It could be perceived as an attitude of mind, rather than a step-by-step affair which proceeds by a process of inexorable logic from a mission statement to implementation.

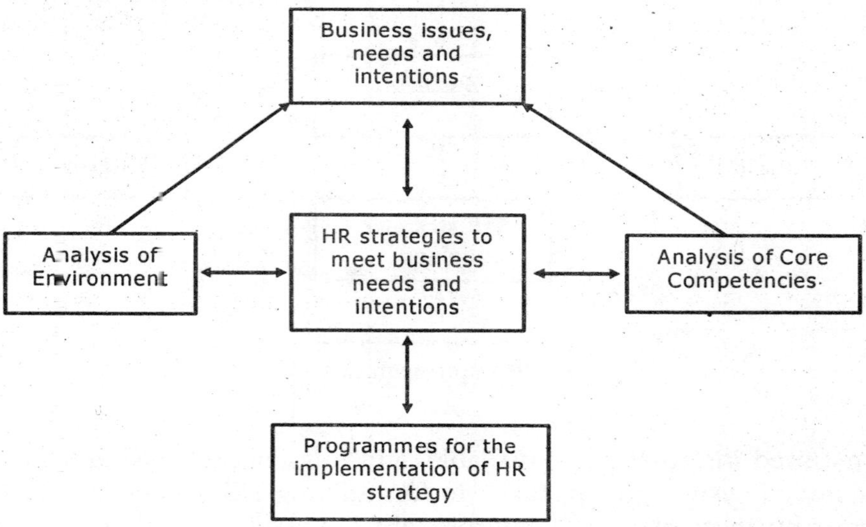

The notion of strategic fit or integration, sometimes described as the matching model, is central to the concept of strategic HRM. The HR strategy should be aligned to the business strategy (vertical fit). Better still, HR strategy should be an integral part of the business strategy, contributing to the business planning process as it happens. Strategic integration is necessary to provide congruence between business and human resource strategy so that the latter supports the accomplishment of the former and, indeed, helps to define it.

Horizontal integration or fit is required between the different elements of the people strategy. The aim is to achieve a coherent approach to managing people in which the various practices are mutually supportive. HR strategies are different, however, in the sense that they are interlinked with all other strategies. The management of people is not a distinct function but the means by which all business strategies are implemented. HR planning should be an integral part of all other strategy formulation. Where it is treated separately, it means nonetheless to be closely aligned.

Five types of *fit* have been identified by Guest (1997) are as under:

- Fit as strategic interaction – linking HR practices to the external context.
- Fit as contingency – approaches which ensure that internal practices should respond to particular external factors such as the nature of the market.
- Fit as an ideal set of practices – the view that there are best practices that all firms can adopt to their convenience.
- Fit as gestalt – an approach that emphasises the importance of finding an appropriate combination of practices.
- Fit as 'bundles' – the search for distinct configurations or 'bundles' of complementary practices in order to determine which is likely to be most effective.

**Vertical fit** – When considering how to integrate business and HR strategies, it has to be kept in mind that business and HR issues influence each other, and in turn influence corporate and business unit strategies. Vertical fit occurs where HR strategies, match the firm's stage of development, take account of organisational dynamics, and are in line with the characteristics of the organization.

**Congruence with Business Strategies:** The whole concept of strategic HRM is predicted on the belief that HR strategies should be integrated with corporate or business strategies. The key is to make operational. The concept of 'fit' – the fit of human resource management with the strategic thrust of the firm. The development of organisational links is an important characteristics of strategic HRM. Congruence with business orientation of the firm. Different organizations require changes in approaches to investing in the firms human capital.

## Matching life cycle stages

Matching the stage of the organisation's development means aligning HR strategy to the business strategies appropriate at each stage of the life cycle of the business – start up, maturity, decline or degeneration, re-generation or transformation. Clearly, the business strategies and the HR strategies will differ, say, between a firm opening up on a green field site and one forced to embark on a comprehensive transformation programme.

**Dynamics:** The dynamics of organisational change exert a marked influence on HR strategies. A transformational programme in any part of the life cycle will indicate what specific organisational development and culture management strategies the organisation should adopt. Managing the transition between the present state and a future state will mean the development of change strategies and, possibly, new strategic approaches to the employment relationship. HR strategies may have to be developed to support business initiatives in such areas as total quality, customer care, organisational restructuring, process re-engineering, product/market development, and require the introduction of new technology or production systems, e.g., computer integrated manufacturing or just-in-time production.

## Organisational characteristics

An alternate way of determining HR strategy requirements is to relate them to the overall characteristics of the organisation. The most familiar classifications produced by Miller and Snow (1978) is:

- 'defenders' who seek stability and believe in strict control
- 'prospectors' who seek new opportunities, focus on continuous development and believe in flexibility.
- 'analysers' who seek to incorporate the benefits of both defenders and prospectors.

## Difficulties in achieving vertical integration

Vertical integration (strategic fit between business and HR strategies) may be desirable but the difficulties to achieve are as under:

- The diversity of strategic processes, levels and styles
- The complexity of the strategy formulation process
- The evolutionary nature of the business strategy
- The absence of articulated business strategies
- The qualitative nature of HR issues
- Differing definitions of what is to integrate with

## The diversity of strategic process, levels and styles

The different levels as which strategy is formulated and the different styles adopted by organisations may make it difficult to develop a coherent view of what sort of HR strategies will fit the overall strategies and what type of HR contributions are required during the process of formulation. To achieve competitive advantage, each business unit in a diversified corporation should tailor its HRM policy to its own product market conditions, irrespective of the HRM policies being pursued elsewhere in the corporation. If this is the case, there may be coherence within a limit but not across the whole organisation, and it may be difficult to focus HR strategies on corporate needs. The only time a serious problem is likely to emerge is when units have to be merged. Admittedly, synergy may have to be sacrificed and the organisation might not reap the benefits of a corporate management development and career planning strategies. But the choice on that has been made by those who are in organisational command, and if it is their loss, it is only they who can do anything about it.

## Complexity of the strategy formulation process

Strategy formulation and implementation is a complex interactive process – heavily influenced by a variety of contextual and historical factors. In these circumstances how can there be a straightforward flow from the business strategy to HR strategy? It has been pointed out by Truss (1999) that an assumption in some matching models of strategic HRM is that there is a simple linear relationship between business strategy and human resources strategy. But this assumption fails to acknowledge the complexities both between and within notions of strategy and human resource management, and is based on a rational model of organisations and individuals which takes no account of the significance of power, politics and culture.

## Evolutionary nature of business strategy

This phenomenon, and the incremental nature of strategy making, may make it difficult to pin down the HR issues likely to be relevant. HR strategies may well therefore be equally evolutionary and just as difficult to pin down to a set of definitive statements. If this is the case, not to bother to peak the holy grail of strategic fit, which presupposes a certain rigidity that is not in keeping with the realities of organisational life and the chaotic conditions in which organisations have to subsist?

## Absence of articulated business strategies

If, because of its evolutionary nature, the business strategy has not been clearly articulated, this would add to the problems of clarifying the business strategic issues that human resource strategies should address. But it should be noted that 'clearly articulated' in this context means that the business strategies are fully understood by those concerned. It does not mean that they have to be written down, although that may help to create understanding.

## Qualitative nature of HR issues

Business strategies tend, or at least aim to be expressed in the common currency of figures and hard data on portfolio management, growth, competition may deal with quantifiable issues such as resourcing and skill acquisition but are equally likely to refer to qualitative factors such as commitment, motivation, good employee relations and high employment standards. The relationship between the pursuit of policies in these areas and individual and organisational performance may be difficult to establish.

## Integration with what?

The concept of strategic HRM implies that HR strategies must be totally integrated with corporate/business strategies in the sense that both of them flow from and contribute to such strategies. But as Brewster (1993) argues, HR strategy may be subjected to considerable environmental pressures for example, in India, by legislation over involvement. Pressures of this type may mean that HR strategies cannot be entirely governed by the corporate/business strategy.

The question may also arise, 'To what latest should HR strategies take into account the interests of all the stakeholders in the organisation, employees in general as well as owners and management? There is now a growing realisation that the overriding concern should be the yield from employees. Yield concentrates on the intricate well of costs and benefits that result from investing in and focusing human resource activities toward a certain set of activities and away from other behaviours and altitudes. Yield recognizes both trade-offs and choices. Yield depends on shared responsibilities and collaboration across functional units and hierarchical levels. Ideally, strategic integration should attempt to achieve a proper balance between the hard and soft elements. The emphasis may be in achieving corporate or business objectives, but it should be a process of planning with people in mind, taking into account the needs and aspirations of all the members of the organization.

Whereas finding the Holy Grail of strategic fit may be desirable, it is still essential to appreciate how resource-based and intellectual capital theories' uniform approaches the development of integrated HR strategies by providing a conceptual framework within which HR strategies that achieve strategic fit can be developed.

## Resource-based strategic HRM

The concept of resource based strategic HRM strategy is derived from the resource-based theory of business strategy. The concept is founded on the belief that competitive advantage is obtained if a firm can obtain and develop human resources that enable it to learn faster and apply its learning more effectively than its rivals.

The aim of a resource-based approach is to improve resource capability – achieving strategic fit between resources and opportunities and obtain added value from the effective deployment of resources. Resource-based theory provides a rationale for strategic HRM but does not attempt to prescribe solutions.

In line with intellectual capital theory, resource-based theory emphasises that investment in people adds to their value to the firm. Resource-based HR strategy can develop strategic capability. The strategic goal will be to 'create firms which are more intelligent and flexible than their competitors by hiring and developing more talented staff and by extending their skill base. Resource-based strategic HRM is therefore concerned with the enhancement of the intellectual capital of a firm.

Knowledge has become a direct competitive advantage for firms selling ideas and relationships. The challenge to organisations is to ensure that they have the capability to find, assimilate, compensate and retain the talented individuals they need. Unique talents among employees, including superior performance, productivity, flexibility, innovation, and the ability to deliver high levels of personal customer service are ways in which people provide a critical ingredient in developing an organisation's competitive position. People also provide the key to managing the pivotal interdependencies across functional activities and the important external relationships. It can be argued that one of the clear benefits arising from competitive advantage based on the effective management of people is that such an advantage is hard to imitate. An organization's HR strategies, policies and practices are a unique blend of processes, procedures, personalities, styles, capabilities and organisational culture. One of the keys to competitive advantage is the ability to differentiate what the business supplies to its customers from what could be supplied to them by its competitors. Such differentiation can be achieved by having HR strategies which ensure that the firm has higher quality people than its competitors, by developing and nurturing the intellectual capital possessed by the business, and by focusing on organisation learning.

It is strategic capability that significantly determines the extent to which the organisation achieves the best possible fit between the unique tangible and intangible assets that it possesses and the competitive position it occupies in its environment. It involves selecting resources, and combinations of resources, most likely to generate the new strategic assets of the business.

## Conclusions

Resource-based strategy can provide a strong base for strategic HRM. It is to do with internal implementation and performance strategies, and change is also important in HRM strategies since their concern is with the future, the unknown, thinking of and learning how to do things differently, undoing the ways things have been done in the past and managing its implementation. This supports the argument that the processes of formulating and implementing HR strategies are mainly about making decisions on what needs to be changed and managing those changes. It is, however, worth bearing in mind that HRM is concerned with the delivery of effective people management services as well as innovating new policies and practices. HR strategies could, therefore, focus on how these services can be maintained at the right level as on what changes should be made to them.

## Case Study

### Net Airlines HRM

Net Airlines (NA) is a highly professionally managed global player in the civil aviation industry. This company has a comparative growth over its past twenty years. Total strength of employees is about 20,000, and has won several awards for its quality service. It may be mentioned that NA was opposed to be one of the partners with the Hook Airlines in the Air-Care disinvestment deal with the national government, which is yet to take shape. It is worth mentioning that the emerging competitive business environment of the 1980s was the resultant effect of the global deregulation of the airline business, which led to cut-throat competition from carriers in the Asia-Pacific region, resulting in air fare reduction. NA took pains to turn the threat of fierce cut-throat competition into opportunity by providing differentiated service against its existing rival groups. It projected an image of high value-based quality service in all areas of its operations, including in-flight internet and telecommunication facilities at the disposal of passengers, as well as service in ticket reservations, etc.

At the operational level, NA effected savings in fuel consumption through a fleet of young aircrafts — average of an NA aircraft being six years against the industry average of twelve years. The NA management was determined to control costs through integrated HR strategies in its sub-systems by changing the existing performance management and rewards, recruitment and selection, career development programme, etc. NA uses personality tests in the selection of outside candidates. Only those who can fit the organisational corporate culture and also found to be high performers are selected. As such, its selection process is quite rigorous and elaborate. Training and development of employees is totally need-based, which enables the employees to perform their best on the job.

Career development of employees receives full attention of the management. Line managers play a very pivotal role for imparting training for on-the-job related skill, e.g., skill in operation of cnc/nc (computerized numerically controlled/numerically controlled machines). On an average, every employee is given eleven days of annual training. Adequate emphasis is given to development of managerial skills. The corporate office the total activity. NA has a well-designed performance. management system for the senior management and the staff. Potential appraisal and career planning of senior cadre management positions is linked to performance appraisal. Juniors are promoted to senior positions as part of their career development programme. Potential appraisal is the basis of staff career progression. There are opportunities for the staff to move horizontally. This helps broadening the experience, which is helpful in career growth. Besides, the staff is allowed to change their jobs at intervals of 3-4 years.

NA's reward system is very lucrative. The company provides medical insurance, ESOPs, as well as travel loans. Though salaries is not very attractive, but the total package is attractive and includes performance and profit-linked compensation. So, the pay with benefits attracts outside potential candidates. The labour turnover rate is very negligible.

To conclude, NA was faced with a dynamic business environment. As part of its strategy to combat the uncertainty, the company, first of all, aimed at controlling the costs, and achieving market differentiation through strategic quality service. HRM sub-systems were aligned to the strategy for the drive for quality service. All efforts were made for the development of employees' commitment and identification with the company. Recruitment processes were well-defined to select the best talents to match the strategic objective *vis-a-vis* the NA corporate culture.

## Questions

1. Define the strategy adopted by NA to survive in the cut-throat business competition.
2. Do you think that the reward system was strategically designed to retain the employees?
3. Strategic HR policy helped NA to survive and earn profit - discuss critically.

## References

1. K. Prasad, *Strategic Human Resource Management,* Macmillan India Ltd. 2005.
2. *Ibid.*

***

# 3 New People Management

## The New People

It could be the perfect partnership of post liberalisation India – between the corporation and its most important resource. Between the learning organisation and its teacher–pupils. Between corporate purpose and individual aspiration. And it can only be brokered by another alliance between business strategy and the management of people. Uniting the organisation's direction with that of its employees, a new human resource management is trigerring a fusion of the knowledge pools of the individual and of the organisation. Culiminating in the combined triumph of both. In brief: articulate the connections between corporate success and individual behaviour, instal institutionalised processes to reinforce these connections and catalyse a chemistry that allows the connectisins to be translated into action which is mutually beneficial for both the organisation and individual. The approach to managing human resources is undergoing a revolutionary change. And it is in acknowledgement of the fact that it is people and not money, machines and materials that must run organisations.

## The New People Management

Coalescing corporate needs with the individual's is crucial. The corporation is driven by the interest of its stakeholders its goals of profit–making, determining its business philosophy. But the individuals bring into the corporation their own ambitions. In the past, however, the corporate human resource function seldom tried to bridge the gap between them. Being in a buyer's market considering the country's huge reservoir of qualified people and operating with systems that did not distinguish one individual from another, corporates had no need to ensure congruence between organisational objectives and an employee's aspirations.

But equal access to all resources is forcing them to rely on other people as the only source of competitive advantage today. And as Sanjiv Goenka, Vice–chairman, RGP enterprises said: "Global competitiveness can be achieved not through the best technologies and plants, but by effectively motivating your employees to perform at global standards. A new approach to managing people becomes absolutely critical have". As a result, the human resource function has acquired a new and critical responsibility, ensuring that corporate and individual objectives are melded into one says, T.V. Rao one of the pioneers of human resource corporations are not in the business of human resourse development. They are in their own business. But human resource development is an important tool which unfortunately is being used in a limited sense. The corporate vision has not been attached to it.

**A Common Set of Objectives**

- Corporate goals must factor in individual career growth
- Company profits must be linked to personal rewards
- Organisational learning must involve employee training
- Job responsibilities must facilitate personal development
- Business strategies must consider human resource issues.

Actually, human resources must become the business of every one in the organisation. CEOs can achieve that goal only by integrating human resouce planning, implementation and validation firmly with their strategic activities, thus giving birth to the new people management (NPM). Its principal mandate is to develop and execute polices, programmes and practices that align all human activity to corporate objectives. The major paradigm shift taking place in the management of human resource is the progressive integration of conceptual values with operational values.

## Anatomy of the New People Management

As the transition from the old human resource development to the NPM materialises, the human resource function is beginning to play a role much broader in scope, much stronger in its impact and much more permanent in its effect. Instead of running laboratory tests on small groups – the only freedom that the human resource specialists in many a company had – the NPM has to make the entire enterprise its arena. The continuously rising need for competitiveness can only result in continuously changing role boundaries for human resource management. Therefore, as the frontiers of its influence are rolled back, components linked seamlessly to each other and to the company's business goals. The challenge today is to sustain continuity, and how you manage your people is critical for that. It is part of the new people management to ensure that organisational exit is handed fairly. The approach to managing human resources is undergoing a revolutionary change.

### Recruitment

Woken into strategic planning, recruitment no longer involves short-term vacancy filling measures or the annual ritual of Campus recruitment. Translating corporate strategies into a manpower plan, and developing a long-term hiring programme accordingly. Corporations are tracking down people with the combination of knowldege, experience, skills, and behaviour best suited to achieving the company's objectives.

## Performance Management

To ensure that the talent they have attracted can help the organisations achieve their goals, companies are using NPM to create appropriate working conditions. The steps evaluating all jobs so as to assign them to the individuals best suited for them – Designing customised jobs if necessary. Using motivational techniques drawn from behavioural sciences and industrial psychology. Creating manpower configurations to boost the ability of individuals. And, through it all, balancing corporate and employee interests by designing individual cases.

## Training and Development

As change overtakes the stable environment in which Indian corporations have so far been functioning, organisations are changing rapidly. And so, naturally are the tasks that people have to perform. The function of the NPM bridge the gap between the abilities that individuals need to perform these tasks–such as self–directed leadership, self–motivated teamwork and self–generated creativity–that they possess.

# The New People Management

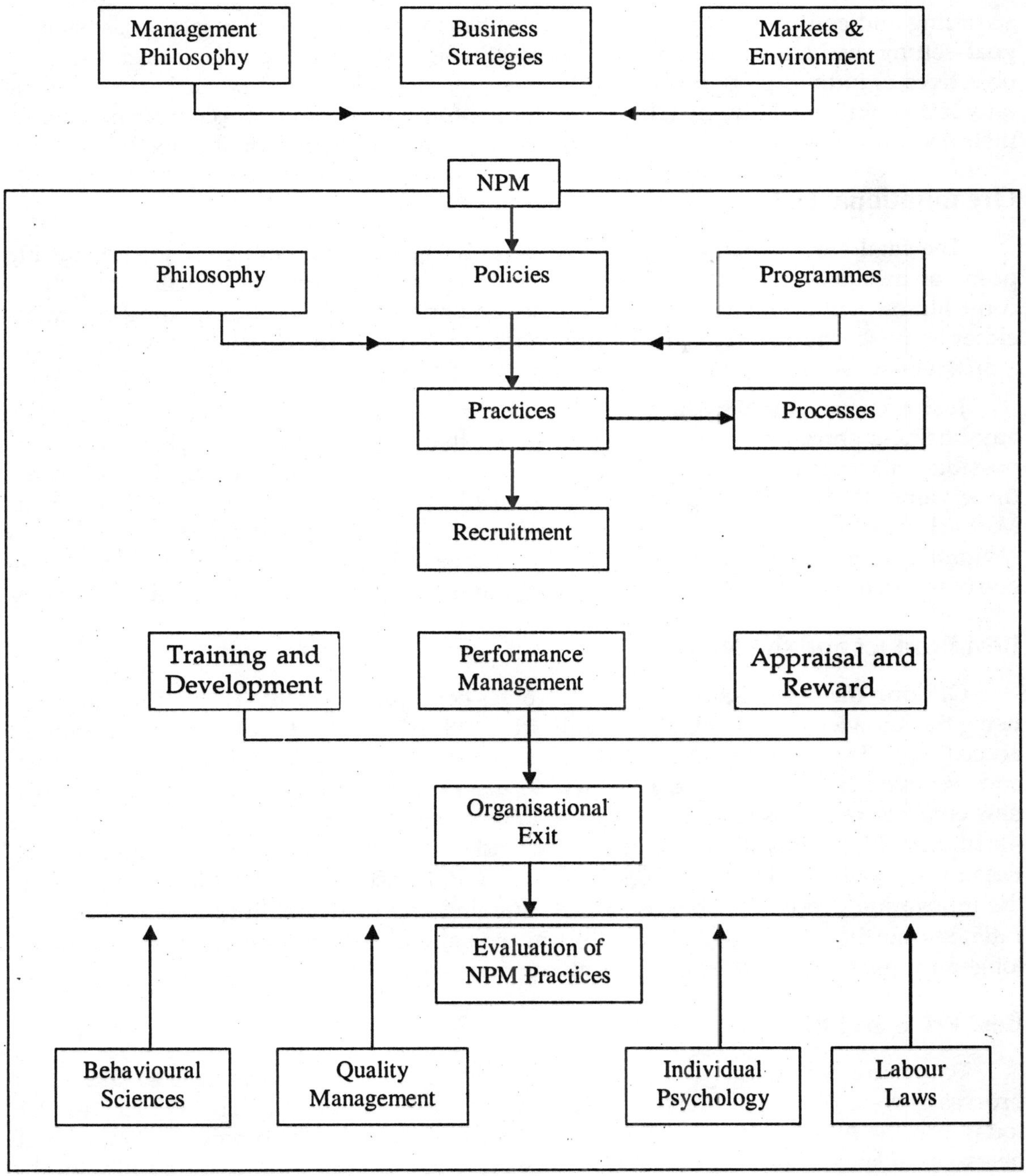

## Appraisal and Reward

With the first three phases of a company's integrated NPM process focusing on acquiring and equipping people with the abilities to fulfil corporate objectives, system of goal–setting evaluation and compensation is being used to directly link organisational objectives to individual performance. By ensuring that individual rewards are available only if corporate goals are met, the NPM successfully preventing people from expending their energies on activities that bear no relationship to organisational objectives.

## Organisational Exit

The final step in managing the life cycle brings the process back to the starting point of manpower planning. For planned separation from the employees whose contribution will no longer add value to a company's processes is becoming essential– either because wage fills have to be rationalised, or because the company has moved into a different stage of its existence where it now needs a new set of skills from its people.

Just how can the NPM help implementing a company's competitive strategy? In any business strategy people are more crucial than plans. Effective implementation is possible only with motivated people. Consider the alignment between the NPM and the three value disciplines adopted by market leaders as revealed by management gurus Michacl Treacy and Fred Wiersema in their newsletter. *The Discipline of Market Leaders* "Winning corporates dominate the market, contend Treacy and Wiersama, by offering one of three competitive benefits to their customers best product, best price, or best service.

## Best Product and the NPM

Offering the best possible product involves continuous process within the company, using the knowledge and abillities of individuals. The NPM strategy has to be customised accordingly. The recruitment process has to focus on identifying people with a original and creative bent of mind. Next, the NPM must create a working enviornment that sets new controls, provides resources for experimentation, encourages risk–taking and failure – without which innovation cannot succeed and provide a high degree of empowerment. Retaining people will be a key objective for the NPM since losing individuals involved in the innovation process can be disastrous. Training and development needs will have to cater to unorthodox skill building while appraisal and reward systems must be tied to long–term gains in the market place rather than short–term achievements.

## Best Price and the NPM

To ensure the lowest price in the product categories, companies have to tailer their process as well. And while the low–price, low quality equation may have sufficed earlier, today can the NPM ensure lowest possible costs Immaculate manpower planning will be essential since wage bills must be kept as low as possible. And since training of the workforce in response to the emergence of cost–cutting technologies will be an essential component of the best pricing strategy, the NPM must manage organisational exit strategically. Choosing people with the right profile —low risktakers and pliable individuals who can adapt their working style to the organisation's needs will be the key to implementing the strategy. And a speical mandate will be to link organisational cost cutting to individual cost cutting goals and reward employees accordingly.

## Best Service and the NPM

Since the cult of the customer rules the corporation that competes with the best service package the role of the NPM is vital. For captivating the customer requires not just internal systems which a company can device, even without the right people, but also individuals with the right mixture of initiative and skills. They have to be multi-talented team–players who are not prevented by the lack of precedents or of establisted procedures from improvising their responses to delight the customer. Importantly, a service–leader's employees have to stay at the forefront of new paradigms and techniques that affect their client's businesses. And it is the company's NPM that has to find the right people and then, institute training programmes that keep their knowledge levels abreast of latest developments. After all, a company provides the best service not only by selling its non products – which is secondary, but by enabling its people to solve its customer's problems. And it is the task of the NPM to set up a system that binds the level of customer satisfaction achieved directly to appraisal and reward.

## The Old HRD vs. The New People Management

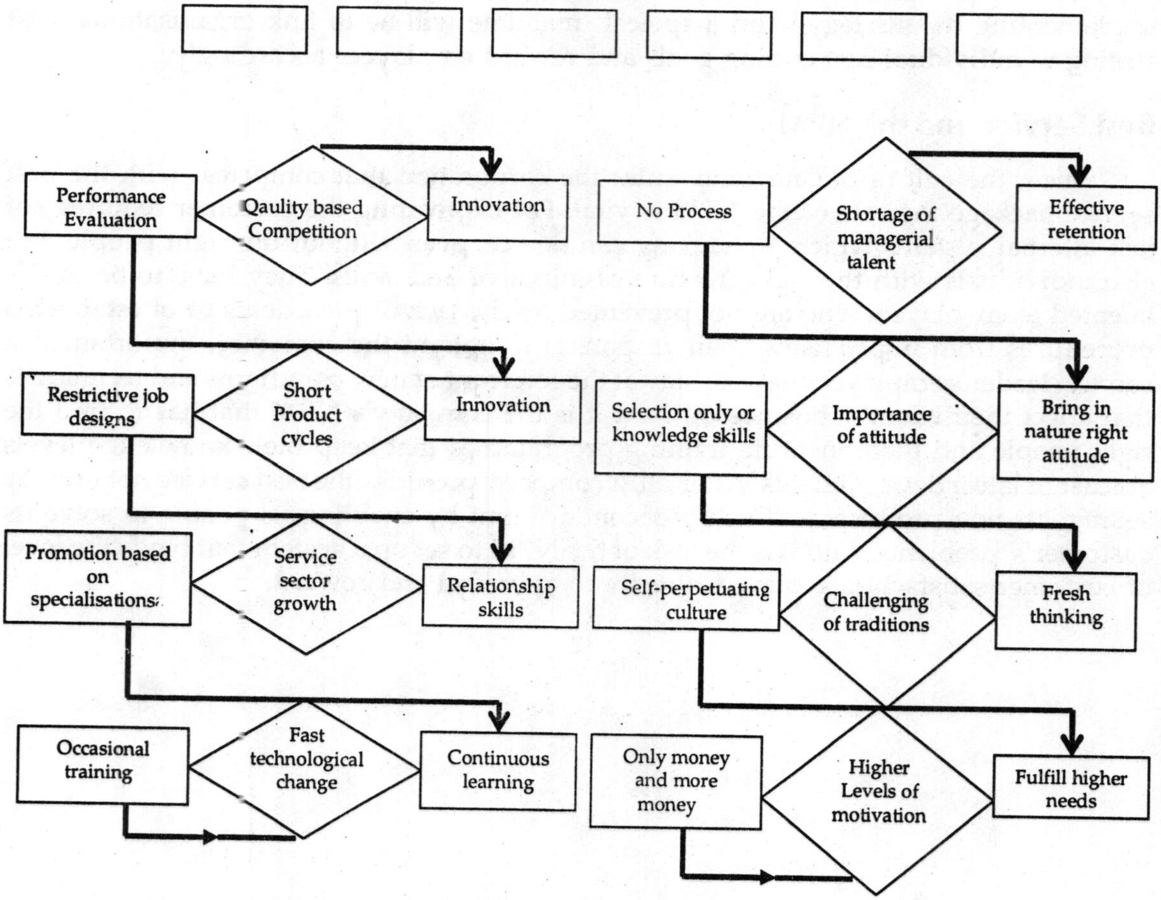


## Change Management and The NPM

To reinvent themselves in order to cope with the post-liberalisation competition. Indian corporations started in the wrong place: transforming organisational practices and processes without changing first the mindset of the people who would manage them. From reengineering to time-based management from total quality management to cellular manufacturing. No attempt to bridge the gap with global standards in quality, costs, product-cycle time, or technology can succed without managing people effectively. Listen for instance to Ashvin Parekh, director. KPMG Peat Marwick: "Companies are realising that effective people management strategies are crucial for the success of reengineering, "In fact, not just half-hearted participation of people at all levels.

For all of them can only be actuated by linking the top management's vision for change to the frontline workers who will be its instrument. And it is the function of the NPM to establish a powerful coalition within the company by communicating that vision, says human resource management guru Udai Pareek. There must be greater involvement and participation of people in decision making, decentralisation and delegation of power. That is the only solution and it must be done pragmaticaly, not philosophically, adds managment guru Mriyunjay Athreya. Top management relies on champions for new process products and processes. Human resource management will play a vital role in providing them. After all the NPM must not only give power to your people. It must in the ultimate analysis also power your profits.

Get six job offers a year from all kinds of companies. All of them offer better salaries and designations than I have but no special reason why I should join them. And surely they all cannot want the same kind of person?" asks a financial analyst, with two years experience in a foreign bank. It proves how retrogressive the rules of recruitment were even recently.

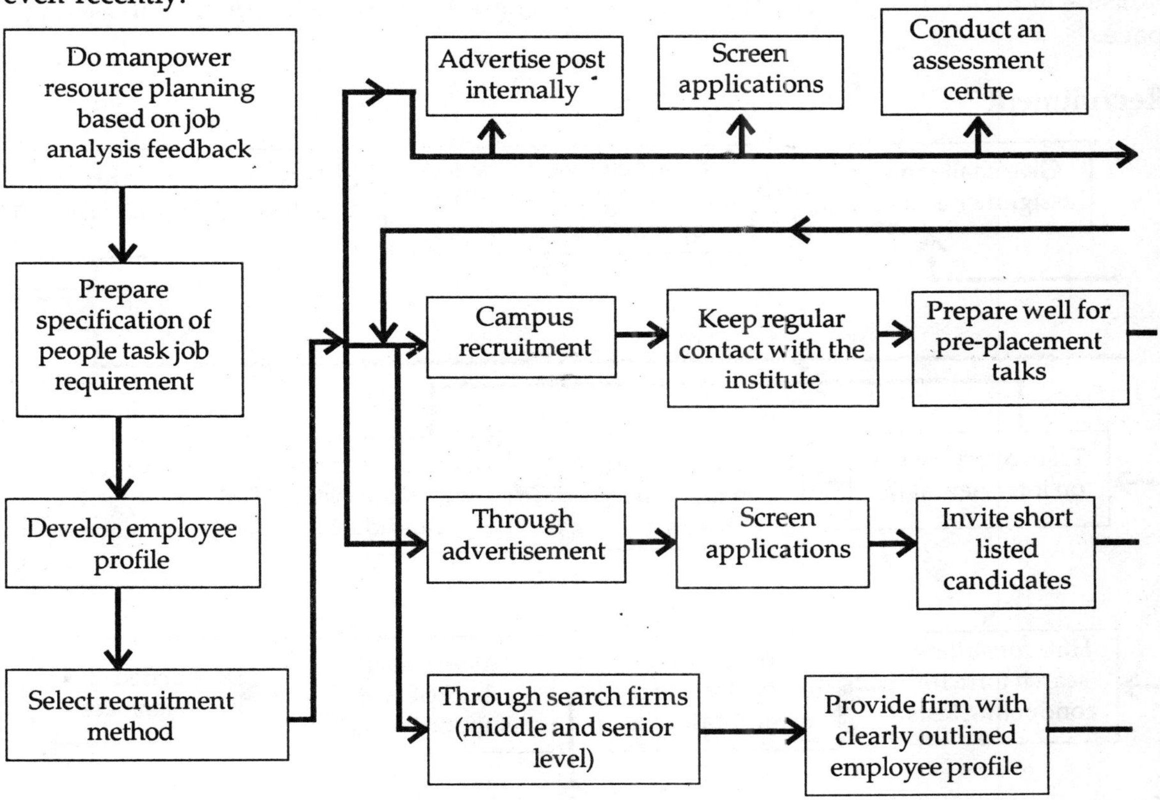


Companies simply hired fresh graduates or MBAs – seeking out the top-rankers – started them off as trainees, paternally oversaw their vertical progress, and repeated the process every year. On the rare occasions that they had to recruit at higher levels, they advertised – the discreetness of the ad matching the stature of the company as a coveted employer – or used the services of a head–hunter, and chose on the basis of the track-record. Job hoppers were never favoured, and companies hired everyone for a lifetime.

Now a recruitment revolution is beginning. And the people whom companies will soon compete for most fiercely will be those who have earned their spurs in different functions, companies and industries – and not the one-company, one-function specialist. Having succeeded in hiring them, CEOs must not expect all of them to stay. Some will leave when the company changes its operational focus – as it must to stay ahead of change – and needs different kinds of people. Others will opt for entrepreneurial careers in favour of employment. Yet others will go back to school to re-educate themselves and proceed to the next phase of their portfolio careers.

Abandoning their old polices of hiring only at the bottom, therefore, companies will have to induct new talent at every level, including those where internal promotions were once *de rigueur*. Even the search for CEOs will intensify as new companies look for team–captains, and existing companies feel the need for new qualities – not available in-house – in their CEOs. In fact, the search for the right people at every level will pick up pace.

## Recruitment

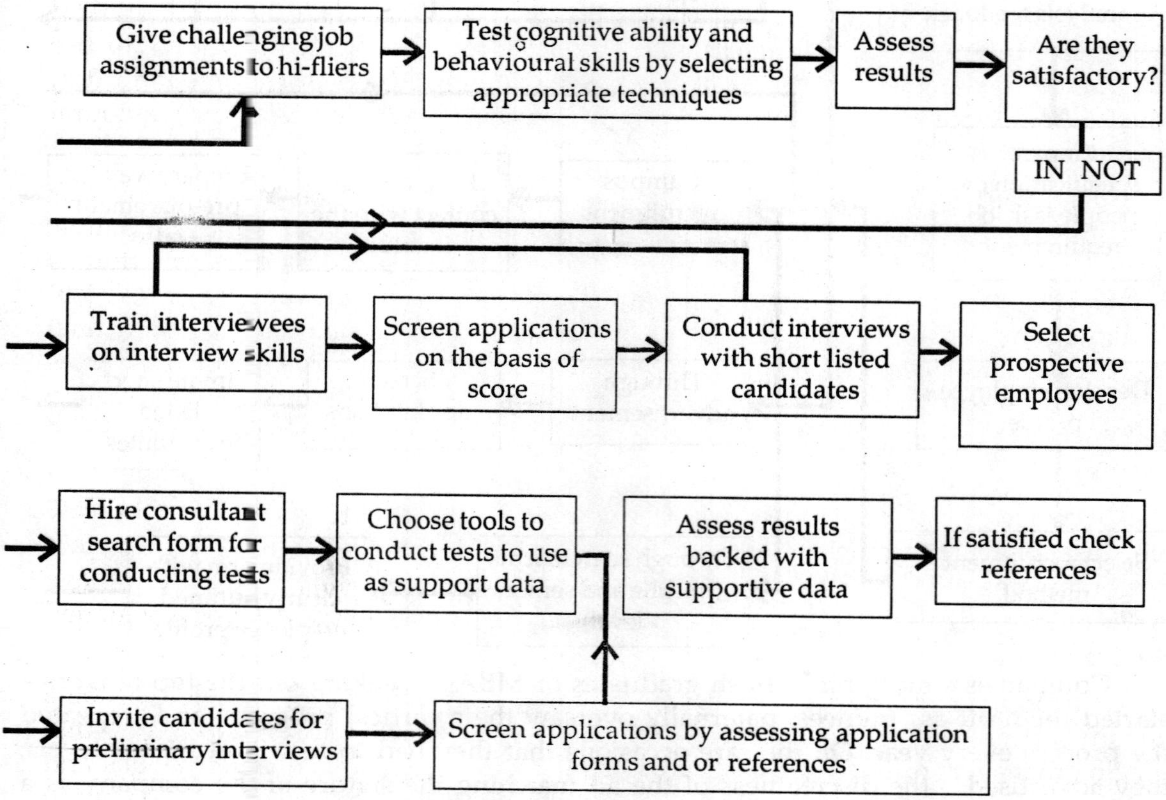


And while companies will have to develop innovative techniques to beat the competition at recruitment hotspots like campuses, they must also look outside their conventional hunting grounds. For that is where people with unorthodox winning ideas will come from. So CEOs looking for breakthrough will have to recruit them from other industries since everyone already in the sector will only offer their ideas. Hunting for knowledge workers, companies will have to raid research laboratories non- governmental organisations, college staff-rooms, and even sports-fields. And the quest for managers with the ability to lead megaprojects will have to be global, and not limited to the country.

At the organisational level, companies must tailor their manpower recruitment plan to corporate objectives, drawing up the profiles of suitable hires accordingly. Companies focusing on new business development will have to seek entrepreneurial abilities, companies planning to withdraw from diversifications must look for pragmatists; companies chasing growth through alliances should hire people comfortable in different cultural backgrounds. Above all, companies must hire for the future, anticipating jobs that may not be in existence yet.

So, recruitment of managers must focus not on functional expertise, but for attitudes and approaches that fit the corporate goals and culture. Among the qualities that companies will have to screen, therefore, will be interests, disposition, attainments, general intelligence, special aptitudes, and even physical make-up. For every job that a company seeks to fill, therefore, it must prepare psychological profiles of the ideal candidate. And to test candidates for a fit with that profile, companies will increasingly have to use psychographic testing techniques such as Thomas Profilling, Myers Brigg Type Indicator, or the PA Preference Inventory that draw up the complete psychological and behavioural characteristics of an individual.

In fact, the test for Personality Traits will involve using unconventional tools like graphology. Also on test will be candidate's result orientation, analytical ability, initiative, communication skills, and innovativeness, giving employers as much information as possible with which they decide whether an individual will be appropriate for the job. To validate the conclusions of the tests, line managers and human resource personnel who conduct interviews will have to be trained in interviewing skills. And companies will have to use multi-session depth interviews instead of one-off interactions to explore different facets of a candidate under different circumstances and varying degrees of pressure.

What are the elements which companies must use to entice top talent? Compensation will be crucial only if it is not absurdly below the competitor's offer. Instead, recruiting teams will have to market their company as a place where employees have fun working, particularly to people that the company is trying to hire from old-fashioned organisations.

A Corporate culture that cares for people and gives them room to grow will be a company's strongest magnet for attracting good people. CEOs will have to ensure that their line managers and human resources department design unconventional jobs and daring responsibilities to create offers that their targets cannot refuse. And if pursuing the right person and convincing him to agree takes time, so be it. After all, in the knowledge economy, the corporate quest for intellectual capital will be a continuous process, comprehensive, systematic and continuous training linked closely to the strategy with which they are planning to fight in the marketplace. For them, it is training that will act as catalyst between people, between strategy and systems, between customers and the organisation.

## Employment and Development

### Employment

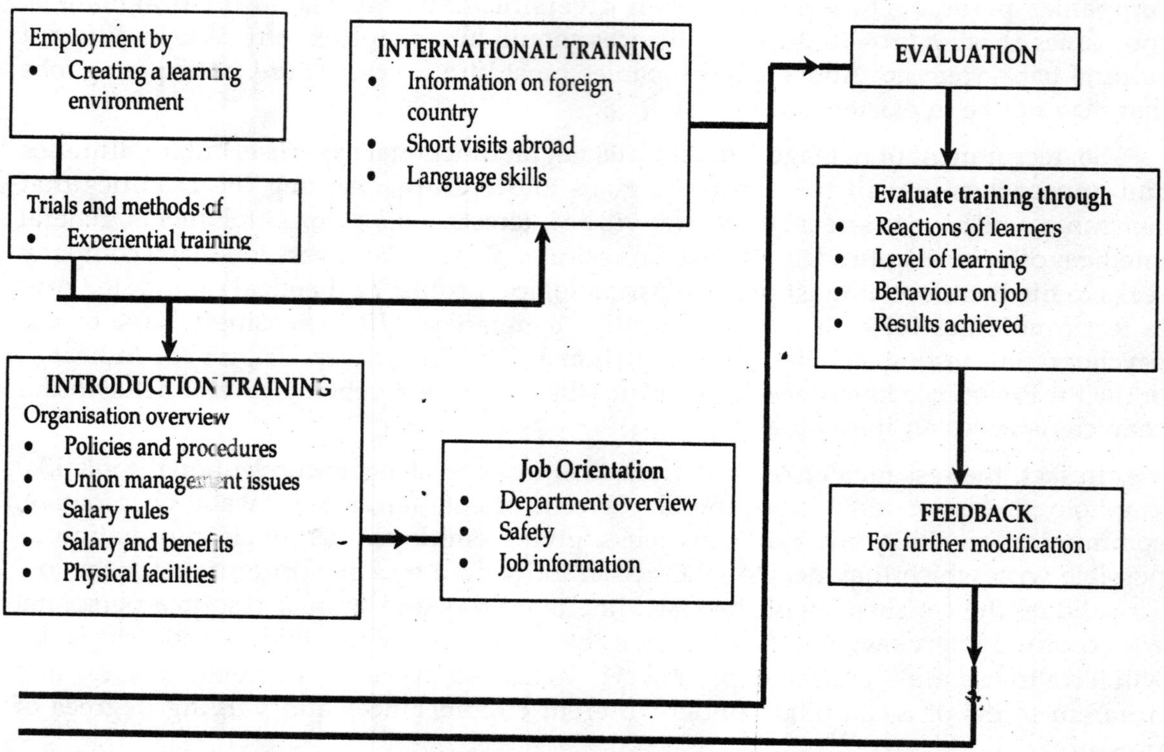


Companies relying on time-based competition – beating rivals to the market with new products, new designs, and new methods of selling – will have to teach teamwork and streamlined production techniques to their employees. Companies competing on the quality platform will have to train their workers in developing the mindset and culture for quality as well as the codified systems without which quality efforts will fail.

Those who choose to compete on the strength of their innovation will have to train their employees for creativity and lateral thinking. Companies whose focus will be on service will have to inculcate interpersonal and communication skills in their front line staff. CEOs who will stay competitive by battling costs will be compelled to train their employees in problem-solving techniques. And companies that globalise in-order to expand their markets will find cross-cultural training for their managers a vital imperative.

Management techniques applied to internal processes will demand training too. As more and more complanies follow the twin of empowerment and teamwork, teaching employees the right attitudes and competences will be crucial. The abilities of employees used to taking orders and avoiding responsibility will have to be developed so that they can decide wisely and bear the consequences. And workers will have to be trained to ask for ideas, seek help listen, and give feedback – the classic elements of successful teamwork.

Prominent on the training agenda of winning corporates must be retraining – which will involve unlearning old concepts and acquiring skills – for workers and managers whose experience has been gained in a non-competitive, low–tech era. The alternative, firing existing employees and hiring new ones, has been proven to be more expensive.

Equally, companies must insist on intensive induction training for new recruits, since they will no longer be able to afford the luxury of a long-drawn-out introduction to the company's business, systems and culture. This will help move trainees quaickly from the threshold of the organisation to the inner circle. And, above all, CEOs will have to take coginzance of the new role of the boss, which replaces autocratic commands with inspiring and facilitating as the key priorities, by training his managers for the post-heroic leadership qualities.

How must companies integrate their diverse training needs into a consistent strategy? Following the formal assessment-objectives-mode-evaluation cycle will be important. An evaluation of organisation, operation, and individuals will help identify training requirements. Setting specific objectives of training programmes will then help determine the form. And for information-rich, experience-poor employees, experiential training such as games, case studies, simulations, behavioural modelling, and outbound training will have to be included in the programme. Ultimately, the real objective of corporate training will be to teach people how to learn: to develop the mindset that craves for a constant upgradation of knowledge and skills. For, any organisation that stops injecting itself with intelligence is going to die.

| TECHNIQUE | DESCRIPTION |
|---|---|
| Induction Training | Orientation programmes for new recruits |
| Stress Management | Training in techniques to contain work-related stress |
| Delegation | Sessions for learning importance of deecentralisation |
| Negotiating | Role–play to develop bargaining skills |
| Lectures | Presentation of introductory material |
| Audio–visuals | Use of films, videos, slides, tapes *et.al.* |
| Self–directed Learning | Learning at one's own pace |
| Programmed Instruction | Methodical breakdown of material into small topic |
| On-The-Job-Training | Dose at the work-site under supervision |
| Computer-based Training | Use of software packages to learn skills |

| | |
|---|---|
| Simulation | Teaching by recreation of working conditions |
| Games | Structured tests of skills and aptitude |
| Ice-Breakers | Games to get team-members to know one another |
| Leadership Games | Exercises to teach different styles of leadership |
| Skill Games | Tests to develop analytical abilities |
| Communication Games | Exercises to build bias-free listening and talking |
| Strategic Planners | Games to test ability to plan ahead |
| Team–building Games | Exercises requiring collaborative efforts |
| Creativity Games | Tests for evolving multitude of solutions to problems |
| In-Basket Exercise | Evaluating managers' response to imaginary |
| Role–play | Adoption of roles other than their own |
| Role Reversal | Exercise to teach plurality of viewpoints |
| Doubling | Brings out ideas that often are not expressed |
| Tag Teams | One role played alternately by two participants |
| Mirroring | Training with an external perspective |
| Monodrama | Insight into a given interaction |
| Shifting Physical Positions | Highlighting of communication problems |
| Structured Role Playing | Role–play with pre-determined objectives |
| Multiple Role Playing | Providing a common focus of discussion |
| Built-in Tension | Teaching the importance of resolving matters |
| Case Study | Problem-solving discussions |
| Shadowing | Working under a senior to watch and learn |
| Coaching | Senior manager leading a team of recruits |
| Outward-Bound Training | Adventure sports for teams |
| Grid Programme | Determination of effective leadership |
| 9 + 1 + 23 | Self–assessment by learner of leadership skills |
| Brainstorming | Discussions for developing innovative solution |
| Lateral Thinking | Thinking randomly to come up with new ideas |

| | |
|---|---|
| Input-Output Technique | Suggesting solutions by specifying input and output |
| Morphological Analysis | Listing of possible alternative solutions to a problem |
| Gordon Techniques | Steering a discussion to crystallise solutions |
| Attribute Listening | Isolation, selection and evaluation of a problem |
| Synectics | Prodding subconscious mind and invoking interest |
| Cross-cultural Training | Programmes to teach specifics of varied culture |

***

# 4 The Environment and Strategic HRM

In arguably, the human resource environment is currently more turbulent than in any other period since World War II. During the last 10 years of the twentieth century, many political developments had massive impacts on human resources. Eastern European countries were freed from occupation by the Soviet Union, the Soviet Union was broken up into independent but unstable nations, civil wars broke out, and in less than one year East and West Germany were reunited. Almost overnight, previously communistic eastern European countries became markets for western goods, suppliers of labour, and business competitors. The economic sphere of the European community became a reality, as did the North American Free Trade Agreement (NAFTA).

Technology also had massive impacts as well. The Internet alone had an impact of epic proportion. Dot Com companies and existing businesses created thousands of e-business and e-commerce operations, employing some of the labour force's most talented workers. Companies providing infrastructure for the internet, such as Cisco systems, Oracle, Sun Micro systems, and Microsoft became some of the largest companies in the world, based on their market capitalisation.

Developments such as these affect business and human resources. It seems clear that the economic turbulence that characterised the last of the twentieth century will continue into the twenty-first century. Dynamic political and technological environments are likely as well. During such times of rapid change, the difficult processes of formulating viable competitive strategies and planning for their implementation become even more difficult as well as more important. Only some of the developments that occurred at the turn of the century could have been forecasted. Nonetheless, those organisations that scanned the environment, developed strategies, and planned alternatives for dealing with changing conditions probably fared better than those that did not.

## Technological Change and Organisational Structure

Technology, particularly information technology, is having a major impact on the structure of organisations and on the nature of managerial work. Enterprise software systems have been implemented to integrate the major areas of business: manufacturing, sales, finance, supply-chain management and human resources. These information systems have enabled organisations to gain numerous benefits such as efficiency gains, quicker response times, better inventory control, enhanced coordination, and speedy and effective decision making. Companies now spend $23 billion a year on enterprise softwares such as oracle, SAP, and People Soft, compared with only $ 1 billion in 1990. Information systems such as these and others have eliminated the need for many middle management involved coordination and dissemination of information, many of its functions have been computerised. With this removal of a level of the organisational hierarchy, a valuable training ground for top executives has been eliminated. Further, the context in which much work is currently being performed is changing. The era of the "Smart machine" and the skilled professionals who operate such machines probably will produce conditions in which there is less need for supervision or a very different type of supervision. Human resource strategies will need to consider changes in the nature of managerial work that will result from the accumulation of knowledge power in non-managerial, technical positions.

Managers who can be effective in such environments require new skills. Not only the number of managerial positions has changed, but also in many settings the nature of management has changed as well because of other developments. Thus, in information based, lean and flat organisations, alternative job assignments and opportunities are needed for the development of tomorrow's high-level managers.

Although the need for middle managers and low skilled employees has been lessened by information technology, it is useful to reflect on these developments before concluding that the jobs of human beings are being eliminated. S Levitan has put the effects of these developments in perspective.

There is nothing new about the prediction that labour will become less important as new technology replaces human labour with machines – this prediction has been heard repeatedly since the beginning of the industrial age. It can be asserted with some confidence, however, that this forecast is no more true today than it was a century ago.

Another important increasing technology is that skill and managerial educational requirements tend to increase. Although managers in advanced technological environments cannot have detailed knowledge of all aspects of the technology with which their subordinates work, they must have a conceptual understanding in order to provide effective support and direction.

Another impact of technology is that manufacturing is moving towards much shorter developmental cycles. New product development approaches based on concurrent or parallel engineering, design, purchasing, marketing, software, hardware, field support, and manufacturing specialists work together, beginning with the earliest product development phases. The availability of highly trained specialists work together, beginning with the earliest product development phases. The availability of highly trained specialists who have the skills to work effectively in such environments cannot be taken for granted. Training programmes and developmental assignments must be planned to ensure the availability of such workers.

## Influence of Human Resource Information Systems

As discussed above, firms have invested heavily in the implementation of enterprise or integrated software such as ORACLE, SAP and People Soft. Such information systems include human resource information system (HRIS) components and provide immediate information to decision makers about the organisation's human resource capabilities. Human resource departments and the activities they perform have been affected dramatically by these enterprise software systems, and executives can now include more human resource information in the equation when making strategic or operational decisions. In addition to their impact on strategic and operational decision making, such systems also have allowed firms to automate human resource processes of a transactional nature. Such automation is described as follows:

For example, managers and employees can now use personal computers or Kiosks to complete many HR transactions. Employees can make simple changes to personal information, such as their home address or contribution to a 401(K) plan, without going through any sign-off loops. Line managers can complete routine tasks, such as appraisals and salary changes, automatically.

The implementation of systems such as People Soft and SAP also has led to the restructuring of human resource departments, jobs and processes. Processes have been changed to conform to the requirements of information systems. Jobs also have been redesigned with fewer transactional activities because of computerisation.

## Redeployment of Human Resource Staff to Operating Units

One of the outcomes of organisational decentralisation has been that human resource generalists have been redeployed from human resource departments to individual operating units. Such decentralisation provides better service to the units because the staff member is on site and typically reports to the units line management while retaining a dotted line or functional reporting relationship to the human resource department. Generalists, who can handle a relatively broad range of issues, are typically the staff members assigned to operating units. These individuals can access specialists in the human resource department when greater expertise is needed for various issues.

Because of the redundancies and costs associated with the deployment of human resource generalists to operating units, some observers have questioned the value of such assignments. Fred Foulkes has provided an interesting account of an exchange between the top human resource executives of two large companies. One argued that his Boston based company had no human resource representatives at its sector location where it had 400 employees. Instead, the company provided a toll-free number for its employees to call human resource representatives in Boston when they needed assistance with major issues, such as attempts of unionisation or sexual harassment. In marked contrast, the other executive supported the deployment of human resource specialists to the operating units. He pointed out how difficult it would be for employees to have productive conversations with strangers on a toll-free line in Boston about such sensitive matters such as the autocratic behaviour of their manager. Thus, although deployment to the operating units has costs, it also adds value that comes from having good human resource staff representatives on site who can sense the atmosphere and organisational climate. There is probably substantial value added by the deployment of trusted, sensitive, and compassionate staff members to the operating units.

## New Organisational Structure

Not only is the nature of work and management changing, but organisations also are changing as a result of advances in information technology. The distinctions between management and labour have become flurried. Workers are becoming increasingly responsible to act on matters that they become aware of through computerised information systems. Further, there is a shift from individual to joint accountability because more group members have the same information for decision making. Because of the knowledge power of skilled technology workers, the structure of many of today's organisation is poorly suited for the future. Regardless of the exact form, many organisations have becomes much less hierarchical. More work is being performed in task force teams and project oriented work groups. Temporary organisations, such as task forces, require different managerial skills. Likewise, there is evidence that organisations are becoming more flexible, porous, and adaptive. In some, the organisational structure may become less pyramidal and more like a set of concentric circles.

Changes entailing more real participation, de-emphasise managerial status, new forms of superior subordinate relations, and rotating leadership roles require different managerial skills. Power shifts from one part of the organisation to another as tasks deemed. Most companies cannot take for granted the emergence of managers with the skills to operate in such environments. As a result, their members and skill requirements must be anticipated and developmental experiences planned so that the organisation will have an adequate number on hand when the need emerges.

There are other views on the structure of future organisations. Aside from the structural changes noted, there are four new structural forms of interest: (1) unbundled corporations; (2) network organisations; (3) cellular organisation, and (4) respondent organisations. All four forms have the ability to adapt to rapidly changing conditions characteristic of the present and likely for the future.

### Unbundled Corporations

Essentially, unbundled corporations employ a portfolio or conglomerate approach toward business units. As a result, units are retained or divested according to profitability and risk criteria. An example of an unbundled corporation is Johnson & Johnson, which has 190 autonomous operating companies in 51 countries. Johnson & Johnson had over 100 consecutive years of profitability and has achieved exceptional growth. The following provides an indication of its willingness to add or divest units based on their performance:

Over the past 10 years, through ongoing mergers and acquisitions, they have added nearly 50 companies and product lines ....... More than one third of each years sales comes from new products introduced within the past five years and from existing products launched into new markets.

In unbundled organisations, many of the traditional support services of bureaucracies are outsourced to consultants and vendors. For example, some traditional human resource management functions such as training are performed by vendors, along with some compensation and payroll functions. An advantage results from the potential to redeploy resources rapidly to more profitable alternatives. In addition, developing managers have more opportunities to exercise general managerial skills in running relatively autonomous business units that function as profit centres. For a small group of fortunate employees who form the core unit of the unbundled corporations there is some job squints. These units, which may be quite small, are composed of high impact employees who coordinate the work of vendors, manage change and manage the portfolio of business units.

While the jobs of the core of permanent employees are more protected, there is lower commitment to the employees of the peripheral units. Essentially, some of the employment security of the core employees comes at the expense of the peripheral's employees. Other implication for human resource strategy are that some of the benefits of using temporary employees may be offset by the reduced control and inefficiencies of dealing with "employees" through a vendor/supplier relationship. Further, when scarce labour is involved, the wage savings of unbundling may be wiped out by the increased costs of components purchased from vendors who must employ such labours.

## Network Organisations or Virtual Corporations

Charles Snow, Raymond Niles and Henry Coleman have used the term network organisations to describe organisations that are similar to unbundled corporations. (They refer to unbundled corporations, consisting of one corporate unit with multiple autonomous units, such as Johnson & Johnson, as internal network). One of the driving forces for the evolution or creation of network organisations is the need to outsource activities that other companies, consultants, or joint venture partners can perform better or more quickly. The term virtual corporation also has been used to describe similar organisations in which there is heavy reliance on outsourcing and a critical need for speed. Membership of the network may include companies from throughout the world. Like unbundled corporations, network organisations also have a permanent core member that performs a broker role. However, the non-core membership of the network may be stable or dynamic with the dynamic network form, the core network member or broker may replace network components with some frequency. For example, a member of a dynamic network performing a manufacturing role may be replaced because its production facilities cannot handle a new product design preferred by customers. However, with the stable network form, the organisation retains the component members for long periods of time.

The managerial requirements in network organisations are somewhat unique and include (i) referral skills, as needed for guiding problems to network components where there are solutions; (ii) partnering skills, such as problem solving or negotiating for outcomes that are beneficial to all parties, and (iii) relationship management, such as being offensive to customer's and partner's needs.

### Cellular Organisations

Another structural form is called the cellular organisation, which has some similarities with classical guilds. Such organisations are typically groups of small technology oriented companies that maintain affiliations over time. Employees of these companies are predominantly technical professionals. Subsets of the organisation companies join forces on various projects when their unique skills and capabilities are needed. One company takes the leadership role depending on the nature of the project. Individual companies also may join projects even when they only want to learn about a new technology that may be involved. The skills required of managers in cellular organisations are technical knowledge, cross-functional experience, international experience, collaborative leadership, sub-management skills, and flexibility.

### Respondents Organisations

Another structural form, the respondent organisation, is essentially an entrepreneurial corporation that exists by filling riches to supply customised services to unbundled corporations and bureaucracies. In such corporations, decision making is quick and likely retained at the level of the central entrepreneurial figure. Unfortunately, these corporations are risky and have high failure rates. The positive trade-offs, form the employee's perspective, are that although there is greater risk and less individual development from participative decision making, there should be opportunities to develop as a generalist and acquire new skills as well as the potential for financial gain. Some of today's smaller Internet players are respondent corporations.

## Stimulus for Entrepreneurial Business

Entrepreneurial firms, medium sized companies, and small businesses are accounting for increasing numbers of jobs as employment accounted for by the largest U.S. corporations has declined. Some of this growth in jobs may be related to their role in providing services or manufactured components for larger companies. In essence, some may be playing the role of respondent corporations. A study by Donald Hicks of Job Creations in the Dallas Metropolitan area found that 61.0 per cent came from new businesses whereas 25.0 per cent came from existing small companies. Some of the human resource knowledge base developed for large corporations may not be directly applicable to quickly responding, lean respondent corporations and smaller businesses. Nonetheless, recent literature describes small business applications of such managerial innovations as open book management and team building. Further, there has been a tendency for some innovative, smaller companies to decentralise the human resource management function by distributing greater personnel responsibilities to line managers. A future challenge for the managers of these organisations will be to develop or adapt existing human resource practices for these settings. Interestingly, some human resource executives who lost their jobs as a result of corporate downsizing now operate successful consulting firms that supply human resource services to smaller businesses.

## Worker Values and Attitudinal Trends

Before examining worker attitudes and values, it is important to note that attributing less work-oriented values to a younger generation has been a long-standing tradition. As a result, popular views on the work values of younger employees may be biased. Jeymour Lipset has observed the following:

Beliefs about the work ethic vary over time and place. There is, however, a general inclination for older people to believe that things were better – or at least more moral, more decent – where they were young.

There are a several arguments that can be used to support the contention that the work ethic in the United States is strong and that it has remained relatively stable. One argument is that employees have worked the same number of hours per week for over 45 years and that when committing is included, they are spending more time in work-related activities. Thus, workers are involved in more hours of work-related activity and are spending less time in leisure. Another argument is that the overwhelming majority of U.S. workers enjoy their jobs, and as a result, work appeals to them. A final argument is that U. S. workers are second only to the Japanese in the proportion who keep working after they reach 65 years of age. The meagre retirement benefits for Japanese workers may explain their tendency to remain employed.

Lipset's warning and arguments notwithstanding, there have been some shifts in work values of importance to strategic management. Among the most important of these are values and attitudes of employees toward their employers. Unbundled organisations typically display low loyalty to the employees of their peripheral units. This lack of loyalty seems to be reflected in the attitudes of the younger cohorts of today's employees as well. Terence Pare has observed the following about young college graduates: "That loyalty toward employers would decline. There is ample evidence that levels of loyalty have probably have declined on both sides, along with shifts in some other fundamental work related values. However, decreased loyalty is probably not a unique characteristic of younger workers. In a survey, 57.0 per cent of the respondents indicated that they were " less loyal to their employees than they were five years ago". Reasons for declining loyalty include executives' receipt of large bonuses during cutbacks and perceived lack of concern on the part of management for the welfare of employees. Indeed, there has been a growth of organism in the workers, probably resulting from such factors as excessive focus on the bottom line to the exclusion of other values and lofty excessive focus on the bottom line to the exclusion of other values and lofty excessive salaries.

An understanding of trends in other work values, particularly those of younger workers, is critical to understanding the future human resource environment. On study of work values analysed data collected from a survey of high school students and young, newly hired male smelter workers and female telephone operators. The study found that high school students tended to place greater emphasis on extrinsic values than the recently hired employees. Conversely, the recently hired employees placed greater values on the intrinsic aspects of work, being involved in their jobs, and performing meaningful work. The initial work experience of young employees, even in relatively low-level jobs, apparently has the potential to shift their work value foci from extrinsic to intrinsic work aspects. Interestingly, it is only after lengthy socialisation in the work environment that these are work value changes from intrinsic to extrinsic. The implications of these findings are that blaming young entrants to the labour market for an emphasis on extrinsically oriented work values may be counterproductive because the real cause for such values may be companies' mismanagement of the socialisation process of young workers.

Further research indicates that younger U. S. workers are not more materialistic than workers from other countries. A comprehensive study compared work values of subjects from the United States, Germany, Holland, Israel, Korea, Taiwan, China And Hungary. The U. S. sample was drawn from undergraduate and graduate business students mostly between the ages of 21 and 39, of which more than 90.0 per cent were employed in full-time jobs from a broad range of occupations. The responses of the subjects who were asked to rank 24 work values, revealed the following:

1. U.S. subjects ranked pay 15$^{th}$, which was about the same for most other countries.
2. Having an interesting job was the most important values for U.S. students, as well as for subjects from Germany and Holland. Subjects from Israel, Korea, and Taiwan also ranked job interest as one of the top three work values. Subjects from China and Hungary viewed job interest less importantly, ranking it at eighth and seventh place, respectively.
3. The second ranking work value for the U.S. subjects was achievement, which was also ranked first or second by subjects from all countries except Germany. Surprisingly, German subjects who were small business managers and employees or business students, ranked achievement in ninth place.
4. When compared to German subjects, U.S. subjects placed much higher emphasis on benefits, security and supervision.
5. A final difference of interest is that while U. S. subjects along with subjects from Germany, Holland, Israel and Taiwan – placed contribution to society in last or next to last place, subjects from China ranked it much higher, fourth place, apparently as a result of their collective culture.

The implications for strategic management of these results are that U.S. workers are interested in the types of jobs that they perform and that they still have desirable work values. Younger workers who currently account for a major portion of the workforce and who will dominate it during the rest of the decade and beyond, feel entitled to meaningfulness and involvement. They want interesting work, to participate in decisions affecting them, autonomy, and opportunities to grow. Pay will remain important, but workers will probably not be as focussed as in the past. These findings are consistent with the changing work values conveyed in the following:

After a decade of excessive consumerism and blind ambition, American workers between the ages of 25 and 49 are beginning to emphasis public service and family life as measures of success.

The trend toward greater interest in aspects of job satisfaction such as autonomy and interesting work, are even reflected in the significant impact such factors have on worker's intention to vote for unionisation. Recent research also has demonstrated the significance of values as determinants of job choice decisions.

The values of older workers also may be important to strategic management. When labour shortages persist, older workers will have to be persuaded to stay on the job or be drawn back into the labour force. One critical element to their return may be job satisfaction. Unfortunately, there is evidence of continuing bias against older workers in various aspects of the work relationship. Although there is empirical evidence of a positive relationship between job satisfaction and age, the relationship is curvilinear and reflects a decline in job satisfaction among older workers, as a result of such factors as lost influence and unmet expectations. Since downsizing organisations also have targeted older, higher paid workers for voluntary early retirement programmes as a means of cutting costs, older workers also may feel unappreciated. In planning for the environmental challenges of the future, strategic managers may need to develop approaches to prevent the decline of job satisfaction of older workers.

## Management Trend

Several managerial trends are having an impact on human resources. Trends discussed in this section include work teams, virtual teams, open-book management, management of diversity, total quality management, reengineering, management of professionals, and managing in the aftermath of mergers and acquisitions.

### Management of Diversity

Because of the increased heterogeneity of the workforce, managers must be prepared to deal with the challenges associated with such demographic changes. Effective management of diversity can increase an organisations' productivity through several avenues, one of which is increased problem-solving ability. Such productivity may result from increases in creativity that have been hypothesized to be related to heterogeneity. For example bilingualism and biculturalism have been found to be related to divergent thinking, which in tern has been hypothesized to be associated with creativity. Recently, it has been demonstrated that ethnic heterogeneity in small groups is associated with increased quality of ideas generated for solving problems. Increased heterogeneity also may bring another benefit – the prevention of the "group think" phenomenon that occurs only in cohesive groups. However,. whether these benefits will be obtained is dependent on how well diversity is managed. Such factors as the amount of diversity, communications, ease of discussing differences, cultural awareness training, and awareness of background information on group members affect the quality of idea generation.

Through such contributions, the management of diversity may enable companies to gain competitive advantages. In addition to diversity related creativity and problem-solving advantages, companies also may be able to tap gender and racially diverse markets better acceptance from these markets as a result of a good public image based on diversity. As an example, the Avon Corporation has had success with this strategy. Companies having good records in managing diversity may be able to attract better employees. Organisations that do a good job of managing diversity also tend to be more flexible because they have broadened their policies, are more open-minded, have less standardised operating methods, and have developed skills in dealing with resistance to change.

Although prejudice still exists, there is evidence that progress has been made. For minorities and females, obtaining jobs with companies is less of a problem than it was in the past. Instead, any apprehension about minorities and females is more likely to be faced as per options of their qualifications. These perceptions are affected by the fact that, on average, minorities and females have less training and education. As Roosevelt Thomas has stated: "Companies are worried about productivity and well aware that minorities and women represent a disproportionate share of the undertrained and undereducated." To the extent that companies generalize from classes to individuals and make unfounded attributions, they underestimate the value and contribution that minorities and females tend to plateau earlier than those of male non-minorities.

Two *caveats* on the implications of the diversity literature seem warranted one is that some of the empirical literature recommends that researchers should seek to determine the optimal level of heterogeneity because there is a curvilinear relationship between heterogeneity and performance. An example of such a recommendation is that "groups should pay careful attention to how much they increase diversity ... too much diversity can lead to communication problems and unavoidable conflict. Unfortunately, if one had knowledge of an optimal level of heterogeneity, the application of such information to increase performance weight lead to specific consideration of race, ethnicity, or gender in making work assignments, which would appear to violàte civil rights legislation. A second *caveat* is that much of the past research on racial diversity has focussed on blacks and whites but has not devoted much attention of Hispanics. Hispanics are the fastest growing segment of the workforce. Thus, managers need to be sensitive to diversity issues for all races and nationalities as well as gender and other forms of workforce diversity.

## Work Teams

Work teams have been of increasing interest to managers in a number of leading companies, such as Procter & Gamble, Eli Lilley and Motorola. These companies have developed substantial expertise in the utilisation of teams. John R. Katzenback and Douglas K. Smith define work teams as "a small number of people with complimentary skills who are committed to a common purpose, performance goals, and approach for which they hold themselves mutually accountable." A number of benefits have been attributed to the use of work teams as an organisational form. These include improved decision making, improved performance, improved quality and increased flexibility afforded by the ease with which they can be created and disbanded. The use of teams may also lead to reduce labour costs, lower employee turnover, greater service efficiency, facilitation of change resulting from reduced individual threat and shorter product development cycle. Empirical analysis of the long-term performance of work teams involved in business simulations has provided some evidence of this effectiveness.

In spite of the advantages, there are also some disadvantages with the use of work teams as they are sometimes subject to the dysfunctional group think phenomenon and norms of production restriction. Further, as researchers Eric Sandstorm, Kenneth P. De Meuse, and David Futrell have pointed out, the literature on work teams provides mixed evidence on their effectiveness and identifies a large number of factors that potentially influence work team effectiveness. These include developmental aspects, the boundaries of the teams, and the organisational context. There are also examples of difficulties with the implementation of teams such as Levi Strauss, where the introduction of teams led to declines in productivity and morale.

Although work team effectiveness is a complex subject, effective work teams have some common characteristics. Such characteristics include relatively small size, dedication to a common purpose, commitment to common performance standards, willingness to be collectively accountable, equitable and effective work and role assignment procedures within the team and complimentary skills. Effective work teams also require compensation approaches that reward teamwork, such as gain sharing or team bonuses.

Aside from their complexity and the potential disadvantages of teams, there is great interest in their potential contributions. For example, in design and production situations, cross-functional work teams have been found to be effective in reducing the time required from initial product design to eventual production. Through simultaneous engineering. Such teams, which typically include both design and production engineering personnel, as well as programme managers who mediate differences, are ideally housed in the same area. Another benefit derived from these teams is the broadening experience that takes place within the teams across engineering specialities.

An example of the use of work teams having a great deal of autonomy is provided by the experiences of Sterlease Inc., which introduced work teams into its new Context Plant. The plant's hourly employees are organised into some 47 work teams, several of which are cross-functional in nature. In addition to normal production work, these teams perform many activities that normally would have been managerial responsibilities, such as scheduling production, scheduling vacations or design materials and purchasing new equipment. Performance evaluation and compensation reviews are still the responsibility of managerial personnel.

Stulcase has divided a number of important benefits from its work groups. One is that the teams, which include machine operators, tend to make better machinery purchasing decisions than managers. Another benefit is savings in labour costs because the proportion of indirect labour costs is lower than other plants in the industry. For examples, there is no need for the position of assistant foreman. An additional benefit is that the context plant has experienced an annual turnover rate lower than one per cent. Furthermore, communication has been facilitated as a result of the use of work teams. Finally, Stulcase has found that its workers have not become complacent because of the sense of ownership produced by the teams.

## Virtual Teams

Virtual teams have members who work closely together even though they are based at different locations, including different locations, including different countries, and may even be indifferent time zones. They typically have members from different functions and work across organisational boundaries as well. Advances in telecommunications, such as the internet, e-mail, cell phones, and video conferencing, have made virtual teams a possibility. In turn, market factors, such as shorter product life cycles, rapidly shifting customer tastes, and international competitive pressures have provided the driving force for the use of technology to develop virtual teams. A team at a Johnson & Johnson unit provides a good example of a virtual team. This team has been assigned the task of developing a new surgical product and bringing it into production. The team consists of representatives of various functions and has members in Arlington, Texas and Juarez, Mexico, where production facilities are located. Team members communicate frequently with each other using e-mail, fax and telephone and the team leader also makes frequent trips between the different locations.

## Human Resource Outsourcing

One of the most significant forces affecting human resource management has been the outsourcing of human resource functions. Human Resource outsourcing is commonly understood as the permanent contracting out of activities that were previously performed inhouse. The trend towards outsourcing has been extremely widespread and recent surveys have focused as many as 91 per cent of responding companies engaging in outsourcing.

The trend toward outsourcing has been caused by several strategic and operational influences. From a strategic perspective, some human resource departments have attempted to shift their focus and resource toward a mere strategic role through the use of outsourcing. To accomplish this, human resource executives have used outsourcing to relieve their departments of some of the mere mundane aspects of the function, such as the involving routine, low-value added transactions. Outsourcing has also been used to help reduce bureaucracy and to encourage a mere responsive and cost sensitive culture by introducing external market forces into the organisation through the bidding process. In addition, outsourcing has been used for political purposes, such as to reduce or control head count in human resources.

Outsourcing has been pursued for several operational reasons as well, such as for greater efficiency or better service in the performance of functions. For example, companies almost universally outsource 401(K) plans because large financial services companies can provide almost flawless low cost administration of the plans. Other examples include medical claims processing and the processing of benefit continuation under the Consolidated Omnibus Budget Reconciliation Act. (COBRA). Outsourcing also has been seen as a vehicle for cutting costs, while cost reduction is an important consideration in many firms, the evidence indicates greater livelihood of successful outsourcing when it is pursued as part of a coordinated plan, such as for strategic focus and service has been used to obtain specialized expertise that is not available inhouse. During the past two decades, downsizing has often reduced the number of human resource specialists in human resource departments. This reduction in staff has required organisations to go to outside vendors to obtain specialized services, such as for test validation or indepth assessments for leadership development.

## Open Book Management

The practice of sharing financial and performance information is often referred to as Open Book Management. Essentially, the practice relies on the notion that empowered employees can make informed decisions and take informed actions on behalf of the firm. Because employer have the information and are empowered, they are almost compelled to take action. Jack Stack of Springfield manufacturing has been credited for being the inventor of open book management. Stack acquired a nearby bankrupt plant from International Harvester and was able to achieve a remarkable turnaround through the use of open-book-management. One of his most critical changes in implementing open-book-management was to help employees think of the firm as a business instead of an organisation that reconditioned diesel engines. Interestingly, "He persuaded employees to view running the business as a game they could learn to play-and win".

Open-book-management is broader than many human resource practices as it combines a number of practices such as profit sharing use of bonuses sure-boarding (reporting results or scoreboards) and training employees to understand the business. It often process heavy emphasis on the use of games in which the objective is to defeat a problem instead of other employees. Typically firms that practice open-book-management develop simplified methods for reporting their financials to employer and train them to interpret various measures of performance. Open-book-management usually combines generous bonuses beyond competitive base pay for a broad group of employee when the firm's goads are achieved.

Such bonuses are carefully spelled out as indicated in the following:

The bonus in open-book companies is an agreed-upon part, a significant part-of everyone's compensation package. It pays out only if the company or business unit hits certain goals, which are determined and spelled out in advance. The bonus is everybody's reward for boosting the company's performance for succeeding in business..... Right away you can see a couple of conditions that an open-book bonus plan must meet. For one thing, it has to be generous — generous enough to matter.... A bonus plan that breaks out any group of regular employees runs counter to the basic ideas of open-book-management. So does a plan with widely disparate rewards.... A bonus in an addition to competitive base pay.

Another positive feature of open-book-management is that the sharing of such information instils a sense of trust among employees. In firms that do not practice open-book-management, financial and performance information is often restricted to high level executives. This restricted information flow conveys to other employees that they are not to be trusted with such information. As a result if its positive features, open-book-management has the potential to enhance employee motivation.

Examples of companies using open-book-management include R.R. Donnelly and Sons, Carolina Safety Associates, and Terminex (North Carolina). The Braelshaw Group, Inc., in Richardson, Texas, provides an example of a small company that is practicing open-book-management. The firm trains its employees to understand accounting and financial terms and stores ten per cent of its firms profits when profit goads are achieved.

## Total Quality Management

While not new, another continuing trend of importance to management strategists is total quality management (TQM). TQM, pioneered by Edwards Derring, is a broad-based, systematic approach for achieving high levels of quality. Many leading companies such as Motorola, Cadillac, and Xerox, wrote strategies that require them to survive against the pressures of world-class competition, have implemented TQM. In a strategic context, TQM is probably most accurately categorised as a tactic for carrying out strategies requiring high levels of product or service quality. Essentially, TQM pulls together a number of well-known managerial principle coherent and systematic framework. Through the systematic interaction of these principles, TQM has the potential to lead to increased quality. TQM principles emphasize:

- Articulation of a strategic vision.
- Objective and accurate measurements.
- Benchmarking.
- Widespread employee empowerment and team-building.
- Striving for continuous improvement.
- Emphasis on a systems view of quality that conceptualises quality related activities as being highly interdependent.
- Leadership correlated to quality.
- Great emphasis on customer satisfaction.

Interestingly TQM programmes have the potential to increase the importance of the human resource management function. Human resource management plays a major role in providing more systematic training, facilitating changes that empower employees, instituting team-based reward systems, and communicating to workers their role in quality. David Bowen and Edward Lawks have described the relationship between TQM and human resource management as follows:

The importance of the HR side of the quality equation provides HR departments with a golden opportunity. Quality can be the "business issue" that truly brings senior managers and HR executives together to move from just HRM to strategic HRM. A major role in the quality improvement effort puts HR in a position to contribute directly and visibly to the bottom line to add value to the company's products and services in the same way that other functions, such as sales, accounting and production add value.

Before the human resource function can make full contributions to TQM efforts, high quality must be assured within the function itself. Unfortunately, measurement of the functions, contributions is often difficult because of their indirect effects. Nonetheless, valid measures of human resource effectiveness can be developed. One means by which this might be accomplished is through external benchmarking, which provides a useful means of both evaluating the quality of human resource programmes, activities, and impact as well as a means of identifying areas in which resources should be concentrated. The following quotation by David Ulrich, Wayne Brockbank, and Arthur Feung describes the practice:

Benchmarking HR practices provide the means of focussing attention on highest value-added HR activities those practices which are more likely to be practiced by successful companies. Rather than fall into the trap of trying to do everything well and please everyone with insufficient resources which results in no one being satisfied – HR professionals could use benchmarking to focus limited resources on critical activities.

Evaluation of the human resource function can also be accomplished by asking other managers in the organisation to evaluate the quality of services provided by the human resource management function. One guide for evaluation is to place greatest emphasis on measuring the most critical human resource management attributes, with secondary emphasis on the precision with which these attributes can be measured. This point is evident in the following statement by Curt Reiman, Director of the Baldridge Award for the U.S. Department of Commerce: "A company does not earn money making measurements. The trick is to avoid great measurements of irrelevant things". Along this same line, proponents of TQM also advocate the use of Pareto analysis. The basis of Pareto analysis is that a small number of factors has a disproportionately large impact on outcomes, such as quality. Therefore, by correcting a few critical problems, disproportionate improvements in quality can be obtained.

One of the important impacts of TQM, from a human resource management perspective, is that it places great emphasis on training. TQM maintains that errors and mistakes, which distracts from the quality of companies products and services, are a predictable result of untrained workers, and therefore training must be provided. Consistent with the emphasis on measurement, in some companies that use TQM, training is evaluated with the use of control groups and experimental designs.

In contrast to training, TQM is sharply at odds with conventional human resource practice in the area of performance evaluation. According to Deming, traditional performance evaluation systems are flawed because they are directed toward the individual instead of the team. Such systems also focus on assigning blame for past mistakes instead of pointing out direction for the future and may even detract from teamwork. Deming also argued that faulty systems and procedures are usually the cause of quality problems, not the performance of individual employees. TQM proponents also maintain that compensation should be directed toward teams instead of individuals. In addition to disagreement over performance evaluation, there also is controversy among TQM proponents over the appropriateness of team-based pay. Even some companies that have won the Baldrige Award for quality have not extended TQM into the areas of performance evaluation or compensation. Instead, companies implementing TQM have focused on problem areas that detract from quality, are relatively easy to fix, and do not involve much risk. For example, many companies focus their TQM efforts on improving training and communications. Fewer companies have shifted from traditional compensation systems to team-based pay, abandoned their performance evaluation systems, or instituted self-managed teams. Motorola and Cadillac are exceptions in that they have instituted such teams. With any managerial innovation, TQM is not without problems. One says that TQM efforts can lead to goal displacement, in which TQM is an end instead of means. In such cases, attention is diverted from pro-activities to gaining approvals from committees, filling out forms, and bureaucratic procedures. The well-publicized difficulties encountered by Flower and Hight and the Wallace company after they won the Baldrige Award for quality provide wonderfully ironic examples of this problem. Finally, although not the fault of TQM-during economic difficulties, companies have reduced the level of employee empowerment. Executives of the companies have blamed employee empowerment for slower decision making. However, this appears to be a short sighted criticism since the critical implementation process is facilitated by employee empowerment. Thus, even in Japan there has been second guessing of employee empowered consensus decision approaches because of their slowness. As a result, the leading Japanies Companies have formed to more top-downsizing of executive officers. Another problem is incompatibility of some of the concepts and downsizing strategies. De-sousa from Cibaca has stated:

> In case the aim of TQM is to add value to all stakeholders in every activity, it is almost of necessity make a company more efficient — increased productivity implies producing more with the same resources or, in a saturated market, produces the same amounts with fewer resources. In the latter case, which is the rule than exception in the industrialised nations today, downsizing is the probable consequence.

De-Sousa claims that layoffs can be avoided, presumably by attrition, insecurity resulting from downsizing or layoffs, would seem to under TQM philosophy.

## Advance Manufacturing

Manufacturing systems provide a new approach for streamlined manufacturing system and are commonly composed of advanced manufacturing (AMT), TQM and just-in-time (JIT) inventory control methods. AMT manufacturing approach based on highly computerized technologies, such as cost aided manufacturing (CAM). JIT inventory control is a method for manufacturing complements to the production line at the shortest practices before they are needed. When these technologies and managerial systems use, integrated manufacturing systems have the potential to provide dissemination of information rank barriers associated with functional organisation, promote collaboration to serve quality problems, and develop control between goals of cost, quality and desired production lead times.

These systems require knowledge workers whose levels of technical and problem solving skills are advanced beyond those needed for earlier forms of manufacturing and have major implications for human resource management. Scott Snell and James Dean conducted an empirical analysis of the types of human resource practices associated with various components of integrated manufacturing systems. In companies in which there is greater emphasis on AMT and TQM, there is more selectivity in hiring, more comprehensive training, greater development on external pay equity. These results are consistent with companies motivations to hire and maintain high quality workforces and to preserve their investments in human resources.

## Reengineering

Reengineering, which is also called process innovation, core process redesign, and business process reengineering, has been practiced since the late 1980s, often by companies facing intense competitive pressures. Essentially, reengineering is directed at achieving large cost savings by eliminating unneeded activities and consolidating work. It also sometimes redirects work across traditional departmental boundaries in order to accomplish work more quickly in cross functional teams. Accordingly, reporting relationships are sometimes changes along with reward structures. The type of service desired by customers is the key to the process.

An example of reengineering is provided by its application at Tatas Instruments. In this application, the driving force was the desire to reduce the time required for making customised semiconductor chips for a customer. In another example, the driving force was increased competition. In this case, GTE revamped its customer service process when it found that customers wanted to call only one number for repair service, to obtain answers to filling questions or to obtain additional services. Prior to reengineering, customers having service problems called repair clerks, who then recorded the information and then forwarded it to repair personnel. These activities were subsequently combined into one role performed by employees called front end technicians who also now operate testing and switching equipment relocated from repair personnel. As a result, the front-end technicians solve 30 percent of all service calls, and a smaller percentage of calls must be passed onto other repair personnel. Another example involves a bank. In order to reduce its operating costs The Banca di America and di Italia (BAI) reengineered its retail banking operations with the goal of becoming a paperless bank. After reengineering activities involved in depositing checks, the numbers declined from 64 to 25. As a result of these and other changes, employees in each branch declined from seven to nine prior to engineering to three to four afterwards. With these labour savings, the bank was able to open 50 new branches with its existing workforce.

Often, reengineering requires cross functional coordination and the crossing of organisational boundaries. Because it may disrupt existing power relationships and eliminate organisation jobs, it has high potential for conflict. Because the process often fails to obtain desired improvements and it has high potential for destructive consequences, organisation should not engage in reengineering unless they perceive a serious need. furthermore, reengineering generally does not achieve the level of improvement desired. The conventional wisdom is that the organisations strategy should be reengineered. Activities are necessary to these business needs are potential targets for elimination. As with early intervention of this nature, the organisations culture will have a major impact on its success. In many contemporary organisational cultures, the broad direction for reengineering should be the responsibility of those other performers. In addition to the recruitment for extensive time commitment from the executive, successful reengineering is more likely to take place where it is needed to a broad range of activities, training programmes accompany work organisation, and there is extensive communication with employees.

As a closing note on reengineering, it should be noted that some high-level employees are not convinced of the ultimate value of reengineering. They have proved the elimination of jobs and such a massive increase in the workload of remaining employees that they have serious concerns about the long-range, environmental human impact of such programmes. Because of such reactions, the use of reengineering may diminish source that in the future.

## Engagement of Professionals

The case of the mature professionals require a different form of management to provide a challenge for human resource management. Important characteristics of professionals are that they often have low organisational loyalty, require financial autonomy, follow a code of ethics established by their profession; standards of the profession and have a high need for intellectual and technical challenges. The availability of managers who can mange the work, the professionals cannot be taken for granted. The difficulties are well-known and there has been a long standing controversy over whether, such managers should be the members of the relevant profession themselves or lawpersons. The problem to plan for the development of managers who can be effective in such things are apparent. Mary Anne Vanglinew has stated:

*Maximizing a professional productivity has led to the adoption or development of new methods of work organisation that limit hierarchical levels of supervision, group link pay and other records to performance, ease the tensions between the computing cultures of professionals and other employees, and give professionals greater participation in the decisions that affect their lives.....* These managerial challenges and their solutions are crucial to the success and long-term survival of every high tech firm. The changes require different and sometimes counter intuitive management skills and practices.

Human resource problem for the future will be to develop career paths for professionals. To move up in an organisation, professionals have traditionally pursued an administrative track. Since they are often unprepared for management or administrative careers, they may not find such work satisfying. As a result, dual career leaders are sometimes provided, one is management and the other within the professional work. Planning for career progressions for professionals will require greater attention to the development of alternative tracks that will satisfy the needs of both professionals and their employing organisations. Large public accounting firms provide a remarkable example of turnover problems among professionals. A study of one such firm found that retention rates, after 60 months with the firm, ranged from 6 to 29 per cent. A challenge for the future will be to develop career tracks of professionals brgnigned that will enhance organisation loyalty.

### Managing in the Aftermath of Mergers and Acquisitions

Although the level of merger and acquisition activity has begrimed, mergers and acquisitions are still a permanent feature of the economy. Whether a merger or acquisition is successful depends on more than financial considerations. Success often depends on how well the two organisation's human resources are integrated. As a result, the degree to which human resource aspects of mergers and acquisitions are planned can be critical. Bruckman and Peters have stated:-

*The amount of time and energy needed to successfully merge two sophisticated organisations, however, is more likely to resemble to planning and execution of the invasion of Normandy, accompanied by the resultant clash of cultures from many elements attempting to work together toward one end.*

There is much evidence of the failure to work through human resource issues when organisations are acquired for their human resources. It also has been argued that planning for the contingencies of a merger is critical because human resources will pay the price. If the company loses a takeover battle, there may be redundant employees and the new entity will have to resort to layoffs. Conversely, if a company is successful in finding to pay the costs of the defensive actions.

## Demographic Trends

Many of the major demographic trends for the future are relatively well known. Nonetheless, these massive changes in demography have important implications for human resource management. Major changes include an ageing workforce, the baby born age glut, the baby bust labour shortage, increased racial diversity, and greater feminization of the workforce. The developments, particularly the variations in growth across different age cohorts, will have major implications for the career potential of individual workers. Planning will be necessary to avoid age bulges, age gaps, and surpluses in job categories or job families.

## Ageing Workforce

Indications for ageing trends, the median age for the U.S. population will increase from 42 in 1998 to 45 by the year 2008, while the median age for the labour force will increase from 39 in 1998 to 41 in 2009. Some of the implications of ageing are that the workforce will be mere productive. However, an older workforce may not adapt as quickly to a dynamic economy. Greater costs will also request from greater pension contributions that is likely to be associated with an ageing workforce. One implication of this trend is that as the workforce ages there should be correspondingly greater health care costs. Huge increases in health care costs have already occurred. Company's age distributions have already begun to affect their production costs of ability to compete. Interestingly, during the post war period in which Japan's remarkable economic growth occurred, it had a relatively smaller proportion of aged people to support than other industrial countries.

## Labour Shortages

At the beginning of the twenty-first century, firms faced the highest US labour market in 30 years. In some states, the unemployment rates for adults fell below three per cent. The combination of an exceptionally strong economy and demographic trends produced the labour shortages that had been predicted solely from demographic trends. Employees were expected to respond to the shortage by hiring retired workers and creating mere varied work schedules to accommodate their needs. Indeed, as the shortage developed, employers responded in many predicted ways like hiring disabled workers such as the mentally challenged and retired workers. Barring an economic collapse, labour shortages also are predicted for the future.

The traditional want ad will be replaced with "situation wanted" ads: workers will place these ads on the internet or other media and wait for companies to call them. They will have good reason to expect a call back. The U.S. Bureau of Labour Statistics Projects 151 million jobs by 2006 and 141 people employees. As often happens today. Many of these workers will be working two jobs.

The availability of jobs with dot.com or e-business companies and the prospects for rapid accumulation of wealth has made the labour market brighter for highly skilled workers who are willing to take risks and live with uncertainty. Nonetheless, the most admired companies in the United States such as Larent Technologies, General Electric, Microsoft and Dell Computer have high ratios of applicants to jobs. The above companies have opened their units in India and attracting the Indian software intellectuals to join these companies. These companies are aggressive recruiters, but ratios of applicants to jobs are high at Southwest Airlines help reinforce the notion that good employees are attracted to companies that have good management even in light labour markets.

The internet has created many of the jobs for highly skilled workers and has helped the labour market work more efficiently by providing information about jobs and applicants and facilitating match-ups. Internet recruiting has become so important that trade journals publish ratings of the top job sites such as Naukri.com or Jobs.com. In addition to its advantages of speed and economy, Internet recruiting reaches the global labour market. Internet sites also offer the potential for tremendous volume. For examples, Naukri.com receive 20,000 to 30,000 resources each year through e-mail. In addition, there is great specialisation. For instance, one site specializes in job openings for morticians.

In addition to recruiting efforts, companies have responded to labour shortages by hiring non-traditional workers. A number of companies have achieved excellent results by hiring disabled employees. Older workers also have provided on excellent source of labour. Although many older workers are not interested in full-time work, they appear to be interested in "fill-in" work of a part-time nature if the jobs provide flexibility and are close to home. Interestingly, the reserve of female workers that provided needed labour in the past has been depleted by their current involvement in the labour force. Liberalised policies that would allow greater immigration of skilled workers also are being viewed as a remedy for shortage of labour.

Unfortunately, for unqualified workers, employers will need entry-level workers whose skills are on par with global standards. Reten Merrison has stated "*when today's first graders reach adulthood they will compete within a global labour market and will need intellectual skills and levels of education and literacy never demanded of their predecessors*". Stated differently " Jobs that are currently in the middle of the skill distribution will be the least skilled occupations of the future, and there will be very few new jobs for the unskilled".

## Greater Racial Diversity

The labour force will become much more diverse in the twenty-first century. The category consisting of Asians and others (Pacific Islanders, Native Americans) is projected to grow by over 40 per cent through 2008, the fastest of all racial groups Hispanic participation is expected to increase by 36.8 percent, and Hispanics will become the largest minority group in the labour force by 2008, accounting for 12.7 percent of the labour force. The participation of black workers is expected to grow more slowly. 19.5 per cent growth in labour force participation of white workers will be the slowest, only 9.7 per cent. As a result of these growth patterns, by the year 2008, over 29 per cent of the workforce will be composed of nonwhites and organisations will need to plan to take advantage of diversity instead of forcing conformity. Likewise, organisations will need to be proactive in helping to create a work environment in which the creativity and innovations of diversity will flourish.

## Changing Occupational Distribution for Women

Females have constituted a growing portion of the workforce for several decades. However, this growth has slowed tremendously as women are predicted to constitute about 48 percent of the workforce by 2008, only one percentage point more than in 1998. While the occupational distribution of women still differs from that of man, they have made great strides in several job categories. Women now account for 68.3 per cent of the workers in training, human resources, and labour relations and for approximately 50 percent of accountants, although they are still underrepresented at the level of partner. Women have advanced most rapidly in cutting-edge industries because the need for pure intellectual horsepower overcomes inclinations for exclusion on the basis of gender. For example, they have fared well as information workers and as computer scientists. In the past 10 years, they also have made impressive inroads as engineers, sales engineers and as support staff for technical sales.

In order to attract talented women, many employers have work arrangements that better accommodates childbirth and, for women as well as man, the care of young children. Such approaches, include part-time schedules, flexitime, flexi scheduling, and allowing employees to work part of the time at home. Experiences with the latter have been reported at General Motors and Citi Bank for managerial and professional personnel. The trends towards greater flexibility are clear. Between 1991 and 1997, the proportion of the civilian labour force working on flexitime increased from 15 per cent to 27 per cent.

### Dual-career Couples

An issue related to increased feminization of the workforce is the number of dual career families. The number of couples having two-wage earners has increased rapidly, having passed the two-thirds point more than a decade age. In order to accommodate such families, many employers offer support services such as "sick child" care programmes and day care — such services are believed to produce reductions in absenteeism, lower turnover, recruiting advantages, and a positive impact on productivity. In order to help such dual-career couples, as well as single parents, employers now provide several forms of support. For example, referral services for child care are provided by one of the large public accounting firms as well as IBM. Other companies have set up child care facilities on company premises. Campbell Soup Company has had success with such a programme. However, such programmes are not automatic successes. Corning Glass and Merck encountered high costs and resentment from employees who did not need such services.

## Trends in the Utilisation of Human Resources

Internet, e-mail, fax machines, cable modems, digital subscriber lines, personal computers, other forms of telecommunications, and express mail make up of forces that have been able to relocate geographically while continuing to perform the same work for their employers via telecommunications technology.

### Telecommuting

Commuting or telecommunicating does not necessarily involve geographic communication but simply involves working at home at least part of the time. In recent times, the number of workers who telecommute has increased dramatically, telecommuting is thought to bring several individual benefits, including savings from the avoidance of commuting as well as at-home child care. Use of working for multiple employers, access to jobs by disabled workers and style advantages. There is a positive impact on the environment as well as fewer workers are on the highways. Organisation benefits include shifting advantages, lower costs in using part-time workers, increased ability of skilled professionals. On an *ad hoc* basis, reduced likelihood of unionization and need for office space, productivity improvements, and better morale for employers given the opinion of telecommuting, and employee retention. States that it is able to retain more of its employees because of telecommuting. Some observers have asserted that telecommuters work more efficiently.

Nonetheless, there are potential problems with such arrangements, including control difficulties, career limitations related to lack of visibility, workers, seems about missing opportunities, social isolation, less sense of belonging, reduced loyalties to both employer and employee. There are also concerns about the security of confidential or competitive information when it is transmitted over telephone lines from to and from the telecommuter. Although encryption technology may reduce such threats, security is a concern for some companies. Telecommuters also need remote office and information technology support. In addition, some managers find it difficult to trust their employees to work at home without their supervision.

## Relocation of Work

Telecommunication advances have allowed information workers to migrate from cities to rural areas and small towns. This migration has created what futurists Naisbilt and Aburdene call the electronic heartland. These workers have been attracted to the heartland because there is less crime, a lower cost of living, and quality of life benefits. Workers who are working on this relocation include owners of home-based businesses, writers, artists, stock traders, composers, software developers and engineers.

Companies are also relocating their operations. In information systems and data processing, companies are relocating their facilities to areas where there are favourable costs. For example, a New York Money Centre Bank relocated its data processing operations to a nearby state where real estate and the cost of living are lower. Information is transmitted electronically and henceforth with no delay in information system responsiveness while achieving substantial cost savings.

It is increasingly common for automobile rental companies and hotels to locate their reservations operations in areas of the country where there are wage advantages. For example, Hertz has its reservations and accounting operations in Oklahoma city. Thrifty and Avis both have reservations operations in Tulsa, and Budget's reservations operations for Hyatt Hotels are located in Omaha, Nebraska. These geographic areas offer wage advantages over many areas in the United States, and location is irrelevant to the nature of the work performed. Recently, manufacturing companies have been relocating out of their operating areas because of the high costs of land and labour as well as regulative environment.

## Growing Use of Temporary and Contingent Workers

Another important human resource issue is the increasing use of temporary or contingent workers. Temporary employees are often used to provide a buffer of protection for the jobs of the core of permanent employees. Further, the use of such workers is increasing and there is likely to be additional unbundling in the future. In contrast to core employees, contingent workers have short-term affiliations with employers. Examples include temporaries, subcontracted workers, part time workers, consultants, life of the project workers and leased employees. Companies also are using more "leased" employees who are "rented" from a temporary help agency on a long-term basis. Not surprisingly, unions typically resist the use of temporary workers.

Although there is growing use of higher skilled temporary employees, the largest category of temporaries is still administrative support of electrical work. The second largest category is industrial help workers such as labourers, equipment cleaners, helpers and handlers. Because demand for such industrial help workers is cyclical and seasonal, the advantages to the employer are obvious. Temporary workers are even being used in the health care industry as registered nurses, practical nurses and X-ray technicians.

As indicated, the nature of temporary jobs is changing as there is a shift toward the higher skill levels. Temporary workers now include accountants, computer specialists, engineering personnel, financial executives, and technical writers. In information systems, temporary management services are being used for project management, installation of new systems, or during transition periods. Temporary management personnel and executives are sometimes early retirees from major computer companies or managers displaced as a result of restructuring.

## Factors Promoting Use of Temporary or Contingent Employees

A number of factors encouraging the use of temporary or contingent employees. Because of economic uncertainty or turbulence, many employers are reluctant to use permanent employees and have increased their use of contingent employees. Another factor is fluctuating workloads. Companies also can avoid paying overtime pay by using temporaries during peak demand periods. Growing and declining companies have been found to use more temporary employers. The use of temporaries who can be dismissed on short notice allows these companies to protect the core of permanent employees. Nonetheless, in tight labour markets, it may be difficult to obtain qualified temporary employees.

Other factors prompting the use of contingent workers include avoidance of recruiting, hiring and training expenses for workers who are to be used only s short time and avoidance of severance costs. The perverse effects of legislation also may have prompted the use of temporaries in some instances. For example, the Worker Adjustment and Retraining Notification Act (WARN), which was designed to provide advance notice to plant shutdowns to full-time employees, may encourage the use of temporary workers. Other advantages for employers in the use of such workers include flexibility, potential savings in labour costs, and acquiring labour needed during hiring freezes.

In addition to benefits for employers, there are some benefits for temporary or contingent workers. These benefits include the flexibility to match lifestyle and family obligations with work and the ease of finding a job. For women, who constitute approximately two thirds of the temporary workforce, the benefits also include exposure in the job market, opportunities to obtain work experience and work skills, and the opportunity to sample employment situations. Opportunities to reacquire work skills and confidence may have appeal for women who have withdrawn from the labour force for substantial lengths of time. Youthful workers also may be attracted by temporary work as opportunities to gain work experience.

## Factors Limiting the use of Temporary Contingent Employees

Although there are several advantages for employers in using temporary employees, there are also disadvantages. One disadvantage is the increased livelihood of missing affirmative action goals. Employers may not obtain desired numbers of female and minority employees in their permanent workforce if they curtail hiring and rely extensively on temporary workers. Another disadvantage is the need to train such workers. With temporary executives, disadvantages may include inordinate emphasis on short-term financial performance and absence of company loyalty. Disadvantages for temporary employees include lower opportunities to receive health insurance and retirement benefits, lower pay and fewer training and educational opportunities. However, temporaries frequently have benefit coverage from spouses employment.

## Employee Leasing

Employee leasing is different from the use of temporary workers because there is no implication that employers will be other than full time, long-term employees. Often, when an employer makes the decision to lease employees, his or her employees then become employees of a leasing firm. The leasing firm then supplies these same employees to the original employer. As with the use of temporaries, there are some advantages with employees leasing. One primary reason for leasing is that small employers can obtain more economical health insurance by virtue of the leasing company's larger numbers of employees and inclusion in order pooled rates. Another motivating factor is that all payroll and administrative services are performed by the leasing company, leaving the management of the small company free to focus on other aspects of the business.

However, there are other disadvantages with the use of based employees. One is that some of the advantages of small size, such as exclusion from coverage by various federal laws based on size limits, are lost because of the leasing company's larger size. The use of the leasing company also may not eliminate liability, as there may be a shared employment relationship. Another disadvantage is that a number of leasing companies have failed, leaving the employers using based employers liable for workers compensation.

## International Developments

Companies competing on a global basis will need to use world-class labour to achieve the quality needed for some product markets. For example, The Motorola uses its training programmes to develop employees who can produce at a level of world competitive standards. One of the Motorola's accomplishments was to develop some of the workers into world class software engineers. One software manufacturer has obtained specialised world class information service by having programming done in USA and routing work done in India.

Moving foreign nationals across internal boundaries is another approach for highly skilled individuals. However, the use of U.S. expatriate enters in overseas holdings may be declining. In some U.S. companies with overseas holdings, the number of U.S. expatriate workers is relatively small. For example, during one year Honeywell had 27,159 employees overseas and approximately 200 were U.S. citizens. Instead, there may be growing tendency to bring foreign nationals to the United States for a few years training through the parent company and having them take on the managerial or professional responsibilities in their countries. The legal restrictions involved in these may be critical. Some large organisations have human resource management specialists who have developed expertise in working through the legalities in such ways.

## Global Sourcing of Labour

Innovative use of labour on a global basis are evident. One example is a large Insurance Company in which claims are processed in Ireland. The combination of a common language, an educated labour force, a shortage of jobs, and relatively low wages more than this is an attractive option. As operations have been setup, its data are sent from the United States using overnight airmail and electronic transmission. An interesting benefit of this relationship is that, in addition to the low cost of labour, there is a time differential advantage as work delivered overnight can be worked on several hours prior to the normal starting time of 8.00 A.M. on the East Coast. Additionally, U.S. companies sometimes have data entry performed offshore in order to take advantage of wage differentials. In some instances, data entry is performed by deistical workers who do not even speak English. For example, American Airlines has data entry performed in China and Barbados

Several Asian Countries such as Korea, Singapore, Taiwan, Malaysia and Indonesia are major U.S. trading and outsourcing partners. Nonetheless, the dramatic changes in Eastern Europe also have implications for labour supplies. Germany is especially intriguing. Although productivity in the eastern portion of Germany is lower because of the residual effects of communism, the prospects for rapid productivity growth are good because the labour force is literate, competent, mechanically adept, and has a strong work ethic. This transition to high productivity is in stark contract to expectations of the labour force in many U.S. cities where illiteracy among workers are high. Although the workforce from the former East Germany may be more skilled than those of some East European countries, the labour forces of these countries are attractive in many respects and are now accessible to western companies.

## Summary

This chapter overviewed several trends and developments that are likely to affect human resources in the twenty-first century. The impact of technology on employee skill requirements and jobs was considered along with the impact on globalisation structure. As a result of information technology, organisations are running less hierarchical and more adaptive and flexible. The emergence of corporations, network or virtual organisations, cellular organisations, and the growth in entrepreneurial businesses were discussed. Some of these new organisational structures or forms that take continuous views towards organisation units and their workers are becoming more common place. The examination of worker values and attitudes reveal that employees also are becoming less loyal towards their employers, more concerned with having interesting jobs that allow them to grow, and more inclined to feel that they are entitled to participate in decisions affecting them.

Several important managerial trends were examined, including the need to manage an increasingly diverse workforce and to harness its capacity for creativeness. The increased use of teams and the emergence of virtual teams was discussed. Team practices, such as rotating leadership responsibilities among team members based on the stage of product development cycles were addressed. The increasing practice of human resource outsourcing was described as a major change in the management of human resources. In addition, there was discussion of the continued emphasis of TQM, which requires a number of changes in the human resource functions, including a stronger service orientation. The implications of several other managerial trends were examined, including integrated manufacturing process, reengineering, and managing an increasing number of professionals. There also was a discussion of how organisations will need to prepared for and deal with the aftermath of mergers and acquisitions.

Several other trends were also examined, including demographic trends such as the ageing workforce, the age gaps and bulges that have resulted from the baby form and baby bust, the possibility of continuing labour shortages, greater racial diversity, changing occupational distributions for women, and dual career couples.

Trends in the utilization of human resources were also examined, including telecommuting and the relocation of work. The implications of telecommuting and the migration of information workers to rural areas and small towns for cost of living and quality of life reasons were discussed. In addition, there was also a discussion of the relocation of companies that are taking advantage of low costs in different locations. The trend toward increasing use of temporary or contingent workers, which has expanded to professionals was discussed. The increased internationalisation of business and global sourcing of labour were also examined along with the implications of NAFTA and the EC.

## Case Study

### My Car Automobile Manufacturing in the Twenty-first Century

In 1990, economists Anirban and Bhupati predicted a resurgence of Indian manufacturing before the new century. They predicted that resurgence would be stimulated by increased investment in the capital base of machinery and tools by which products are manufactured. When they made their prediction, many Indian manufacturers were using outdated tools and machines, compared with those of global competitors. As a result, some Indian products were not competitive in price or quality. Factors expected to drive the resurgence of manufacturing included a low rate of inflation and the demographic influences associated with the baby boom. The country's manufacturing investment stagnated during earlier periods of high inflation, which reached 15 percent in 1982. High inflation caused investors to purchase tangible assets, such as hotels and office buildings, as inflation hedges. Since stocks and bonds do not provide the same hedge, they become less attractive investments and funding for the plant and equipment needed for production of goods became more difficult to obtain. The attack on inflation during the 1982s and tax reforms made tangible assets less attractive as inflation hedges and tax shields. Stocks and bonds then became relatively more attractive.

One foundation for the economists' prediction was ageing of the baby boomers. When the economists made their predictions, the baby boomers had reached their mid-forties and were predicted to start to save more. The savings of this huge age cohort were expected to serve as major sources of funding for the new plant and equipment needed to make the country's manufacturing competitive in world markets. The oldest of the baby boomers were in their mid-fifties in 2004 and will be in their mid-sixties in 2014. This is a huge cohort and is expected to push the median age of the country's labor force to 45 in 2010. As a result of the baby boomers and past layoffs based on inverse seniority, some Indian manufacturing houses in the year 2004 had workforces with an average age in the mid-fifties. Employment in manufacturing was fairly stable in the 1992s while manufacturing productivity increased. With increased productivity, fewer workers were needed to manufacture the same amount of goods (The health of the industry is not necessarily indicated by whether there is a growing or declining level of employment.) Furthermore, some manufacturing employment shifted to the services sector as a result of outsourcing. (Employees of firms supplying services, such as information services for manufacturing companies are not counted in manufacturing employment.)

Interestingly, in automobile manufacturing the capital requirements for assembly plants has declined as indicated in the following:

We could be seeing a radical transformation in where and how cars are built, predicts one of the senior most professor of a premier technical university in the department of Automobile Engineering of the country in one of his landmark survey. But will we? Assembly plants can now be built for 10K crores, instead of 500 crores they historically cost. These "disposable plants" could, at least in theory, be readily written off, making site selection decisions extremely flexible and short-term. 'We've learned a lot about plant design and about designing with less redundancy," explains the professor.

In addition, experts on the automobile industry say that labour costs are increasing in northern parts of the country and that it actually costs more to build a plant in around Faridabad.

Faridabad is still generally a cheaper place to do business, but not as cheap as it used to be. Labour, for example, is getting more expensive. The labour force in northern India is getting increasingly sophisticated, and wages have gone up.".... Building a plant in around Faridabad also entails a number of unexpected costs... "Simple materials like concrete may be cheaper, but overall, I can build a plant cheaper in southern India than I can in north."... That's because there are few to no local suppliers for more sophisticated building systems like air conditioning, and because the energy and water constraints mean the plant has to be built for greater efficiencies than would be necessary in the country.

Interestingly, the labour costs of producing automobiles in coastal part of western India are lower than central India, and productivity is substantially higher. Additional developments in the automobile industry are that the manufacturers would like to sell automobiles over Internet booking, which they predict would reduce the average price of automobiles. However, there is stiff resistance from the dealers who have been able to obtain legal restrictions making direct sales more difficult for manufacturers. Finally, the country's auto workers has lifetime employment agreements with the automobile manufacturers association.

## Questions

1. Consider all of the information provided in this case and your knowledge of current economic and business conditions, what human resource issues should managers in the automobile industry be prepared for in the future?
2. How might the employee skills, management practices, and automobile manufacturing companies change in the future? How would you expect the managerial trends to affect in human resource practices and policies in future automobile manufacturing?
3. Describe how the human resource and managerial environments of automobile manufacturing firms in the twenty-first century differ from the same environments in the 1975s?

## References


1. Charles R. Greer, *Strategic Human Resource Management-A General Managerial Approach*, second Edition, Pearson Education, 2006.
2. Rutledge, John, and Deborah Allen. *Rust to Riches*, New York: Harper and Row, 1989.


***

# 5 Strategic Human Resource Planning

Human resource is part of the strategic planning process. It is part of policy development, line-extension planning and the merger and acquisition process. Little is done in the company that does not involve employees in the planning, policy or finalization stages of any deal is not going to attract employees in achieving the goal. In terms of competitive advantage in the global economy. However, the good news is that most foreign competitors also conduct their HR planning and recruitment in a reactive manner rather than as a fully integrated system. Thus, there is opportunity for competitive advantage in terms of organisational capability for companies. Recent survey results from small business and the continuing trend to downsize in large corporations underscore the importance of human resources in strategic planning. The focus of small business in recent years has been on growth and expanding the customer base, while the focus of the largest companies has been on controlling overhead by reducing labour costs and shedding workers. HR planning should be an integral part of either strategy. The most effective approach to staffing, whether adding workers or eliminating them, is to assess staffing needs with a focus on meeting customer requirements and for most products or services, expanding the customer base.

The goal for organisations of all sizes is quite simple: keep the cost of labour as low as possible while meeting (or exceeding) customer demand and, if this is part of the strategic plan, expanding the customer base. The realisation of this goal for HR practice is difficult. This goal can also be applied to the internal customers who require products or services from internal suppliers, including HRM staff. For example, an internal customer could be a District Manager in retail who must hire a Store Manager for a store in the District. One option could be to use an external head-hunter group that specializes in retail or perhaps the company relies on internal recruiters to compile a list of qualified candidates. The company is very interested in the cost of the recruiting effort, and the District Manager may be particularly interested in filling the position quickly with someone who requires little or no training.

Two of the most important aspects of staffing are HRM planning and recruitment. Planning is the forecast of HR needs in the context of strategic business planning. The human resource planning process of the past was typically reactive in nature, with business needs defining personnel needs. However, with major changes in the business environment and increasing uncertainty, many organisations are adopting a longer term perspective and integrating human resource planning with strategic business planning centered on a consideration of core business competencies.

Recruitment is the process of attracting applicants for the positions needed. This process should be fully integrated with the HR planning process and other HR activities, especially the selection process. Most experts maintain that recruitment and other HRM activities are interdependent. For example, recruitment success affects selection success and the use of selection procedures can affect recruitment success.

This chapter provides an overview of the planning and recruitment process. We will discuss the relationship among planning, recruitment, and the other HRM functions, the process of downsizing and reengineering or restructuring, the various sources available for recruiting and their relative effectiveness; the advantages and disadvantages of internal and external recruiting; and the role of equal employment opportunity in the planning and recruitment process.

## What is Human Resource Planning?

E.W. Vetter viewed human resource planning as "a process by which an organisation should move from its current manpower position to its desired manpower position. Through planning, management strives to have the right number and right kind of people at the right places at the right time, doing things which result in both the organisation and the individual receiving maximum long-term benefit".

According to Leon C. Meggison human resource planning is "an integrated approach to performing the planning aspects of the personnel function in order to have a sufficient supply of adequately developed and motivated people to perform the duties and tasks required to meet organisational objectives and satisfy the individual needs and goal of organisational members."

The United Kingdom Institute of Personnel Management in 1989 defined human resource planning as:

*"The systematic and continuing process of analysing an organisation's human resources needs under changing conditions, and developing personnel policies appropriate to the longer term effectiveness of the organisation. It is an integral part of corporate planning and budgeting procedures since human resource costs and forecasts both affect, and are affected by longer term corporate plans".*

Human resource planning may be viewed as foreseeing the human resource requirements of an organisation and the future supply of human resources and (i) making necessary adjustments between these two and organisational plans; and (ii) foreseeing the possibilities of developing the supply of human resources in order to match it with requirements by introducing necessary changes in the functions of human resource management. In this definition, human resource means skill, knowledge, values, ability, commitment, motivation etc., in addition to the number of employees.

## Strategic Human Resource Planning Process

The above definitions emphasizes several important features of the formal human resource planning activity:

(i) It is conducted within a dynamic not static environment it constitutes an ongoing process or activity. In other words, a human resource plan should be regularly updated to accord with changing circumstances.

(ii) The plan itself allows the organisation to react to such changing circumstances with some degree of order and control.

(iii) The human resource plan both affects and is affected by financial considerations.

(iv) A human resource plan is an aid to longer-term strategic organisation activity.

The Human Resource Planning process is outlined in Figure 5.1. An examination of this figure shows that the human resource plan is, in the short-term at least, a product of the business plan of the enterprise. As such, the organisation's human resource planning is conducted not in a vacuum but in an environment mindful of and responsive to organisation needs.

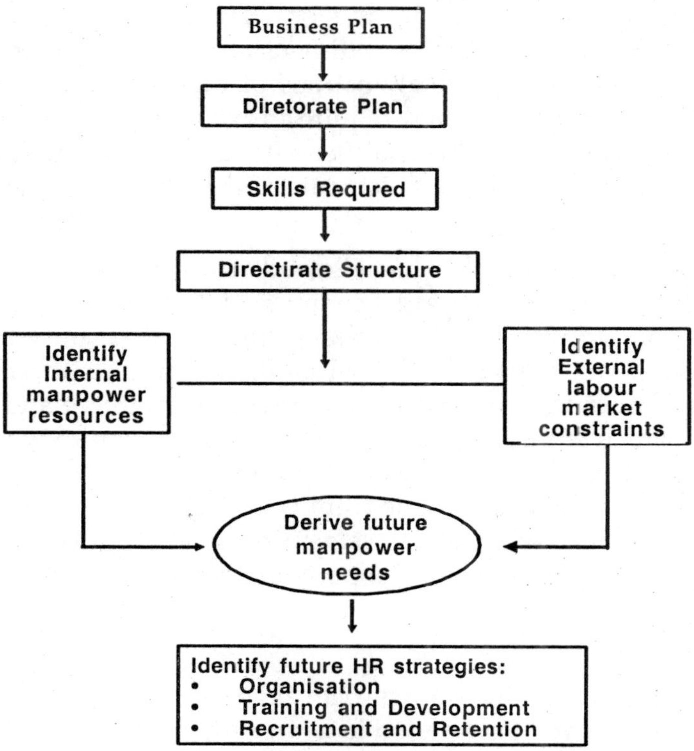


**Fig. 5.1: Strategic Human Resource Planning Process**

From these objectives an assessment of the tasks needed to fulfil these needs are made. From the assessment of these required tasks an assessment of the skills required to effectively address these tasks are made. This will necessitate a thorough examination of the numbers of employees required, the timings of such requirements, and the skills required of these employees at the various stages of the operational plan.

The human resource plan than attempts to organise the human resources of the organisation in such a way as to achieve organisation goals and produces a formal plan that is well placed to evolve an organisational structure which affords the environment necessary to achieve the organisations objectives. Alternatively, it could be concluded that any organisational structure which is evolved without examining the problem at the manpower level is likely to be deficient.

The process, then necessitates an examination of the existing manpower resources within the organisation: the numbers of employees, their existing skills, their age structures, the present way in which these employees are grouped or structured. It may well be that existing employee members, skills and structural deployments will not be conducive to the fulfilment of the organisations objectives and plans. It may well be that the organisation needs to examine how it can improve its human resources. This may involve the organisation employing new people. However, a good human resource plan will examine the constraints of the external market. Desirable though it might be to employ a specified number of people with specified skills in the future, the practical feasibility of employing such people needs to be examined. For a typical large organisation this will require the analysis of national, regional and local labour market information and indeed, in certain circumstances, an international dimension may need to be assessed. This will require the determination of the likely actions of their organisations to which future employees might be attracted. This may require an examination of the job content afforded by such likely competitors. The financial benefits likely to be offered, the training and development opportunities and other elements of the job environment, such as attitude to flexible working practices.

So far as human resource plan has allowed an assessment to be made of current employee altitudes, loyalties, skills and a comparison to be made with likely demands at future specified points in time. It has effected this comparison whilst examining the future state of the labour market. The final and most important part of the plan is an assessment of the future training and development, recruitment and retention needs of the organisation, which employees and in what numbers require what types of training and development? What new types of employee, and in what numbers, does the organisation need to employ at specified times in the future? Furthermore, the human resource plan necessitates a formal assessment of what employment strategies will be needed to retain those employees for the period of required by the operational plant.

## The Issue of Retention

It may be that the human resource plan reveals that so called natural wastage is excessively high. During any time period in a large organisation employees will leave for a number of reasons beyond that organisation's control; they or their family may leave the area; they may reach retirement age; they may leave as part of their normal career development; they may become ill; they may leave to look after their family. Indeed it might be claimed that such a natural throughput of labour brings to an organisation much needed new approaches and enthusiasm.

However, such a change in the workforce brings with it costs; new employees need to be recruited and selected, new employees need to be inducted; new employees need initial training; new employees involve some disruption of the working group.

An organisation needs regularly to question whether its natural wastage is excessive. Under such circumstances the organisation will be required to scrutinise the reasons for employers leaving; this can be relatively easily achieved by exit interviews whereby employees are questioned as to their reasons for leaving. If the organisation finds that some of the causes are not 'natural' but due to problems emerging in the organisation, it might wish to rectify these problems rather than commit itself to the costs of recruiting, selecting, inducting and training new employees.

Thus, the issue of increasing the retention rate of employees becomes a legitimate management project for an organisation. If this excessive wastage is due to low remuneration, the organisation might give consideration to reassuring its remuneration package by way of rewarding employees for staying in the organisation. If it is caused by limited promotion possibilities it might reconsider its promotion policies. However, it must be admitted that, in time of flattening organisational structures, pure promotion may not be readily available: under such circumstances the organisation might have to direct its attention to wider developmental issues such as job variation, job enlargement, and job enrichment. If the excessive wastage is confined to one section of the organisation, there may be clear signals that some aspect of management is remiss in that section. The organisation should then be obliged to rectify this problem.

### Reduction in Staff Numbers

An examination of real life human resource planning reveals that on many occasions the plan demands an actual reduction of staff numbers. This reduction in staffing needs to be professionally and effectively managed. In shedding of staff an organisation will have two objectives:

(i) Complying with law;

(ii) Striving to retain the goodwill and motivation of those remaining after the reduction.

## The Legal Environment

In the United Kingdom the primary legislation applying to this area is the Trade Union Reform and Employment Rights Act 1993 (TURER). TURER obliges an organisation seeking reduce its workforce to undertake certain actions before it institutes compulsory redundancy:

1. It must restrict recruitment in the areas of employment concerned.
2. It must ensure that employees beyond normal retirement age are retired.
3. It must not allow paid overtime in the areas of employment where reductions are taking plan.
4. It must institute short-time working.
5. It must strive for transfer or retaining of staff where possible.
6. It must terminate the employment of temporary or contract staff.
7. It must seek early retirement of voluntary redundancy before instituting compulsory redundancy.
8. In all these actions it must seek the co-operation of employee representatives.

## Ensuring goodwill and motivation of remaining staff

The goodwill and motivation of remaining workers is extremely important. The established working groups of remaining staff will have been disrupted, previous colleagues will have been seen to have lost their jobs. This is hardly the environment to retain the goodwill and consequent motivation of those remaining.

It could be claimed that many organisations would consider instituting the legal provisions just mentioned even if the legal environment did not prescribe their introduction. Many of the matters introduced by the law can be seen as attempting to limit the harmful consequence of termination. Such action will at least ensure that remaining workers will feel that the organisation has tried to limit the harm done to its workforce.

However, with this objective assuming primary, it might be that an employer seeking to reduce the workforce could voluntarily pursue additional activity to mitigate the negative consequences which might ensue. It might be useful to examine what, in addition to the matters just discussed, an employer could voluntarily institute:

1. It could seek to gain new employment for those staff leaving by approaching other employers, by approaching employment agencies, by advertising vacancies in other organisations.
2. It could prepare these staff for future employment by helping them with future career plans; it could help them prepare CVs and application forms for other employment; it could tutor them in the skills required at selection.
3. It could seek to mitigate the financial consequences of loss of employment by advising on entitlement to benefits or by advising or handling personal finances and investment.
4. It could focus on counselling for all those affected, both, those no longer employed and those who continue to be employed.

## Some practical issues which should be addressed

The human resource plan, and specifically the examination of external market conditions, will reveal whether the likelihood is that the organisation will need or more particularly, be able to employ full-time or part-time employees. If the analysis reveals that it is the part-time section of the labour market which is likely to afford the organisation with its required skills, then the organisation might have to reconsider its present employment hours to make it more attractive to potential recruits. The overwhelming majority of part-time employees are women with family responsibilities and it may be that the organisations present working patterns conflict with the family responsibilities of these future potential recruits. The organisation must then either adjust its working practices or accept the consequences of failing to adjust.

Finally, the concentration of this analysis has been upon human resource planning conducted in situations where the labour market or budgetary constraints are such that the original plans of the organisation are found to be achievable. It must be recognised that the human resource planning exercise can itself highlight unachievable plans, desirable though the operational plan is, the required labour either cannot be provided or the cost of providing it will be prohibitive. It is extremely important to note, therefore, that the human resource planning exercise can be an invaluable tool in assessing the practicality of operational plans.

# Who should produce the Human Resource Plan?

The production of the human resource plan will be a complex exercise; it will involve inputs from all operational managers, the finance manager and the human resources expert. The operational managers will be responsible for advising what needs doing and upon the skills required of the workforce. The finance manager will need to impose financial discipline on the process, human resource plans can so easily become an expression of the ideal but unachievable. The role of the human resource expert is more problematic; he has the skills to contribute to the assessment of the capabilities of the staff.

### Objectives

The important objectives of human resource planning in an organisation are as below:

1. understand the importance of human resource planning (HRP) to the organisation.
2. identify the six steps in the HRP process.
3. identify the methods by which an organisation can develop forecasts of anticipated personnel demand and understand labour markets.
4. understand how an organisation can stay apprised of and evaluate its personnel supply and, if necessary, implement a low range programme.

5. determine which recruitment methods are best for given situations, including the growing business of automated recruiting through the internet and other online services.
6. understand the pros and cons of internal versus external recruiting.
7. know the most important features of recruitment advertising.
8. know the EEO implications of recruitment and planning.

## Effective Human Resource Planning

We have so far discussed human resource planning as a problem solving process conducted in the context of an organisations strategy and policy. Strengths, weaknesses, opportunities and threats, SWOT analysis is critical for the strategic planning and recruitment processes. Effect HRP closes the gap from the current situation to a desired state of affairs in the context of the organisation's strategy. The process of determining this match is outlined in Figure 5.2. Effective HRP should involved:

1. Environmental scanning,
2. Labour/Demand forecast,
3. Supply forecast,
4. Gap analysis,
5. Action programming, and
6. Control and evaluation.

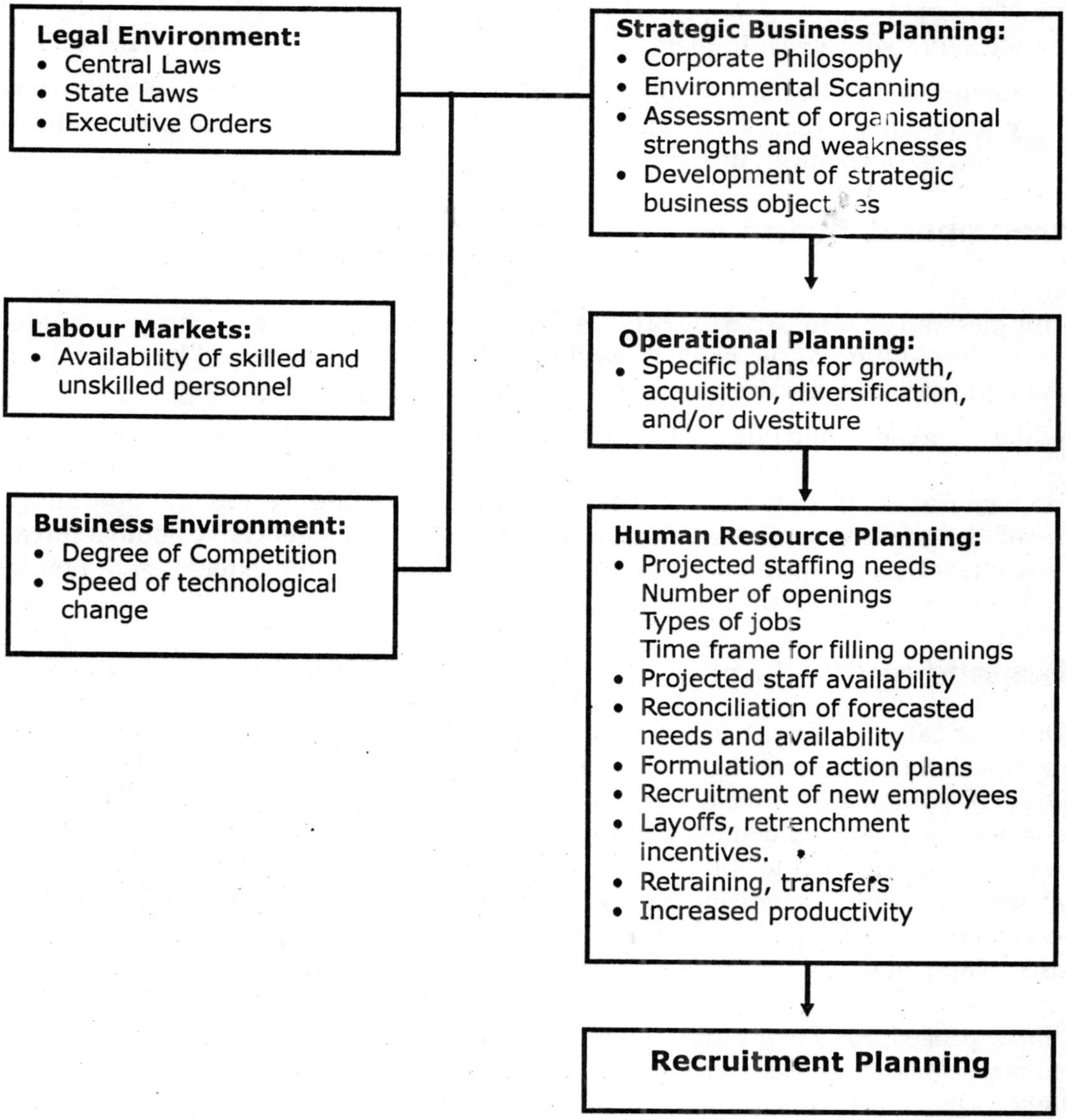


**Fig. 5.2: Simplified Model of External & Internal Factors that Influence Recruitment:**

1. *Environmental Scanning*: Identify and anticipate sources of threat and opportunities, scanning the external environment (competitors regulation) and internal environment (strategy, technology, culture).
2. *Labour Demand Forecast:* Project how business needs will affect HR needs, using qualitative methods (e.g., Delphi, nominal) and quantitative methods (trend analysis, simple and multiple linear regression analysis).
3. *Labour Supply Forecast*: Project resource availability from internal and external sources.

4. *Gap Analysis*: Reconcile the forecast of labour supply and demand.
5. *Action Programming*: Implement the recommended solution from step – 4 .
6. *Control and Evaluation*: Monitor the effects of HRP by defining and measuring critical criteria (e.g., turnover costs, breakeven costs of new hires, recruitment costs, performance outcomes).

## Environmental Scanning

Environmental scanning helps HR planners identify and anticipate sources of threats, opportunities and should drive the organisation's strategic planning. Scanning provides a better understanding of the context in which HR decisions are or will be made. Both external and internal environmental scan is critical for effective planning.

While there can be and often are situations with ambiguous threats and opportunities, the probability of reducing or eliminating the ambiguity is increased by a more thorough environmental scan. The idea is to at least attempt to turn a threat into an opportunity. In general, the greater the amount of relevant information managers have about a threat, the more likely that threat can be turned into an opportunity. Both external and internal environmental scans are critical for this information.

## Understanding the Labour Market for HR Planning

One critical component of HR environmental scanning for HR planning and recruitments is an understanding of the relevant labour market. Labour market conditions influence HR planning in terms of both the number and types of available employees. In a loose labour market, qualified recruits are extremely tight. For example, there are current shortages in cutting-edge technologies (e.g., optics, laser technology, electromagnetic, composites technology), medicine and medical support, computer science and support services, electrical engineering, manufacturing engineering, plastics, languages and statistics. Tight markets limit the availability of labour, drive up the price of those employees who are selected, and limit the extent to which the organisation can be selective in its hiring procedures. For example, many hospitals hesitate to administer valid selection tests to applicants for physiotherapist jobs because applicants are in such short supply. Private security guard and trucking companies use psychological tests for screening mainly because of fears of negligent hiring lawsuits. However, because of the level of competition in this area, the demand for services, and the tight labour market for largely unskilled labour, these companies cannot be very selective in hiring people despite what the tests may predict.

There is now a mad scramble among companies to assess the implications of the world wide web on strategic plans, positions in the market, and, in general, the threats and opportunistic of this fast paced movement. Experts on the intricacies of all aspects of the web are in short supply and in great demand.

The relevant labour market for an employer is usually defined by occupation, geography and employer competition. Obviously, the job and the skills or job specifications play the greatest role in the definition of the relevant labour market and the ease (or difficulty) with which positions can be filled. The labour market for most jobs can also be greatly affected by geography. Bechtel, the giant international construction company received several million dollars in contracts with Kuwait to rebuild the country after the 1991 war with Iraq. However, the company had difficulty recruiting civil engineers and other specialists to go to Kuwait. Even high wages did not attract the necessary number of qualified professionals. There was such a chronic shortage of qualified teachers for the 1997 school year in Texas, schools were hiring almost anyone with a college degree to fill classes. The state of Michigan, which pays teachers about 30% more to start, had no such shortage.

Competing employers are the third factor defining the labour market. The number and type of employers seeking similarly qualified personnel or offering similar compensation in the same geographical location can also define the labour market.

## The Global Labour Market

The technological and communications revolution has changed the relationship between geography and labour supply. The world is now the labour market for both skilled and unskilled labour. The outsourcing of the manufacturing/assembly process to a foreign location is now common in many industries. What is also becoming more common is that skilled labour positions are being turned out to lower paid overseas workers. Digital Equipment, Hewlett Packard, IBM, Texas Instrument, and Compaq Computer all employ skilled workers in Bengaluru, India. Many of whom write software packages for these companies. The programme costs are estimated to be about half the cost of an American Programmer. However, this difference could change rapidly as the demand for Indian Programmers grows.

E-mail, fax machines, private satellite links, and the worldwide web have made workers from all over the world very accessible and have expanded the labour market. The result is lower labour costs and thus greater profits. Companies that do not take advantage of the global labour market for labour will be at a competitive disadvantage as long as consumers do not place a heavyweight on the extent to which a product or service involves the workers. Figure 5.3 presents a summary of the relevant labour market as defined by occupation and geography.

| Relevant Labour Market | | | | | | | |
|---|---|---|---|---|---|---|---|
| | **Geographic** | **Production Scope** | **Office and Clerical** | **Technicians** | **Scientists and and Engineers** | **Managerial Professionals** | **Executive** |
| | Local: Within relatively small areas, such as cities or metropolitan statistical areas – MSAs (e.g., Kolkata Metropolitan area) | Most likely | Most likely | – | – | – | – |
| | Regional: Within a particular area of the state or country or several states(e.g., Hyderabad) | Only if in short supply or critical | Only if in short supply or critical | Most likely | Likely | Likely | – |
| | National: Across the country | – | – | – | Most likely | Most likely | Most likely |
| | International: Across several countries | – | – | – | Only for critical skills or those in very short supply | Only for critical skills or those in very short supply | Likely |

**Fig. 5.3: Relevant Labour Markets by Geographic and Employee Groups**

Managing the labour market and the cost of labour is a crucial HR activity. Companies usually look at labour first when their corporate performance measures do not meet expectations. The need is to be more flexible in this dynamic and global economy. Employers need to be creative in solving their staffing needs.

### Labour shortage in services

Companies sometimes have to expand the geographical base for labour because of supply and demand. They may also have to expand the supply of labour by increasing compensation. Companies are also looking at technology and software to replace at least some humans without affecting customer satisfaction. Technology has reduced the need for certain categories of employees in numerous industries.

### Affirmative action/diversity programmes and the law: A threat or opportunity?

Government regulations also influence HR planning and must be considered in any environmental scan. The most contentious situation, however, is one in which the employer shows some form of preferential treatment toward members of one group when there is no proven history of discrimination, no court mandate, or no consent decree. HR planning often includes very detailed programmes directed at increasing the diversity of an organisation's workforce. The planning converts to recruiting efforts designed to increase the supply of workers to meet diversity criteria. The ambiguity has been fostered because of the current state of the law regarding the manner in which such diversity is achieved. We return to this issue since diversity goals are an important part of HR planning and recruitment for government and most large corporations.

Despite the legal confusion, organisations are continuing their efforts to promote diversity in their workforces. Walt Disney Company, for example, has minority hiring targets at every level, according to Marc Pacala, Disneys general manger. Kentucky Fried Chicken maintains separate lists of minority candidates for its executive positions. Xerox continues with its "balanced workforce" programme, which has measurable hiring goals for all levels of management. One survey found that 70 per cent of Fortune 500 companies engage in race based hiring while only 14 per cent said they hired by merit alone.

## Qualitative Methods

The simplest method for preparing labour demand is a centralised approach in which the HR department examines the current business situation and determines staffing requirements for the rest of the firm. While this approach is simple, it is generally not accurate. A top-down approach assumes that the central HR office has an accurate understanding of the business as well as the needs of each unit or function. In large complex firms, these assumptions typically do not hold. A more preferred method involves a decentralised process wherein each unit or functional manager subjectively derives his or her own staffing needs. These projections are aggregated to create an overall composite forecast for the company.

For example, top management of a company set a goal of 30 per cent cost reduction for each functional unit. Unit managers were asked to conduct job analysis of each job under their jurisdiction and after analysis to submit proposals for workload reduction and other cost reduction options. A procedure was established to present the various reduction options including a method for the presentation of a rationale if the manger failed to move the 30 per cent target reduction.

Other firms have experimented with formalised problem solving methods such as the Delphi technique to minimise interpersonal and jurisdictional conflicts. The Delphi technique avoids face to face group discussion through the use of an intermediary. Experts take turns presenting a forecast statement and assumptions. The intermediary passes on the forecasts and assumptions to the others. Revisions are then made independently and anonymously by the experts. The intermediate then pools and summarises, the judgements and gives them to the experts. This process is continued until a consensus forecast emerges or until the intermediary concludes that more than one perspective must be presented. The Delphi techniques has been shown to produce better one year forecasts than with linear regression analysis, but there can be difficulties in reaching consensus on complex problems.

The full Delphi process can take considerable time. For example, a clothing retailer took over four months to forecast the number of buyers needed for the next year using a Delphi method. The use of networked computers can reduce the time required for Delphi forecasting.

The nominal group technique is similar to the Delphi method. Experts join at a conference and independently list their ideas with the group. As the ideas are presented, a master list of the ideas is compiled so everyone can refer to them. The ideas are discussed and ranked by member vote.

## Quantitative Methods

Quantitative methods are based on the assumption that the future is an extrapolation from the past. Trend analysis incorporates certain business factors (e.g., units produced, revenues) and a productivity ratio (e.g., employees per units produced). The company's external environmental scanning data indicated more favourable ratios. By projecting changes in the business factor and/or the productivity ratio, we can forecast changes in the labour demand. There are six steps involved in trend analysis:

1. Find the appropriate business factor that relates to the size of the workforce.
2. Plot of historical record of that factor in relation to the size of the workforce.
3. Compute the productivity ratio (average output per worker per year)
4. Determine the trend.
5. Make necessary adjustments in the trend, past and future.
6. Project of the target year

The use of the appropriate business factor is critical to the success of the trend analysis. The business factor should be directly related to the essential purpose for the business. Universities typically use student enrolment by discipline, hospitals use patient-days, manufacturers typically use output needs, and retailers use sales adjusted by inventory.

Learning curves predict that the average numbers of units produced per employee will increase as mere units are produced. Such an increase is expected because workers learn to perform their tasks efficiently over time. Learning curves are evident in virtually all industries.

Simple linear regression and multiple linear regression are the most commonly used statistical procedures. Simple linear regression uses information from the past relationship between the organisation's employment level and some criterion known to be related to employment. For example, most companies can establish a statistical relationship between sales or work output and level of employment. Such a relationship, however, is also influenced by the learning curve. Learning curves can be used to make more accurate projections of future employment levels. More complicated quantitative methods involving multiple regression and linear programming further this process by incorporating operational constraints (i.e., budgets, mix of labour) into the mathematical models. Through this elaboration it is possible to forecast demand under varying business scenarios. Multiple regression may use several factors that correlate with labour needs. For example, in preparation of its collective bargaining negotiations, companies can use several different sales figures, gross national product, gross domestic product, capital investments and other factors to forecast labour needs for the coming years.

While our discussion of labour demand may suggest that planners attempt to establish a singular forecast, the outcome of this process is typically a set of potential scenarios. A scenario is a multifaceted portrayal of the mix of business factors in conjunction with the array of HR needs. As such, each scenario/forecast is an elaborate set of "if-then" statements; that is "if" the business context presents us with scenario A, "then" our labour demand forecast would be B. Ideally, HR planning is as comprehensive as possible to provide leeway for a variety of business activities.

## Step three: Labour supply forecast

Whereas the labour demand forecast projects HR needs, the labour supply forecast projects resource availability. This step of HR planning is vital in that it conveys an inventory of the firms current and projected competencies. This skill base sets an upper limit on the commitments and challenges the firm can undertake (all else being equal). From a problem solving perspective, labour supply represents the raw materials available to address threats and opportunities. Supply forecasts are typically broken into two categories: External supply and Internal supply.

*Internal Supply:* Internal labour supply consists of those individuals and jobs currently available within the firm. Data from personnel/skill inventories are used to make projections for the future based on current trends. These trends include not only the number and kinds of individuals in each job, but also the flow of employees into, through, and out of the organisation. Specifically, a skills inventory includes an assessment of the knowledge, skills, abilities, experience, and career aspirations of each worker. This record should be updated at least every two years and should include changes, such as new skills, degree completions, and changed job duties. These inventories also aid in the internal recruitment process. If these skills inventories are not updated, present employers may be overlooked for job openings within the organisation. This may result in increased search costs in addition to dissatisfaction among employers who were overlooked. Accordingly, internal supply forecasts must consider the company's current practices pertaining to hiring, firing, transfer, promotion, development and attrition. The performance appraisal system of the organisation should be part of any personnel/skill inventory.

Succession planning and replacement charts are also used by some companies to identify individuals to fill a given slot if an incumbent should leave. These techniques are most useful for individual level problems with short-term planning time horizons.

Two of the most important concerns regarding the use of electronic databases for personnel are privacy rights and securing problems. The latter issue can be handled with the right systems and software provisions. The privacy issue is much more difficult. Many states and central governments have privacy laws that may pertain to the use, content and access of a HRIS. More complicated transition models such as Markov analysis are used for long-range forecasts in large companies. Markov analysis used historical information from Figure 5.4.

| **Screen – 1: Current Employee Data** |
|---|
| Name: |
| Department: |
| Position: |
| Supervisor: |
| Period in Position: |
| Date of Joining: |

| **Screen – 2: Educational Qualification Data** | | | | | |
|---|---|---|---|---|---|
| | School Attended | Degree | Major | GPA | Year(s) |
| High | | | | | |
| Position: | | | | | |
| Supervisor: | | | | | |
| Period in Position: | | | | | |
| Date of Joining: | | | | | |
| Additional Training Recommended: | | | | | |

| Screen – 3: Company Employment Data | | | |
|---|---|---|---|
| | Title | Date in Job | Performance Ratings/Dates |
| Present Position | | | |
| Previous Position | | | |
| Positions in Company Qualified for: | | | |

| Screen – 4: Educational Previous Employment Data | | | | | | |
|---|---|---|---|---|---|---|
| | Company | Title | From | To | Reference | Quality |
| Prev. Employment | | | | | | |
| Prev. Employment | | | | | | |
| Prev. Employment | | | | | | |
| Prev. Employment | | | | | | |
| Prev. Employment | | | | | | |
| Additional Training Recommended: | | | | | | |

**Fig. 5.4 Sample Elements in Skills Inventory**

Personnel movements of the internal labour supply to predict what will happen in the future. An estimate is mode of the livelihood that persons in a particular job will remain in that job or be transferred, promoted, devoted, terminated, or retired using data collected over a number of years. Probabilities are used to represent the historical flow of personnel through the organisation, a "transition matrix" is formed from these probabilities, and future personnel flows are estimated in this matrix.

*External supply:* External supply consists of those individuals in the labour force who are potential recruits of the organisation (including those working for another organisation). The skill levels being sought determine the relevant labour market for highly skilled jobs whereas for unskilled jobs, the relevant labour market is usually the local community. Determining the relevant labour market will also determine what type of recruitment approach should be used. Several government reports regularly forecast the supply of labour and estimate available workers in general job and demographic categories. These forecasts are also extrapolations into the future based on current trends.

## Computer Modelling

Computers are used in the most sophisticated forecasting approaches. Various mathematical formulas are used in computer models that simultaneously use extrapolation, indexation, survey results, and estimates of employment changes to compute future human resource needs. Over time the computer's formulas are refined with actual changes in human resource demand. Computer modelling for the most part found only among large organisations with years of experience in human resource planning. Our armed forces probably have the most sophisticated computer modelling approaches to planning and recruitment in employment today. Some federal agencies also use computer modelling. The IRs, played for years by shortage of auditors and accountants, relies in a computer model to develop college recruiting plans.

## Step Four: Gap Analysis

Gap analysis is used to reconcile the forecasts of labour demand and supply. At a minimum, the process identifies potential shortages or surpluses of employees skills, and jobs. In addition, however, planners can juxtapose several environmental forecasts with alternative supply and demand forecasts to determine the preparedness for different business scenarios. From a problem solving perspective, gap analysis is used to pair up potential strengths and opportunities with solutions in order to evaluate how the firm might attack the future. This decision making process involves (1) a search for alternative solutions (2) an evaluation of alternatives, and (3) a choice of solutions.

### Is there an optimal way to downsize?

This type of gap analysis has been used in employee downsizing or reengineering programmes for a majority of the Fortune 1000 firms and even by some of the most successful and profitable firms. More than 85 per cent of the Fortune 1000 firms downsized their white collar staff between 1987 and 1996. The evidence on the effects of downsizing is mixed. Most of the companies had implemented downsizing as a reaction to a loss of market share, increased competition, or lower productivity. Most also looked at downsizing as simply as a workforce reduction process rather than a restructuring or reengineering of jobs in the context of corporate strategy or planning.

### What are some alternative or additional solutions based on the SWOT analysis?

As discussed above, the HRP there are likely to be multiple scenarios worthy of consideration. Environmental scanning and labour forecasts identify a range of possible options. HR planners must exercise their ingenuity to create a range of possible solutions based on the SWOT analysis. At this stage, the range of possibilities can be increased by seeking input from executives, line managers, employees, customers, and consultants in a "brainstorming" process. A qualitative approach such as Delphi can be used at this point as well.

As part of its HR planning process and after a thorough job analysis a line manager can be asked the following questions:

1. How does each job relate to the strategic plan of the work unit?
2. Are there alternatives to a full-time job that should be considered to accomplish the same objectives (e.g., temporary workers, part-time employers, employee leasing, consultants, contract, overtime)?
3. What are the projected costs of each job?
4. What impact will the job have on critical and clearly defined effectiveness criteria?

## What is the role of temporary employment?

More and more companies have been asking similar questions regarding their workforce and coming up with creative answers. One of the strongest trends in this country is the use of labour that is not full time. Temporary employment, part-time workers, job sharing, and employer leasing are among the most popular solutions to controlling labour costs and responding to fluctuating demand. Another alternative to deal with the increasing diversity of the workforce is job sharing. Job sharing divides a single job into two or more workers.

### Internal Programming

Many of the solutions in the HRP rest on actions inside the firm with the current workforce. For routine SWOTs, in particular, bureaucratic adjustments in HR practices can be easily programmed internally (e.g., job design/assignments). Taking a closer look at organisational design around changing technologies is one such example.

### External Programming

Other solutions in HRP require going outside the firm to interact with constituencies in the environment (e.g., labour unions, competitors etc.) in particular, when HR plans require drastically different skills from what employees currently posses and/or the time frame for change is quite short, the firm will likely need to recruit from the outside labour market.

## Step Six: Control and Evaluation

Control and evaluation monitor the effectiveness of human resource plans over time. Deviations from the plan are identified and actions are taken. The extent to which human resource objectives have been met is provided by the feedback resulting from the outcomes of human resource planning. Essentially it has been suggested that long range planning activities require the attainment of short run objectives. Examples, include performance or productivity data, turnover costs, workforce reduction effects from early retirement programmes, breakeven costs of new hires, and analysis of costs of recruits compared to the training and development costs of existing employees. Obviously, actual staffing levels compared to projected levels should be evaluated for accuracy. Doing evaluation such as cost-benefit analysis makes it easier to determine whether long-run planning objectives will be met.

The issue of evaluation in planning can be considered along with the evaluation of recruitment efforts since the criteria used for the evaluation are often the same. The critical consideration here should be identification of the vital measurement criteria that will provide for an assessment of the HR planning implementation in the context of the business strategy.

When HR planning involves adding to the labour force, the organisation must rely on the recruitment function to meet its employment needs. The point of the planning exercise is to provide the optimal number and quality of employees to put internal and external customer requirements. If the gap analysis determines that employees are needed, that is where recruitment comes in.

## The Recruitment Function: Putting HRP into Action

Moving from HRP to recruitment is essentially a process of translating broad strategies into operational tasks. The major responsibility for this process typically rests within the HRM department, although most tasks are shared with line managers. While HR managers are responsible for determining recruiting policy, ensuring EEO compliance, and training and evaluating the recruiters, many organisations such as Xerox, IBM and Proctor and Gamble actively involve line managers and employa as recruiters. As mentioned above, conflict between HR and line managers can occur when their priorities diverge. For example, line managers may be more concerned about filling a position quickly (i.e., when the new employee is needed) while HR managers may be more concerned about affirmative action guidelines or complying with EEO regulations. Their goals should be the same: hiring the most qualified person(s) when needed and without violating any laws or regulations.

## Recruitment and Other HR Activities

Recall our earlier statement about the interdependent nature of recruiting and other HR activities. Decisions regarding employee testing, work policies and programmes, compensation, and corporate image can all have a profound effect on recruiting. For example, one large retailer required high level managerial candidates to travel to the company headquarters (for some over 2000 miles) to go through a two day assessment centre that was offered only at headquarters. Because of these requirements, many experienced managers, who were working for other companies dropped out of the pool of candidates because they didn't have the time of commuting to a two-day assessment centre with two additional days of travel.

A company institutes a comprehensive drug testing programme that includes random drug testing with no probable cause for all employees. The company assumes the policy will only have an impact by deterring applicants who would be most likely to use drugs. Another company installs a binding arbitration policy for all employee employer disputes. A new employee must sign off on the policy as a condition of employment. Once again, the company does not consider the effect of this new policy on the ability to recruit and retain the most qualified applicants. Another company decides to reduce indirect compensation by reducing health benefits for new employees and increasing the premium. It has no idea what the change in policy will do to its ability to recruit, the company finds out later that recruitment costs have grown up along with the rate of offer rejections. It finally conducts an actual cost benefit study of the change in policy and discovers the company lost money because of the interactive effect of the policy on staffing and the retention of valuable employees. Recruitment, selection, and personnel policies are indeed interdependent.

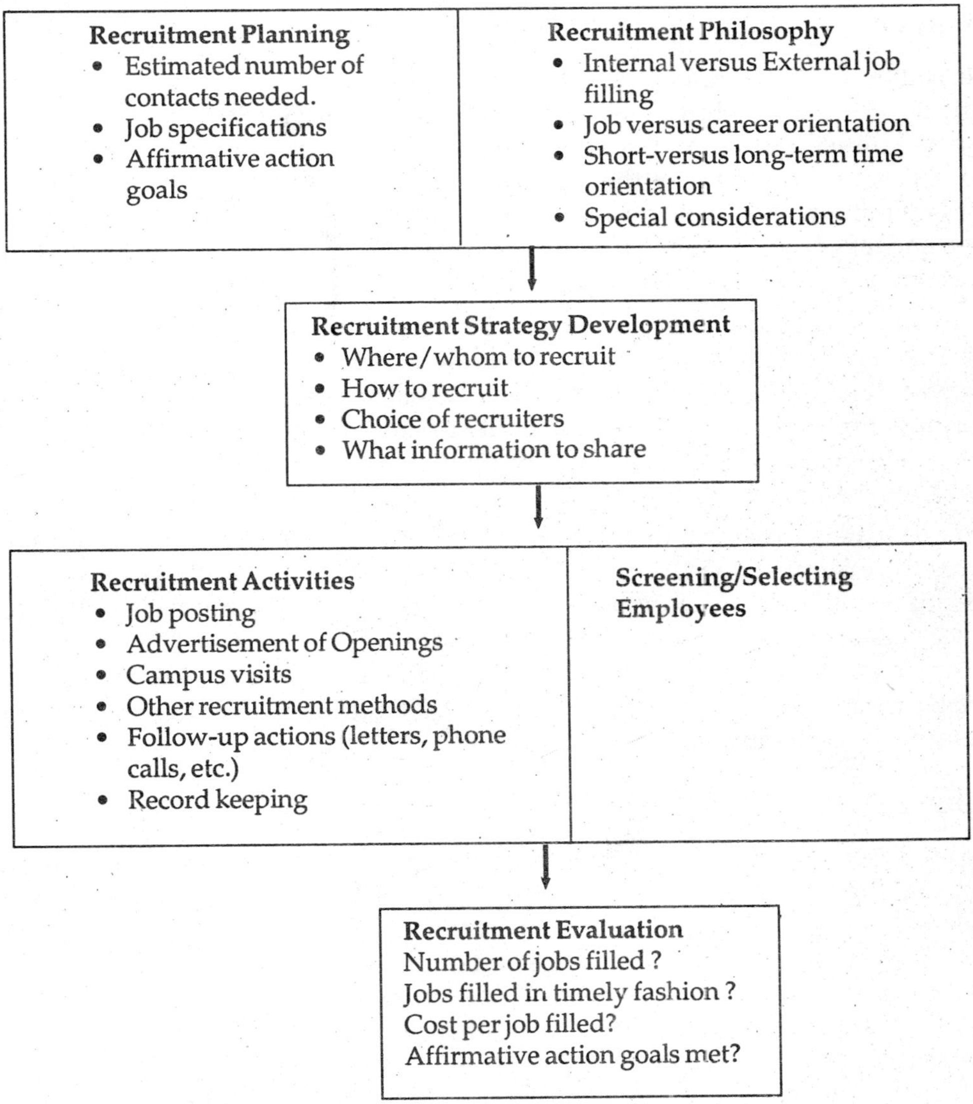


**Fig. 5.5: A Simplified Model Of The Recruitment Process**

## Three Essential Steps for Recruitment Planning

Based on the HR Plan (more specifically, the gap analysis), the organisation has a fairly good idea of its overall recruitment or downsizing needs. However, this information must be operationalised and communicated to others who will be taking the action. Three essential steps for translating future needs into specific operational terms are (1) job analysis (2) time lapse data, and (3) yield ratio.

## Job Analysis

Recruiters and HR Planners rely on two aspects of job analysis information to identify the critical skills for which they will recruit. First, job descriptions provide an outline of the responsibilities, duties, and tasks to be performed by the potential employee. Second, the job specifications outlines the KASOCs required of the applicant. In general, the more specific the recruitment design, especially in terms of job specifications, the more efficient and effective it is, assuming the same is important for job. Poorly designed recruiting is more expensive and takes longer.

For example, sometimes job specifications are not essential for the job and are unnecessary and costly. One retailer stipulated five years of experience as a district manager to be eligible for consideration as a district manager for the company. One retail manager made this decision unilaterally based on his "sense" of what was required in the job. The result was a small pool of applicants, high advertising costs, and fewer backward and minorities who were eligible for consideration.

Job analysis information that accurately reflects the requirements needed for the job can have a direct impact on the effectiveness of any recruitment and planning effort. Job analysis information can also be used in a downsizing as jobs are restructured based on the new organisational structure. HRP provides the number of jobs needed and job analysis provides the requirements of the jobs, management must know when to start a recruiting process and how extensive the search should be. This is where time lapse data and yield ratios come in.

## Time Lapse Data

Time lapse data (TLD) provide the average time that elapses between points of decision making in recruiting. For example, if the recruitment plan calls for newspaper advertisements, records may reflect that the job is filled on an average of two months after publication of the ad. Thus, the ad should be placed at least two months before the job has to be filled. Data may also be available on the time lapse between interviews and offers and acceptances. When combined with yield ratios, the TLD can provide useful information for planning a recruitment efforts.

Time lapse data has been reduced for companies taking advantage of the automated recruiting options available through the world wide web. For example, a database known as " provides online services for both job hunters and job employers. Recruiters that use the service report shorter time lapses with no loss in candidate quality. There are over 20 new recruiting web sites, some of which are narrowly focused on particular jobs or occupations or industries (e.g., nursing, professors, health care, computer technology) to further reduce the time lapse. Some of the countries largest newspapers now have a job testing service on the Internet.

## Yield Ratios

A yield ratio for any recruiting step reflects the number of candidates available at a step and the next step. For example, a series of newspaper ads may result in 1,000 applications for employments. Of these 1000 applications, 100 are judged to much some minimum qualifications. Thus, the yield ratio at this initial stage is 10 per cent of the group of 10 candidates, 50 accepted invitations to be interviewed (yield ratio is 50 per cent for this stage and 5 per cent as the cumulative yield ratio); of the 50, 10 were given job offers (20 per cent yield ratio; 1 per cent cumulative). Assuming the labour market has not changed dramatically from when the yield ratio was derived and that similar methods of recruiting are to be used (e.g., advertising in the same papers, using a web site or a head-hunter), this ratio can then be used as the basis for planning for future recruitment efforts. By going backward from the yield ratio, the recruiter can estimate how many applicants will be necessary to fill a certain number of positions. The recruiter can then adjust the recruiting effort accordingly with more (or less) advertising, more (or fewer) trips to college campuses, and so on.

## Discrepancy Between Academic Research and Practice

The use of time lapse data and yield ratios is another area where there is a wide gap between what academic texts and scholarly research recommended and the extent to which such data drive recruitment planning. While almost every scholar on the subject recommends a recruitment evaluation process to assist decision makers in efficient recruitment planning, few companies actually collect the data as part of recruitment evaluation.

Recruitment is a never ending process for many jobs where there are critical shortages of highly specialised skills. There are tight labour markets for many occupations today and strong indications that markets will get even tighter, particularly for knowledge intensive jobs. Many high tech manufacturing firms recruit for engineers and computer programmers year round as well. Some companies have difficulty in filling even unskilled positions.

## Internal Recruitment Sources

There are two general sources of recruiting:

Internal and External. Internal recruiting seeks applicants for positions from among the ranks of those currently employed. With the exception of entry-level positions, most organisation try to fill positions with current employee.

There are three major advantages to internal recruiting. First, it is considerably less costing than external recruiting. Second, organisations typically have a better knowledge of internal applicants skills and abilities than that which can be acquired of candidates in an external recruiting effort. Through performance appraisal and other sources of information about current personnel decision makers will typically have much more extensive knowledge of internal candidates and thus make much more valid recruitment decisions. The third advantage to internal recruiting is that an organisational policy of promoting from within can enhance organisational commitment and job satisfaction. One advantage of detailed job analysis is that succession planning programmes can be developed so that management (and employees) can have a good idea of the sources for internal recruiting. For example, associates complete a competency based job analysis describing their current knowledge and skills required for their present job and what knowledge or skills they would like to acquire. These responses are then linked to vacancies within the company, descriptions of which have already been completed by managers of the vacant positions.

There are disadvantages to internal recruiting as well. Continuity is not always such a good thing. If the organisation has decided to change its business strategy, for example, entrenched managers are probably not the "change masters" you want. One theory of internal recruiting is that the approach simply promulgates the old ways of doing things; creative problem solving may be hindered by the lack of new blood or a sort of "managerial in breeding".

One well-documented managerial blunder is to irrationally stay committed to an initial course of action, particularly if you initiated the action. Irrational commitment, misdirected persistence, and escalation bias are much more likely when internal versus external recruitment is emphasised. For example, one company faced new competition to an established product line from a foreign competitor. The senior managers, all of whom had been at the company for at least 15 years and had great ownership in the product and how it was marketed, agreed to deal with the new competition as they had always dealt with competition, by competing on price. This matter was unfortunately out of step with the upstart competitors strategy, which included competing on price.

Entrenched managers sometimes have difficulty understanding that time and money already invested are "sunk-costs" and should not be considered in planning, managers who had something to do with a present course of action seem to have more difficulty in understanding this. Some organisations complain of unit raiding where divisions may compete for the same people. Reading in common in universities for classical positions where position descriptions can be written in such a way that a secretary can move to another department for a higher salary.

A third possible disadvantage of internal recruiting is that politics probably has a greater impact on internal recruiting and selection that it does on external recruiting. Thus, while more job related information may be known about internal candidates, personnel decisions involving internal candidates are more likely to be affected by the political agendas of the decision makers. HR managers must constantly monitor very lightly defined job descriptions or job specifications. While this may constitute well focused recruiting based on precisely what the organisation requires. It can also mean a position has been 'wired" for an internal candidate. An effective HR manager should be able to make the distinction. The manager writing the job description and job specifications should be required to stipulate why highly specific credentials or areas of expertise are required in the context of the organisations or units strategic plan.

Internal recruiting programmes must be carefully integrated with other HR functions. Effective HR succession planning, job analysis, personnel selection, and performance appraisal are all important for an effective system that can fill required positions with the most qualified personnel in the shortest time. Administrators of such programmes should be knowledgeable of EEO legislation and litigation because numbers of lawsuits may come up related to internal recruiting and placement decisions. While most large companies have formal succession plans at the managerial level, a much lower percentage of small to medium size firms have formal systems. A job posting system can enhance the effectiveness of internal recruiting. In job posting, announcements of positions are made available to all current employers through company newsletters, bulletin boards, and so on. Surprisingly, only a small percentage of organisations have formal systems of job posting for vacant positions within the organisation. When properly implemented, job posting systems can substantially improve the quality of job placements and protect the organisation from EEO problems.

## External Recruitment Sources

External recruiting concerns recruitment from outside the organisation. One big advantage of external recruiting is that the approach can facilitate the introduction of new ideas and thinking into corporate decision making. The new blood comes with no ownership of past strategies, which often hinders an objective assessment of future strategy. A major disadvantage of external recruiting is that the introduction of new personnel may have a negative impact on work group cohesion and morale. Also, new personnel from outside the organisation typically take longer to learn the ropes. Another possible disadvantage is that external recruiting can be very costly.

The internet is already having a profound impact on the cost and the time involved in recruiting personnel. Most Fortune 1000 companies now post available jobs on their web sites and more and more skilled employees are applying for these jobs through these sites.

The final disadvantage of external recruiting is that you typically have less reliable performance data on external candidates. Good assessment procedures can be costly and bad assessment procedures can be deceptive. Inflated letters of recommendations or confidential interviews can lard a job outside the organisation for a troublesome employer. This is probably the main reason that letters of reference have almost no validity; there may be an incentive on the part of evaluators to inflate references to move a job candidate (out of an organisation).

**Plan**
Outline details of system
**Involve the employees in planning**
**Determine Eligibility Requirements**
Tenure with Company
Time in present position
Allowable number of annual bids
Allowable number of Simultaneous Bids.
Lateral Transfer
Status with company
**Outline Job Requirements and Content**
Job title and department
List of specific tasks. Duties, Responsibilities.
List of job specifications(e.g., Training, experience, education) Salary ranges
Application process
Deadlines
Work schedule
Format
Affirmative action statements

**Establish Employee Awareness**
Maximise employee awareness of Positions
**Establish Time Frames**
Time between posting and Application deadline.
Time to notify applicants of hiring Decisions.
Time given by the superior before His or her subordinates switching of jobs.
**Determine Policies for Notifying Present Supervisor**
Informed before bidding?
Informed only if subordinate seriously considered?
Informed only if employee selected
**Determine Applicant Review Procedures**
**Provide Applicant Feedback**
Notification of decision in writing
If not hired, outline reasons.
**Establish an Appeals Procedure**

**Fig. 5.6: An Effective Job Posting System**

## Methods of External Recruiting

Several methods are available for external recruitments: Walk ins and unsolicited applicant files:

The most common and least expensive approach for candidates is direct applications where job seekers submit unsolicited material (i.e., resume) or simply show up in person seeking employment. Direct applications can also provide a pool of potential employees to met future needs. While direct applications are particularly effective in filling entry level and unskilled positions, some organisations, because of their reputations or because of their geographical locations, compile excellent pools of potential employees from direct applications for skilled positions. Such an example is interactive employment network provides a resume database that is accessible from several online service providers. The network is used by most Fortune 1000 companies and search firms and do not forget about the online service offered by the newspapers.

The reputation of the company has a great deal to do with the usefulness and size of the pool or unsolicited applicants and resumes. Organisations such as Coca Cola, Merck, Microsoft, GE, IBM receive thousands of unsolicited applications every year. Many excellent candidates can be found in this poll. One reason companies actively campaign to make one or more of the many top 10 lists of the "best companies to work for" is because the rate of unsolicited resumes is directly related to this honor. Not only do unsolicited resumes reduce the cost of recruiting, but they also increase the probability of hiring the best employees. Many companies now scan resumes or applications and then conduct keyword computer searches to quickly get to a reasonable short list of candidates when positions become available. Software now exists to match fairly detailed job specifications with resume information. The result is usually a much more efficient (and fresh) recruiting effort.

## Referrals

Some organisation have formal systems of employee referral for occupations with great demand. Some leading MNCs pays current employees a lumpsum amount of bonus who are referred are ultimately hired and work for the company for a reasonable period. While formal systems of referral are/were effective in attracting interested applicants, some evidence reveals that the quality of the applicants is less than that which results from an informal system of referrals. Microsoft is offering referral incentives to its employees for internet experts of all shapes and sizes.

## Advertising

A third common method for recruiting is advertising. Advertising can range from a simple classified ad to an elaborate media campaign through radio or television to attract applicants. The approach can be quite versatile in its ability to provide information about job opportunities while targeting specific labour markets in particular geographical areas. While the majority of advertising is in newspapers, many organisations go beyond the typical newspaper ads for tight labour markets commercials extol the virtues of starting your "career" in our armed forces/operation desert storm has had a positive effect in armed forces recruiting. Employer advertising is common on the world wide web. "Career Magazine", for example, includes employer profiles, interactive discussion groups, and a directory of executive recruiters. Employers can also place ads for specific jobs right on the web site.

Most experts agree that advertising through any media (including the internet) should contain the following information:

1. The job content (primary tasks and responsibilities)
2. A realistic description of working conditions, particularly if they are unusual.
3. The location of the job.
4. The compensation including the benefits.

5. Job specifications (e.g., education, experience).
6. To whom one applies.

Since advertising can be very expensive, record keeping on the successes of the various media sources can help to identify the approaches with the biggest potential payoff for future recruiting. This chapter presents a summary of some of the advantages and disadvantages of the various media options. In general, while advertising or job listings on a web site are relatively cheap, we do not know how effective they are in attracting qualified applicants. There are several excellent outlets for targeted advertising to minorities and women.

## Employment Agencies

Employment agencies are used by many companies for identifying potential workers. Publicly funded agencies provide free placement services, and private agencies charge either the employee or the employer for a placement or referral. These agencies increase the pool of possible applicants and do preliminary screening. Private agencies are most effective when: (1) the organisation has had difficulty building a pool of qualified applicants, (2) the organisation is not equipped to develop a sophisticated recruitment effort, (3) there is a need to fill a position quickly, (4) the organisation is explicitly recruiting minorities or females, and (5) the organisation is attempting to recruit individuals who are not actively seeking employment.

**Search Firms:** In selecting a search firm, experts recommended the following criteria:

1. The firm has restricted its recruiting to specific industries.
2. The firm pays its sales personnel based on the completion of an assignment.
3. The firm uses primary data sources rather than secondary sources such as computerised lists of potential candidates and association directories.
4. Firms that also do outplacement services are not recommended (outplacement is professional services for terminated employees, which may include placement in another job).

Many recruiting firms now specialise in targeted recruiting for many jobs. The fee for search firms can be very high, with estimates ranging from 20 to 50 per cent of the first year salaries of the individuals placed. Reviews on the effectiveness of search firms are mixed. According to one review, 50 per cent of the fulfilled job searches take twice as long to fill as promised. Less than 50 per cent of contracts to fill positions are ever fulfilled, job searches take twice as along to fill as promised. Less than 50.0 per cent of contracts to fill positions are ever fulfilled. "By charging a flat rate we are able to remain objective in presenting candidates to the client. We do not show only the high priced candidates; we show the most qualified". Many companies have begun to demand the flat-fee approach because of the tendency of percentage based recruiters to recommend high priced candidates.

## Campus Visits

One major source of recruiting for professional and managerial positions is the college campus. Numerous organisations, in particular the larger organisations, send recruiters to campus once or twice a year to inform graduates and future graduates about career opportunities. One survey found that about 65.0 per cent of all managers and technical professional were fixed through college recruiting. There is no question that college recruiting is successful at filling vacancies. There is a question as to the extent to which the vacancies are filled with people most likely to be successful within the organisation. Some companies report turnover rates in excess of 50.0 per cent for new college graduates after only one year.

The cost of college recruiting can be enormous. One conservative estimate of the cost is almost Rs.15,000–20,000 per hired graduates. Despite this substantial cost, programme evaluation is rarely done and little attention is given to recruiting. When evaluation has been done, the criteria for evaluation was simply filled vacancies or number of offers accepted rather than a measure of the quality of those who are recruited or retention rates. Recruiters often receive little guidance on interviewing procedures, despite evidence that the interviewing format is important for the accuracy of predictions.

The recruiting process should commence long before any visits to the campus. Recruiters should be familiar with the University/College and University/College personnel before their visit. Job descriptions and specifications should be mailed to the campus before the recruiters arrives. Another good strategy is to set up internship programes through the university. In general, the most effective college recruiting efforts are those that facilitate a long-term relationship with the college through a variety of cooperative programmes between the school and the organisation. Again, record keeping on past experiences will be very helpful in planning future campus recruiting. For example, the Institutes uses a computer to centralise its college recruiting operation. Resumes are entered or scanned on the computer upon receipt alongwith applicant preferences for certain job characteristics. Recruiters can also instantly receive extensive information about particular candidates. Due to the expense of college recruiting, reliable yield ratios are even more important. Computerised systems are ideal for planning.

Many companies now employ computer technology to conduct recruiting. Other companies use video conferencing at college campuses. This allows for more cost effective interviewing than traditional face-to-face interviewing. The extent to which videoconferencing is an effective approach to recruiting is another empirical question. There is now a need to compare the effects (and costs) of campus visits to recruiting (and interviewing) through the internet. Most college graduates can go online and may not be hampered by highly efficient, computerized recruiting and interviewing.

One large recruiter of college graduates is the software industries and government sectors. Recent research on the governments ability to attract the most qualified graduates is not encouraging. One survey found only 38-40 per cent of graduates were interested in careers with the government. The private sector was viewed as offering more prestige and power than the public sector. The research also indicated that the government could do a much better job recruiting graduates through more on campus visits and a concerted effort as changing its negative public image. If anything, the public image has gotten worse in recent years.

Two other sources for recruiting are professional associations and computerised services. College faculty for management departments, are often recruited through the ISTE, IEF, AIMA, EDIL etc.

## Electronic Recruiting on the World Wide Web

Electronic job descriptions and resumes are now retrievable from numerous computerised job listings. Numerous computerised resume data bases are available for employers. Technology has created all virtual recruiters" where a software programme turns resumes into a database that is then searched to fill job openings. For example, if a MNC was looking for an engineer with programming skills, five years experience and who can speak English, the software could screen the resumes to identify applicants who meet these specifications. While the efficiencies of this approach should be obvious, little problems with the software as it reads the resumes can create errors in the search and eliminate applicants who may have otherwise survived at least the initial screening. For example, if you misspell a key word, you could be out of luck.

Excellent software tracking is now available. The Restrack System has a manster board (http://www.manster.com) where resume and job postings are matched over the internet. Companies can then download a resume and fold it into their resume database.

Recruiting in the near future may go something like this for most large companies:

1. A line manager completes a standardised job analysis questionnaire on the internet identifying employment needs for the unit; the questionnaire may include job location and other details of the job in addition to the critical job specifications.
2. The completed questionnaire is then automatically converted into a job posting on the internet and matched with a current database of applicants whose credentials are entered using the same terminology as the job analysis.
3. A list of candidates is identified based on the match of job specifications with job credentials.
4. Almost instantaneously, the line manager has a list of interested and qualified candidates with whom he or she can interact.
5. A testing and interview format, in compliance with all EEO guidelines, is derived from the same job analysis information completed at step 1.
6. Using the testing/interview material, additional data are collected on the candidates through e-mail and/or video and a list of top candidates is compiled.

The Internet has great potential for expediting the recruiting process. The scenarioabove should be contrasted with the typical methods of recruiting , we described earlier. Of course, the Internet approach depends on potential job applicants being aware of this convenient approach and amenable to the process.

## What Recruiting Method is Most Effective?

Few studies have compared the effects of different recruitment methods. The Internet is too new for significant work related to it. The criteria used in the studies that have been done also differs and include: cost per hire, number of resumes, time lapse from recruiting to filling the vacancy, interview/invitation ratio, applicant performance on the job and job turnover. A recent emphasis has also been placed on minority hiring pattern as a function of the recruiting effort and relative to population statistics and census data on potential employees. These comparisons may be critical if EEO litigation is pending. Figure 5.5 presents a list of some of the most important criteria that could be used to evaluate different approaches to recruiting.

## The Discrepency Between Research and Practice

Unfortunately, there is very little systematic research on the effects of recruiting options using any of these criteria. Despite numerous calls for systematic research on the effects of various approaches to recruiting, little indication were found.

### Two Philosophies of Recruiting : Fly Paper Versus Matching

The traditional philosophy of recruiting has been to get as many people as possible to apply for a job. The idea is based on trying to obtain the lowest possible selection ratio given a fixed recruiting cost. A Selection Ratio (SR) is the proportion of job openings to applicants. An SR of .10 means there are 10 applicants for every job opening. A lower selection ratio is frequently more desirable because it enables the organisation to choose a job candidate from a larger pool – thereby increasing selectivity. This assumption holds true as long as the cost of recruiting and subsequent screening is not exorbitant and applicants for the job are at least minimally qualified. In general, selection ratios goes down when companies are admired by the working public. In circumstances where "quality" criteria are important, the "matching philosophy" of recruitment may be more efficient. A persuasive argument can be made that matching the needs of the organisation to the needs of the applicant will enhance the recruitment process. The result will be a workforce that is more likely to stay with the organisation longer and perform on a higher level of effectiveness for a longer time. In the context of this matching philosophy, a process of realistic recruitment is recommended. An important component of realistic recruiting is a realistic job preview (RJP). RJPs provide the characteristics of the job to applicants so that they can evaluate the compatibility of this realistic presentation of the job with their own preferences. RJPs can result in a sub-selection process that screens people most likely to have difficulty on the job. Those applicants who are hired after being exposed in the RJP are also better able to cope because of more realistic expectations about the job. It is said that RJPs "vaccinate" applicants by lowering their unrealistic expectations and bringing them more in line with actual work conditions.

Many companies doing international work provide extensive RJPs for potential expatriates and their families. Research on realistic recruiting shows lower rates of employee turnover for employees recruited with RJPs, particularly for more complex jobs, and higher levels of job satisfaction and performance at the initial stages of employment. RJPs are more beneficial for organisations hiring at the entry level, when there are low selection ratios (i.e., many applicants per position), and under conditions of relatively low unemployment (i.e., where people have more job options). Otherwise, the approach may increase the cost of recruiting by increasing the average time it takes to fill each position. RJPs can be developed by using job analysis information. The critical incident technique is particularly effective for developing RJPs. RJPs could also be incorporated in job postings on the Internet to facilitate the self-selection process.

Another staffing approach that fits into the matching philosophy is the use of Job Compatibilities Questionnaire (JCQ). The JCQ provides a quantitative match between job applicant preferences and the actual characteristics of a job, including compensation system characteristics, benefits, work schedule, and of course, the characteristics of the actual work to be performed. The JCQ has also been used to construct a realistic job preview. A study of the customer service representatives found that whereas many managers still perceive overseas assignments as a banishment of sorts, corporations now place more weight on overseas experience as a requirement for high level executive assignments. With the increased sophistication of international communications and the growing importance of international operations for corporate strategy, studies showing overseas managers perceiving a loss of visibility at headquarters probably apply less today than few years ago.

Underlying all HRM challenges is the strategic position of the multinational Corporation regarding the relationship of the overseas operation to the parent company. The recruitment strategy for overseas assignments is directly tied to this strategic position. The use of nationals in overseas operations can reduce language and cultural problems, the need for expensive training programmes, and the tremendous cost of placing expatriates and their families in overseas assignments. This is becoming more and more common these days. For corporations maintaining a close strategic relationship to the overseas division (as opposed to a philosophy of autonomous operations), the most common strategy for managerial recruitment and job placement is a balance between expatriates and nationals. Sales and Production personnel are typically recruited from the national pool. Companies that have a "hands-off" managerial philosophy to autonomous foreign operations typically use expatriates in coordination with nationals until the present company is comfortable with the operation and profits of the foreign division are acceptable.

## Summary

Human Resource Planning seeks to place the right employees in the right jobs at the right time and at the lowest possible cost, thereby providing the means for the organisation to pursue its competitive strategy and fulfil its mission. Planning improves the organisation's ability to create and sustain competitive advantage and to cope with problems, threats and opportunities arising from change — technological, social, political, and environmental. HRP and all its derivatives should always keep the future customer in focus. Reengineering or downsizing problems that lose this focus may ultimately have a negative impact on the organisation. HRP systematically attempts to forecast personnel demand, assess supply, and reconcile the two. Personnel demand can be assessed using qualitative methods. Internal supply may be forecast by using Human Resource Information Systems (HRIS), replacement charts, and Markov analysis. Internal shortages are resolved through training and/or recruitment. This information is used in action planning to develop human resource strategy. HRP is an ongoing process where control and evaluation procedures are necessary to guide HRP activities. Deviations from the plan and their causes must be identified in order to assess whether the plan should be revised.

Recruitment is the process of finding and attracting applicants who are interested in and qualified for position vacancies. Recruitment should encompass both the attraction and the selection of the most qualified personnel. The ideal recruitment programme is one in which a sufficient number of qualified applicants are attracted to and ultimately accept the positions in an efficient manner. Unfortunately, the typical assessment of recruitment policies, programmes, and personnel in the past has focused on simply whether positions were filled and the cost and speed of filling positions rather than evaluating the quality of the personnel who were hired and placed a greater emphasis on the quality of the recruiting effort. There is increasing evidence that the various approaches to recruiting result in different outcomes for the organisation. The evaluation of recruiting programmes in the future is thus more likely to focus on the quality of the people who are hired in addition to the "body count" criteria, which are more typically used. We have emphasized the quality criterion in this chapter and the need to establish a match between job seeker's needs and desires for certain job characteristics and that which the organisation can offer.

## Discussion Questions

1. How should HR Planning involve a comparison to competitors? What critical data are required?
2. Why is planning an important activity? What are some advantages of effective planning?
3. Some organisations do have a thorough job analysis first and then human resource planning as part of a restructuring process. What makes more sense to you?
4. Discuss the possible pros and cons of the two qualitative methods presented for forecasting labour demand?
5. If actual performance of the human resource plan differs from desired performance, what remedial steps might you use?

6. Employee referral is a popular method of recruiting candidates. What are its advantages and disadvantages?
7. What are the advantages and disadvantages of the various external recruitment sources?
8. Can you think of some examples of escalation bias applied to HRM?
9. Suppose a key employee has just resigned and you are the department manager. After you have sent your request to personnel for a replacement, how could you help the recruiter find the best replacement?
10. Discuss the advantages and disadvantages of using the Internet to find a job and to fill a job.

## Notes


1. Lawrence, S. (April 1989). Voice of HR Experience, *Personnel Journal*, p.70.
2. Martell, J. and Carrole, S. (July 1995) *HR Magazine*, pp.48-52.
3. Jackson, S.E, and Schuler, R.S. (1990). Strategic human resource planning. *American Psychologist*, 78(3), 223-239.
4. Tichy; Fombrum, C; and Devanna, M. (1982). Strategic human resource management. *Sloan Management Review*, 23, p.47.
5. Bass, D.D. (April 1996), Help Wanted desperately. *Nation's Business*, pp-16-19.
6. Heneman, H.G. Heneman, R.L., and Judge, T.A. (1997). *Staffing Organisations*. Burr Ridge, IL: Irwin.
7. Hooper, J.A., and Catelanello, R.E. (1981). Markov analysis in human resource administration: Applications and limitations. *Academy of Management Review*, pp 535-542.
8. Buller. P.F., and Maki, W.R. (1981). A case history of a manpower planning model. *Human Resource Planing*, 4, 129-138,
9. J.L. Rastogi (1998). Human Resource Management: Need for Positive Approach. *Human Resource Development*, pp. 10-15.
10. B.B. Tandon (1998). Strategy and Technique of Manpower Planning. *Human Resource Development*, pp. 187-195.
11. Dinesh K. Gupta (1998). The Lev and Schwartz Model based Human Resource Accounting System and the Use of Appropriate Discount Rate. *Human Resource Development*, pp. 392-402.
12. Bernardin. H.J. (1989). Innovative Approaches to Personnel selection and performance appraisal. *Journal of Management Systems*, I. 25-36.
13. Dowling, P.J; Schuler, R; R.R.S, and Welch, D.E. (1994). *International Dimensions of Human Resource Management*. Boston: PWS Kent.

14. Dowling, P.J. (1989). Hot issues overseas. *Personnel Administrator, 34*, 68-72.

15. Meyers, M. (1987). Is your recruitment all it can be? *Personnel Journal, 66*, 56; and Brown, B.K.; and Campion, M.A. (1994). Biodata phenomenology: Recruiter's perceptions and use of biographical information in resume screening. *Journal of Applied Psychology, 79* (6), 897-908.

16. Bernardin, H.J. (1997). A Survey of recruiting practices and methods of assessment. Paper presented at Virginia Polytechnic Institute, Blacksburg, VA.

## Case Study

### Effective Manpower Planning

Professor Rahul Kanungo, a very eminent consultant in human resource management was delivering lecture on strategic manpower planning in the present environment in a textile mill in Surat. He contended that the answer to flexible and effective manpower planning for many corporations might lie in what has become known as placement agencies. Gradually, many placement/outsourcing agencies have been developed in India to cater to the needs of several organisations in the country. Almost all types of organisations both in government and private sectors are utilizing the services of placement agencies in which they are now free from the problem of employing permanent staff. The agencies are primarily engaged in supplying personnel to client businesses on their "need" basis. Temporary workers are under the supervision of the client business, but they are on the payroll of the temporary help agency. The agencies help companies to recruit and screen applicants, check references, administer employment tests, and even train new temporary workers. Once an employee is hired, the agencies look after the social security and other benefits of those people who work for them.

A company may resort to outsourcing agencies' help when it is faced with peak business periods or during the festival season when many permanent employees remain on leave. They may also enable companies to avoid costly overtime payments to permanent employees. Companies with expensive employee benefits package may use the support of outsourcing agency to reduce medical insurance and retirement plan costs. These agencies can also be used as a hedge against economic uncertainty, when business slows; temporary workers are "returned" to their agencies. In a similar vein, temporary workers who prove unsuitable are simply replaced by the client business. Office workers such as secretaries, typists, clerks, sweepers, gardeners and office peons, etc., mainly comprise the largest segment of the outsourcing. The industrial segment of the market includes labourers, material handlers, and food workers who are unskilled and work at a low rates of pay. The medical market within the temporary help industry consists of registered nurses, licensed practicing nurses, attendants. Engineers and technical workers are also employed on a temporary basis to help client companies with special projects. After Prof. Kanungo finished his lecture, the following questions were raised by the participants:

## Questions

1. Do you think that the outsourcing agencies can help the organisations in effective manpower planning?
2. "Outsourcing of manpower will affect the brand image of the organisation" - Critically discuss.
3. What advantages and disadvantages are there to work as an employee in an outsourcing agency?

***

# 6 Human Resource Evaluation

The concept of the value of human resources is derived from the concept of general economic value of all resources. The value of any resource may be interpreted in terms of its utility and is known as **'value in use'** or **'use value'**. The concept of value may also be interpreted in terms of the purchasing power, which the possession of a resource gives rise to. Value is, then, termed as 'value in exchange' or 'exchange value'. The value of human resource is interpreted in the former sense of use-value, i.e., in-terms of future services expected to be rendered by people. This concept may be applied to individuals, groups and the human organisation as a whole. The final component of the conceptual framework is human resource evaluation. With the increasing emphasis placed on strategic contribution, competitiveness, and cost control, there has been a greater need to justify the existence of human resource practices, activities and programmes. As will be noted in this chapter, the evaluation of human resource programmes has not been a high priority in most organisations. Nonetheless, evaluation will be more important in the utilization of resources. The impact of human resource practices and systems increases overall firms, performance. This chapter will explain how to conduct such evaluations of practices and systems. It will deal with several aspects of evaluation, beginning with an overview and a description of different analytical approaches. The chapter will discuss approaches for evaluating the strategic contributions of traditional human resource areas as well as emerging areas. Explanations of the different analytical approaches to evaluation will be provided along with specific guidance for evaluation in the various human resource functional areas. Finally, there will be a discussion of macro-level evaluations of human resource effectiveness.

Several human resource theorists and practitioners have presented compelling arguments for the evaluation of human resource management, and the human resource function. Such evaluation have been advocated for a number of reasons including :

- Promotion of the human resource function, for example, through demonstration of bottom-line contributions through reduced turnover.

- The demonstration of accountability in utilization of resources.
- Promotion of change by identifying strengths and weaknesses.
- Introduction of financial assessment as a decision tool in human resource programme selection.
- Highlighting key human resource practices.
- Gauging the performance of the human resource function.
- Demonstrating the function's role in the accomplishment of company goals.

The intensive emphasis on cost control, justifying efficient allocation of resources, contributing to the bottom-line, and capability of human resources to provide a competitive advantage, appear likely to result in more emphasis on evaluation.

## Overview Of Evaluation

Before evaluating human resource management, a suitably comprehensive definition of evaluation must be accepted, as well as the criteria and measurement approach. From an organisational perspective, organisational effectiveness is generally viewed as a multi-dimensional construct and typically involves multiple criteria, such as productivity and flexibility. Productivity measures sometimes tap efficiency, quantity, and quality, while flexibility measures may also tap the effectiveness with which the organisation deals with schedule changes, adaptability is operationalised separately and includes measures of problem anticipation, knowledge of new technology, and adaptation to change. Because of the multi-dimensionality of the effectiveness concept, policies capturing statistical procedures have been developed for constructing multiple measures of submit effectiveness.

## Scope Of Evaluation

Within the narrower confines of human resource management, there has been substantial progress in the evaluation literature. Although dozens of effectiveness measures have been proposed for evaluation of the function, including composite indexes, the literature has suffered from a lack of an organizing, theoretical framework. This shortcomings has since been filled by some other researchers in comprehensive conceptual framework. Their framework differentiates between outcomes or processes affected by line management and those under control of the human resource management function. In order to evaluate broader human resource performance, a company might examine turnover, grievance rates, or workers' compensation claims, which are largely affected by the actions of the company's line managers.

In contrast, a narrower evaluation of the human resource management function would focus on its efficiency in administering a benefit programme or recruiting and screening applicants. Thus, with broader evaluations, measures of the company's use of human resources would be affected by the performance of the company's line managers.

With narrower evaluations, the measures are affected only by the performance of the human resource staff. Human resource departments are unique in that their activities and responsibilities apply to all managers and employees in all departments. Thus, the evaluation of human resource departments is a complicated but important matter. While it may be tempting to simplify matters with a narrower evaluation, there are shortcomings with this approach. Therefore, it may be cautioned that isolated evaluation of human resource departments run the risk of communicating that others have no responsibilities in the area. Because all managers and departments affect the quality of human resource management and have related responsibilities, this would be an undesirable side effect of evaluation. In addition, another aspect of the scope of evaluation involves a time dimension.

The length of time between implementation of a programme and its impact on performance can vary depending on the nature of the programme. Likewise, its effects may be stable or diminish or increase over time. In addition, different stakeholders, such as shareholders, executives, and production workers may have a very different perspective on the time frame that should be used for evaluation clearly, there are problems when evaluation is performed on only a one-shot basis instead of a continual and systematic basis. There are obvious advantages with longitudinal approaches as opposed to cross-sectional approaches because of the latter's inability to provide insights into casualty.

## Strategic Impact

Another aspect of human resource evaluation is that the nature of the process is changing from a reactive focus on how well a problem is solved or how successful a programme has been to emphasised on the organisational and employee impact of human resource policies, programmes and activities. For example, in contrast to past evaluation practice in which a company might have examined narrow criteria such as turnover rates, a more strategic approach would examine whether it is losing high performers. Essentially, more strategic approaches to evaluation recognize the organisational interdependences and relationships between human resource policies, systems and activities. As a result, they have moved from narrower determinations of whether human resource activities are working to broader analysis of their contributions.

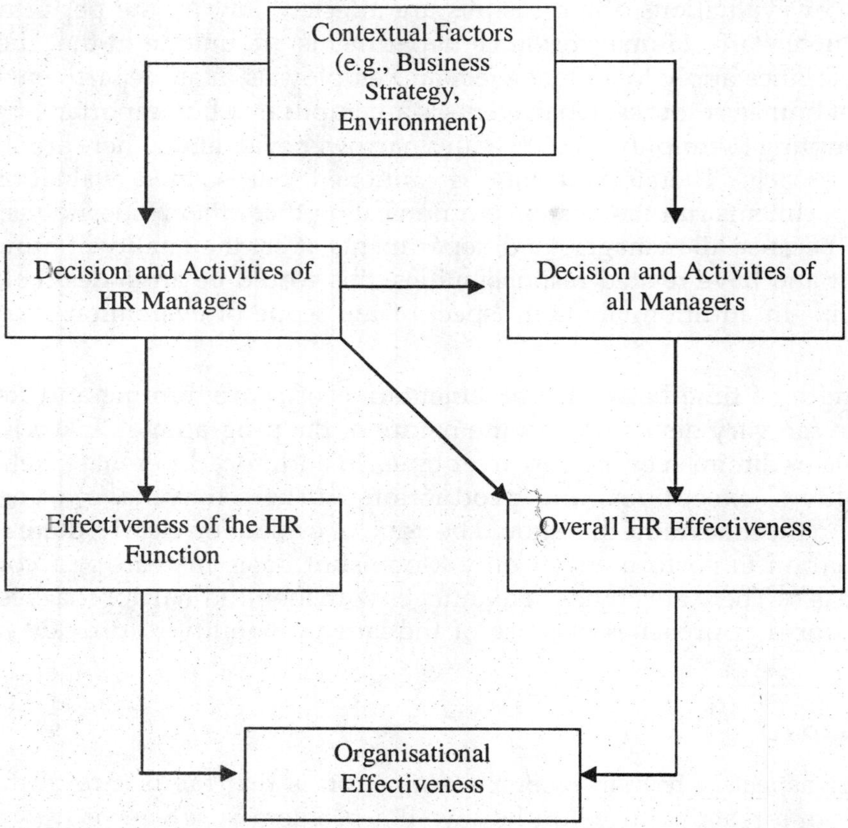


**Fig. 6.1: Model of Human Resource Effectiveness**

## Level of Analysis

Another dimension of evaluation involves the level of analysis, which is the level of aggregation or level within the organisational structure. Generally, there are three levels of analysis in human resource management evaluation; strategic, management, and operational. The objective of evaluation at the strategic level is to determine whether human resource policies and programmes are consistent with the company's strategy. At the management level, the focus is on control, such as the cost effectiveness of a benefit programe. At the operational level, the focus is on the quality of human resource services and programmes. Since there are multiple constituencies at this level, the service provided and level of satisfaction with the human resource department may vary across these constituencies.

## Criteria

In another comprehensive study, the criteria by which the effectiveness of human resource departments can be assured was identified. The results emphasise that the various constituencies of human resource departments have differing views of the importance of the various services provided. Results of factor analytic statistical procedures indicate that there are five clear categories of effectiveness criteria for human resource departments:

(1) responsiveness;

(2) managing cost and negative performance;

(3) pro-activity and innovativeness;

(4) training and development; and

(5) affirmative action accomplishments.

## Level of Constituents

Another finding is that the level of constituents has a major impact on the effectiveness criteria they apply. Managers and non-supervisory employees tend to place importance on the department's ability to provide services on matters of immediate or short-term importance. Operating line executives, who have production responsibilities, also hold similar views. In contrast, when corporate level human resource executives evaluate human resource departments, they tend to place greater importance on such activities as organisational development and human resource planning, which have strategic implications. Thus, human resource departments are subject to incompatible expectations that that need to be taken into account in an evaluation strategy.

## Ethical Dimensions

In addition to determining the impact of human resource practices and programmes should be evaluated from an ethics perspective. While human resource management operates within a highly regulated environment, compliance with the law or regulation does not always ensure ethical behaviour. Fortunately, the investment perspective of human resource is consistent with high ethical standards. Employers who invest in their employees are more likely to treat them ethically because they have an investment to protect. Nonetheless, the investment perspective is not sufficient to ensure ethical behaviour. In addition, the technological advances that have done so much to enhance productivity, make job less monotonous, and allow greater flexibility in where work is performed also have brought new ethical challenges. Information technology and the rapidly evolving Internet and Software Industries pose special challenges, as described in the following account of ethical problems in the Silicon Valley.

*Among the common infractions*: Companies stealing one another's intellectual property, cheating employees out of promised stock options .... or intercepting private e-mails, as when Interlock, the corporate predecessor started collecting messages sent from its customers.

Nonetheless, the guidelines for evaluation of the ethics of various practices and programmes are available, and it is often the role for those in human resources to take the lead when it comes to ethical treatment of employees. Advocacy and ethics are important for any profession, but they are especially significant roles for human resource managers. It is customary that the HR executive makes his or her contribution by first and always being a member of management. At the same time, HR executives are paid to understand their communities, workplace, employee attitudes, and Government regulations and requirements. It is up to the HR professional to balance and advance the interests of all parties within the business and strategic thrust of the organisation. On occasion, the HR executive may even find it necessary to put him, or herself at risk in order to balance these interests. This is especially the case when situations are not clear cut or where a double standard may appear to exist.

## Approaches to Evaluation

There are a number of general approaches to human resource evaluation, as well as various measures and criteria of effectiveness. Some of the classifications of these components of evaluation are not mutually exclusive – they may fit several categories.

### Audit Approaches

In addition to different evaluative foci, criteria, and levels of analysis, there are also two general approaches that have been traditionally used in human resource evaluation. The first is the **Audit Approach**, which relies on:

(1) Personal indices, such as per capita recruiting costs, absenteeism rates, or worker's compensation experience rates, or

(2) Service/user reactions, such as the perceived equity of the job evaluation system. Typically, data pertaining to the latter would be obtained through the use of surveys or interviews. Usually, items for such surveys can be obtained from published sources. Audit approaches also may be referred to as stakeholder approaches. Stakeholder approaches determine the satisfaction of key users or consumers of human resource services. Such stakeholders may be individuals or units within the organisation. There also may be external stakeholders, such as unions, community organisations, or suppliers. An example of a stakeholder approach to evaluation is provided by the Defence Division, which has used the process to clarify the human resource department's role in the Company.

### Analytical Approach

The second approach is analytical and involve either:

(1) experimental designs, such as the pre-test /post-test control group design, which will be discussed later in the discussion of evaluation of training, or

(2) cost-benefit analysis, such as uplifting theory.

Although the cost-benefit analytical approach has been used with success, the valuation of benefits poses a major problem for human resource applications. Utility analysis is a specific type of cost-benefit analysis, which has applicability to human resource evaluation. It has the advantage of expressing evaluations in economic terms, which are probably more understandable by decision makers from other functional areas. Several human resource activities have been evaluated with utility analysis, including appraisal systems, equal employment policies, recruiting, selection, training, and turnover. Although utility analysis has broad applicability and represents a quantitatively superior means of evaluating human resource activities, the process is quite difficult for some applications. As a result of these difficulties and the amount of resources and effort is required for analysis, its use has been limited to only selected applications. Human resource practices such as succession planning and career development, which may have greater strategic impact, often defy quantitative measurement.

## Quantitative and Qualitative Measures

Other evaluation issues are whether to use quantitative or qualitative measures. A number of quantitative measures can be constructed to measure the effectiveness of a company's human resource or the human resource function. Quantitative measures can sometimes be combined in the form of composite indices, and, as indicated earlier, weighing schemes necessary for such indices can be developed through policy capturing approaches. Further, the human resource function can also be evaluated as a cost center. Additionally, the benefits resulting from human resource management programmes, such as reduced turnover or improved percentages of good hires, can sometimes be determined in Rupee values. In such cases, the effectiveness of the function can be measured as a profit center. It is worth noting that an inordinate emphasis on quantitative evaluation measures can become dysfunctional. This occurs when the focus on goals or objectives, as operationalised in-terms of such measure does not contribute to accomplishment of strategic goals. Changes in the attitudes of an organisation's workforce also can provide a partial indication of the effectiveness of the human resource function. These indicators, although inherently more qualitative than many other organisational characteristics, can be captured in measures that allow them to be subjected to statistical analysis.

## Outcome and Process Criteria

A final evaluation is whether the criteria will involve outcomes or processes. The distinction between the two types of criteria is that outcomes are results or end products of work while processes concern behaviour or how activities are performed. An example of an outcome criterion might be productivity ratios for a company's workforce. In-spite of measurement, and objective nature, outcome or output criteria are often contaminated by external factors unrelated to the activity being evaluated. For example, high turnover rates could be more indicative of low unemployment rates in the local labour market than weaknesses in a company's selection or compensation systems.

Conversely, an example of a process criterion could be whether a unit meets affirmative action milestones according to a schedule, such as completing a utilization analysis by the end of the first quarter, and soon. Many managers experience difficulties in defining objectives in terms of processes. When they have difficulty in articulating a desired process by which an activity should be performed, it is sometimes useful to reverse the question and ask them if they can describe how the activity should not be performed. Almost without exception, they can describe how the activity should not be performed, which then helps to stimulate and organize their thinking on desired or efficient processes.

A matrix of these two categories of evaluative criteria are presented in Figure 6.2 of the company's human resource management function itself.

## Balanced Scorecard Perspective

Another perspective on measures is presented in the balanced scorecard approach developed by Robert Kaplan and David P. Norton. Kaplan and Norton's work on evaluation concluded that companies commonly use three measures in human resource evaluation :

### Employee satisfaction; retention, and productivity

Kaplan and Norton explain that satisfaction is a pre-requisite for improvements in productivity, quality, responsiveness and customer service. They note that the relationship with customer service is straightforward, as satisfied employees tend to have more satisfied customers. They also endorse annual surveys of employee satisfaction or monthly rolling surveys of samples of the workforce. Similarly, they endorse the measurement of employee retention for its importance in preserving the organisation's investments intellectual capital.

Their most pointed advice is reserved for measurements of employee productivity. While ratios such as revenue per employee are commonly used, there are problems with such measures. More specifically, the preferable approaches to improving productivity ratios involve actions directed at increasing the numerator (output or revenues). However, the same improvement in productivity ratios can be obtained by less preferred actions. Actions directed at reducing the denominator (downsizing or outsourcing) are often dysfunctional because of the long-term loss in organisational capabilities. The following provides more specific advice on the use of measures of revenue per employee :

One way to avoid the incentive to outsource to achieve a higher revenue per employee statistic is to measure value-added per employee, subtracting externally purchased materials, supplies, and services from revenues in the numerator of this ratio. Another modification, to control for the substitution of more productive but higher paid employees, is to measure the denominator by employee compensation rather than number of employees. If a revenue per employee measure is used to motivate higher productivity of individual employees, it must be balanced with other measures of economic success so that the targets for the measure are not achieved in dysfunctional ways.

| | Overall HR Effectiveness | | HR Function Effectiveness | |
|---|---|---|---|---|
| | Quantitative | Qualitative | Quantitative | Qualitative |
| Process | Cell 1 | Cell 2 | Cell 5 | Cell 6 |
| | • Absenteeism rate<br>• Minority Turnover<br>• Grievances<br>• Job acceptance rate | • Lack of conflict<br>• Innovativeness<br>• Union relations<br>• Flexibility | • Average time to fill jobs<br>• Cost per employee<br>• Number of Minority applicants<br>• Training hours per employee | • Time to answer inquiries<br>• Quality of HR Services<br>• Cooperativeness of HR Staff<br>• Quality of HR Programmes |
| Outcome | Cell 3 | Cell 4 | Cell 7 | Cell 8 |
| | • Revenue per employee<br>• New inventions<br>• Loss of key employees | • Employee morale<br>• Stakeholder approval<br>• Company reputation for HR | • Value added on HR investment<br>• HR budget per employee<br>• Number of new HR programmes<br>• Personnel ratio | • Executive satisfaction<br>• Line manager satisfaction<br>• Employees' opinion of HR |

**Fig. 6.2: Effectiveness Criteria**

## Benchmarking

In addition to these approaches, criteria, and measurements, another general evaluation approach has been applied to human resource practices in recent years. This approach is called '**Benchmarking**'. In essence, benchmarking involves studying how competitors, and sometimes even companies in unrelated industries, are better at certain activities. For example, Ford studied 400 different features of the automobiles of competent manufacturers, with the goal of designing and producing a car that would be better than, or at least as good as, the best competitor in each feature.

Similarly, benchmarking in human resource applications involves the collection of information about specific human resource practices, from large number of respondents across many companies. At a macro-analysis level, Brockbank and Yeung at the University of Michigan collected information on 21 human resource practices in the general areas of staffing, development, performance appraisal, rewards, communication, and organisational design. Questionnaires composed of five interval response scale items (where 1 = low and 5 = high) were used to measure these practices. The questionnaires were completed by 11,300 respondents in 91 companies. Of the respondents, 1,315 were human resource professionals, while 9,985 were from associates of these professionals from various functional areas throughout their companies. The data provided by this large number of respondents provide benchmarks for various human resource practices in 10 different industries. Much of the data concern practices and perceptions of the human resource function's competencies in such areas as recruitment, training, and designing benefit programmes. The data also provide benchmarks of perceived competencies across the various other functional areas (e.g., finance, marketing, research and development) and allow a comparison with the human resource function on competencies in such areas as business knowledge, change management, and the like.

Through benchmarking, a company can compare its human resource practices and competencies with other companies. In addition to some of the benefits of evaluation noted earlier, benchmarking can also enable a company to see how its competencies in human resource practices stack up against those of world-class competitors and whether it has improved over time when longitudinal data are collected. An implication of benchmarking of particular relevance to human resource management's strategic role is that it enables a company to better concentrate its resources so that it can obtain a competitive advantage.

Benchmarking HR practices provides the means of focusing attention on highest value-added HR activities – those practices which are more likely to be practiced by successful companies. Rather than fall into the trap of trying to do everything well and please everyone with insufficient resources – which results in no one being satisfied – HR professionals could use benchmarking to focus limited resources on critical activities.

## Industry Influences

One important consideration in evaluating human resources is industry differences. What may constitute effective human resource practice in one setting may be ineffective in another. A study of high-technology entrepreneurial start-up firms provides some good examples of industry differences in effective human practices. This study points out that the entrepreneurial and high-technology literatures provides contradictory guidance in the areas of human resource planning, compensation, and the work environment. For example, in high technology industries, higher company performance is associated with the use of internal sources for managerial recruitment. Extrapolating from this relationship, the researchers reasoned that human resource planning would be needed to ensure the availability and development of internal sources of talent. Thus, they hypothesized that in high-technology companies, human resource planning is associated with company performance. In contrast, the entrepreneurial literature suggests that there is insufficient time for such planning, relative to other demands, and that planning is inconsistent with the rapid rate of change and flexibility required in entrepreneurial companies.

The researchers also examined compensation issues. The high-technology literature argues that high-technology firms should exercise salary leadership in-order to attract talent. Although the entrepreneurship literature recognizes these benefits, it maintains that cash-flow problems in entrepreneurial firms typically preclude salary leadership practices. The high-technology literature also argues that since its key employees, scientists and engineers, adhere to norms of autonomy-oriented work environment will be associated with company performance. However, the entrepreneurial literature argues that a control-oriented work environment is necessary to focus employee's efforts on short-term goals.

The study, which tested the hypothesis in high-technology entrepreneurial start-up companies, found no relationship between human resource planning and performance. In contrast, compensation leadership was found to be related to sales growth and measures of innovation, as predicted by the high-technology literature. Also, as predicted by the high-technology literature, work environments emphasizing professional autonomy were found to be associated with company performance. An important conclusion from this study is the following:

Researchers interested in the effects of HR policies and practices on organisational effectiveness are advised to take into account such contingencies as industrial setting, stage in the lifecycle, and business strategy. Failure to do so may result in prescriptions which are inapplicable or inappropriate in particular settings.

### Prevalence of Evaluation

Inspite of advocacy for evaluation, a relatively small portion of companies conduct human resource management evaluations. Likewise, few companies express the results of their evaluations in economic terms. Even in billions of rupees being spent on training every year, many companies do not even evaluate training. There are several potential explanations for this difference between the normative views of the human resource literature and industry practice. These explanations include human resource executives' fears of the outcomes of evaluation, difficulties in obtaining meaningful and valid measures of human resource activity and lack of meaningful evaluative framework. Nonetheless, important variables are positively correlated with the conduct of such evaluation, including financial performance, aggressiveness in marketing strategy, economically-oriented goals, and top level involvement of human resource executives in setting the strategic direction of their companies. Because of these positive contributions of evaluation and the cost consciousness resulting from the pressures of the global economy, evaluations should become more prevalent in the future.

### Evaluating Strategic Contributions of Traditional Areas

There are many areas within the traditional functions of human resource management that probably should be evaluated. Major human resource functions of obvious strategic importance are human resource planning, staffing, performance evaluation, compensation and reward systems, training and development, and labour relations. The first to be considered is human resource planning. The potential strategic contributions of human resource planning and the evaluation of this area should be of importance to general managers.

## Human Resource Planning

The effectiveness of human resource planning can be viewed from a behavioural perspective. This includes the degree to which managers accept human resource planning as an activity that helps them perform their jobs. Line management's willingness to supply information to be used in the development of forecasts and actually use human resource forecasts in their own planning provide other indicators of human resource planning effectiveness. Even when forecasts are inaccurate, the human resource planning process has value. This is because, as in any planning effort, the process of forecasting is often more valuable than the forecast itself, because managers are forced to reexamine fundamental operating assumptions. Such reexamination and resultant communications are often valuable side effects.

From a quantitative perspective, for companies that have strong preferences to fill vacancies from internal sources, the extent to which the organisation must hire in the open labour market, may be an indicator of the effectiveness of the human resource planning process. To the extent that shortages in certain skill areas are forecasted and prepared for with the development of employees, the organisation has less need to hire externally. Companies that hire from external market only at entry levels must have effective human resource planning programmes. The failure to plan is probably no more obvious than in professional sports when a team finds itself with a roster of ageing athletes and then must endure years of rebuilding because it did not have an effective planning process for bringing in younger players.

Another standard or criterion of human resource planning and development effectiveness is provided by the just-in-time talent, which means that vacancies can be filled quickly from within the company by a person qualified for promotion. The promoted individual should have been developed by previous assignments and training but should not have to wait in a holding pattern in which his or her skills are underutilized. The concept of just-in-time talent has a great deal of appeal because from the company's standpoint during the period in which the individual is underutilized, the company is not obtaining a return on its investment in development. From the individual's perspective, there is the obvious advantage of not having to spend time in positions that underutilize one's talents. Such situations lead to turnover, which has costly implications for the company as well.

It is interesting to speculate about a potential cause for inaccuracies of human resource forecasts. This explanation points to the rationales for planning. Although, planning in comparison to the effects of global expansion or recession, demographic influences, immigration, and intensified international competition, at the micro-level individual companies probably plan for the forecasted shortages. For example, when expecting labour shortages, companies may invest heavily in labour saving equipment. This may be evident in industries in which productivity is growing rapidly. Such investments helped many companies in India and abroad to meet international competitive pressures by increasing the productivity of their employees. Awareness of forecasted shortages in labour supply may contribute to companies' decisions to make investments in technology development. Thus, increased investment in labour-saving equipment may be influenced, to some extent, by companies' awareness of forecasted labour shortages through their environmental scanning activities. At least in some small portion, forecasted labour shortages may not materialize because companies do human resource planning and take appropriate actions.

This speculative explanation is also consistent with a general description of an effective human resource management function. James Walker has explained the same as follows:

One Company suggested that the most effective function is the one that ensures that there are no pressing human resource issues to concern management. The most proactive, strategic approach to managing resources anticipates and addresses emerging issues before the "pain" is felt. Because conditions continually change, however, there are always issues to be addressed. Through human resource planning, the function may bring these issues to management's attention and create a sense of urgency for action.

## Staffing

Obviously, a company's recruitment and selection procedures are critical to its ability to acquire the human resources needed to obtain competitive advantage. Further, human resource effectiveness is influenced by factors outside the human resource functions. Accordingly, evaluation approaches for staffing functions must control these other influences before valid assessments can be obtained. In addition to the traditional approaches to selection, which attempts to match applicants with job requirements, some new views of selection may pose different evaluation challenges. For example, some companies are now placing primary emphasis in matching applicants with the characteristics or culture of the organisation, instead of the job. Thus, future evaluations may need to focus on developing measures of staff compatibility with organisational characteristics.

There are several measures that can be used in the evaluation of recruiting effectiveness (e.g., cost per hire, number of resumes received, recruiter activities). In turn, the effectiveness of recruiting has an impact on the effectiveness of a company's staffing. To the extent that a company performs staffing functions poorly, the impact may be potentially manifested in problems such as excessive turnover, line management dissatisfaction, poor quality, litigation, under-representation of minorities and women, and so on, which detract from human resource effectiveness. Utility analysis may be used as an evaluation approach for assessing the effectiveness of selection processes. An interesting feature of the utility analysis approach to cost-benefit analysis is that it can be linked with capital budgeting processes. In turn, this link with capital budgeting may make such evaluation of much greater interest to general managers. Like capital budgeting, utility analysis of selection procedures deals with projected cash flows, such as in the form of savings from increased productivity. The results of the utility analysis of such cash flows can be expressed as net present values.

## Training

As noted earlier, one of the most neglected areas in human resource management is the evaluation of training effectiveness. Such failures to evaluate training have been identified by Steven Kerr, as a classic example of misdirected reward structures, or "rewarding **A** while hoping for **B**". In a typical scenario, the proponent of the training, who championed the financial outlay, will collect anecdotes and testimonials that provide "evidence" of the success of the programme.

The last thing many desire is a formal, systematic, and revealing evaluation. Although members of top management may actually hope for such systematic evaluation, their reward systems continue to reward ignorance in this area. Expensive training programmes, strong forms of evaluation are sometimes unlikely because of personal risk to the proponent of the programme, in the event of failure. The alternative in such cases is a trade-off of risk for a weaker form of evaluation, such as participant's reactions or satisfaction with the programme.

However, as noted earlier, because of international competition and increased focus on costs, human resource programmes have been subjected to greater scrutiny. Consequently, human resource managers have had to become more sophisticated in justifying their programmes because the costs of investments in training can be substantial. For example, during one year training costs for IBM were more than $2 billion. Thus, conducting credible evaluations of training effectiveness should be more important in the future.

Although training should normally be expected to contribute to increased productivity, reduced expenses, reduced turnover, improved morale, and so on, training is also conducted for other reasons that may be difficult to quantify. For example, training is sometimes conducted in attractive off-site locations to reward performance and to communicate to those being trained that they are important to the organisation. It may also be conducted to allow employees to build informal relationships and to develop personal networks that facilitate communication and coordination. Training also may be conducted for the purpose of allowing a managerial coalition to propagate its views at the expense of another or for other political purposes that cannot be acknowledged in assessment measures. Further, some companies' cultures may require objective data before an evaluation will have any credibility, while in others, elaborate evaluations of training employing objective measures may be rejected because they are incompatible with the company's culture.

Nonetheless, inspite of such difficulties, training can normally be evaluated with relevant, acknowledgeable criteria. Traditional levels of evaluative criteria are (1) reaction; (2) learning; (3) behaviour; and (4) results. In addition, some researchers consider attitude change as another category of evaluative criteria.

Measures of reaction criteria typically tap participant's satisfaction with training or their perceptions of its quality or relevance. Student evaluations of professors are examples of such measures. Whether reaction criteria actually provide valid standards of effectiveness is arguable because they may indicate only satisfaction. In most industrial settings, some level of satisfaction with training probably is necessary, although insufficient, condition for effectiveness. The essence of this intuitive interpretation has been supported by a recent empirical study that found no linear relationship between reactions and learning. Instead, the study found that reactions moderate the training motivation and learning relationship. It also found that reactions have a complex relationship with other facets of training and effectiveness criteria. In fact, the best training results occur under conditions in which trainees are highly motivated to learn and have a positive reaction to the training.

Learning criteria are concerned with whether participants have absorbed the concepts or content of training. As such, they are concerned with whether the trainees have learned facts, information, techniques, strategies, and the like. An application of this criteria would be a test to determine whether stockbroker trainees have learned the content of training on Securities and Exchange Commission Regulations.

Behaviour criteria go a step beyond whether the trainee has learned the relevant concepts. These criteria are concerned with whether the lessons of the training programmes are translated into changes in the behaviour of the trainee on the job. For example, there should be changes in the managerial behaviour of employees who have completed a management training programme. Unlike the other criteria, a period of time is usually needed for the training to become manifested in behaviours. Therefore, a minimum of three months between the completion of training and measurement of behaviour is ideal.

Finally, results criteria are bottom-line criteria. Measures of such criteria might be breakage and scrap rates that are affected by the skill levels of production workers. Similarly, measures of turnover and morale could be relevant applications of results criteria for managerial training programmes. With results criteria, it is easy to visualize potential contaminants of broader or more global customers, such as , morale, because a multitude of factors other than training may impact morale.

Criteria can also be classified as internal and external. Internal criteria are reactions, attitude change, and learning, while external criteria are behaviour and results. External criteria have an advantage of going beyond the measurement of satisfaction with training or learning of material as they provide information on whether the training has an impact on job performance. A final point on evaluation criteria is that when measuring the effectiveness of training methods, such as lectures, behavioural modeling, role-plays, and so on, the choice of evaluative criteria makes a difference. In other words, the effectiveness of different training methods depends upon the types of criterion to be measured in the evaluative process. For example, a comprehensive meta-analysis of 70 studies by Michael Burke and Russel Day found that when objective performance standards are applied, evaluations of general management training indicate that it is usually quite effective. These findings differ from the conclusions of evaluations applying learning and subjective behavioural criteria.

In addition to the criteria used, it is critical to have an appropriate and practical research design that guides the collection of data and the choice of the measures of the evaluative criteria. The potential contaminants to valid measurement of training effectiveness must be eliminated or controlled through use of an appropriate research design. Both experimental and quasi-experimental designs can be used in a wide range of evaluative applications. Two experimental designs have particular relevance to the assessment of training effectiveness in many organisational settings. Experimental designs are presented in Figure 6.3

The first is the pre-test-post-test control group design, which includes experimental and control groups. Assignment of participants to these groups is based on random selection in order to control such contaminants as differences in ability, experience, and the like. Prior to the commencement of training, both groups are pre-tested on the effectiveness criteria (e.g., knowledge of concepts, skill levels). The experimental group then receives the training which the control group does not. After completion of the training, and any appropriate time lags for behaviours to be manifested, both groups are post-tested. The statistical approach for assessing the significance of results involves the computation of gain scores, in which each individual participants' pre-test score is subtracted from the post-test score. Mean values of gain scores are computed within the experimental group and the control group. The significance of the difference in means of the gain scores between the two groups can then be tested with a t-test. In realistic company settings, a control group should not be too difficult to obtain. Members of the control group can be employees, who may even participate in the same training at some point in the future, after its effectiveness has been determined. When assigning employees to control groups, evaluators must be able to provide justifications as to why control group members are not being trained when they know that another group is receiving training. Another aspect of control groups, of which evaluators should be aware, is the groups' knowledge of the training. In work settings, it is often likely that members of the control group may receive substantial information about the training through discussions with other employees.

**Pre-test-Post-test Control Design:**

| Assignment | Group | Pre-test | Training | Post-test |
|---|---|---|---|---|
| Random | Experimental | Yes | Yes | Yes |
| Random | Control | Yes | No | Yes |

**Posttest – Only Control Group Design:**

| Assignment | Group | Pre-test | Training | Post-test |
|---|---|---|---|---|
| Random | Experimental | No | Yes | Yes |
| Random | Control | No | No | Yes |

**Fig. 6.3: Pre-test/Post-test Control Group Design**

The second experimental design is the post-test-only control group design. This design also utilizes an experimental and control group with random assignment of participants. Unlike the pre-test-post-test control group design, there is no pre-test. With randomization and sufficient sample size, the two groups may be assumed to have equivalent characteristics, such as ability and experience. This design is useful where a pre-test can not be used because it may sensitize employees to a subtle objective of the training and therefore defeat its purpose. An example might be where "asking questions of the members of the control group regarding their management style might cause them to become sensitized to this aspect of their behaviour and inadvertently, cause them to change their style in some systematic way. Further the statistical testing with this design is straightforward, as the significance of the difference in the means between the experimental and the control groups are truly equivalent. This is a crucial point because decision makers, who must be convinced of the value of the training, may not truly understand randomization and research design.

Although these two experimental designs should be adequate for most evaluation needs, the Solomon four-group design may eliminate other threats to the validity of evaluation. However, the exceptions that require this level of analysis are probably beyond the scope of interest for most general managers.

A final research design appropriate to the assessment of training programmes is the quasi-experimental design based on a time series. This design may be appropriate in situations in which no control group can be obtained. The essence of the approach is to obtain measures of evaluation criterion at repeated intervals, such as every month for six months, prior to the conduct of training. After the training, the measures would be collected again at repeated intervals. Unfortunately, analysis of the significance of the results is not as straightforward as with the two experimental designs because of the non-independence of the observations. In some cases, the interpretation of the results may rest on a simple visual examination of observation trend lines.

For example, BHEL has used the quasi-experimental design to assess the effectiveness of its basic management skills training programme. In one Unit, repeated measures of productivity were collected for several months prior to and after the training in-order to assess the programme's effectiveness. In another unit, measure of outstanding collectibles were collected in the same manner. Additionally, projections of collectibles were also developed in this unit to indicate the performance that would have occurred in the absence of the training. These projections allowed the calculation of financial returns on the training investment. Other aspects of its programme provide an indication of the comprehensiveness of CIGNA's evaluation approach. In addition to these evaluations based on the time series quasi-experimental design, the Company also used reaction, learning, and behavioural criteria to assess training effectiveness. In the case of assessments of behaviours, the company had the participants' supervisors assess their managerial behaviours prior to and after the training on such dimensions as leadership, setting standards and planning.

## Performance Evaluation Systems

Unfortunately, in-response to complaints and unfavourable comments, many organisations may respond in a technical manner by changing their performance evaluation format instead of addressing more basic problems, such as inadequate training for evaluators, absence of linkage between ratings and rewards, or failures to consider strategic contributions. Maintaining an effective performance measurement system requires training for evaluators, adequate time to perform evaluations, adequate time to conduct performance counseling, and rewards to distribute according to performance. Periodic surveys of managers' views on these aspects of the performance evaluation system can provide indicators of its effectiveness. Another effectiveness indicator can be obtained by correlating employees' ratings with their percentage merit increases in compensation. Although structural adjustments for external equity or other adjustments can sometimes legitimately alter the relationship, on average there should be a positive correlation. While it is hoped that an effective performance evaluation system will reduce the frequency of litigation, another indicator of effectiveness may be its track record in litigation.

## Compensation Systems

It has been observed above that the human resource function has been faulted for the existence of compensation systems that are not congruent with organisational strategies. Several aspects of compensation systems must be evaluated in order to determine their value in strategy implementation. The compensation mix is a critical issue that needs monitoring. Unfortunately, where there is movement toward more variable compensation, the compensation mix does not yet promote workforce stability, as it does in Japan. One means of providing more employment stability is to change the compensation mix by building in a larger proportion of variable compensation, such as profit sharing or bonuses, which is the approach used in Japan. When profitability and demand decline, compensation costs also decline, making it less necessary to lay off employees.

Another critical issue in evaluating the effectiveness of compensation systems is their flexibility. The traditional compensation systems mainly based on job evaluation and determination of internal equity among jobs tend to be inflexible. The process of job evaluation commonly performed according to the point system, assigns different scores of points for various levels of classifications, such as "know-how", which refers to the operational knowledge of different jobs. But for some non-managerial jobs, there are no "know-how" points in the evaluation system. Thus, the job evaluation system places some employees in "non-thinking" categories. One consequence of placing employees in such pigeonholes is that some tends to stop thinking and maintain a level of ignorance in order to conform to the job requirements. Another consequence is that some employees who are dissatisfied with the "non-thinking" requirements, proceed on their own to develop other knowledge. As a result, these employees' initiatives, managers attempt to have their positions upgraded, which introduces another source of distortion to the wage structure.

In addition to these major issues, there are several other aspects of compensation that should be evaluated for their contribution to the strategic goals of the company. These may include subjective measures of the extent to which the compensation system provides for internal equity; conforms to legal requirements for race and age; and provides pay satisfaction. Objective measures of compensation system effectiveness may include overtime utilization, payroll complaints, and comparisons of the company's wages for various jobs with those in the existing labour markets.

## Labour and Employee Relations

It is important for companies where strong trade union is existing to evaluate the effectiveness of their labour relations functions and the managers' conduct and attitude for maintaining industrial relations. For unionized companies, there are numerous indicators of labour relations effectiveness. Such as the frequency or length of work stoppages, degree to which collective bargaining agreements are restrictive, degree of co-operation between the union and management, managerial flexibility in work assignment, ability to impose reasonable work rules, other management prerogatives, discretion to promote or layoff on the basis of ability or merit, ease of administering the labour agreement, and the company's grievance experience. In the case of grievances, caution must be taken in drawing inferences of effectiveness, because there is multitude of potential influences of effectiveness, because there is multitude of potential influences on the incidence of grievances. Such influences include managerial behaviour, the working environment, the personality and motivation of union representatives, the company's relationship with the union, and individual employee characteristics.

It is also important for non-union companies to evaluate the effectiveness of their employee relations functions. For such companies, the prospects of unionization should not be discounted even though overall union membership is small in number. However, because of competitive pressures, many such companies have abandoned their policies of downsizing and layoffs and are able to remain non-union. In addition, the casual approach of many companies to downsizing and the emergence of unbundled or network organisations have probably reduced employee loyalty to the extent that more employees may be willing to unionize in order to gain job security. The question remains as to whether employees will consider unionization as an instrument for their job security or as a futile effort.

In the past, unions were often able to confine layoffs to the most junior employees, as the vast numbers of layoffs were conducted according to inverse seniority. They were successful to the extent that they could organize extensively in an industry and make all competitors pay the same wages and offer similar working conditions. Their strategy was to "take wages out of competition". The cost of wage increases and favourable terms of employment were then largely passed on to consumers in the form of price increases. However, in today's international market place, the power of unions has declined. Unions cannot organize all international manufacturers in a given industry, as demonstrated by abortive attempts at multinational union cooperation. As a result, there will be adverse employment effects to the extent that employment security agreements put domestic manufacturers at a disadvantage to international competitors. Further, unions seems to be unable to prevent domestic manufacturing companies from shifting production facilities to other countries. It will be interesting to see whether unions will be able to devise strategies to help employees obtain greater job security. Regardless of the eventual direction of unionization in the future, unionization is very much a reality in many industries.

## Evaluating Strategic Contributions in Emerging Areas

There are number of challenges from emerging areas related to human resource management that have major implications on most of the companies. Two of the most important of these are: (1) equal employment opportunity and the management of diversity; and (2) quality readiness. The details are as below:

### (1) Equal Employment Opportunity and Management of Diversity

The relevance of the management of diversity to the topic of evaluating human resource effectiveness is that effective management in this area enables organisations to tap the potential of their workforces. Thus, management of diversity can be related to the effectiveness with which companies avoid labour shortages. Evaluations of effectiveness in this area should measure turnover of minority and female employees.

From literature survey, some suggestions appear to have value in enabling organisations to be more effective in the management of diversity. One suggestion deals with the advancement of minorities and females. Advancement to upper level positions requires information that is obtained through informal networks from which minorities and females are often excluded. Because the pathway to promotion for companies' highest level jobs becomes more subtle and ill-defined with moves up the organisational hierarchy, it is desirable for organisations to devote more attention to these subtleties. Being networked and acquiring upward pull from a mentor are critical before minorities and females can rise to the top.

Unfortunately, performance evaluation processes frequently do not provide managers with the feedback that they need to advance to the highest level positions. This weaknesses of performance evaluation is often offset by informal feedback through personal mentoring or networks. When lack of access to networks deprives an individual of honest feedback, performance appraisal systems must be improved for increased effectiveness.

A second suggestion for improved effectiveness is that, where the problems of minorities and females are unrelated to prejudice, remedial efforts should facilitate the advancement of all groups of people. In contrast, when remedial programs give special consideration only to particular groups, they become enormously time consuming and are inconsistent with the spirit of diversity. A third suggestion is that, since the management of diversity is not an exact science, mistakes will be made and setbacks will occur. Accordingly, in the interests of fairness, managers should not be penalized for their efforts. A fourth suggestion is that the focus of the management of diversity should be a broad one, extending even to education, personality, background, and age. Such a broad orientation should facilitate the development of a heterogeneous culture, instead of attempting to assimilate those who differ into a dominant culture of white males. A fifth suggestion is to conduct training courses on diversity, which may deal with communication style differences, increase self-awareness, and reduce biases through skill-building exercises. Leading companies in this type of training include Hewlett-Packard and Ortho Pharmaceuticals. Such training can be evaluated with the approaches discussed above. A sixth suggestion is to incorporate management of diversity into the company's performance evaluation and reward system so that those managers doing a good job in this regard are rewarded. Companies providing leadership in this area include Coca-Cola and Exxon-Mobil.

## Quality Readiness

Although total quality management (TQM) has received a great deal of attention, the importance of the role of human resource management is not well-known. Christopher Hart and Leonard Schlesinger have pointed out that TQM is relevant to the evaluation of human resources in at least three respects :

1. The quality that can be achieved by a company's workforce is in part determined by its motivation and training.
2. The quality of the activities and services of the human resource function are evaluated in TQM approaches.
3. The Malcolm Baldrige National Quality Award framework provides a TQM guide for evaluation of human resources.

Interestingly, human resource management and development make up one of the seven major components on which companies are evaluated for the Baldrige Award, comprising 150 of the total 1,000 points. The importance of the Baldrige framework, however, is not attributable to its role in the granting of awards of quality. Instead, its importance lies with its usefulness in providing a guide to obtaining quality and its value in evaluation or assessment.

Under TQM, the ultimate objective is to provide customer satisfaction. By satisfying customers, a company increases its market share and enhances the likelihood of increased profitability. The traditional objectives of the human resource function, which seek to improve performance, productivity, employee satisfaction, and motivation, are indirectly related to customer satisfaction. This is because employee retention and a well-trained workforce is required for the production of quality goods and services. TQM emphasizes the importance of a systematic, comprehensive approach toward quality, the interrelated role of the human resource function and its indirect impact on the workforce make it critical to this objective. One outcome of TQM is that a stronger case is made for the importance of funding training.

As a model for evaluation, the Baldrige guidelines make several important points. Among those most relevant to human resource management are its emphasis on (1) the use of objective performance data and (2) benchmarking based on external comparisons or based on the company's own performance in earlier time periods. Hart and Schlesinger have noted that the guidelines also deal with the specifics of assessment, such as described below:

What Baldrige examiners look for, though, is objective evidence, like job definitions that include clearly delineated quality responsibilities. The criteria ask, among other things, for "indicators, benchmarks, or other bases for evaluating and improving organisational structure", and "key methods and key indicators the company uses to evaluate and improve awareness and integration of quality values at all levels of management and supervision".

By using the Baldrige framework as a questionnaire, a company can use the guidelines like the award examiners do to evaluate its strengths and weaknesses in quality. This assessment would be a first step towards adoption of TQM and improvement of quality. Following this evaluation or assessment, a triage process would be undertaken in which priorities would be established for actions to be taken. One practical suggestion is to fix first those problems that have easy solutions or pick the "low-hanging fruit" first. Another TQM-related suggestion is that the human resource function should adopt a perspective that is similar to an independent contractor providing services to a customer. When viewed from this perspective, those in the human resource function would begin to ask themselves whether the customer, the company, would renew their contract. When viewed in this manner, the importance of customer satisfaction is more evident.

Finally, the use of the Baldrige framework as a guide for evaluation and its emphasis on objective data deserve comment. Many important phenomena may not meet all parties' definitions of objective. Dysfunctional results occur when important phenomena are ignored because they cannot be expressed in an objective format.

## Case Study

### Simulation and Role Play

Kapil Agarwal has recently joined as manager of a famous resort located in Shankarpur called "Kutir". Agarwal has received a mandate to ensure that the resort maintains the best destination of choice for foreign tourists. He has also been instructed to bring down the operation cost to 25% without affecting the goal. Agarwal recently participated in an executive development programme at Kolkata on accountability of a human resource manager. He put this item in the agenda for the management meeting scheduled for next month. He collected the data very meticulously and attached with the agenda regarding the ongoing HR activities of his resort with a comparative chart of the competitor hotels in the region as per the details given below:

| Components | Score on HRM Effectiveness (Number of hotels=20) Score of 1 = very low, Score of 6 = very high |
|---|---|
| Customer Satisfaction | 4.50 |
| Employee Commitment | 2.10 |
| Employee Satisfaction | 3.90 |
| Employee Absenteeism | 4.20 |
| Employee Turnover | 5.10 |
| Overall Productivity | 3.80 |

### Adapted from Bratton and Gold 2003

Kutir employs 500 during the peak season. The HR department hires and trains employees from the labour market, administers salary and benefits, and maintains harmonious trade union relationship. There were five managers including Agarwal in the routine monthly meeting. When Agarwal presented about the accountability of HRM, the other members responded as stated below:

**Rajat (Associate General Manager)** HR activity should be outsourced in case the existing HR cannot perform its job effectively and optimally.

**Sumit (Front Desk Manager)** Does HR follow best practices? How does HR help the management reducing operating costs? How does our HR practices compare with the competitors?

**Bipasha (Food and Beverage Services)** HR department has conducted the training programme very nicely and as a result, increase in sales and profit has taken place.

**Abhijeet (HR Executive)** It is nice to evaluate the overall role of HR in achieving the organisational goal, but it is very difficult and time taking.

**Gopal (Corporate HR Head)** I think Agarwal this point needs attention.

- Six students are required for this role play exercise, each assuming the role of one of the managers present in the monthly management meeting.
- Each student should support the viewpoint of the manager. There should be a discussion on the different views of the managers expressed during the meeting. All members should contribute in the discussion.

- After listening to the managers' views, the student playing the role of Corporate HR Head, must persuade the HR manager about the effectiveness of measuring the HR contribution and of demonstrating its value. He should also suggest some measures the HR manager should do to demonstrate the value added by the HRM department.
- The group should then discuss the pros and cons of various HR evaluation methods, such as Balanced Score Card, HR Scorecard, Benchmarking, and Business Excellence Model, in measuring the contribution of HRM to the resort's performance. Every member should offer arguments to support his/her viewpoint.
- The role play should end with the members reaching a consensus on making HR accountable, and the HR evaluation approach to be adopted by the resort and why.
- After the role play is over, the facilitator should open the discussion to the rest of the class and seek their reactions on the role play, as well as the views expressed.
- The facilitator should summarize the discussion at the end.

## Reference


- Tanuja Agarwala, *Strategic Human Resource Management*, Oxford Higher Education, 2007.


***

# 7 Human Resource Accounting/Human Resource Audit

## Concept of HRA

Accounting is a code language used by the accountants to translate business transactions into a definite quantitative framework which can be further interpreted and analysed to derive meaningful qualitative conclusions. Accounting helps in rational decision making as it provides objective information to the decision maker.

Human resource accounting has been defined by the committee on Human Resource Accounting of the American Accounting Association as "the process of identifying and measuring data about human resources and communicating this information to interested parties." According to Flamholtz, "Human resource accounting means accounting for people as an organisational resource. It involves measuring the costs incurred by business firms and other organisations to recruit, select, hire train and develop human resources. It also involves measuring the economic value of people to organisations." Human resource management's planning and control functions. The following diagram shows the team and their interrelationships, which corporate managers generally recognise that employees constitute the most important and the most valuable assets and often take decisions involving expenditure which may be justified as investment in human resources, traditional accounting requires such expenses to be charged to income without considering the timing of expected benefits. Thus, expenditures made for recruiting, engaging, training and developing people are treated as, expenses, and no attempt is made to formulate rules to distinguish between their asset and expense components. It has been increasingly realised that although outlays for human resource have been traditionally conventional foundations of the concept of an asset, and not because of the real nature and timing of benefit that result from such outlays.

Accounting being a practice – engaged in the collection and presentation of economic information to assist a wide ranging decision making process is based on certain rules, procedures and techniques which have evolved over a period of time as a consequence of social, economic, political, legal conditions, restraints and influences. Many managers believe that the accounting function has failed to adjust its objectives and activities to the decision-making requirement of a changing business world. This belief gets reinforced when one finds that the human resource – but for whose direction and effort "plants, offices, computers, automated equipment and all else that a modern firm was/are unproductive" – find no place in the annual report of a business enterprise just because of the simple reason that the customary accounting system is based on the conventional of monetary valuation and the doctrine of verifiable objective evidence which tritly rule out the ease of accounting for human resources.

The practice of regarding all costs incurred on human capital formation as 'expired cost' is conceptually wrong and in assistant with the treatment given to the similar expenditures on physical capital or physical assets. This is done inspite of the fact that the benefits may accrue to the entity not only in that period but in future also. This treatment is elected because "investment in people seen more tenuous than investments in machines, and because there are special difficulties involved in distinguishing between the future benefits of such expenditures and the portion consumed currently. We also have difficulty in thinking of people individually as assets since they are not legally owned by the firm and because of cultural constraints or taboos on the notion of valuing an individual in monetary terms. This view may be countered on several grounds. Human valuation is not concerned with humans *per se*. Its primary concern is with the performance of human services. The concept is not concerned with any other activities of the employee services qualify as assets? To resolve this issue, one must consider the economic viewpoint. According to the American Accounting Association, accounting is primarily concerned with events and objects that have economic significance, and this does not necessarily involve legal ownership. As Sprouse and Moonitz have observed, "the value of assets, indeed their existence, depends upon the future economic services they are capable of rendering to the business enterprise." Based on the accounting definition of resources, Hendriksen's view is that there must be a legally enforceable claim to the rights of services of the resources, but this does not mean that the firm must have a formal title or even a formal contract. Rather, the accountant must rely upon the apparent intent of those who may have all interest in the asset rather than the strict legality of the right. It follows that to be classified as an asset, a resource must have service-potential for the future, extending over more than a year.

All economic theories of value are faxed explicitly or implicitly upon the premise that the attribute determining whether, and to what extent, an object possesses value, is the perceived ability to render future economic 'utility, benefits', or 'services'. Von Mises observed, "whoever wants to construct an elementary theory of value and price must first think of utility. To put it differently, if an object is not capable of rendering future economic services then it has no value. A resource may be defined as an object that possesses expected future services, that is, objects which do not possess expected future benefits can not, by definition, be resources. Live all resources, people possess value because they are capable of rendering future services. From a macro economic viewpoint, the services which people can potentially provide constitute a form of capital. In the same way, people employed in the organisation are resources because they possess expected future service potential. If the accounting system incorporates the value of a firm's human resource and its changes over time, the 'net income' might be adjusted to reflect changes in the value of human resources. So as to avoid the illusion of 'Profits' derived from the liquidation of human resources. The adjusted figure would give a more realistic measurement of managerial effectiveness. Besides, the trends in the adjusted net income figure would also provide an improved basis for the projection of future earnings.

Managerial planning involves search for alternative solutions to problems and evaluation of the alternatives in decision situation. The search for alternatives requires an awareness of the critical nature of all human resources. A conscious recognition of this factor in the development of alternatives can be possible with a regular assessment of the value of human resources.

Likewise, the impact of capital budgeting decisions on human assists is often considered to be a qualitative factor and its critical significance, if not ignored, is not given due importance. Measures of the value of human resources are expected to make a lot of difference in capital budgeting decisions. Human assets are not included in the asset base used to calculate the rate of return on investment. Human assets are assumed implicitly to be cost free. But human as well as physical assets have opportunity costs associated with their use. This cost needs to be quantified and considered in evaluating alternative proposals.

Evaluation of investments in human capital is generally based on a qualitative assessment of the alternatives. Moreover, investments in human assets are often made without evaluation the expected pay off or return on such investments. The value of managerial training and development programmes is usually taken on faith and expenditure on these accounts is incurred by firms which can afford it with ease, given a high level of profits. Systematic programmes of employee training and executive development obviously need evaluation of the yield or return on the expenditure involved in such programmes.

In the decision models, used in the process of selecting among alternatives, human resource information and changes in the value of human resources over time are important ingredients of decisionmaking. For example, if the management has to choose among alternative locations for a new plant, involving transfer of existing employees, it is necessary that a survey of employee attitudes should be undertaken towards the alternative locations and attempt should be made to determine the expected turnover, associated with each location, and the expected cost of turnover calculated. This may be a critical factor in the choice of location for the new plant.

The use of human resource accounting for reporting on actions taken and results achieved may also be of crucial significance in the management control system. Human resource data may include information about the composition of investments in human resources and analysed to determine standard costs of recruiting, firing, training, and developing employees to bring them upto a desired level of competence. Besides, these data may be useful to estimate the replacement costs of filling up various positions.

Replacement costs, in turn, can be used to make budget allocations for investment in manpower, planning and development. In other words, human resource data may provide the basis of setting up a standard cost accounting system for human resource costs, similar to that for manufacturing costs.

Flamtoltz has specifically underlined the primary role of human resource accounting as that of providing information essential for management to perform the functions of acquiring, developing, allocating, conserving, utilising, evaluating and rewarding human resources. The first step in human resource acquisition is to forecast manpower requirements, the management must then translate the manpower forecast into a manpower acquisition budget, which is essentially a process of cost estimation. HRA can provide measurements of the standard cost of recruiting, selecting and hiring people, for estimate of amounts to be incorporated in the manpower acquisition budget. Again, in making selecting decisions, managers need measurements of the value of candidates for particular jobs, so that the person selected is one who possesses the greatest future value to the organisation. Instead of using non-monetary measures of potential abilities desired through qualitative tests, the potential economic value of candidates may be a better criterion for selection. Using monetary measurements of the expected value of people, decision rules may be designed to optimise the expected value of the firm's human resources.

Budgeting for training and development programmes for employees involves assessment of the value of proposed investment in such programmes and estimating the cost of such programmes. HRA can be helpful for decision making, involving the allocation of resources to training and development programmes by measuring the expected rate of return on proposed investments. By providing estimates of the historical and current costs to acquire and develop people for various positions, HRA can also help management to assess the trade-off between the costs of recruitment from outside and development from within.

Allocation of human resources, i.e., assigning people to various organisational roles and tasks, needs to be decided on the basis of the efficiency of the employer, opportunity of self-development and job-satisfaction expected to be derived by the employee. HRA can help qualify the variables required to be considered in the process of allocation expressed in terms of the common dominator of monetary units. The management may, thus, be enabled also to apply linear programming for an optional solution of the manpower allocation problem. Otherwise, allocation decisions may be costly to individuals as well as to the organisation.

Conservation of human resource is yet another area in which HRA can be can be of great assistance to management, conservation of human resources is the process of maintaining the capabilities of people as individuals and the effectiveness of the human system developed by an organisation. This needs monitoring the effectiveness of the human organisation to assess the extent to which it is being maintained or depleted. Measures of employee turnover rates, traditionally used to assess the conservation of human resources, are inadequate, first because there are historical figures and, second, because they do not fully reflect the economic impact of turnover. Through monetary measures and reporting of socio-psychological indicators of the condition of human organisation, HRA can help management by providing an early warning system to take law of human resource conservation. HRA can further help management in the utilisation of human resources effectively and efficiently by providing a conceptual framework, so as to develop strategies with respect of acquisition development, allocation and longer-vation, designed to influence the value of people. Human resource evaluation involves the measurement of productivity and promotability of people. HRA can be useful in the evaluation of human resources by developing appropriate methods, including both monetary and non-monetary measurements. Moreover, human resource valuation can be used for organisational rewards to be administered in relation to an employee's value to the organisation. Further, the efficiency of personnel management function *per se* can also be assessed through human resource accounting. The standard costs of acquiring and developing people may be compared with the actual costs incurred for the purpose, and the variances from the standard may be analysed to identify the possible lapses in the personnel management functions.

## Benefits of HRA

The rationale of human resource valuation for manpower management essentially arises from the fact that the collectivity of people happens to be the key to organisational efficiency and effectiveness. At the national level, the quality of people determines the state of the national economy as much as the social and political ethos. Similarly, in an individual firm it is the organised group of human beings that determines the quality of day-to-day performance as well as the growth and prosperity of the firm. One can speak of human capital being a necessary and vital component of the organisation just as human capital or manpower happens to be the major component of any economic system. The success of an organisation hangs ultimately on the efficiency of its HRs. Hence, the objectives of an organisation should, therefore, be to acquire their services, to develop their skill, to motivate the people to enhance their level of performance and ultimately to ensure that they continue to maintain their commitment to the organisation. These operations are performed by all the organisations, whether they are profit seeking or non-profit seeking to achieve their desired objectives.

Growth in size and complexity of organisations are inseparable features of modern society, so are complexities of management. Managing people has become increasingly more complex in today's organisations. The trend towards organisational proliferation for economic advancement has led to the pursuit of goals, which require increasing size and complexity to be accepted for the sake of efficiency. New type of organisations have come into existence over the years with technological advances and increasing control of man over his environment. In the context of all these changes, the role of people in the organisations has come to be recognised as of vital significance. Along with the concern for the management of the manpower is achieving corporate objectives, attention has also been drawn in recent years to the necessity of measuring the value of human resources and changes thereof. The assumption underlying the valuation of and accounting for human resources is that information relating to the value of human resources is an important ingredient of managerial decisionmaking. Over and above, the usefulness of human resource value for internal management, the relevant data are also expected to be useful to investors, creditors, financiers as well as government agencies. The impact of human resource data on managerial decisions and its usefulness to external uses of corporate reports has been the subject of inquiry in a number of research studies. Approaches to the methods of measuring the value of human resources have been developed by a number of researchers keeping in view the nature of use of such data.

The Benefits of HRA in an Organisation can be as under:

### 1. Provides Status of Overall Functioning

The traditional accounting system does not provide information about HRA. The expenses incurred during the process of selection, hiring, training and development, etc., are treated as current revenue expenses rather than an investment for the purpose of being capitalised over its useful economic service life. Resulting in the conventional balance sheets failing to represent the value of HRs and hence these financial reports are unable to reflect the true value of the organisational and the rate of return on actual investments. The rate of investment shows a brighter image than what is the actual position. This is why the information on HRs is necessary to provide a complete picture of the assetsholding of an organisation.

### 2. Effective Control

The data retrieved from sources can be used as a tool by the management for effective control of the functioning. The basic purpose of HRA is to provide information pivotal for management to perform the functions of acquiring, developing, allocating, conserving, utilising, evaluating and compensating HRs. The result so derived through using HRA for reporting may also be of crucial significance in the management control system.

### 3. Information to Interested Parties

HRA information could also be of great use to other beneficiaries through its periodical publication. Such as the bankers giving loans, agencies making investments are interested in the profit and success of the organisation at par the Board of Directors and Chief Executives in having these periodic measurement of the casual and intervening variables. Where the causal variables denote the strategy, skill and policies of leadership, the intervening variables denote the strategy, skill and policies of leadership, the intervening variables reflect the internal health, state and performance capabilities of the organisations.

### 4. Information of HRs Performance

HRA can attract investors through publication of information regarding the skill, efficiency and whether HRs of the organisation are able to achieve the organisational goals, for they feel that an entity with skilled, efficient and wise HRs are more desirable for investment, as they may get higher rate of capital gains from their securities and expects greater service potentials than from those with efficient working force. Moreover the efficiency of HRs can be measured through the HRA.

## 5. Indicator of Prospective Profits

The investment in human assets ratio may be regarded as a very useful tool to forecast the relative position of HRs in comparison to investment made by the organisation in other physical assets, and also service as an important indicator of future profit performance to the investors and other interested parties.

## 6. Information on Non-monetary report

If the non-monetary performance of the organisation is published annually, the beneficiaries can feel more secured because the measurement of services and reporting of such non-monetary report will make the information system more logical and authentic. HRA would first identify the variables which determine a person's value to an organisation that would suggest in developing monetary measures fo human value, and by identifying the variables, it would facilitate the development of non-monetary surrogate measures of human value.

## 7. Development of Employee Behaviour

If information received through financial statement regarding the organisational human resources can help the management in developing employee's behaviour and skill, monitoring their efficiency of performance, reducing employee turnover, absenteeism and improving human relations. The HRs, once treated in the Balance Sheet as assets of the organisation, may achieve some psychological impetus, which ultimately influence their performance in the organisation.

## 8. Facilitator for Preparing Comparative Analysis

Comparison of performance between monetary and non-monetary aspects can be made based on the received information, which will be of great help to management for effective control. For this comparison, a few financial ratios may be suggested such as: (a) Ratio of human to non-human; (b) Rates of the value of scientific staff to the total value of human capital. These ratios will help determine the value of HRs in comparison to the total assets, as well as their performance in the organisation.

## 9. Effective Managerial Decision Making

The financial statement gives the information related to HRs and the changes in the value of HR assets from time to time to the interested particles, which helps them taking appropriate decisions and choosing the alternatives. The resource providers may decide on their intended investments on the basis of the rate of return of the entity.

### 10. A precursor of Profitability and Productivity

The funding agencies of the profit-making organisations are generally interested in the organisation's higher profit, and HRs is the prime mover for achieving maximum productivity. Hence, HRs should be shown as assets in the financial statement to give a meaningful and comparable measure of productivity. The profitability on the other hand, presents the performance and creditworthiness of an entity and such information can only be portrayed by incorporating the value of both human and non-human assets in the financial statements.

### 11. A system for optimum use of human resources

HRA also helps the management in utilising the organisational human resources in the most effective and efficient manner by a pre-decided policy for acquisition, development, allocation, conservation, designed to influence the value of the people.

Based on the above discussions, we can say that HRA depicts more realistic financial picture of the organisation. Through financial statements which ensures more comparability and completeness of accounting reporting. Thus, it provides a more useful information as an edge to financial analysis.

## Difficulties to implement HRA in an organisation

Human Resource Accounting is the process of identifying and measuring data about human resources and communicating this information of interested parties. Inspite of various benefits of HRA for organisational excellence, there are still several difficulties in introducing HRA in an organisation. The following are the difficulties.

1. On scanning through literature it has been found that a good number models have been developed by different researchers for the valuation of HRs of an organisation, as per primary requirement of a module data required to fit the model, which is very difficult.
2. Besides above, the authorities are reluctant to recommend introduction of a particular model, because no uniform standard has so far been established for the measurement of HR value.
3. The management of organisations does not show interest in the valuation of HRs on the following pretext.
   (a) The valuation models have their own complex standards and difficult to implement,
   (b) Most of the management are least interested to disclose the organisational value of their HRs,
   (c) Another difficulty to human resource accounting is that by introducing HRA an organisation cannot get any tax relief.
   (d) There is no legal binding for disclosure of the HR value.

4. The ultimate motto of a profit-seeking organisation is to earn maximum profit. The system of HRA, in fact, neither helps in profit maximisation, nor facilitates in presenting the financial data in a greater way.
5. Since the values are based on estimates than on exchanges, the resultant statements are sometimes considered subjective, surmisive and imaginary.
6. The last, not the least, difficulty is that the people are not owned by the organisations like other physical properties. As no ownership can be claimed on HRs, they loose their sales value. Most of the people concerned are, therefore, reluctant to measure and report such resources in the financial statements.

Inspite of all the difficulties mentioned above, it can be rightly claimed that HRA has opened a new vistas in the accounting world so that there will be a scope for evaluating and reporting HRs associated with the entity.

## Methods of Valuation of Human Resources

Accounting purists must be perplexed by a novel addition that computer education and software firm APTECH has made to its annual reports. For a couple of years now, the company has been publishing a double-spread entitled "The knowledge score-board". Its simple format provides an easy-to read snapshot of how the company has performed on the human resource (HR) front. Novel presentation apart, APTECH is not a pioneer in this respect, though. As far back as 1996, Infosys began including quantifying the value of its employees in its annual report. This data used to be mentioned in a section titled "Additional Information to shareholders" in the company's Annual Report. This section, looked at, apart from human capital valuations, such issues as the company's overall intellectual capital brand value, and all.

Unlike the U.S. where the markets were awarding heavy premiums to knowledge companies, human capital valuation in India is still restricted to a handful of firms. The reasons vary, ranging from the desire to conform to the U.S. Generally Accepted Accounting Principle (GAAP) ahead of raising money from markets abroad, or to communicate the worth of one's human resource to investors or, as you will set, for purely internal reasons. This early adopter phase is hardly surprising, as these are early days yet for HR valuation systems globally. The concept of (both) HR valuation and valuing other intangible assets is still in the realm of academic discussion even in the most advanced country like us.

The proponents of HRA have suggested several methods of valuation for human resources. They are as under:

**A. Cost-based Approaches**

(i) Historical Cost

(ii) Replacement Cost

(iii) Opportunity Cost

**B. Monetary Value-based Approaches**

(i) The Hermanson Model

(ii) The Lev and Schwartz Model

(iii) The Eric Flamhortz Model

(iv) The Myers and Flowers Model

(v) The Sadan and Auersach Model

(vi) The Jaggi and Lace Model

**C. Non-monetary Value-based**

(i) The Likert Model

(ii) The Flamhortz Model

(iii) The Pekin organ Model

## A. Cost-based Approaches

(Brummet, Flamhortz and Pyle)

### (i) Historical Cost Method

The cost of acquisition, training and development of individuals capitalized with subsequent amortization over the years to reflect the value of the individuals and the organisation. It is based on the Historic cost approach. This may not truly represent the HR value of an organisation. Capitalisation of cost contrary to its expense nature in traditional accounting practices may not be acceptable. Accumulated cost of HR acquisition and development may not reflect their value. Cost amortization inappropriate due to performance rating of individuals.

However, this can not fulfil the requirement of developing a system of HRA based on systematic valuation of internal as well as external human resources, which may improve the quality and utility of accounting reports from the viewpoint of rational decision making.

### (ii) Replacement Cost Method: Flamhortz Method

The cost of replacing individuals and rebuilding cost of human organisation to reflect the HR asset value. The replacement cost may be relevant only for key individuals. Human resource is not traded in the market, hence replacement cost may not exist. Replacement alternatives may be many and assessment of correct alternative may be subjective.

It is difficult to find identical replacement of the existing human resources in actual practice due to the absence of arriving at proper replacement cost of an employer, this model is not useful.

### (iii) Opportunity Cost-based Approaches (Competitive Bidding Model-Hekimian and Jones)

It is based on competitive bidding amongst the investment centre managers to win the individual employees for use based on the highest bid price to be included as value of human asset along with investment in physical assets while assessing the return on investment by individual investment centres. More and more individuals may be out of the bidding process and may have no value in the organisation. It requires assessing the likely contribution from each individual for future assignments.

It is more subjective and may not be uniform across the company. The assessment may be based on the perception of the individuals involved in the bidding. It is more subjective and hence cannot be used effectively.

## B. Monetary Value–based Approaches or Economic Models

### (i) (a) Goodwill Method

**Hermanson Model:** Extra profits earned by organisation as compared to industry average rate, i.e., HR value = Goodwill, Investment in HR/Total investments. The rate of earnings may be influenced by other external factors also and cannot be purely linked to HR. Goodwill may be attributable to investment in suppliers, the customers, the public image etc.

This model cannot be implemented if the rate of earnings of the company is less than the industry average. This model is more subjective and unless relationship of various factors to the company's goodwill is established, this model is debatable.

### (b) Adjusted Discounted Future Wages Method – Hermanson Model

Present value of future wages payable for next five years discounted at the adjusted rate of return is the HR value. The adjusted rate of return refers to average rate of return on owned assets of all firms in the economy multiplied by the efficiency ratio in the organisation during the last five years on a weighted average basis.

Rate of return of a specific organisation may not be comparable with other firms in the economy. The model is subjective with respect to Pv being restricted for five years, efficiency ratio calculated for past five years, and assignment of weightless for past rate of return, it is too subjective, and hence can not be used.

### (ii) Lev and Schwartz Model (Capitalisation of Salary Method)

All Pv of likely future earnings of an employee till his retirement. The estimation of wages and consequently HR value on a group basis. Wages are calculated as a function of age alone. Possibility of employee leaving the organisation is not considered. It has to be seen with the Pv of future contribution receivable from the employees.

This is easy to implement and use. Also it is the most widely used model as it can be easily adopted.

### (iii) The Eric Flamhortz Model – Replacement Cost of Human Resources

Replacement cost of human resources as a valuation model has been suggested as an alternative to, and sometimes in addition to, historical cost. The model involves measurement of a cost to replace a firm's existing human resources, i.e. costs to the firm to recruit, hire, train and develop replacements to the level of proficiency and familiarity with the organisation and its operations currently experienced with existing employees. Flamhortz, who used this model, has referred to two different concepts of replacement cost, *viz.*, "individual replacement cost" and "positional replacement cost'. The model is considered to be useful in different phases of the Manpower Planning and Control Process as measures of the cost of people *per se.* It may also be potentially useful in developing valid and reliable surrogate measures of the value of people to formal organisations.

The applicability of the replacement cost concept in the valuation of physical assets has been questioned on the ground that changes in technology may not permit replacing one asset with an identical one. This problem becomes more serious in the valuation of human resources because individuals, especially higher level managers of an organisation, are unique in their talents and capabilities. Even otherwise, the applicability of this model is limited because it demands considerable amount of estimation.

### (iv) The Myers and Flowers Model

An employee's attitude governs his productive behaviour on the job. The employee's attitude inlet multiplied by the wages payable could reflect the likely benefits to the organisation and hence the HR asset. Individuals attitude matters more than the group's attitude. High ratings based on job grade level and tenure of service may not be appropriate.

Attitude is not the only parameter to influence employee behaviour. It is difficult to assess the attitudes of the individual employees and the model is more subjective.

### (v) The Jaggi and Lau Model

HR value depend on rank and performance rating. Assuming the past trend to continue in future estimation on retirement, death and service movements need to be arrived at. The Pv of likely services from employees relevant to different service states considered as HR value.

Past trend is not an indication for the future. The model does not recommend any method to evaluate the extent of services that may be available from the employees. It is based on the past trend. In a technology intensive industry like software, past trends may not be representative of the future.

## C. Non-Monetary Value-based Methods: Behavioural Models

### (i) The Likert Model

The model aims to establish through psychological test results, how a set of causal variables reflecting the management systems adopted by an organisation determine the depreciating or appreciating of human asset.

Establishing valid relationships between organisational health and performance is difficult. In the absence of a valid relationships, the condition of HR may not be a true reflector of the HR Performance. Hence, it is mere difficult to implement and is more subjective.

### (ii) The Flamhortz Model

Flamhortz has specifically underlined the primary role of human resource accounting as that of providing information essential for management to perform the functions of acquiring, developing, allocating, conserving, utility, evaluating and rewarding human resources. The first step in human resource acquisition is to forecast manpower requirements; the management then must translate the manpower forecast into a manpower acquisition budget, which is essentially a process of cost estimation. HRA can provide measurements of the standard cost of recruiting, selecting and hiring people, for estimates of amounts to be incorporated in the manpower acquisition budget. Again, in selection decisions, managers need measurements of the value of the candidates for particular jobs, so that the person selected is one who possess the greatest future value to the organisation. Instead of using non-monetary measures of potential abilities derived through qualitative tests, the potential economic value of candidates may be a better criterion for selection.

In the absence of arriving at proper replacement cost of an employee, this model is not useful.

### (iii) The Pekin Organ Model

Pekin organ's model presents a new concept of determination of certainty – equivalent net benefits stream for each employee in an organisation, which consists of two elements – (a) his or her net benefits and total cross; and (b) a certainy factor which is comprised of the employees probability of continued employment and probability of survival.

The model presented by Pekin organ is certainly an improvement over other models presented earlier. This organisation, which the other models have ignored. It also makes use of the 'certainty factor' designed to measure the probability of continued employment and probability of survival.

### Limitations/Deficiencies

A major shortcoming of this model is that it can be applied only in these organisations where costs and benefits of employees can be traced fairly objectively.

### Aims and Objectives of HRA

Human Resource Accounting aims of following objectives:

1. Managers are more aware of the value of human resources.
2. Based on the effective management information systems, better and suitable decisions are taken about people.
3. Greater accountability on the part of the management for its human resources.
4. Effective and optimum utilisation of human resources is made by developing new models.
5. Enability of longer time horizon for planning and budgeting.
6. Effective human resource planning.

## The Indian Scenario

The following two major issues emerge with regard to HRA valuation in India:

### Issue No. I

Do the organisations, which are publishing HRA information, use the appropriate model for valuation of human resources in India? The basis for this issue is that the model which may be applicable in one economy, may not give dependable result in another economy.

### Issue No. II

Do the private sector undertakings not have HRA systems? The basis for this issue is the non-availability of HRA information in the annual reports of private sector undertakings. As majority of the organisations which publish such information are public sector undertakings.

As regards the first issue, the preliminary survey conducted by the researcher shows that few organisations (Nine in the public sector, one in the joint sector, and one in the private sector) publish HRA information in their annual reports. Most of the organisations use the Lev and Schwartz model for valuing the human resources using employees' anticipated future earnings as a surrogate of his economic value.

Measurement of HR under this method involves the following considerations:

1. Divisions of employees according to their age, grade of pay and designation.
2. Determination of the average annual earnings per employee in each group.

3. Calculation of the total earnings based on the remaining tenure of their service life.
4. The total earnings will be discounted on the basis of average rate of return on investment.

The human resource can be valued on the basis of the following formula:

$$V_n = \sum_{T=n}^{T} \frac{I(t)}{(1+r)t-n}$$

Where $V_n$ = The human capital value of a person 'n' years old,

T = The person's retirement age

I(t) = The person's annual earnings up to retirement

R = A discount rate specific to the person

This model was refined later by the authors considering the possibility of death of an employee before his retirement. Then the formula stands as below:

$$E(Vy^*)=Py \sum_{i=y}^{T} \frac{I^*}{(I+r)t-y}$$

Where E(Vy*) = Expected value of the human capital value of a person 'Y' years old.

T = Person's retirement age

Py (t) = Probability that a person's retirement age 't'

I* = Expected earning of the person in period 'i'

r = Discount rate specified to the person.

## Criticism

This model is criticised on the following consideration:

1. An individual may have an organisation prior to his retirement, death or due to various factors whether personal or impersonal. Those factors are not considered here.
2. The promotional aspect of an employee is not highlighted here. It may appear as if there will be no personal betterment of an individual during his service life.
3. The ratios based on the value of HRs calculated through the application of this model is of little consequences to the investors and management.
4. The discounted factor may vary from firm to firm, as there is no specific rate for such valuation.
5. The cost of recruitment, selection, training, placement and retaining the HRs are not considered here.

6. Here the underlying assumption is that the benefit derivable from an employee is just equal to the cost of salary paid to him. If that be the case, there is no need of valuing HRs.

Despite the above limitations, it may be claimed that the application of this method of valuation is least debatable, as data on the basis of which such values will be determined are objective in nature.

The use of the Lev and Schwartz model provides with fascinating results when the information of human resource value, for the years 1983 to 1986 of three public sector undertakings (Oil and Natural Gas Commission, Steel Authority of India, and Cement Corporation of India) are analysed and interpreted in relation to value added sales growth and production value growth (Appendix-I).

The growth in average value per employee (Col.5) leaves no relation to growth in average value-added per employee (Col.9). In case of SAIL, growth in the latter for years 1983-84 and 1984-85 comes out to be 69.01% and for 1984-85 and 1985-86 43.11% but the growth in the former is 7.45% and 0.19% respectively. Similar is the case with ONGC and CCI. It means that the model that uses salary as a surrogate for the contribution of an employee to the organisation during his stay does not even remotely reflect the actual values of human resources. This becomes more evident from the Col.4 which shows the average value of per employee in lacs. It clearly emerges that average value of an employee of ONGC is the highest, followed by SAIL and then by CCI. The reason is simple; the employees of ONGC are highest paid out of the three organisations. It is because of this reason the value per employee is highest. If we analyse the results of growth in average value added per employee (Col.9), then SAIL is first, then CCI and then ONGC. Even if we look at growth in sales (Col.13) and growth in production value (Col. 11) SAIL is on the top. Hence, no relation exists between the operational results generated by employees of an organisation and the value of employees given by the model. The results based on Lev and Schwartz model might hold good in a highly competitive society where an employee is fairly compensated in relation to his contribution to the organisation but in a society like India where welfare considerations dominate work culture, the model should be used continuously.

As regards the second issue, the researcher believes that the current notion that the private sector undertakings are not using HRA systems is not correct. If one glances at the information regarding average annual growth in sales and in net assets of the top fifty industrial units in India (Appendix 2-a) one gets a clear idea that the managements of private sector undertakings are more concerned about the growth of net assets than the growth of sales. In case of private sector undertakings 7.6% organisations have shown more growth in net assets than in net sales as compared to 48% organisations in the public sector (Appendix – 2b). On the basis of this analysis the researcher is of the opinion that the private sector organisations are highly physical assets growth conscious which presupposes that their attitude towards the growth in human assets is highly positive. By not publishing HRA information, it does not mean that they are not generating and using such information for variety of decision making purposes. It is possible that somehow they do value the human resources, though not using HRA models available. It is a matter, which requires further research.

## Appendix – I

Table 1: HRA System in India Practised by Different Companies

| S. No. | Name of the Company | Published HRA informati on since | Model Adopted | Discount factor considered |
|---|---|---|---|---|
| 01 | Bharat Heavy Electricals Ltd. (BHEL) | 1974-75 | Lev and Schwartz | 12% |
| 02 | Cement Corporation of India Ltd. (CCI) | 1980-81 | Lev and Schwartz with reference as suggested by Flamhortz and Jaggi and Lau | 15% |
| 03 | Engineers India Limited (EIL) | 1980-81 | Not reported | 10% |
| 04 | Oil & Natural Gas Commission (ONGC) | 1981-82 | Not reported | 12.25% |
| 05 | Minerals and Metal Trading Corporation of India Ltd. (MMTC) | 1983-84 | Lev and Schwartz | 12% |
| 06 | Steel Authority of India Limited (SAIL) | 1983-84 | Lev and Schwartz with reference as suggested by Flamhortz and Jaggi and Lau | 14% |
| 07 | Metallurgical and Engineering Consultants (India) Limited (MECON) | 1984-85 | Lev & Schwartz | 14% |
| 08 | Madras Refineries Limited (MRI) | 1985-86 | Lev & Schwartz | 15% |
| 09 | Oil India Limited (OIL) | 1984-85 | Lev & Schwartz | 10.5% |
| 10 | National Thermal Power Corporation Ltd. (NTPC) | 1986-87 | Lev & Schwartz | 12% |
| 11 | Associated Cement Co. Ltd. (ACC) | 1983-84 | Lev & Schwartz | Not reported |
| 12 | Southern Petro-Chemical Industries Corpn. (SPIC) | 1983-84 | Lev & Schwartz | Not reported |

The information as provided in Table – reveals that most of the enterprises in India, reporting HRA in their annual accounts, adopted Lev-Schwartz model for valuation of their HRs. BHEL one of the leading undertakings in India is the pioneer in implementing the concept, publish HRA since, 1974-75 based on the Lev-Schwartz model. However, SAIL another frontline undertaking in India adopts the Lev-Schwartz model with modifications suggested by Flamhortz and Jaggi and Lau.

One point is to be noted here that in most cases the discount factor is around 14%. But the rates ranges from 10% to 15%. The logic of considering such values of this factor is not mentioned in the report. However, the maximum of the rates (i.e. 15%) is near to the rate of interest on fixed deposit payable by a nationalised bank in India during the period of study. The maximum rate is used for discounting with a view to providing a conservative measure of the HR values. So far in India, HRA has been practised very little, and whatever small has been done in this direction that has been confined to profit seeking organisations only. The basic reason for such limited spread of the idea is perhaps that the conventional accounting system is capable of reflecting, though to a less extent, how far the basic objective of earning profit has been realised. Non-adoption of HRA therefore, does not make any barrier to reflect the profit earning capacity of the business.

## Achieving an HR Return on Investment

In analysing the value of HR talent as an asset, there are two ways of looking at the issue – from the point of view of the executives themselves, and from the corporate angle. It is all a question of maximising return on investment (ROI) – for both parties. How can individual executives most effectively manage their career and make the most rewarding career moves, and how can companies attract, develop and retain their executives at different stages in their careers to maximise the benefit to the company?

Recent observations by an international executive search firm in New Delhi and Mumbai reveal many high-flying executives are effectively managing their careers to maximise their cash and prospects, putting pressure on their employees to up the stakes. Meanwhile, by contrast, many companies are being taken for a ride in terms of handling HR ROI and many are making a net loss. Taking an holistic view, companies are "renting" the value of their executives for a period of time, making inputs in terms of their performance – but many are often falling short on obtaining a high level of ROI.

## The Real Costs of Losing People

In making an analysis of HR return on investment, it is important to quantify the real costs of losing people as opposed to keeping them. "Our company is currently suffering from 27 percent staff turnover", revealed one media-sector multinational H R Manager in New Delhi, "this means that last year 600 years of company experience walked out of the door." What does this mean in terms of bottom line costs? Factored in should be the recruitment costs incurred in identifying and hiring the replacement staff, including the fees charged by executive search firms, and management time and travel expenses in interviewing candidates. The costs of employing a temporary replacement could also be included, to say noting of possible reduced morale among officemates, loss of productivity, clients, intellectual properly and confidential company information.

This is especially alarming in view of the fact that job-hopping is between competitors. One multinational company in the construction sector lost a key staff member to one of its own clients, with whom it had an overlooked no-poach agreement. In considering this the 'poacher' company calculated its costs as around ten times the cost of the lost staff member's salary, insofar that these costs can be quantified.

## Making the most of what the company is offering

Other companies whose HR assets may be more successful in achieving pecuniary self-improvement rather than in enriching their employers include some multinational businesses which, for various reasons, have decided to scale-down in the Indian market. One company in the utilities sector with operations across India recently made several staff redundant, but not before these employees had successfully lobbied for unconditional severance pay-offs of a year and a half salary for every five years worked with the company. One staff member in particular was still sent on previously promised Rs. 5 lakhs worth of training courses despite his imminent redundancy. Previously, he had enjoyed a company sponsored MBA and several all-expenses paid overseas trips. Cumulatively, his salary (Total cost to company) over the years would have added up to around Rs.40 lakh, with around Rs.25 lakh worth of training and travel benefits, topped by nearby 25 lakhs of severance pay. He was no doubt a diligent and able employee, but in a staff role and predominantly involved in implementing head office directives rather than creating anything new. Did he really bring in over Rs. 85 lakhs of value to the company? He could have chosen to stay on – but, like a careful gambler, he chose to take his winnings and move on to the next game.

## Companies Growing their Own – or not?

Hindustan Lever is a good example of a company that "grows their own" and has developed strong management training inputs, and is able to retain staff long-term. HDBC, headquartered in Mumbai, is another example. Their challenge in the HR ROI context is to ensure that staff are still working to peak productivity and are still stimulated by their jobs, in an environment, which may be seen as "comfortable". They also have to work hard to resist being used as hunting-grounds by aggressive hirers of early and mid career talent.

Given the cost of campus – recruiting exercises and running assessment centres for selection purposes, training, cross training and job rotation upto two years employment before becoming proactive – a company like Lever must keep staff members for seven to ten years to achieve HR ROI.

## Raiding the Opposition

Companies taking a different view, which tend to hire early-or-mid-career talent from other companies, may be achieving a higher ROI than their "home grown" competitors. Bringing-in-top talent, even at higher salary levels, can work out to be more profitable for the company concerned, having avoided the cost of the down-time of the person coming upto speed and all the training costs involved.

Multinational companies newly entering the Indian marker – new especially in the consumer products sector have little choice but to cream off this pre-trained talent. Dotcoms and other internet related start-ups are the same and these are the companies in India who have been making the most effective forays into the fashions of home-grown talents. Some of India's oldest multinational company brands are feeling the effects of these raids – but so far, most of them have built up so much stack over the years of low staff turnover that reinforcements have been immediately available. Clearly, this situation of replacing from within cannot last indefinitely, especially as the new crop will have taken years to mature.

## Starting Young

From the point of view of the postgraduates entering the workforce from India's premier Institutes, the issues and choices facing them are becoming increasingly complex and bountiful. Arguably even some of the best postgraduates centres are limited in their ability to prepare these young executives for a top management career. It has been suggested that these bodies do not really keep in touch with the needs of the market, and that the company they join needs to make the real training inputs.

In terms of companies attracting and choosing the right graduates, management trainee programmes need to live up to the young executives expectations or their retention rate will be further reduced. Post graduates, especially with MBAs are already savvy about positioning themselves to win the best opportunities.

## Making the Most of Young Talent

The big challenge is how companies can retain graduate trainees after the traineeship is over, given the calculations of length of tenure of that first job to be cost effective for the company and to make career sense for the individual. Certainly, completing a graduate traineeship and immediately moving on not only means zero ROI for the company, but also smacks of extreme opportunism and a certain ingratitude on the individual's part, which would not be attractive to even the most opportunistic new employer.

The other viewpoint of hiring mid career letting other companies do the training and development work and make all the investment is arguably more cost-effective. There can be negative effects on the corporate culture, which will be more influenced by other programmes and borrowed compensatory, constantly even rewarding to the latest talent brought from outside.

However, on the other hand, there is the benefit of being more cutting edge, with more new blood, being more in tune with the market, more flexible and more responsive. People changing their jobs – but not too often – have to keep proving themselves, keep adding value for the first six to twelve months in a new job as always is a challenge to deliver. Executives who regularly put themselves through these paces will be producing a higher ROI than those just hanging out.

## The Bottom Line

Despite the sophistication of the HR some in India and the associations of many senior HR Managers, few companies are achieving strong HR ROI and most do not know whether they are or not. For the executives, it is a different story – they have it all worked out. "I do not bother with these salary surveys", one claims, "Many HR Managers do not want to admit everything they are paying. I take to the search consultants and get a real picture of where the salary deals are heading – especially for people in demand, with overseas exposure, premier institute education and able to deliver results in the hot new business areas".

## The Metrics you Choose

Ranbaxy's using Human valuations for reasons that are more organisational (than valuations) driven. "For an Indian Pharma Company that aims to become a research based, International pharma company the key to success is R & D," says Vice President – HR Rajendra Singh. Mindful of its investment in employees, the company is using the cost of replacement model to retain employees. Here is how.

As can be guessed, the cost of Replacement model calculates the worth of employees in terms of their replacement cost. The rationale is in replacing an employee, a company takes financial fits on recruiting, training, initial dips in efficiencies while the recruit comes up to standard, and so on. This overall cost, says the model, is the actual human capital.

Ranbaxy decided to go in for human capital valuations about two years ago. A pace was constituted to identify "critical" and "important" employees on such parameters as the impact of business if, say, an employee were to leave, the value that s/he adds to the company, the availability of similar people in the market, the time that could lapse before a replacement is found, and learns enough to step into the incumbent's stores. After so identifying its most valuable employees, Ranbaxy estimated their worth, used some industry-benchmarking, and offered competitive salaries, ESOPs and locked in performance bonuses.

Since retaining people is the toughest challenge any company faces today, why are not more opting for this model? The problem with this approach, says Vohra of Ernst and Young, is it calculates the basic minimum value. It too does not factor in an employee's expertise, he says.

Take say, a management consultant. He might be getting Rs.50,000/- a month. But to say that his replacement cost will be just "new salary + training costs" will not be entirely accurate. Not only does the consultants own expertise that will put him ahead of any replacement. This might manifest itself, in an extreme case, in the form of lost clients and so on. But with debate still raging on how companies should manage their human capital, it is difficult to judge which works the best. Even the most complex models require companies to make subjective judgments. This partly explains why consumer electronics multinational Philips HR head says the company has stayed away from HR valuations. "The methods in use currently have stayed away from HR valuations. "The methods in use currently are not objective enough" he says.

Also valuations (at least in their present form) cannot replace subjective judgements of equality in any case. Significantly, in Ranbaxy, R&D and Infotech executives attend analyst nuts along with the finance people. This is not unusual, says Ganesh Natarajan, worldwide CEO — APTECH. "An analyst would look at a company's employees to gauge if they are even capable of ensuring that the company meets its commitments".

All this boils down to the fact that, Bar says, such factors as cost to company and productivity putting a money-value to human capital is a tough task. Felian say Industries is among the first "Old economy" Indian companies to opt for human capital valuation, but it has recognised this essential flow. A company spokesman says, "The rupee value of intellectual capital is not a value that can be marketed. That is, you cannot exchange anything at that stated value if you desire. While there is a strategic benefit in valuing your workforce as intellectual capital and acknowledging their role, whether there is a benefit in converting that value in rupee terms is debatable.

So, when Reliance first published an annexure on its intellectual capital, it prefaced that section saying it hoped to redress the imbalance between non-financial and financial data. In this annexure, the company provides data like number of workers, hours of training, educational background, revenues and profits per employee. Importantly, the company has made no attempts to put a rupee value on the worth of its employees.

"That is because," says the company spokesman, "there is a multiplicity of methodologies and people do not perceive the same thing in the same form. So it is best to present the basic data and let people come to a conclusion rather than put a number that people are likely to consider as unreal." As Reliance suggests, the real challenge for companies undertaking HR valuations is presenting a realistic picture of their human resource.

One of the leading thinkers in this area of valuing employees (financially, of course) is Karl-Erik Sveiby in www.sveiley.com. he says "The problem with translating actions into money is that very few people in an organisation handle money directly. Most of them work by using their competencies in the service of customers. Money is merely a proxy for human effort, and the 500 year old system of accounting sheds little light on the vital processes in organisations whose assets are largely non-monetary and intangible .... Knowledge flows and intangible assets are essentially non-monetary. He needs new proxies of all their attempts to find such "new proxies", some of the most pioneering work in this area has been done by Swedish Insurance firm Skandia. It accounts for its intellectual assets by documenting on parameters that are not normally used in standard accounting.

The Skandia system maps its performance on various key, but non-financial parameters. It incorporates about 30 key indicators in various areas, which are monitored on a yearly basis. The areas are financial, customer, process, human, and development forces. In 'human', the key indicators include turnover, proportion of managers, proportion of female managers and training costs per employees.

Therefore, for example, a company like Ranbaxy could decide that the most relevant metric for measuring the value of its employers is innovation and institute a system that would monitor the number of new drugs launched, or the number of patents it filed. By bringing in comparisons with previous years, it can offer analysts a qualitative look at its HR capabilities. By presenting this information as an adjunct to the balance sheets, a company might help investors develop a better understanding of its operations, and its prospects.

**A Flow Chart of Business Activities**

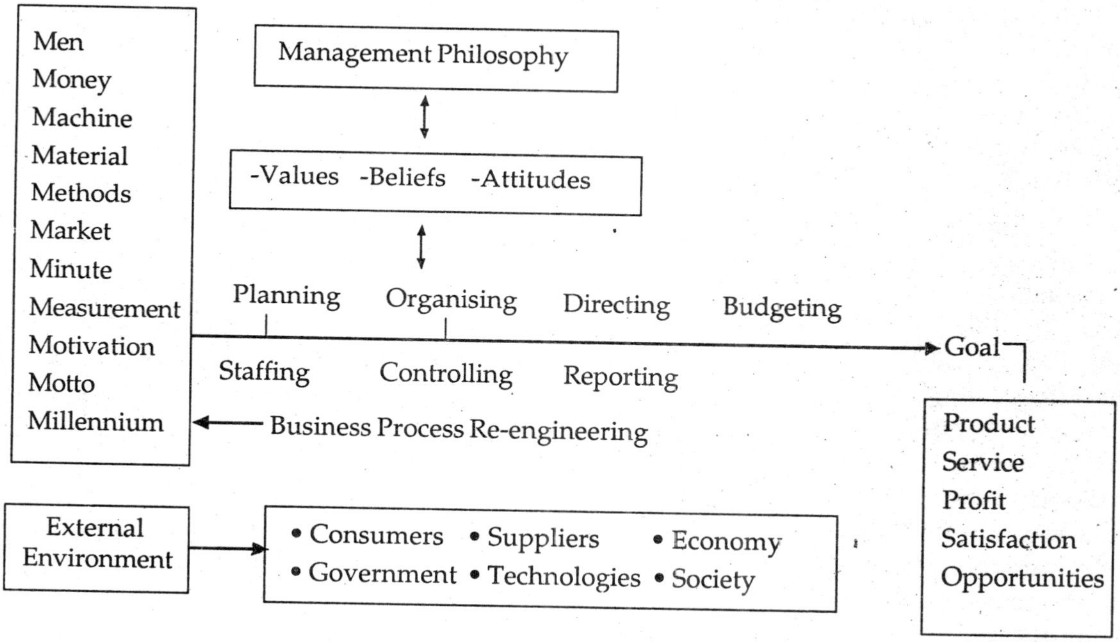


## Summary

Efficiency in any industry stems from the human being and not the machines nor the technical process. However, while the latter tangible aspects can be measured, gauging the human resource for its worth is a difficult task which has to be handled with care. Human Resource Accounting (HRA) is method with which such task is sought to be achieved.

There has been a lot of research in the area of quantification of human resource. The measurement of human resource value and its value and its valuation approaches have been suggested in the literature by the following proponent of HRA:

a. Hermanson's Adjusted Discounted Future wages Model.

b. Lixert's Socio Psychological Model of Human Resource Valuation.

c. Flamhortz's Model of Human Resource Valuation: A Stockastic process with service rewards.

d. Morse's Model of Human Resource Valuation as Assets and Capitals.

e. Jaggi & Lau's Model of Human Resource Valuation of Career Movements of the employees.

f. Lev and Schwartz Compensation Model of Human Resource Valuation.

g. Firedman & Lev's Measure for the firm's investment in Human Resources.

h. Myers and Flowers Five dimensional Model of Human Resource Valuation.

i. Pekin organ's Model of Human Resource Valuation for professional service.

It can, thus be seen that using different models, accounting of human resource is a fairly simple affair. Since we are dealing with human resource, there will naturally be certain limitations and deficiencies in different models of HRA. A high number of employee in every company also possesses problems for HRA. Notworthstanding these difficulties, HRA today are being implemented by most professionally managed companies like BHEL, ONGC, SPIC, EIL, VSNL, etc.

The success of HR depends on the extent to which the function can be driven through the management. The 'how' of implementing HR interventions, particularly through a consensus of the 'what'. HR works if the interventions are simple and practical. The 'buy-in' of line management is most, if the interventions planned are bounced off them and they in turn bounce off the proposed interventions or changes with the community. An HR professional must possess a sense of detached involvement, even in the ideas that he/she generates of everyday follows that float up in the form of ideas, even if nine are shot down or just fade away, it is the one that stays up that matters. The analogy of a balloons that float up in the form of ideas, even if nine are shot down or just fade away, it is the one that stays up that matters. The analogy of a balloon seems particularly relevant when the success stories of HR intentions are revisited. When the effort to keep up the pressure on an HR intervention wanes even for a short period, all the good work done for years, just deflates. The skill of an HR professional depends largely on the ability to build a consensus and guide an organisation's change process through consensus. This skill demands tremendous patience, emotional intelligence and the ability to stand up to corporate bullies. The chief executive's commitment and the credibility that the HR professional develops with the CEO are not to be under-estimated. At times, the HR professional has to walk the tight rope between being the conscience keeper of the community and the CEO's alter ego. The function requires firm convictions without intellectual arrogance, the ability to challenge assumptions and to develop glasnost. Finally, when the HR function in an organisation is praised for functioning in guarantee, the true success of the HR professional will be determined by his/her ability to attribute the success to line management.

## Balanced Scoreboard

The balanced scoreboard from work can be extremely helpful to organisations (Table)

**Table: A Sample Balanced Scoreboard**

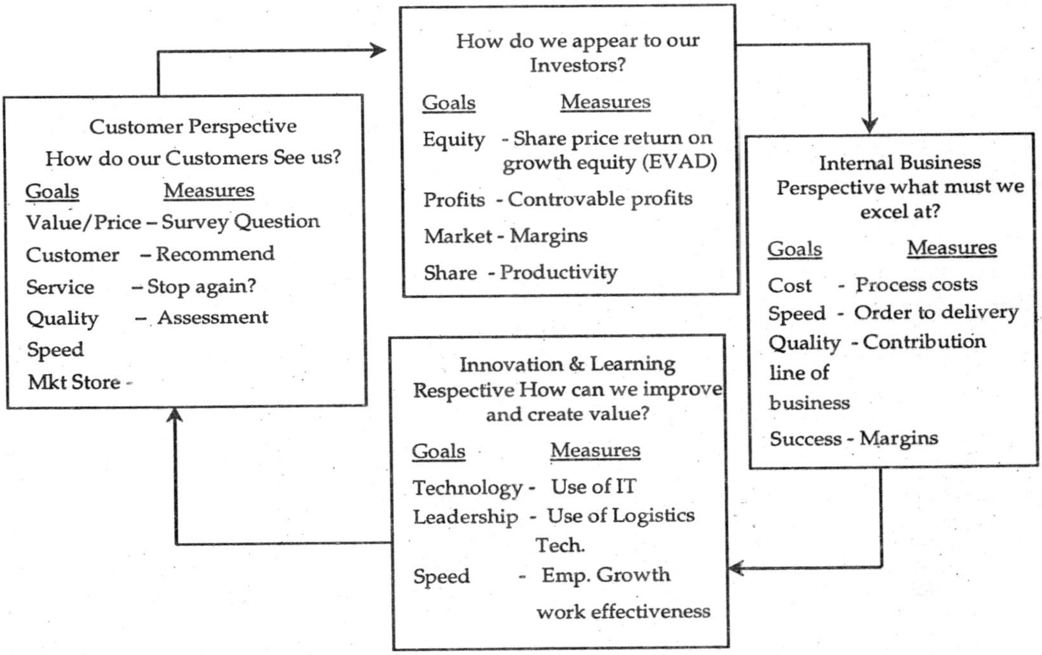


The following guidelines may be useful for balanced scoreboard:

- Determine the human capital impediments and/or contributors to your strategic performance drivers.
- Ask: Which HR issues (employee skills, motivation, work design, alignment) are the very human capital drivers of your strategy? Use interviews, focus groups, questionnaires.
- Operationalise the human capital drivers.
- In partnership with the managers, specify the employee behaviour required to provide the strategic human capital drivers.
- Analyse the entire HRM system and evaluate the influence of the practices individually and as a system, on strategic behaviours.
- Ask: what behaviours does our current HRM system elicit?
- And how must the system change if we are to flawlessly implement our strategy?
- Capitalise on positive synergies.
- Eliminate misalignment.

- Understand the presence of particular practices as well as their effectiveness.
- Redesign the current HRM culture into a high performance work culture.
- HR is the expert on the system elements, but should be guided by a 'map' of the firm's value chain.
- HR Managers must adopt a system approach rather than functional 'Silos' of compensation, training, staff find and so on.
- Measure and evaluate HR's strategic impact.
- Establish objective and subjective links between the H R System and strategic performance drivers through financial performance.
- Partner with line managers to develop legitimate and acceptable measures of impact at each point in the value chain.

The strategic capabilities of a HR manager are the key to this re-positioning. Amongst other things he/she:

- Anticipate the effect of internal and external changes.
- Exhibits leadership for the function and the corporation.
- Demonstrate the financial impact of all HR activities.
- Defines and communicates the HR vision for the future.
- Educates and influences the line managers on HR issues
- Takes appointment risks to accomplish objectives.
- Has broad knowledge of many HR functions.
- Is knowledgeable about competitor's HR functions.
- Focuses on the quality of HR services.
- Has international experiences
- Influence Peers in other companies.
- Has significant external customer contact.
- Is computer literate.
- Possesses highly specialised knowledge of a few HR functions.

Once the capabilities come into operational use, HR would then be poised to occupy a strategic position to give value both to the organisation and to the function.

***

# 8 Organisational Culture (OC)

The internal working environment of every organisation has certain commonly perceived psychological characteristics or traits which are collectively called its climate, culture or mileu. These traits generally vary from organisation to organisation, are relatively stable over time and influence the behaviour of people in the organisation. Thus, every organisation has its own unique culture. Not only this, even different departments of the same organisation may have different cultures depending upon the perceptions of members of these departments. Various personal characteristics such as values, needs, attitudes, expectations, etc., determine the manner in which members are likely to perceive the various aspects of internal working of their departments.

## Components of Organisational Culture

Organisational culture or climate consists of the following components or dimensions:

1. *Individual Autonomy,* i.e., the degree to which employee are free to manage themselves or are not accountable to others.
2. *Position structure,* i.e., the extent of formalisation, centralisation and direct supervision.
3. *Reward Orientation,* i.e. the extent to which rewards are related to performance and the required system of behaviour in the organisation.
4. *Consideration,* i.e., the extent to which people in the organisation offer socio-emotional support to each other and work as a team whether the supervision is production-oriented or people-oriented.
5. *Conflict,* i.e., the extent of differences present between individuals and departments and the way in which they are resolved.
6. *Growth and Development,* i.e., the scope for self-development and growth in the organisation.

7. ***Risk-taking,*** i.e., the degree of freedom to experiment with new ideas, take risks and correct honest mistakes without fear of punishment.
8. ***Control,*** i.e., the extent to which people are formally controlled. Whether the organisation is rule-oriented or result-oriented. Whether informal groups are opposed by management or are supported.

## Determinance of OC

Factors which influence the above dimensions of OC are as follows:

### 1. Economic Conditions

An organisation's economic condition influences its structure in several ways. The more prosperous an organisation is, the more it can afford to spend on research and development and the more it can afford to take risk and be adventurous.

### 2. Leadership Style

An organisation's leadership style plays a profound role in determining several aspects of its culture. Thus, an authoritarian style may make the organisation's culture characterised by high position structure, low individual autonomy, low reward orientation, low warmth and support and so on. Opposite may be the culture characteristics of an organisation with goal-directed leadership style.

### 3. Organisational Policies

OC is also influenced by organisational policies. A policy to resort to lay off only as a last remedy during business downturn will boost a cordial and supportive climate. Similarly, a policy to reward employees for increase in profits will make culture more reward-oriented.

### 4. Managerial Assumptions about Human Nature

Douglas McGregor in his book, "The Human Side of Enterprise," points out that virtually every act on the part of management that involves human beings is predicated upon some assumptions, generalisations and hypotheses relating to human nature and human behaviour – in other words, on some theory of behaviour. This, inturn, affects OCs McGregor has postulated two opposing theories which he refers to as Theory 'X' and Theory 'Y'.

#### Theory 'X': The Traditional View

This view followed in most of the organisations is characterised by the following assumptions about human nature.

(a) The average person has an inherent dislike of work and tries to avoid it as far as possible.

(b) The average person is by nature self-centred and indifferent to overall organisational goal achievement.

(c) The average person is resistant to change.

(d) The average person lacks ambition, dislikes job responsibilities and prefers to be closely directed.

(e) The average person desires job security and economic rewards above all else.

McGregor says that the above assumptions about human nature gives rise to the need for coercion, control, and fear punishment in organisations.

## Theory 'Y': The Integration of Goals

In the author's opinion, money of the above assumptions about human nature are incorrect. He, therefore, says that Theory 'X' should be replaced by another set of assumptions which he calls Theory 'Y'. The assumptions of this theory are as under:

(a) The average person is not by nature passive or resistant to the organisation's needs.

(b) External control and the threat of punishment are not the only means for bringing about effort toward organisational objectives. The average person exercises self-direction and control in the service of objectives to which he is committed.

(c) Commitment to objective is a function of rewards associated with their achievements.

(d) The overage person, under rewarding conditions, not only accepts but seeks responsibility.

(e) The capacity to exercise a relatively higher degree of imagination, ingenuity, and creativity in the solution of organisational problems is widely, not narrowly distributed in the population.

(f) Under the conditions of modern industrial life, the intellectual potentialities of the average person are only partially utilised.

The core of these assumptions is the value placed on the integration of individual and organisational goals on creating those conditions in which the members of an organisation can best achieve their goals by directing their efforts toward achievement of organisational goals.

Theory 'X' and theory 'Y' are very important theories because they draw management's attention to a very important phenomenon called the pygmation effect which is also referred to as self-fulfilling prophecy. This means that employees tend to mould the way the management expects them to perform there is a tendency for people to conform to other people's perception of them. The children who are perceived to be bright do in fact become bright then those who are thought to be dull. Management which wants its employees to become active, responsible and innovative should behave to them as if they already are active, responsible and innovative. It will find that its behaviour is justified for most of its employees have come up to its expectations. In brief, a manager should always watch his thoughts for they become his actions – he must watch his actions for they, in turn, become his subordinate's character which we have seen is an important dimension of O.C.

## 5. Managerial Values and Ethos

In the earlier point, we have indicated how managerial assumptions about human nature determine managerial actions which contribute to organisational culture. In this point we are describing the norms and values held by managers about what is good management practice and what is poor management practice. This point tells us about their high or low orientation in the following eight important dimensions:

| Dimension | High | Low |
|---|---|---|
| 1. Authoritarianism | Emphasis on orders, threats and punishment | Emphasis on autonomy and persuation |
| 2. Bureaucracy | Emphasis on rules and procedures and on formal relationships | Emphasis on results and on informal relationship |
| 3. Participation | Emphasis on group decision | Emphasis on individual decision |
| 4. Technocracy | Reliance on sophisticated planning techniques | Reliance on experience, rules of thumb and intuition |
| 5. Risk- taking | Preference for innovation and growth | Preference for *status quo* and stability |
| 6. Self- awareness | • Proactive<br>• Open to feedback<br>• Continuous effort for self-improvement | • Reactive<br>• Closed to feedback<br>• Deadwood |
| 7. Employee's Security and growth | Treating people as an important resource | Practising hire and fire policy |
| 8. Equity | Justice in rewarding performance | Indiscriminate distribution of rewards |

## 6. Employee's Characteristics

An organisation with educated, ambitious and young employees is likely to have a different type of OC than what may be expected of an organisation whose employees have opposite characteristics. The former set of characteristics may foster a competitive, risk-taking and open climate in the organisation..

## 7. Organisational Size

Small organisations with few levels of management are generally mere amenable to democratic and participative functioning than big organisations. Systems of communication are also more open in small organisations. Hence, these organisations foster a different type of climate than what one comes across in big organisations.

## How is OC Maintained?

What makes OC enduring, is the socialisation process of an organisation. This process, which familiarises a 'fresher' both the various characteristics of culture and forces him to adjust to it, continues throughout one's entire career in the organisation.

Socialisation process has 3 stages: pre arrival, encounter and metamorphosis. Selection of only "right type" of persons who "fit" the eligibility requirements (which are laid down in the light of prevailing OC) is an attempt to maintain and perpetuate the existing organisation culture even before the outsider has joined the organisation. If a "wrong" person (whose individual characteristics do not match with the prevailing OC) gains an entry into the organisation his encounter with the new forces begins. These forces try to change him according to OC. The person may decide either to surrender himself to these forces and get completely changed or to leave the organisation if he finds the impact of these force is unbearable. He may even think of fighting against these forces and changing the OC. This, of course, is not so easy.

The various forces which a person has to encounter on his entry into the organisation and which subsequently brings about his metamorphosis are long-standing unwritten rules, rituals, taboos, jargons and the prevailing work culture. Every organisation has some long-standing unwritten rules of conduct which its members meticulously follow. Rituals refer to ceremonies which organisation performs on specific occasion. Taboos refer to the prohibitions imposed on certain forms of speech or acts, e.g., not calling superiors by their first names, not discussing each others personal lives in public, not coming to the place of work in a drunken state and so on. Jargon refers to the special language which only the members of the fraternity understand. This is sometimes referred to as 'code language', and may include micknames for persons, events and processes etc.

### Rituals in Petrofils

Petrofils Co-operative limited, Baroda which has nearby 2000 employees, is one such company in our country which has recognised the culture building role of rituals. The company has woven a number of rituals into the fabric of its corporate life. One such ritual is destruction of gifts to its employees on their achieving production targets. Employees themselves select gifts of a particular value. The gift is given to every employee of the company and not just to those who belong to production development. In another ritual the company celebrates the birthday of every employee from the chairman right down to khalasi by inviting him to the Boardroom and presenting him a token gift, such events foster team spirit, dissolve the manager–worker dichotomy and increase the employee's sense of belonging.

### Work Culture in Maruti Udyog

In Maruti Udyog Ltd. there is a strong emphasis on adopting certain norms of work and quality consciousness. There is no question of compromise on issues like zero defect production, cost cutting, coming in time and systems discipline. Maruti has obliterated hierarchial differences through open offices, common uniforms and canteens. There are no articles in the office. The directors and divisional managers sit in the open halls along with their subordinates. This arrangement makes it easier for communication and removes the elements of hush-hush and secrecy which often breeds an atmosphere of conspiracy and intrigue in companies. Everybody, right from the chairman down to the lowest paid employee, wears the same uniform and eats in the same canteen.

## Instruments for Data Collection

There are no set tools for collecting data on organisational climate and culture. The researchers use their own ingenuity in developing their instruments according to the variables identified for study. Because of this the validity and reliability of these instruments suffer, inter-organisation comparisons become difficult and general inability of conclusions becomes limited. Also, it becomes difficult to delineate the syndromes of illness and to accord a label or a name to a syndrome for ready reckoning of a particular organisational illness as the medical diagnosticians do.

In India, Parikh and Rao have prepared a directory which provides exhaustive lists of different types of instruments developed and used in Indian organisations as well as those adopted to suit Indian conditions. Somnath Chattopadhyay has developed a questionnaire to study organisation environment. It collects data on 12 dimensions on a 5 point scale. These dimensions are: decision making, recognition, growth, grievance management, team support, supervision, communication, creativity, standard, trust, structure and overall identity. Another instrument which has been developed by Udai Pareek is motivational analysis of organisational climate (MAOC). It collects data about the dominant motivation pattern consisting of 6 motivations – achievement, influence, extension, control, dependency and affiliation. In the early 1980s when BHEL completed 25 years, an opinion poll was conducted among its 75,000 employees to know their perception about the management culture. This included questions on several aspects such as job satisfaction, teamwork, working conditions, motivation, remuneration, pride in the company etc.

## Societal Culture

Like organisations, societies too have some commonly experienced stable characteristics. These characteristics make each society unique and differentiate it from others. Some of these characteristics are fatalism, tolerance for ambiguity, contextualism, time amenation, collectivism, parochialism inner directness, androgyny and tolerance for power distance. Since these characteristics produce both functional and dysfunctional consequences for an organisation a brief description of them is relevant for our discussion.

People in some cultures are more fatalist than those in other cultures. Fatalist culture has both good and bad results. Its good result is that it makes people more realistic because they easily perceive natural constraints as dominating about which nothing can be done. Its bad result is that it lowers people's self-confidence. They become passive and tolerant of conditions that need to be changed. Their exploratory tendencies to search for solutions to problems are reduced.

People in some cultures may have greater tolerance for ambiguity and uncertainty such culture develops high role flexibility in people. But it also makes them less attentive to structure and time cause confusion, delay and anxiety.

Contextualism means the importance which a culture gives to the context in interpreting an event, phenomenon or behaviours. In low-context cultures, no importance is given to the context and all events and behaviours are judged by one standard. In high context cultures, behaviour is interpreted in the light of its context. Such cultures develop greater insight into social complexities. People in such cultures quickly understand why many others differ in behaviour or deviate from the known norms.

Some cultures with orientation toward their past gives more importance to their historical glory. Some others emphasise their present and get involved. These present oriented cultures, develop competencies of working and develop temporary systems. But such cultures generally act to develop in people long-term perception and commitment. Collectivism means a culture's preference for a tightly knit social group. This culture develops in people a high sense of belonging, high mutual trust and good relations. But people lose their individual identity and always look to the group to protect their interests.

Parochialism is a culture's tendency to classify people in several in groups on some identifiable basis such as religion, caste, etc. This develops in people a very high sense of identity with their groups. But it also reduces people's objectivity because they become biased against other groups. Moreever, they spend more time in forming sides than in achieving results.

In some cultures people's behaviour is innerdirected i.e. people set their own standards and do not bother for the norms laid down by the collectivity. In some other cultures opposite is the case, i.e. norms of behaviour are laid down by the collectivity. This helps in reducing improper individual behaviour but its greatest dysfunctionality is that there is difficulty in internationalisation of norms.

In some cultures there is strong differentiation of set roles. Roles involving achievement and physical activity are largely assigned to male and females are given only tender roles. Some other cultures do not make this differentiation. These are called androgynous cultures. Such cultures helps individuals develop concern for the weak. But they also reduce competition which is so much needed in societies and organisations.

Some cultures show greater tolerance for unequal distribution of power in society and organisations. This encourages respect for seniority and age. It also encourages more value being given to ascribed status than to achievement.

An organisation many times finds that its surrounding societal culture is in conflict with the culture which it needs for achieving its goals. For example, the organisation may require achievement culture which values results but the society's culture may be affiliative which values good relationships and harmony. In such cases, the dilemma before the organisation is whether it should adapt itself to the culture and produce the kind which is needed for its future effectiveness. Obviously, it would be a great pity, if an organisation were to merely perpetuate the culture which prevails in society not withstanding its dysfunctional aspects. The correct course would be to evolve the right type of culture. In other words, the organisation must be proactive and take action to introduce change. It may be useful to do for a field analysis of facilitating and fingering forces in the culture use and reinforce the facilitating forces, produce counter forces and pay enough attention to process and strategy.

## HRD Climate and Organisational Climate

HRD Climate is an integral part of organisational climate. It can be defined as the employee's perceptions about the developmental environment of their organisation. This may include a number of characteristics such as the following:

- Importance given to human resource.
- Opinions of communication
- Encouragement given to risk-taking and experimentation.
- Feedback given to employees to make them aware of their strengths and weaknesses.
- A general climate of trust.
- Faith the employee's capabilities.
- Employees tendency to help each other and to collaborate with each other.
- Team spirit.
- Tendency to discourage stereotype and favouritism.
- Supportive personnel policies and practices.

The essence of HRD climate is the importance which it gives to the development of OCTAPACE culture in an organisation. The term stands for an important cultural characteristics, *viz.*, openness, confrontation, trust, autonomy, proactivity, authencity, collaboration, and experimentation.

Organisations differ in the context to which they possess the above characteristics. The centre for HRD at the Xavier Labour Relations Institute, Jamshedpur has prepared a questionnaire for finding out the HRD climate of an organisation. This questionnaire has 38 statements. The employees have to give their assessment of the HRD climnate of an organisation. By rating their organisation on each statement using 5 point scale. A rating of 5 indicates that the statement is almost always true; a rating of 4 indicates that the statement is mostly true; a rating of 3 indicates that the statement is sometimes true; a rating of 2 indicates that the statement is rarely true; and rating of 1 indicates that the statement is not at all true about the organisation. Average of all the scores of all the items is taken as the HRD climate. The greater this score the more conducive the OC is for the success of HRD programme.

## University of HRD Practices

There are two views on the question: How far are HRD practices under different perceptions? According to one view management is management wherever practised an universal profession whose principles can be applied to every form of organised activities. F. Harmanson and C. A. Myers in their classic study of management practices in 23 countries conclude that management does not differ fundamentally from country to country. According to the second view held by Winston Oberg, William Newman and others. The management rules and practices are different across countries which have different cultural and social context. After extensive research across 40 countries Geer Hofstede has identified 4 basic cultural dimensions which account for differences in management and HRD practices across cultures. They are:

- The extent to which a society emphasises collective rather than individual activity.
- The extent of power distance or tolerance for social morality.
- The extent of acceptance of uncertainty, and
- The extent to which a society emphasises "masculine" values and behaviours such as assertiveness, ambitiousness, domination etc.

According to the above study, Indian culture is characterised by moderate collectivism, a high tolerance for social inequality, a general acceptance of uncertainty and a moderate masculine orientation. Translated into HRD practices this would suggest that HRD practices which emphasise on collaboration and are uncertain in their results can well succeed in our country.

***

# 9 Recent Techniques in HRM

## Competitive Advantage Through Human Resources

Organisations face increasing competition and more critical scrutiny from investors, managers have been confronted with greater challenges in securing organisational survival and competitive advantage. Today's managers face a conflicting set of demands – they are expected to minimize costs while increasing quality and fostering innovation and creativity. Consequently, they have sought strategies and practices to meet outside pressures. Mergers and acquisitions, strategic alliances, downsizing, reengineering, outsourcing and restructuring have been common responses to the new challenges facing organisations. Companies can choose from an array of alternatives in trying to achieve improved performance, including such options as pyramid flattering, empowerment, total quality management, continuous improvement, paradigm shifting, searching for "white space opportunities", and becoming "learning organisations". In the 1990s, the importance of developing an organisational strategy, or a vision of the organisation's long-term direction, became a major focus of top management.

The most effective approach to strategic planning involves people from all levels of the organisation, as well as key suppliers and customers, in a process-oriented toward transforming the organisation and changing the rules of its industry to its own advantage. The effective use of human resources showed be an integral part of organisational strategy. A company that seeks to achieve competitive advantage must align its human resource management processes with its business strategies. This is one of the most critical tasks facing management today.

## What is Competitive Advantage?

Competitive advantage refers to the ability of an organisation to formulate strategies that place it at a favourable position relative to other companies in the industry. Companies achieve competitive advantage through effectively leveraging their capabilities. A firm's capabilities include all of its physical and financial assets as well as all capabilities, competencies, organisational processes, firm attributes, information, knowledge, and so forth that are controlled by the firm and that enabls the firm to both design and implement its competitive strategy.

## Employees for Lease

Presently, organisations employ specialists as well as generalists for their various operations/activities. In addition to these specialists the organisation depends upon consultancy agencies or individual consultants for their expertise to tap and utilise their expert knowledge. Even so there is the possibility that the present generalists and specialists will become brain absolute after continuous work in the same organisation and their level of operation will also be limited.

The consultancy agencies offer their expert advice and the execution of the organisation. The employees with their limited knowledge and/or lack of executing abilities may fail to convert the know-how into a project. Hence, the consulting agencies which cannot provide the human resources for implementing the project will also become obsolete.

Under such circumstances new types of organisations will emerge, which will be called as employee leasing organisation. These organisations will provide expert advice and consultancy and further they will also supply human resources for executing their projects. These organisations employ different kinds of candidates and lease them for various organisations. These leasing organisations will be principal employers and send the required number and kind of employees to various organisations on lease basis. They collect the fees and other charges from various industries and pay the salaries, provide benefits to the employees. The leasing company will pay complete salary and benefits to the employees irrespective of the number of days that the employee is sent to various organisations on lease.

This type of arrangement is beneficial to the leasing company specialist employees and the industry. The industry with limited expenses can utilise the expert advice and services of most competent human resources.

The employees will get continuous employment with better salaries and benefits while the leasing company derives surplus resources from its charges and fees.

## Moonlighting by Employees: Blue Moon to Full Moon

Wages and salaries are provided to employees for their services or contributions to the job and organisation. Organisations also pay dearness allowance to effect the decline in purchasing power of the employee due to rise in cost of living. Similarly, a number of allowances are provided to the employee. Further organisations also provide various fringe benefits to enhance the living standards of the employees. Despite all these allowances and benefits, employees feel that their wages are low, allowances are inadequate and fringe benefits are insufficient. They feel that employer enjoys the increased profit and they are being exploited by the employer. Consequently, they agitate for hike in wages, allowances and benefits so as to improve their living standards. But a few employees in most of the organisation realize that all their demands cannot be met by their organisation alone. Hence, they depend either on some other organisations for part-time job, part-time business or take up a business or start an industrial unit in order to earn more money and become much stronger financially. This type of activity, i.e., taking up another part-time job or business or industrial unit simultaneously with that of the original job is known as Moonlighting by Employees (double jobbing).

### Blue Moon

Employees in future will demand the management for hike in wages and benefits. The management will also respond positively to the employees demands. Some employees will be satisfied with the increased wages and benefits and adjust their expenses with the level of wages and benefits from time to time willingly. Some employees will not be satisfied with the level of wages and benefits and will not go for second job in future because of their inability in getting a second job. Such type of employees will have a conflict with organisational wage level as this category of employees need a second job for additional income and it will not be available to them. Thus, if their efforts to earn additional income through second job will not bear any fruit. Such type of efforts and the consequent results may be called Blue Moonlighting by Employees.

### Quarter Moonlighting

A candidate immediately after completing his school/college education joins an organisation in lower level position. He spends his bachelor life comfortably with his salary. Later, he finds it difficult to make both ends meet as his family grows. He could not spend)for the education of his children etc. Then the employees prefers to take up a part time job during the off hours of the present job. Thus, he starts earning additional money to meet the basic needs of himself and his family. Similarly, other employees also take-up part time business to meet the increased expenses mostly due to increased demands of the family and/or lower level wages and salaries in present jobs. This part of moonlighting is called a quarter moonlighting by employees.

### Half Moonlighting

Some employees will not be satisfied with their wages, salaries and benefits as they cannot afford to buy any luxury items with their wages/salaries. Hence, they take up those jobs or business to earn money sufficient to purchase luxury items and to lead a comfortable life. This category of employees spend 50 percent of the available time and/or resources for the second job/occupation as they have to earn sufficiently large additional amount. This extent of moonlighting is called half moonlighting by employees.

Employees in banks and financial institutes grant loans and advances to entrepreneurs, business people, traders and industrialists. They follow-up the implementation of the project, evaluate and check it in various stages of the progress. When the project becomes sick and borrower's repaying capacity becomes red, the bank officers apply their minds to recover principlals, policies and plan of action of the bank. Thus, they will be in the banker's shoes, suit and mind. If the entrepreneur is skilful, tactful, efficient and if the environment also favours him, his project will be successful. It will fetch him continuously an inflow of cash increases, profit generating capacity etc. Then the beneficiary flourishes with the bank's money. The bank officer also feels happy for having generously granted loan to deserving entrepreneur. He will also think that he should also become financially strong and stronger within no time not by resigning the job and taking up the same or similar product as his successful entrepreneur. But it is difficult to take up the project and simultaneously doing the job. This type of situations are responsible for change in values and aspirations of employees for becoming stronger financially with a shock absorber. If the employee makes any loss in the project or if he is pushed out of the project, his job will provide a cushion and acts as a shock absorber.

Similarly, employees in other professions also take up business or start industrial units to become stronger financially. It may not be possible for them to earn that much income which can be earned in business or industry. Hence, the employees take up other occupations and spend more or less 75 per cent of their time and resources for their business or industrial units. Second job activity to this extent may be called three quarter moonlighting by employees.

### Full Moonlighting

Employees in some professions/occupations find relatively free times whereas employees in some organisations generally feel that their income from the job is almost zero compared to their expectations. Some employees have friends or relatives earning huge money more than their salary. Similarly, some employees view that their friends or relatives with lower educational qualifications/abilities enjoy their level social status due to their ownership of and earning from business and/or industry. Employees-who realise that their jobs are almost negligible from the point of view of and/or social status, venture to start/establish a business unit/industrial unit. They spend most of their time and resources in starting, developing, expanding and diversifying their business or industrial units. They keep on staying on the job as it will be useful for them as a shock absorber in times of need. Their financial and social position will almost be determined by the second occupation. The extent of second jobbing may be known as Full Moon lighting by Employees.

## Effect of Moonlighting of HRM in Future

Moonlighting by employees affects almost all the functions of human resource management. The effects of moonlighting would be mostly negative and it possesses challenges to the personnel manager. Presently very limited numbers of employers do moonlighting. But the number of employees who will do moonlighting will go on increasing due to change in employee values and expectations.

Management will have to take all possible precautions in selection process about the possibility of moon lighting by the prospective candidates. Moonlighting will affect human resources development as employees would not be interested in the human resources development as planned by the organisation.

Employees will go on demanding for the hike in wages and other benefits. The moonlighting will be increased, i.e., from dark to full moon and expanded to dark moon-lighting employees if the management does not accept the demand of the employees.

The relations between the superior and subordinate will have an adverse affect in case of moonlighting by subordinates. It will also deteriorate the disciplinary procedure. Managements will face a challenge in motivating the moonlighting and non-moonlighting employees due to varying values, aspirations and goals. It reduces the interest of employees in participative management, quality circles, etc. Thus, different degrees of moonlighting by employees will affect Human Resources Management in future adversely. It will become a challenging task to the human resource managers.

## Dual Career Goals Management

As more and more women enter the working world and pursue careers, organisations will increasingly confront the problems of dual careers. In the past, many companies would not employ both a husband and wife. Now there are so many dual career couples in the workplace that organisations are actively seeking ways to accommodate the unique pressures that exist when both adult members of a household are employed.

One very obvious source of difficulty arises when one member of a dual career couple is offered a promotion that involves relocation. This places the individual in a difficult situation because promotions offer considerable success for many managers. However, since many talented people can be lost if the organisation is too inflexible, many organisations are now implementing special career planning programmes for dual career couples. Spouse career relocation counselling is, in fact, an important part of many of these programmes.

The issue of paternity leave also has overtones for dual career couples. Taking six months off is assumed to be fatal to a person's career. Peer pressure helps perpetuate the belief that paternity leave unfairly burdened co-workers with extra assignments.

Following are the points for organisations dealing with dual career couples:

- An organisation should conduct a survey of employers that gathers statistics and information regarding the incidence of dual careers in its present and projected workforce. The survey should determine (a) how many employees are at present part of a two-career situation, (b) how many interviewed for positions are part of dual career situation (c) where and at what level in the organisation the dual career employees are, (d) what conflicts these employees now have, and (e) whether dual-career employees perceive company policy and practices to be helpful to their careers and to the careers of their spouses.

- Recruiters should devise methods that present realistic previews of what the company offers dual career couples. Orientation sessions conducted by HR departments should include information that helps such couples identify potential problems.
- Policies regarding career development and transfers must be revised. Since the usual policies are based on the traditional one-career family, they are inapplicable to dual career situations. The key is to provide more flexibility.
- The company should consider providing dual career couples with special assistance in career management. Couples are typically ill prepared to cope with the problems posed by two careers. When wives earn more than their husbands, marriages often face strain and a need for adjustment.
- The organisation can establish cooperative arrangements with other organisations. When an organisation wants to relocate a dual career partner, cooperative organisations can be sources of employment for the other partner.
- The most important immediate step is to establish flexible working hours. Allowing couples the privilege of arranging their work schedules so that these will be compatible with family demands is an effective way to meet some of the problems of managing dual career marriages.

It would be a mistake to believe that dual career problems exists only for managerial and professional personnel. Non-managerial personnel are also members of dual career families. Managers will confront problems in scheduling overtime for these people and in transferring them to different shifts.

An especially difficult dual career situation arises when one spouse is relocated abroad. Such factors as Home visits, extended vacation benefits, family culture training, and electronic connections via e-mail must then be considered. When both parties in a marriage take their career seriously, it is important to address the problem of separation before the assignment begins. Unless both partners are being relocated overseas at the same time and to the same location, the issue of adjustment, stress, and distance should be seriously addressed. Dealing creativity with dual career expatriates is necessary before the assignment is made.

## What is Competitive Advantage?

Competitive advantage refers to the ability of an organisation to formulate strategies that place it at a favourable position relative to other companies in the industry. Companies achieve competitive advantage through effectively leveraging their capabilities. A firm's capabilities include all of its physical and financial assets as well as all capabilities, competencies organisational processes, firm attributes, information, knowledge, and so for that they are controlled by the firm and enable the firm to both design and implement its competitive strategy. One highly regarded core competency calls for reconceptualising the organisation into a portfolio of underlying functions, or core competition. Core competencies are essentially what the organisation does, or could do, best.

Two major principles – perceived customer value and uniqueness-describe the extent to which an organisation has a competitive advantage.

## Competitive Advantage Principle

### Customer value

These unique capabilities or core competencies can help build competitive advantage by improving the value that customers receive-or perceive that they receive from the company's goods and services. When a company fails to take advantage of its unique capabilities the results can be disastrous. IBM virtually owned the computer industry from its inception through the 1970s. By failing to identify and perceive the importance of the emerging personal computer market, IBM lost as much as Rs. 90 billion in market capitalisation and was forced to undertake drastic repositioning and organisational restructuring actions. An emphasis on customer value as the framework for sustained competitive advantage has a great deal to do with the human resources of an organisation understanding customer value and building HRM programmes with a customer orientation in the contest of core competencies may be the underlying aim of the HRM function.

Competitive advantage occurs if customers perceive that they receive more value from their transaction with an organisation than from its competitors. Price has a lot to do with value. Proctor and Gamble made a strategic decision in 1992 to compete on the basis of low prices, even for its premium brands. Customer research had indicated price was becoming relatively more important in the buying decision. That data drove a strategic decision to cut costs throughout the organisation. The result was an increase in profit margins by more than 5 per cent despite reducing prices on several major brands. But customer value is far more complicated than a simple assessment of product quality relative to price.

### Does Corporate Image Affect Customer Value?

The notion of customer value is more complicated than it may seem to be unlimited. For examples many customers seek out products and services to some extent as a function of the reputation of the organisation selling the product or services in matters not directly related to the cost or quality of the particular product or service. One reason companies (and politicians) wrap themselves around the Olympics tends to rub off into the company. Marketing research shows that perception of product quality is positively affected by affiliation with the Olympics. Thus, the theory is that customer value is affected by this connection.

Likewise, the reputation of companies' environmental policies as well as the use of child labour or pitiful labour conditions in international facilities affects the decision making of some consumers. An organisation's reputation regarding issues such as corporate ethics or social responsibility, pro-family policies, or affirmative action/diversity practices can go into a "customer value" assessment at least for some customers. Such issues not only affect customer behaviour but also, perhaps, just as important, the ability of an organisation to recruit and retain valuable employees. There is no question that corporate image has an impact on organisations ability to attract and retain qualified workers. This is one reason companies compete so vigorously to make the various socially desirable lists that appear on the covers of popular magazines.

While customers undoubtedly place greater weight on the quality of the particular product or services they are considering relative to its costs, there is no question that "Customer value" can include tangential variables such as corporate responsibility, environmental impacts, diversity policies, political issues, and affiliations with other products or services. Thus, a company's business strategy must include consideration of these important environmental factors.

## Competitive Advantage Principle 2: Maintaining Uniqueness

The second principle of competitive advantage derives from offering a product or service that your competitor cannot easily imitate or copy. For example, if you open a restaurant and serve hamburgers, and a competitor moves in next to you and also serves hamburgers that taste, cost, and are prepared just like yours, unless you quickly offer something unique in your restaurant, you may lose a larger part of your business because your competitor will continue to attract customers. Competitive advantage comes to a business when it adds value to customers through some form of uniqueness.

### Sources of Uniqueness

A key to any businesses sustained competitive advantage is to ensure that its uniqueness lasts. Three traditional types of resources exist to offer customers uniqueness. These three resources are financial capital, physical capital and human resources capital. In addition to these three resources, business may offer customers uniqueness through a non-traditional capability, namely organisational capability. The four mechanisms for offering uniqueness are as below:

First, a business needs financial, or economic, capital. This uniqueness comes when a business receives special access to financial funding or is able to produce a good or service cheaper than someone else.

If, in your hamburger restaurant, you have received a financial gift from family or friends to build the restaurant, without repayment of the gift, you may be able to charge less for your product than a competitor who borrowed money from a bank or financial institution. Your cheaper hamburgers would then become a source of uniqueness that customers value. Large organisations are frequently at an advantage over smaller competitors interms of their access for financial capital it has acquired through its sales of operating software products. Microsoft's available financial capital has allowed it to launch an aggressive strategy for its Internet browsing software, including spending millions of dollars on free subscriptions.

The second source of uniqueness rests in the organisation's physical capital. This includes all the company's plants and equipment as well as its ability to purchase necessary supplies. Specific examples of physical capital that could be used to create competitive advantage include specialised company hardware and software, robotic manufacturing systems, and control of prime geographic locations. Physical capital helps create competitive advantage by allowing the company to develop a unique technological capability. That is, a business can have a distinctive way of building or delivering its product or services. In the hamburger restaurant, the different types of cooking used to prepare hamburgers may distinguish restaurants from each other (boiled vessus flame grilled).

The third source of uniqueness that an organisation can use to achieve competitive advantage is it human capital. Human capital refers to the skill and abilities of the individual members of the organisation, including their training, expertise, experience, creativity and relationships. Many examples exist of organisations that have succeeded because of the skills and abilities of their human assets.

The fourth but related source of uniqueness helping a company gain competitive advantage may be derived from organisational capability. While human capital refers to the skills and abilities of individual members of the company, organisational capability refers to the synergies that they create collectively. Organisation capability represents the business's ability to manage organisation systems and people in order to match customer and strategic needs. Organisation capability helps a company achieve competitive advantage because the manner in which it contributes value to the organisation's products or services is rare, hard to substitute for, and difficult to imitate. A competitor cannot reverse engineer organisation capability and create a copy of it as it can an end-product because organisational capability is so closely matched to the unique characteristics of the company. Human capital and organisational capacity have a great deal to do with the organisation's core-competencies what the organisation does best and how it differentiates itself from the competition. The increased pace of change required by technology, globalisation, profitable growth and customer demands places workforce competence and organisational capabilities at centre stage.

In a complex, dynamic, uncertain and turbulent environment (e.g., changing customers, technology, suppliers, relevant laws and regulations) organisational capability derives from the organisation's flexibility, adaptiveness, and responsiveness. In less dynamic environments, organisational capability derives from maintaining continuity and stability of organisation practices. In a restaurant organisational capability may be derived from having employees who ensure that when customers enter the restaurant, their customer requirements are better met than when the customers go to a competitor's restaurant. That is, employees will want to ensure that customers are served promptly and pleasantly and that the food is well prepared.

## How does strategy evolve from uniqueness?

The creation of strategy repairs an alignment between the organisation's environment and its unique capabilities. HRM is critical for exploiting these capabilities, some of which may interact. Many experts maintain that organisational capability may be the most important source of sustained competitive advantage. An organisation's ability to sustain competitive advantage depend on its ability to attract and retain those individuals with the skills needed to give the organisation the edge. Attracting and retaining individual with skills related to the poor competencies of the organisation are key HR activities directly relevant to organisational capability. Developing HR systems to take full advantage of the potential competitive advantages are also critical to sustained advantage.

## Human Resource Management as a Competitive Advantage

The previous discussion provides a basis for thinking about human resources as a competitive advantage. Below, we review three specific ways that Human Resource Management activities can build organisational capability and sustain a business's competitive advantage. These three are: implementing a strategy, dealing with change, and building a strategic unity.

*Human Resource Management and Strategic Implementation*: Strength, weaknesses, opportunities, threats (SWOT) analysis:

Strategy is defined "a process through which the basic mission and objectives of the organisation are set and a process through which the organisation uses its resources to achieve its objectives". Strategy deals with the future, providing the organisation with answers to such questions as:

1. what opportunities are available to us, now and in the foreseeable future ?
2. what threats do we face from our competitors, regulatory bodies, technological changes, or shifts in customer preferences?
3. what are our unique strengths and internal availabilities and how should we leverage them in developing competitive advantage ?
4. what are our weaknesses, and how can we improve these areas ?

Organisations with a "well articulated strategic vision" are more likely to achieve sustained competitive advantage over organisations that lack such a vision. Strategies pursued without thorough answers to all four of these questions are more likely to fail.

Implementation of strategy requires the involvement of people from every functional area and level. An organisation can perform at its maximum capability only when the HR strategic planning focus is fully integrated with the organisations strategy in a form of reciprocal interdependence. This should be the first consideration within the organisational design domain of HRM.

The development of a human resource strategy requires future thinking, integrated decision making, formalised procedures, and programming, all done in the context of the organisation's overall mission and ideally, in the context of the potential sources of uniqueness.

Human resource planning (HRP) incorporates each of these components as well in the context of this strategy. While we typically focus on the particular techniques used by HR planner, these techniques are simply tools for solving internal organisational problems related to the strategy of the organisation.

Identification and analysis of strengths, weaknesses, opportunities, and threats (SWOT) is central to the strategic planning process. SWOT analysis involves developing a strategy that respond to external threats and opportunities by exploiting internal strengths and avoiding or improving internal weaknesses. Effective SWOT analysis include most of the organisational design activity. An organisation employing the SWOT approach has to first analyse its competitive environment to identify potential opportunities and threats and then match the opportunities and threats to its internal strengths and weaknesses. The perceived fit between external conditions and internal capabilities articulates the organisation's strategy.

## Identifying Environmental Opportunities and Threats

Strategy development is an analytic exercise, requiring research and assessment of the threats and opportunities presented by the company's external environment. The organisation must view its competitive environment as a business lean system, complete with the opportunities to form mutual beneficial alignments and partnerships as well as threats from aggressive competitors. The successful organisation must accurately discern and respond to the environmental changes that will most directly affect the organisation's future. One approach to identifying potential threats and opportunities is environmental scanning. Environmental scanning involves studying and interpreting social, economic, political, regulatory and technological trends that can effect competition in the industry generally, environmental scanning addresses the overall economic conditions in the industry, driving forces that are changing industry conditions, the nature of competition in the industry and regulatory and social trends.

**An Analysis of the Strenghts, Weakness, Opportunities and Threats**

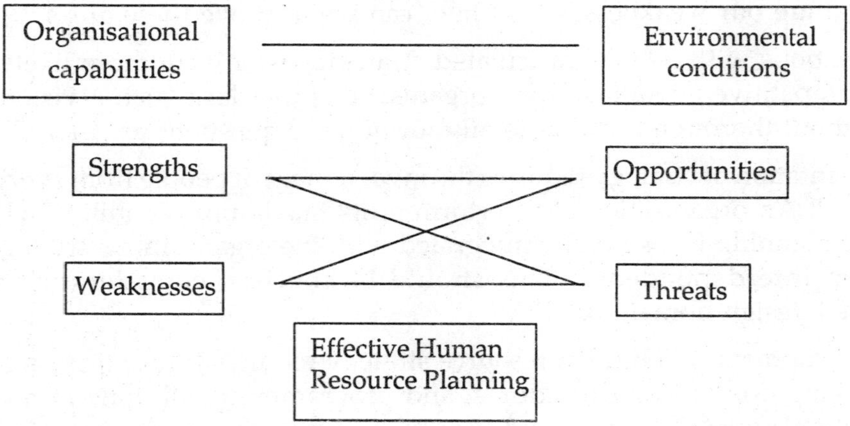

Environmental scanning helps strategic planners identify and anticipate sources of threats and opportunities. The big picture of scanning should focus on the future customer base. This focus provides a better understanding of the context in which HR decisions are or will be made on the one hand, environmental scanning is used to analyse or tease apart, the individual sources of threats and opportunities. At first glance, the environment is a middle array of positive (opportunities) and negative (threats) events. Whether a problem is viewed positively (e.g., opportunity) or negatively (e.g., threat) has a great deal to do with the solution adapted. Some of the best planners are those who can turn a threat into an opportunity. For example, while most companies in smoke-stack industries view unions as a serious threat to performance, the executives at national skill work side by side with the unions to improve quality and productivity. In this case, a potential threat becomes an opportunity. Analysis of competitors characteristics (e.g., costs, overheas, pricing, quality, image, reputation, safety etc.) is a critical part of the environmental scan. The mass marketing of one of its test requires an extensive study of this possible opportunity. On the other hand, environmental analysis is also used to synthesise the wide variety of threats and opportunities into an integrated whole. The variety of demands placed on the organisation requires some methods for typing them together to access their joint effects. For example, in an organisation, HR planners were able to synthesise more than 50 HRM programmes into a least of 10 that were of top priority to the firm in the context of its strategic plan. In addition to their variety, some of these threats and opportunities place competing demands on the firm. For example, the need for efficiency and the need for innovation sometimes lead to inconsistent HR policies. Environmental scanning helps strategic planners set priorities, fine synergy among activities, and create future opportunities.

Industry competition has a profound impact on HR strategic planning. Changes in the labour supply and demand are also a critical consideration. As argued above, businesses must realise their human capital and organisational capabilities as effectively as their financial and physical capital given the importance of managing for competitive advantages. Organisations are increasingly aware that talented employees are vital to their success. Since labour can constitute as much as 80 per cent of operating expenses, and most businesses compete atleast partly on a price/cost basis, managing the labour market is a crucial HR activity. Infact, the control of labour costs in the context of the supply and demand for labour is considered by some experts to be one of the most important components of environmental scanning for competitive advantage.

Government regulation and labour laws also influence HR strategy and planning and must be carefully considered in any effort to reduce the cost of labour or increase productivity. Virtually every decision made by a business owner, a supervisor, or a manager that involves personnel could have legal consequences. Firing employees, the terms and conditions of their employment, the monitoring of their behaviour at work, discrimination, disability, unemployment benefits and labour union issues are just some areas where there are legal minefields for decision makers. For example, many states now have laws that govern how employees are treated in mergers and acquisition and that protect workers right of privacy. Of course, any international expansion requires a thorough understanding of labour laws where expansion is being considered. Many companies provide extensive training in labour laws for their decision makers.

## Identifying Internal Strengths and Weaknesses

External threats and opportunities do not, in themselves, define a company's ability to achieve competitive advantage. As stated above, the most effective organisation blend HR planning with the organisation's overall strategy to ensure that the goals and resources deployment and HR work in concert with those of the organisation as a whole. Issues related to the internal environment are often related to the external environment. For example, mergers and acquisition require redesign of structures and jobs. Geographic expansion and consolidation require managerial succession planning and development and an assessment of labour markets in the areas planned for expansion. International expansion requires an extreme case of this type of business growth. But expansion does not always mean concurrent growth in employment. For example, during the 1990s many firms had aggressive plans for business growth, while either reducing or holding headcount constant. Instead of requiring new employees, this type of strategy required job reducing, retraining, outsourcing, and reassignment of human resources. Some competitive strategies may require considerable employee downsizing or redeployment, these types of HR activities are evident in a host of companies such as AT&T, IBM, HRB Singer, Honeywell. For AT&T to position itself after passing of the 1996 Communication Act., it had to reorganise and divest. The substantial restructuring and downsizing effort was designed with the company's strategic plan in mind. AT&T understood that rapid response environmental change required a long, flexible organisation. The company had to be reduced in size, layers of hierarchy had to be eliminated, and business units spun off to operate as autonomous divisions.

Other corporate and business strategies suggest different HR requirements. While downsizing was at an all time high in 1996, the rhetoric regarding restructuring changed because of adverse publicity regarding job elimination and evidence that some companies may be overdoing their workforce reductions and ultimately hurting revenue growth. It is becoming more and more obvious that downsizing must be done carefully and with a long term perspective. Growth strategy is now making a comeback. As a recent Business Week article put it, "strategy gone with new prospects are in".

In addition to human capital, technology evokes an important set of potential internal strengths and weaknesses for HR strategy. The internal strengths and weaknesses of an organisation may reflect its culture. Personnel Assessment Systems had ready cash and a high motivated workforce of people with very limited experience in the expansion areas. It is at this point that HR strategy often turns into HR planning. Such planning may involve a gap analysis, for example, which is used to reconcile the forecasts of labour demand and supply. As a minimum, this process identifies potential shortages or surpluses of employees, skills, and jobs based on the organisation's competitive strategy. HR planners can juxtapose several environmental forecasts with alternative supply and demand forecasts to determine the firms preparedness for different business scenarios or competitive strategies. From a problem solving perspective, gap analysis is used to "pair-up" potential opportunities and threats and internal strengths and capabilities in order to evaluate how the firm might attack the future. This decision making process involves:

(1) search for alternative solutions,

(2) evaluation of alternatives, and

(3) choice of solutions.

Gap analysis may have revealed a need for employee downsizing for a majority of the Fortune 1000 companies in recent years. Approaches to downsizing are many and varied. Some companies adopt a "last in, first out" policy where layoffs are based strictly on employee seniority. Many organisations are constrained by collective bargaining agreements that require such a policy. The most effective firms look at downsizing as an opportunity to create or improve he company's competitive advantage through restructuring and overhead reduction. The most effective downsizing efforts are those conducted in the context of some important measurement orientation or benchmark, such as productivity and not with under consideration of the stock price for the next quarter. Ford, for example, set a goal of 18 employee hours per vehicle for 1996, a figure superior to GM and Chrysler but still a few hours more than Honda, Nissan, and Toyota. Downsizing was just one of several programmes aimed at the employee hour reduction goal. The goal was met in 1996 through these efforts and a 16-hour goal was set for 2000.

Multiple scenario are likely to be worth considering in meeting the strategic goals of the organisation. Environmental scanning and forecasting in the contest of the strategic plan identify a range of possible opportunities and threats some of which are routine, others uncertain, and still others ambiguous. Strategists must exercise their ingenuity to create a range of possible solutions to the opportunities and threats they identify. The extent to which the current HR policies and practices are consistent strategic plans is a critical consideration.

The choice of any strategy should be made relative to the present and potential organisational capability of the company. The choices should also be driven by what is viewed as actual or potential sources of competitive advantage in the financial, technological, or human capital areas as well. However, since there are likely to be several solutions that are equally viable/desirable, the choice is likely to be heavily influenced by the values of the decision makers (e.g., executives, HR planners, line managers etc.). Some of these decision makers may differ in their attitudes regarding resource constrains (time and money spent), employee morale, financial performance, customer satisfaction, and so on. These differences may result in a political debate. Ideally, it is advisable to choose a solution that takes advantage of all potential competitive opportunities that minimises threats, seizes opportunities, capitalises on strengths, and ameliorates weaknesses. This approach balance the many varied demands placed on the organisation and HR functions and maximises degrees of freedom for future action. For example, Personnel Assessment System (PAS) had to decide to what extent it should risk its core business in order to embark on a new line of business with much uncertainty.

Most problem solving fails due to lack of action, and most plans fail due to poor implementation. Action programming is the final step of HR strategy that takes the adopted solution and lays out a plan for the sequence of events that needs to be executed to realise the strategy. Any business continually assesses and formulates new strategies in order to meet the needs of its customers in more effective ways. PAS involved its customers in its plan to expand into international staffing. PAS staff members gathered information regarding customers, globalisation plans, and a short survey of international staffing objectives are sent to the HR department of each customer.

## Strategy Implementation

It is important that employees be informed about the organisation's strategic mission. For examples at Motorola, employees are kept apprised of their company's strategic plans, goals and subsequent performances. Employees receive corporate performance data relative to goals and benchmark data on a quarterly basis. PAS developed a reward system for information regarding customer global expansion plans and knowledge of major PAS competitor products and services. All PAS employees are asked to gather data on the mass-market appeal of the personality test.

HRM practices should be the mechanism used to focus people's attention in the major strategic issues in the organisation. In general, by addressing the choices and issues, organisations can determine how they should alter their HRM practices to achieve consistency between HRM and strategic goals. For example, if the organisation is emphasizing cost differentiation strategies, several changes in HRM activities can enable those strategies to become a major focus in the organisation. A cost oriented strategy, for example, calls for multi-skilled employees; smaller, less experienced staffs; a focus on performance based pay with a great emphasis on efficiency and financial impact. A differentiation strategy calls for specialists in product design and development, higher budgets for research and development, rewards for innovative ideas related to quality, a flat organisational structure, and customer based performance appraisal. Involving employees and customers in strategy development can facilitate the development of a more effective strategy. Unfortunately many business fail to carefully consider the HRM issues as part of their strategic planning and implementation efforts. These businesses often end up with "strategic plans on top shelf" (SPOTS). These SPOTS are elegantly drafted, documented, and detailed descriptions of what the business strategy should be, but they fail to include the means for accomplishing the strategy.

## HR and the Capacity for Change

In a constantly changing business world, organisations must be able to adapt to changes or risk failure, and yet the first reaction that most people have towards change is one of resistance. Typically, individuals express concern over changing habits, norms and ways of doing things. In organisation the capacity for change may be increased by correctly using HRM tools and expertise. For example, organisations interested in becoming more adaptable to environmental pressures and changes should hire people who are more flexible and develop people so they realise that change is an important part of growth. Further, the company should set performance standards for people to encourage flexibility and diversity and should reward employees for being innovative. In an increasingly competitive environment, organisations with a greater capacity for change are more likely to satisfy customers and expand the customer base. We have already mentioned the Internet revolution and its potential for retail sales. Companies that think doing business over computer is just a passing fad and do nothing to adapt will probably get buried by this revolution in retail.

In the automotive industry, the lead time for new cars was about seven years in the 1970s. That is, it took about seven years to go from new concept to a prototype to production. In the early 1980s, Ford introduced the Taurus/Sable cars in about three and a half years, cutting the lead time by half. This reduced lead time came, in parts, from extensive training of all employees involved in the Taurus/Sable project. The lead time was further reduced by creating a product team of suppliers, engineers, manufacturers, distributors, assembly workers, and customers who all worked together offering input into the design and building of the new cars. This novel group effort of involving all important parties, coupled with other HRM changes (e.g., training, staffing, communication, rewards), allowed Ford to increase its capacity for change and significantly reduce its lead time. Consequently, the increased capacity for change had a dramatic impact on Ford's profits and performance.

## HR and Strategic Unity

Strategic unity represents the extent to which Stakeholders inside (e.g., employers) and outside a business (e.g., shareholders, customers) share a core set of values and assumptions about the business. For example, if the stakeholders believe that customer service is of central importance to corporate performance, this core value can be developed and nurtured among employees, suppliers, and customers of the business.

Strategic unity can be more easily realised by focusing HR on deliverables to internal and external customers. HR must focus on what HR professionals "deliver". The key to strategic units is the measurement of outcomes or deliverables that are most important for assessing strategic accomplishments. These outcomes should be defined in terms of meeting customer requirements and expanding the customer base.

The issue of conflicting stakeholders is most contentious today and underscores the difficulty in attaining strategic unity. Some research suggests that management has become too responsive to stock price and investor demands for a quick return and that some HR decisions are not in the long term best interests of the organisation. HR professionals can and should play a vital role in successful organisation design efforts that call for downsizing, reorganising, and business expansion for the long range success of the organisation. This approach first calls for a detailed strategic plan with a stipulation of the core competencies necessary to achieve it. The core competencies are then used to construct a performance-based approach to assessing employees as part of the strategic plan. Research shows that this approach to strategy implementation can get a company both short and long term gains and that all stakeholders will ultimately benefit.

## Skills Required for Human Resource Management Competitiveness

For HRM practices to be used to gain competitive advantage, both general managers and HRM professionals must have a set of skill or competencies that build competitiveness. Competencies represent an individual's knowledge, skills, abilities and activities performed. That is, individuals should know the business, keep aware of current HR developments, manage the process of change, and integrate all these roles in the context of the organisation's mission and strategy. To refine these broad skills, general managers and HRM professionals must be proficient in oral and written communications, decision making, change process, leadership, innovative thinking, planning and organising, computer skills are also becoming a must for HRM professionals because more and more products and services released to HR Activities are now available on software or through the internet. Without a working knowledge of software requirements for example, it is almost impossible to determine whether a given product is right for the organisation.

### General Manager Skills

General Managers have primary responsibility for ensuring that businesses have a competitive advantage. To do this, they must integrate financial, strategic, technological, and organisational capabilities, these are: creating a need for HRM changes, creating a vision of the importance of HRM practices, generating support of HRM activities, and becoming proficient in the delivery of HRM practices.

#### Competency 1: Create a Need for HRM Changes

Individuals must be convinced that they need to change before they will be committed to any programme for change. Until employees feel a need to pay attention to HRM activities, they are unlikely to do so. Since HRM practices are central to business competitiveness, general managers must encourage employees to be aware of effective HRM in the organisation and to take them seriously, some research indicates that technologically-oriented managers and supervisors tend to place less value on HR activities such as performance management, staffing procedures, and training in equal employment opportunity. Generally, managers of these individuals have a greater challenge.

One approach to increasing perceived value of HRM is to share outcome of data about HRM practices and how they relate to "bottom-line" measures for the success of the company. Effective managers share results of organisational effectiveness criteria (e.g. productivity indices, customer satisfaction data, absenteeism records, grievances filed, reconciling costs) and their relationship to particular HRM programmes (e.g., staffing, training, appraisal).

## Competency 2: Create a vision of the Importance of HRM Practices

Most successful businesses have identified the direction in which they are headed. This direction reflects not only short-term goals (muting this quarter's profit plan), but also more importantly, a longer term vision (e.g., a 5 or 10 year plan). The long-range vision reflects the organisation's strategic goals and core principles and values.

General managers who want to use HRM practices for competitiveness need to relate the company's strategic vision to its HRM practices. That is, general managers must emphasise the important role that employees play in the company's ability to meet its long-term business plans.

## Competency 3: Generate Support for HRM Activities

General Managers need to demonstrate their personal support by participating in staffing decision (e.g., selecting managers, succession planning) or serving as trainees or trainees in management development programmes. They can also use effective performance management practices (e.g., providing timely feedback to subordinates), encourage their supervisory subordinates to do the same, and hold their subordinates accountable for the extent to which they subscribe to HRM recommended procedures. General Managers also need to build commitment among employees for using HRM practices. They may do this by sharing information.

***

# 10 Competency Mapping and Career Management

## Concept of Competency

Survival, smartness, growth and governance of organisations depend on their competencies. Organisational competencies are essentially competencies of people who constitute the organisation. Any training programme instituted in organisations must address ways and means of effectively building competencies of people of the organisation. "Competitive advantage derived from physical assets is seldom maintained in the long run. Organisation that finds, develops and motivates talented people to a common goal will be winner in the competitive world in which we operate". Competitive advantage stems from a firm's unique resources and capabilities and most organisational competencies start with individuals. Training designed to make organisational people competent and to enhance their competencies is critical to organisational excellence.

The Oxford Learner's Dictionary describes competency, "as a skill that one needs in a particular job or for a particular task". Richard Boyatzis (1982), the American who has done a nice work on job competencies, "as the underlying characteristics of a person, which can be a motive, a trait, skill, an aspect of one's self image or social role or a body of knowledge which he or she uses". Thus, competency can be described as a set of knowledge, skills, abilities and behavioural attributes which are required to deliver superior performance in a job position.

## British and American Approach

The Americans prefer to use the term 'competency',. While British prefer to use the term 'competence'. American approach is individual oriented. Americans consider the characteristics of individuals casually related to superior performance on the job, while British approach is to take competencies as the job, task and outcome requirements.

# Components of Competency

Competency is a cluster of knowledge, skill, ability, motive, talent and trait, self-concept, attitude, values etc.

## Knowledge

Knowledge is a basic component of competency. Knowledge is knowing the information. In the present knowledge era, individuals are valued and respected for the level of professional and job-related knowledge possessed and demonstrated by them. Knowledge underpins the performance of employees in the workplace. Expanding horizon of knowledge by re-learning, learning new things and experiences keep the individual in the forefront of competency domain.

## Skill

Skill is application-oriented knowledge. It refers to specific capability to do things well. According to Milan Kubr and Joseph Prokopenko (1990), "skills are the abilities to do things, to effectively apply knowledge and personal aptitudes and attitudes in work situations". Skill is learnt mostly not under formal education and over the period of time by practice.

## Ability

Ability refers to capabilities of an individual to perform a particular task in an effective way. Ability plays an important role in the performance of individuals. While skill is the specific capacity to physically manipulate objects, ability is a broad and stable characteristic responsible for a person's maximum—as opposed to typical performance of mental and physical tasks. Ability includes the natural aptitudes and learnt capabilities required to successfully complete a task.

## Motive

Motive is the inner accelerating force or self-drive that spontaneously spurs one to perform exceedingly well. In general, in any role the characteristics that are important for outstanding, rather than merely competent performance lie at a deeper level than skills and subject knowledge, but it is their attitudes, behaviours, values and characteristics that make the difference.

Motives move or tend to move a person to a particular course of action. Motives differ from person to person. These depend upon the needs, attitudes and values of individuals, and performance is a function of abilities (knowledge and skills) multiplied by motivation, i.e., the unconscious decision about the amount of energy the individual invest in any activity.

## Trait and Talent

Trait is called an attribute or a distinguishing quality. Dilum Jirasinghe and Geoffrey Lyons (1996) define trait as any enduring characteristics of a person leading to regularities and consistencies in behaviours. Talent refers to a special natural ability or aptitude. Trevor T. Bentley (1996) says, "talents are those particular abilities which transcend competency and become much more exciting and creative". Trait and talent add special values to the individuals, make them distinguished people and help them to achieve success.

## Self-concept

Self-concept refers to the way we view ourselves. Our behaviors to a great extent depend upon the way we view ourselves. If we view that we are important in the organisation and the organisation success depends mainly on our performance, we do the job effectively. Self-concept is often divided into four parts. These are: (i) self-image; (ii) real self; (iii) looking glass self; and (iv) ideal self.

## Self-Image

Self-image is the true feeling of the people about themselves. It shows their identity. Its significance gets reflection in the old saying that "they are able because they think they are able".

## Real Self

Real Self, is also called as self-awareness, refers to knowing oneself. Compared to self-image, real self is difficult to get. It should be discovered by having deep thinking and by asking and answering a number of questions to oneself. It is one of the pre-requisites for personal relations.

## Looking Glass Self

It is another part of self-concept. It refers to knowing other's real feelings about us, which is very important for the self-development and for maintaining smooth inter-personal relations.

## Ideal Self

Ideal Self, is the vision of our future selves, which may be clear or vague depending upon the individual. Everyone has some goal or vision of what we want to become. The parents, teachers, peer group, etc., play a critical role in shaping the vision of a person.

## Attitude

Richard Pettifogger (2000) defines attitudes as, "the mental, moral and ethical dispositions adopted by individuals to others and the situations and environments in which they find themselves". Attitudes not only influence the behaviour of individuals, but also their approach to others or to particular events.

When employees have positive attitudes about the work and the organisation, they will become motivated and committed ones and work hard for the organisation. On the contrary, people who have the negative attitudes always behave with pessimistic views, find fault with other people, things, and systems and raise much number of questions to do/not to do a particular activity.

Attitudes are determined by various factors like bringing up, teachers and schools, peer group, media, national culture, etc. As knowledge, skills and abilities without right attitudes become waste; attitudes are considered an important component of competency.

### Values

Values are concerned with matter of human preference and result from choices between competing interests. Values are the worth or importance we attach to different factors in our lives. Depending upon the various factors, values differ from individual to individual, organisation to organisation, and country to country. As the utilisation of an individual's knowledge, skills and abilities (for the development and success of the individual and the organisation) depend upon the value system of the individual and the organisation, values become vital component of competency.

Even though, all these above mentioned components are underlying characteristics of individuals, some components are more visible and observable than others. Knowledge, skills and abilities are more visible and observable than motives, traits and talents, self-concepts, attitudes and values.

Knowledge, skills and abilities are not only more visible and observable, but also more conscious and trainable. On the other hand, values, traits and talents, attitudes, self-concepts and motives are less conscious and trainable besides less visible and observable. Therefore, assessing the underlying elements of competencies at the time of recruitment and selection of employees will benefit the organisation in many ways inculcating and developing good value system, developing positive work and organisation culture will help the organisation for the total development of competencies.

Competencies are the skills, knowledge or abilities that enable good performance in a particular role. They may be learned in a formal education (Principles of Management or Basic Accounting Theory for example), or picked up working on the job (troubleshooting electrical circuits or using a word processing programme). Some competencies are clearly ones that are learnable (project management or C++ programming), while others can be developed but are related to your basic values or way of working, demonstrating customer focus, or striving for quality.

## Competencies and Careers

Making sense out of careers can be a challenge. Knowing just where you are, what you are good at, where and how you want to grow, and where you want to be in five years – or at retirement – can all involve major effort. So much so that many people put the questions off, preferring to make do and stay where they are rather than make changes that could help them lead happier, more productive work lives. One way of sorting through career challenges that become popular in recent years involves focusing on competencies.

## What is Competency Mapping?

It is about identifying preferred behaviours and personal skills which distinguish excellent and outstanding performance from the average.

A competency is something that describes how a job might be done, excellently; a competence only describes what has to be done, not how. So the competencies might describe the form, the project also describes the roles using competencies.

## Competencies and Career Management

Knowing your competencies can be helpful in two main ways. First, think of the basic career management question. **"So, what do you want to do ?"** We're used to answering that question in-terms of a job title, but it is actually more helpful to answer by naming the competencies that you want to use. Finding a job that fits your competencies is easier and more effective than thinking of a job that might fit and then trying to figure out if it would be satisfying. If you know pretty clearly what you like doing and what you are good at (in other words, the competencies you have and enjoy using), then it is going to be easier to say what you want to do. It will also help in reviewing NASA's needs and determining where there is a potential "Strategic Career Management" match of your interests and abilities with the organisation's situation.

## Competencies and Career Development

The second big pay off from knowing your competencies lies in the area of career development. The best way of developing your skills and capabilities lies in focusing clearly on competencies, and using them to create goals for skill growth. They can drive individual development planning, help in picking training and education, or suggest developmental activities. Also, they can be of great value in forming long-term skill growth goals.

Organisations are spending considerable time as well as expertise to arrive at competency models clusters of knowledge, skills, attitudes, motives, and values required to turn out superior performance. This becomes the basis for decision about hiring, training, appraisal, promotion, and other human resource issues. And in the past decade, thousands of organisations throughout the world have joined the quest for competencies.

Many organisations are faced with the dilemma of choosing the right kind of measurement tools for competency mapping. Although tools like assessment centres are valid instruments, they are too costly as well as impractical to be used for large scale requirements.

## Benefits of Competency Mapping

Competency maps have many potential benefits for students and teaching staff. Of course, because staff and students share many goals, these benefits are not entirely divisible, some aspects of competency mapping will benefit both staff and students. A partial list of potential uses for competency mapping follows. It is likely that more benefits will be discovered as the technique matures.

### Benefits for Staff

If competency mapping can actually give a picture of the structure of the course as the students experience it, teaching staff will be able to use that picture as the basis for course refinement. The identification of key concepts is the first step towards designing a syllabus. The information gained can also be published to the students, for example by including it in the subject information handout that students usually receive in their first lecture, or by putting it on the courseware web page.

Of course, it is quite possible that the structure revealed by analysis of student results does not match the lecturer's idea of the conceptual structure of the course. In this case, the revealed structure may suggest ways in which the course can be improved. For example, if two competencies that should be revealed (for example, C pointers and passing by reference) are not clustered together, it could indicate a need to make the connection more explicit to the students. If the competency map uses all the coursework marks as input, this will not help the students of that year, however, it may well help teaching staff to refine the coursework for the next delivery of the course. It would also be useful to staff who are teaching follow-on courses, as they would gain a better idea of which topics need revision.

A competency map using only the marks for half of the course can be produced if staff wish to refine the course on the fly, but care must be taken that the data are sufficient; if the only marks on record are the first six practical marks, it is unlikely that any useful conclusions can be drawn. It is not yet certain how many points are needed for competency mapping to be useful, but it is likely to depend on the amount and complexity of the course material.

These uses assume that competency mapping will educate the structure of the course. If, however, the technique does not do this, then there are still potential benefits; logically, we would expect that activities that test strongly related competencies should show correlation's in their marks; if this is not the case there must be some reason. For example, written exam questions about linked lists might not correlate strongly with practical questions about linked lists if success in practical is more closely related to factors other than subject knowledge. This could be the case if some students find their work environment operating system, compiler and editor-difficult to use. In this case, practical questions will tend to cluster much more strongly with other practical questions, and much less strongly with theory questions. The competency map can show that there is a problem, it is then up to the teaching staff to investigate that problem. Of course, competency mapping over subsequent years of the course will help the staff to know when they have ameliorated the problem.

In a University setting, competency mapping can be used to compare demographic subsets of students to students' access to education, for example, if there is concern that students of non-English speaking background are finding a particular activity especially difficult because of the complex language used to explain it, then competency mapping can be applied separately to the results from students belonging to that group and the results compared to a competency map derived from the marks of the rest of the student body. In this case, a problem with English would result in a distorted cluster arrangement; written-answer questions and questions with complex requirements would tend to cluster together. The technique may also be used to determine whether female students conceptualise the subject differently to male students. Again, if a problem is found, competency mapping over subsequent years will show staff whether the remedies are working.

## Benefits for Students

The primary benefit of competency mapping for students is the increased understanding of the student viewpoint that the teaching staff will have, and resulting in likely course improvements. However, students should also benefit directly from it. A constructivist view of the teaching process suggests that students will assimilate new knowledge and gain new skills more readily if they can be made aware of how those new competencies interrelate with knowledge and skills that are already mastered. Of course, Lecturers know this, most new topics begin with an explanation is almost always exclusively verbal. Information about relationships is often best presented in visual form, especially if the relationships are multidimensional, but words are one-dimensional map of the course structure, may help students construct their understanding of the course material.

If it is possible to use competency mapping to break the subject down into components that are close to orthogonal, it should also be possible to design assessment on the basis of that break down. Once the components are known, assessment tasks can be designed that test them individually, or (since it is virtually impossible to test anything in isolation) as close to it as possible. Thus a test can be delivered to students that is quite small, but gives results that are interpretable in terms of the course's competency map.

Because competency mapping measures correlation between task marks across students, it is obviously impossible to generate a competency map based on a single student's data, however, numeric results can be presented alongside the group competency map for example, by shading regions that correspond to topics that the student needs to work on. In this way, a student may be able to use her test results to determine her own weaknesses, and then consult the map to see how they relate to the rest of the course; using this map and compass, she may find it easier to navigate through the material.

If she still has trouble understanding the material, she may ask a staff member for help. In this case, if the staff member has access to her test results, it would be easier to pinpoint the misconstruction that is at the heart of the problem. Experience shows that determining the problem is almost always harder and more time-consuming than solving it; figuring out what needs to be explained is more difficult than developing an explanation, especially considering that teachers can develop a set of explanations that work and reuse them. This means that the student need not worry as much about coming to consultation, and (because consultation time can be used more effectively) the teaching staff are more likely to be free to help her.

To generate a concept map, cluster analysis and multidimensional scaling are applied to proximity data generated from the number of times, concepts were clustered together. Competency maps are generated in a similar way; after student marks, data is collected, cluster analysis and multidimensional scaling are applied to proximity data generated from the matrix of correlations between the marks.

## Sample Question

My Company is undertaking a Job Evaluation exercise, along with competency mapping. Competency mapping is an area which has been least explored in India. I would like relevant information on competency mapping, along with reference so as to develop my skills.

## Answer

Competency Mapping is a process to identify key competencies for an organisation and/or a job and incorporating those competencies throughout the various processes (i.e., job evaluation, training, recruitment) of the organisation. To ensure we are both on the same page, we would define a competency as behaviour (i.e., communication, leadership) rather than a skill or ability.

The steps involved in competency mapping with an end result of job evaluation include the following:

- Conduct a job analysis by asking incumbents to complete a position information questionnaire (PIQ). This can be provided for incumbents to complete, or you can conduct one-on-one interviews using the PIQ as a guide. A sample PIQ that we use when conducting this step with our clients was provided to this client. The primary goal is to gather from incumbents what they feel are the key behaviours necessary to perform their respective jobs.
- Using the results of the job analysis, you are ready to develop a competency based job description. A sample of a competency based job description generated from the PIQ was provided to this client. This was developed after carefully analysing the input from the represented group of incumbents and converting it to standard competencies.
- With a competency based job description, you are on your way to begin mapping the competencies throughout your human resource processes. The competencies of the respective job description become your factors for assessments on the performance evaluation. Using competencies will help guide you to perform more objective evaluations based on displayed or not displayed behaviours.

It is generally not advisable to carry out these tests uniformly all across the board for all levels. We divide the management team into four levels, namely Junior, Middle, Senior and Top Management. They are further sub-divided into homogeneous groups as far as possible. Depending on the group profile we decide on the Tests that are to be carried out. For example, it is not necessary to test the Junior Management for motivational skills as this is the responsibility of higherups. At this level we go into job knowledge, intelligence, interpersonal, time management and communication skills. There is a gradual rise in the complexity of tests as the level of management goes up.

Each test is different and the questions are carefully framed for the group profile. Any effort to cook up, fudge or give false information will reflect in some other area and we will be able to detect this anomaly. Such cases are dealt with very severely as honesty in replying to such questions is of paramount importance. Unlike most profiling methods which heavily depend on computers and standardized databases, the tests are to be designed for conducting the test:

For MM, SM and TMT the following tests are carried out:

- Job or Functional knowledge
- Leadership Style profile
- Decision Making profile
- Professional Style profile
- Power and Empowerment profile
- Action Orientation profile
- Leadership and Management profile

Depending on the levels we are required to evaluate, we have to, depending on the levels we are asked to evaluate, decide which of the above tests are to be carried out. Most importantly, we rank people based on the above results. This rankings are relative, as they are based on the human resources that are available in the organisation. The objective is to find out the performers, likely performers with training and motivation and finally the non-performers. They are classified into A, B and C categories.

It should be clearly understood that a person ranked in the upper percentile with a particular client may not fall in the same bracket in some other organisation, under identical conditions, because the other organisation may consist of better qualified and trained people and also because of both external and internal equity. Best companies attract the best people. We identify the best people available within the organisation. Each test for each group is tailor-made and this ensures the accuracy.

Taking the competency mapping one step further, you can use the results of your evaluation to identify in what competencies individuals need additional development or training. This will help you focus your training needs on the goals of the position and company and help your employees develop towards the ultimate success of the organisation.

## Career Assessment (Test)

The practice of career assessment involves helping an individual discern the most appropriate career choice, in light of the person's abilities, interests, goals, values, and temperament, as well as the requirements of a given occupation. Few areas of life are as important to people as their occupations, not only because of the great amount of time most persons spend at work but also intrinsic and extrinsic rewards. In addition, the current climate of rapid changes in the nature and conditions of employment is just once but often several times within their lifetimes. Thus, it is not suspiring that theorizing in the field of career choice and career development is proceeding at a very lively pace. Already in the 1990s the number of major new theoretical formulations in the area has equalled or exceeded those produced made their first significant contributions to the field.

From the point of view of testing, we have already considered the instruments that are most directly applicable in the career counselling of individuals, namely the interest inventories and the multiple-aptitude batteries, as well as in the occupational testing section. Choosing a career often implies the choice of a general lifestyle, with its characteristic set of values. Because interest in topics essentially assess the individual's value system, they are coming more and more to be regarded as focal in effective career planning. We examine below two more specialized kinds of instruments that have been particularly designed for career counselling; comprehensive programmes for career exploration and measures of career maturity.

### Comprehensive Programmes for Career Exploration

Several multiple-aptitude batteries have been incorporated into career guidance systems. An example is provided by the Differential Aptitude Tests (DAT), which can be used in combination with the Career Interest Inventory (CII – Psychological Corporation 1991 a, 1991 b). These two instruments were jointly developed in order to facilitate comparisons between their results in the process of career guidance.

The DAT comprises of the following eight tests: Verbal Reasoning, Numerical Reasoning, Abstract Reasoning, Perceptual Speed and Accuracy, Mechanical Reasoning, Space Relations, Spelling, and language usage. A Practice Test covering all eight areas is available for advance use with examinees. There is also a special form, the Differential Aptitude Tests for Personnel and Career Assessment, in which each of the eight test has been shortened and printed in a separate booklet with this form, particular tests may be chosen for relevance to specific operations and used singly. Like most major current tests, the DAT can be completely administered in a Computerised Adaptive Testing (CAT) from (DAT Adaptive) available since 1987. As in all adaptive for this performance level. For this CAT version, the items used were from an earlier DAT (Form V) and were analysed by the Rasch Model, a simplified, one parameter model of item response theory.

An extensive collection of DAT validity data has been assembled over the years, both by the test publisher and by independent investigators who applied the battery in different occupational settings or included it in research projects. Most of these data are concerned with predictive viability in terms of high school achievement in both academic and vocational programmes. Many of the co-efficient are high even with intervals as long as three years between test and criterion data. The results are somewhat less encouraging with regard to differential prediction. Although, in general, verbal tests correlate more highly with English courses and numerical tests with mathematics courses, there is evidence of a large general factor underlying performance in all academic work. Verbal reasoning, for example, gives high correlations with most courses. It is chiefly for this reason that the VR + NRS core was introduced as an index of Scholastic aptitude. Being the sum of the score on the Verbal Reasoning and Numerical Reasoning subtests, this index correlates in the 70s and 80s with composite criteria of academic achievement. Norms are provided for this index, which is one of the scores regularly included in the DAT profile. There is also a Partial Battery, containing only the VR and NR subtests, which can be used only if a general index of scholastic aptitude is wanted.

From another angle, there is a growing evidence that traditional tests of "general intelligence" or "Scholastic administration – yield substantial validity coefficients against a wide variety of educational and occupational criteria. Such tests include essentially the same cluster of cognitive skills and knowledge assessed by the VR + NR score from the DAT. Thus it can be seen that the early gap between intelligence and multiple aptitude tests is being bridged from both ends. Tests like the DAT have been placing more emphasis on the use and interpretation of broad scores, such as VR + NR. At the same time, the initially general tests were putting more emphasis on the use and interpretation of separate subtest scores and profile analysis.

**Verbal Reasoning**

Choose the correct pair of words to fill the blanks. The first word of the pair goes in the blank space at the beginning of the sentence; the second word of the pair goes at the end of the sentence.

..... is to fin as bird is to ......

A water – feather
C fish – wing
B shark – nest
D flipper – fly
E fish – sky

The correct answer is C

Numerical Reasoning

What number should replace R in this addition problem?

| 7R | F | G | H | J | K |
|---|---|---|---|---|---|
| +R | 9 | 6 | 4 | 3 | None of these |

the correct answer is F

Mechanical Reasoning

Which load will be easier to pull through soft sand?

The Correct answer is C

**Space Relations**

Which of the following figures could be made by folding the pattern at the left ?

# Session – 2

## The Pitfalls and Limitations of Psychological Tests, Process to Overcome Limitations

### Nature and use of Psychological Tests

Psychological tests are tool. To reap the benefits that tests can provide, one must keep this essential fact in mind. Any tool can be an instrument of good or harm, depending on how it is used. Testing has been growing at an increasing pace, and it is contributing effectively in more and more areas of daily life. A psychological test is essentially an objective and standardized measure of sample of behaviour. Psychological tests are like the tests in any other science, insofar as observations are made on a small but carefully chosen sample of an individuals behviour. In this respect, the psychologist proceeds in much the same way as the bio-chemist who tests a patients blood or a community's water supply by analysis one or more samples of it.

Organisations are spending considerable time as well as expertise to arrive at Competency Models—Clusters of knowledge, skills, altitude, motives, and values—required to turn out superior performance. This becomes the basis for decision about hiring, training, appraisal, promotion, and other human resource issues. And in the past decade, thousands of organisations throughout the world have joined the quest for competencies. Many organisations are faced with the dilemma of choosing. The right kind of measurement tools for competency mapping. Although tools like assessment contents are valid instruments, they are too costly as well as impractical to be used for large scale requirements.

While Psychological Testing may not be able to completely replace other tools/ practices of Competency Mapping, experiences of hundreds of organisations point towards its wide acceptance. With the growing emphasis on competency Based Human Resource Management, the Psychological Testing has become a vital tool in the task of minimizing risk on all sides in recruitment and in career management decisions. There is a veritable factory of Psychometric tests on the market, that the designers claim, provide insight into the mind that can sort the sheep from goats. But which psychological test or tests should be used, in which circumstances, and why ?

It is clearly evident that psychological tests are currently being employed in the solution of a wide range of practical problems. One should not, however, lose sight of the fact that such tests are also serving important functions in basic research. Nearly all problems in differential psychology, for example, require testing producers as a means of gathering data. As illustrations, reference may be made to studies on the nature and extent of individual differences, the organisation of psychological traits, the measurement of group differences and the identification of biological and cultural factors associated with behaviour differences. For all such areas of research and for many others – the precise measurement of individual differences made possible by well–constructed tests is an essential prerequisite.

Similarly, psychological tests provide standardised tools for investigating such varied problems a life-span development changes within the individual, the relative effectiveness of different educational procedures, the outcomes of psychotherapy, the impact of community programmes and the influence of environmental variables on human performance.

The many kinds of tests designed for these diverse purposes differ also in other major characteristics. They very in the way they are administered as in the individual testing of each person by a trained examiner, the simultaneous testing of large groups, or the administration of tests by computers. Tests also differ in the aspects of behaviour that they cover. Some differ on the assessment of cognitive traits, or abilities. These may range from broad aptitudes – such as readiness to profit from college work – to highly specific sensor motor skills required to perform a simple manual operation.

## Personality Testing in the Workplace

In the mid–1980, Bernardin and Bownas (1985) noted that the use of personality evaluation techniques – including such unscientific methods as handwriting analysis - was flourishing in industrial setting, while the academic community had largely neglected the subject for almost two decades. Since then, a tremendous resurgence of work in the area has occurred, prompted by methodological and theoretical developments. From a methodological viewpoint, the application of meta-analysis and the use of casual modelling the techniques have stimulated research on the non-cognitive traits that can affect job performance. Meta-analysis have been employed primarily to investigate the validity and utility of personality constructs across setting. Path analysis and structural equation modelling techniques are used to study the inter-relationships among predictors and to explore the attributes and conditions leading to differing levels of job performance. The extent to which some critical variables, live ability level and job autonomy, moderate the relationship between personality and performance is also under study.

The more methodologically sophisticated research of the past decade or two has provided considerable support for the use of carefully constructed personality tests in employment decisions across a variety of settings. An important issue that still leaves further investigation is that of determining the most relevant personality dimensions example, whereas a high degree of sociability might be required for some jobs, the opposite may be case for others.

## Behavioural Assessment - The Best for Competency Mapping: Pitfalls and Ways to overcome

The various techniques subsumed under the general concept of behaviour modification represent a direct utilization of major learning principles in the practical management of behaviour change. Basically, these techniques involve the application of conditioning principles to the acquisition and strengthening of wanted behaviour and the gradually broadened to comprise an expanding variety of psychological problems, an ever expanding repertoire of intervention technique's and the consideration of cognitive and effective along with overt motor.

## Assessment Techniques

In the early applications of behaviour therapy, assessment received little attention. Since the mid–1970s, however, the importance of assessment procedures has been increasingly recognised. The principal functions to be served by assessment procedures in behaviour therapy can be subsumed under three headings. First, assessment techniques help in defining the individual's problem through a functional analysis of relevant behaviour. Essentially, such an analysis involves a full specification of the treatment objective – such as overcoming a phobia or obsessive thoughts – and includes a description of the stimuli that elicit the target behaviour, the situations in which such behaviour occurs, and the nature, magnitude, and frequencies of particular responses. A second way in which assessment proceeds can guide the behaviour therapist in selecting appropriate treatments. Third, there is a need for assessing the between change that results from treatment. Such assessments should include techniques for monitoring – change so as to permit evaluation of treatment effectiveness and the introduction of procedural alterations if necessary – as well as terminal measures to establish attainment of a satisfactory status and to plan for follow–up procedures as needed.

In considering specific assessment procedures, we should note, first, that the same procedure can often provide information relevant to all three functions. Second, the choice of procedures depends on the nature of the problem, the characteristics of the client-including the environment in which he or she must operate and the facilities available at the particular clinic. Third, a combination of several assessment procedures is desirable in most cases.

Available assessment procedures can themselves be classified under three major types: Sub-report by the client, direct observation of behaviour, and physiological measures. Although not every centre can afford the facilities required for psychological measures, these measures provide supplementary objective data in the assessment of certain conditions, such as anxiety, sexual arousal disorders, and sleep disorders. Examples, include measures of electro-dermal, muscular, and electro–ocular activity, as well as of cardiovascular, sexual and cerebral functioning.

Direct observation of the target behaviour can be conducted in naturalistic situations by parents, teachers, institutional personnel, or special observers. Observational aids such as chemists, rating scales, and daily schedules may be employed. Such observations are subject to several weaknesses for this reason, analogue situations are often employed in clinics. There is also increasing exploration of the use of mechanical sensors or monitors that can provide a continuous, objective record of behaviour in both real life and contrived situations.

Self-report by the client comprises a diversity of techniques. They include clinical interviews by the therapist, sub-monitoring records of target behaviour and associated conditions kept by the client, and a variety of written checklists and inventories. Some standardized self–report inventories are used, in either the original or adapted versions for preliminary screening and identification, as well as for monitoring of target behaviours.

## To Overcome Pitfalls of Psychological Tests

For competency mapping the Assessment centre, though can be considered as one – among other tools for implementation, the main difficulty is its higher investment, time consuming and the assessors competency to map.

Till date, a good number of Psychological Test models have been developed but their true implementation is quite difficult on the following grounds: No identical model can be used for each category.

- Change of behaviour, altitude, skill may vary with the same person but at different situations.
- Nature of test may not help to come out with correct answers.

## Suggestions to overcome pitfalls of Psychological Tests

Suggestions for overcoming pitfalls of Psychological Test are as follows :

- Selection/Recruitment process to be designed assuming the mapping of employee, as well as employer.
- To assess the questionnaire based on the organisational requirements.
- To identify the gaps between the employee's mapping and organisational mapping areas.
- Evaluate techniques/methodologies to bridge the gap.
- 360° performance appraisal – so that the gap can be reviewed.
- To benchmark the competency area.
- To develop a competency software for evaluation.

## Case Study

### Selection or Promotion?

CRR Industries Ltd., Elore is producing electric bulbs, water coolers, air coolers and refrigerators. Recently it added a new line of production, i.e., electric motors both for domestic and agricultural purposes. It needed one electric engineer with B. Tech. qualification to look after the new plant producing electric motors. Presently five electric engineers with B.E. qualifications as Assistant Engineers are working with existing plant. The company advertised for the post of chief Engineer (Electric) for its new plant. It received twelve applications out of which five are from the Assistant Engineers working in the existing plant.

The company used techniques of preliminary interviews, tests, final interview and medical examination and finally selected Mr. C.B. Sastry, employed in the existing plant of the company. He is fourth in the seniority list of the Assistant Engineers in the present plant. The company served the appointment order to Mr. Sastry and he joined as Chief Engineer in the new plant. But the three Assistant Engineer's in the existing plant moved the issue to the court of law contesting that the selection of Mr. C.B. Sastry is not valid as he is not the senior one amount the Assistant Engineers in the existing plant.

### Questions

1. What would be the management's version in the case?
2. Predict the court management regarding the issue.

# Session – 3

## Six Sigma Leadership in Competency Mapping and HR Planning

### Six Sigma Leadership: The key to sustaining contemporary quality programmes

Six Sigma methods represent a very significant advance in the application of quality principles to produce business impact for many companies, these enhanced quality techniques have had a profound impact on business results because they represent a more systematic method (VS. a focus on compliance with standards). Part of this leader approach has historically focused on human factors – training and recruitment in particular.

### Human Resource Competencies: The Wave up Call

Human Resource Departments in organisations are undergoing remarkable transformations. These changes will not only require new human resource strategies, structures, and processes, but also a range of new roles and competencies performed by professionals. The study surfaced a range of common or core competencies across four domains : Three sets of level – specific management and functional; three sets of level – specific competencies; and three key HR roles : Product/Service specialist, generalist, and strategist each requiring an additional set of separate competencies. The study also identified a range of critical needs for functional development. The final section of the report details these needs and presents a practical approach for designing and implementing competency systems that work for HR or any other function.

### The Sigma Logic Strategy

*Sigma Logic* (sm) is a break through improvement strategy. It is applied to projects linked to our business goals, Sigma Logic is based upon the systematic application of tools to analyze data and tools to enhance process knowledge. The application of these tools is driven by a desire to understand and challenge how our processes work and make them significantly better.

Implementation of the *Sigma Logic* strategy requires leadership commitment and involvement, teamwork and specialized training. Individuals recognized as process owners participate in intensive training in the tools and methodology of *Sigma Logic*. The training model provides these Process Catalysts a chance to work on a project in the classroom and facilitate application of the tools in the workplace as a team works to achieve the project business goal. Members of the team who will work with the Catalyst will also possess an understanding of the process and will bring the additional skills and tools to assist in getting the work done. In addition, significant support will be needed outside the team.

For example, a very significant part of *Sigma Logic* is understanding our measurement systems. Quality Control and analytical testing laboratories will be called on to do special analysis to help us understand the measurement process. Employees who work in the process every day will also be called on to help closely monitor the process or share the knowledge they have about how the process operates.

*Sigma Logic* can be applied to any process. Reduced costs, increased throughput, increased yield, reduced waste, reduced cycle time, increased efficiency and enhanced knowledge are examples of results that can be achieved. There is an opportunity for every one in the organisation to contribute to achieving business results through *Sigma Logic* tools and methodology.

## Career Planning

Your Soul at Work – Five Steps to a More Fulfilling Career and Life

By Stephen C. Schoonover and Nicholas W. Weiler

A Fortune Magazine cover story reports a "growing quest for spiritual renewal in the workplace."

A group of middle-aged rebels in business suits meet to discuss how they can spend more time working from their "souls".

The Washington Post says "Talk of soul and spirituality is flowing freely in the workplace these days."

Executives at a business school conference meditate briefly as preparation for a discussion of "how to find one's true calling."

Fortune describes, "a counter culture bubbling up all over corporate America that wants to bridge the traditional divide between spirituality and work." They quote a Harvard Business School research fellow who follows the topic and agrees; "spirituality in the workplace is exploding."

Hearing all this, how should we as HR professionals respond? Is there a practical and acceptable way HR organisations can help people "bridge the divide between spirituality and work"? And should we even be trying to help people work "from their souls"? Is it appropriate for us, or our organisations, to get involved in something that is so uniquely personal for each individual?

We believe the answer to these questions is "yes". Why? Because the need to address this "exploding" issue may be impossible, or impractical to ignore. And because there souls too work. Also, Those organisations that recognize and respond positively to this emerging need will have more satisfied, more productive employees.

## A New Urgency

The new, more introspective trend may in part be a natural reaction to the booming, possessions–oriented–90s. Fortune speaks of aging baby boomers starting to notice something is missing beginning to feel a need that stock options and opulent lifestyles are not satisfying. Many are asking, "Is this all there is?" One successful executive is quoted as saying, "You get to the top of the ladder and find that maybe it's learning against the wrong building."

Now, with the added shocks of September 11 and additional rounds of downsizing, a new reality is setting in. The need to integrate what I do at work with a larger purpose that has personal meaning has taken on a new urgency, even among the twenties and thirties crowd who have never known anything but good times.

At first glance, already overworked HR professionals may be discouraged that another layer of employee need is coming down the pike. They may think, "Is not it enough that with an already overloaded schedule I now have to deal with downsizing and the morale of those who are not downsized?" How can I deal with people's spiritual needs, especially in a climate where most organisational leaders feel uneasy and at a loss to address their employee's inner lives"?

While such a reaction is certainly understandable, there are some very practical ways to cope with these challenges. We have been developing techniques to help people who really succeed in their career and lives with, do or without the help of their organisations that we were able to build a truly effective process and tools to help others succeed.

## Quiet Revolutions

Through our work, we have been able to tap into and enable the higher aspirations of employees in Fortune 500 companies without setting off alarms. At GE's no-nonsense corporate headquarters we introduced inner-needs focused career and performance development programs that were so successful GE exported them to its businesses worldwide. Part of this practical approach has included the development of models articulating what competencies distinguish successful people with tools for developing them. These competency-based tool kits have been applied successfully across a full range of large Fortune 500 companies and small organisations, for profit and non-profit.

Our roadmap for helping people find and succeed in jobs they love got started years ago when we were asked to help a large company deal with unexpected layoffs. While initial efforts to help showed limited success, we noticed that some individuals were enormously successful at helping themselves. While others fell apart, these individuals "took charge" and negotiated themselves into new careers, many more rewarding than the jobs they lost. There was a clear pattern in what they did. We started capturing and translating that pattern into tools and techniques that help others succeed.

From the beginning, we believed that it's a myth that there has to be an irreparable split between spirituality and productivity at work. We have always found that the myth disappeared, or never came up, if we used a language that addressed both dimensions – and if the tools and techniques we proposed clearly enhanced both. It also helped that we base our action proposals not on theory, but on research and practical lessons from the trenches. Our research team has interviewed over 5000 people in large and small organisations worldwide.

### Your Soul at Work

We're not theologians but we highly respect those who are. We think people should work with their spiritual advisors to define "soul" in their own specific terms. Instead, we focus on a specialised definition that most people, no matter what their unique spiritual beliefs, can apply practically to their work lives.

For career purposes your soul is the inner you the centre of your being. It's that part of you that knows your deepest needs and aspirations and that's the source of your energy. If you leave your soul at home and have no time for it later, your job won't be very fulfilling.

If we define the issues in operational terms and look at what people really want in their work, the problem becomes a little less daunting. We've discovered most people's souls want four things at work. They want to :

Love their jobs and find jobs they love.

Succeed in their work.

Navigate successfully through predictable life stage transitions.

Tie their work to a higher life purpose that has personal meaning for them.

We've learned that, to be effective, we have to address all four in our career and life planning process. To do this at a practical level we've developed a "taking charge" process that leads people through an integrated roadmap of discovery and decision. This process includes:

Giving people a proven step-by-step roadmap for finding and marketing themselves into jobs they really like.

Teaching them how to identify and develop the most important non-technical behaviours research shows, distinguish those who succeed from those who don't, no matter what their career specialties. Providing criteria and a process for updating career and life plans through each life stage.

Showing them how current psychological research and the wisdom of history's spiritual leaders can be applied to tie work into a higher life purpose that energizes and adds meaning to everything we do. Providing a "Career and Life Workbook" with exercises and tools that can be used individually or in group learning experiences to help people implement each step in the roadmap.

## The Other End of the Microscope

While our "taking charge" roadmap was designed for individuals on a career quest, it's also important to turn the microscope around and take a look at our own profession in light of what we've learnt. In addition to providing practical steps and tools to help people keep their career's on track, we've also found we have to address a number of myths that create false barriers to progress. These myths hinder people from seeking rewarding work. Most of us wouldn't accept these myths if we really thought them through. But we don't take time and, often unconsciously, HR professionals and the people they counsel behave as if they were true. A few of the most common myths we encounter include:

## Myth: Someone else has the answer for my life

In the context work, this translates as, "If I focus on my company's or my boss' expectations somehow this will eventually bring me satisfaction". Buying into this myth, even at the unconscious level, prevents people from defining their own self-expectations and needs. People who abdicate responsibility for their own career growth are unlikely to find satisfaction. If they fail to get in touch with their own inner needs and march solely to their company's drum decrease, eventually their energy and productivity will decrease.

## Myth : Meeting my company's success criteria will fulfil my needs

How may smart people seem to ultimately base their self-esteem on-or-measure their personal worth by the same criteria their organisation uses to measure its success (e.g., beating the competition into the ground at my cost)?

Or

Other criterion that may be implicit in one's corporate or personal culture (e.g., fast track movement up the organisational hierarchy is the ultimate value, you can never work enough hours)?

If talented people derail themselves by not getting in touch with their own more personal success criteria, again energy, motivation and ultimately even productivity will flag.

## Myth: As the organisation improves, my needs will be met

Even when there is no conflict in values, people should not rely on any managerial hierarchy or human resource organiazation to meet their needs. Even the best-intentioned organisational leaders rarely have good career counselling skills and generally can only offer advice based on their own personal career paths and aspirations. It's much more productive to have a process in place that helps people define their individual, possible very different aspirations.

When held by an individual, these myths are often self-defeating. When promulgated by an organisation, however, they are Orwellian. Ask yourself, does your company really live by its values in its relations with employees? In the final analysis, will you feel that your work did more to liberate people's spirits and help them grow in jobs where their energies flow naturally or to manipulate them into adapting to the corporate agenda? Which approach do you think will have the highest ultimate pay-off for the organisation?

What is called for is a paradigm shift in many HR organisation's purpose the objective of aligning the workforce with business goals. HR typically expresses a philosophy of fostering employee satisfaction and fulfilment. However, the tools and processes used have often worked from the outside in: The company needs certain qualifications, competencies, or skills, and therefore, is going to hire, train, or incentive people to those standards. Often, this unintentionally results in making the square peg fit the round hole. Most everyone would agree that is not ultimately productive.

## The Whole Person

We've found that challenging people to express and seek what they truly want in a career is critical. When we first started teaching people to march to their own drums, independent of their employer, many saw that as a risky tactic. In practice, however, individuals who seek their own fulfilling path tend to contribute more to the organisation and are less likely to leave.

Similarly, the application of a clear process and practical performance development tools not only has enormous positive impact on individual careers but also improves the bottom line. Individuals get significantly increased satisfaction because the tools help them become more successful in whatever career paths they choose and their success makes them more productive for their employer.

It is important to note that we are not talking about spiritual or value-based programs introduced by management primarily to move employees in directions the organisation wants them to go.

Stephen C. Schoonover M.D. is the president of a management consulting firm specializing in competency-based performance development and career planning systems. Nicholas W. Weiler is an independent consultant who spent over 18 years developing and implementing career and leadership programs at GE's corporate headquarters. Steve and Nick have encompassed their collaborative ad independent experiences around career and performance development in their recently published book, Your Soul at Work – Five Steps to a More Fulfilling Career and Life.

Based on our experiences, we recently wrote a book called "Your Soul At Work – Five Steps to a More fulfilling Career and Life." It outlines our "Taking Charge" process and contains a step-by-step Career and Life Workbook with exercises, tools and checklists we've described. Additional information and sample excerpts/materials can be found on the book web site at http://www.yourslulatwork.com or you can order the book directly at http://www.amazon.com.

## Brief Reflections for HR leaders

Our book contains a number of "brief reflections" to help individuals warm up to the large project of later completing the Career and Life Workbook exercises. Here we suggest a few different reflections for HR leaders to stimulate self-examination around the issues we present.

- Do you feel your organisation can and should play a role in helping people align work with their inner aspirations and values? Do you have what you consider an effective program in place to do this?
- Would you find resistance in your company, either from management or from employees, to the idea of an "inner-needs" oriented career and performance development program ? Do you agree there is pay-off for the company as well as the individuals in such a program?
- Do you feel a universalized lexicon using such phrases as "individual life values", "inner aspirations", "personal success criteria", "large purpose" and "life stage transitions" can be helpful in bridging the gap between corporate culture and the spiritual needs of employees.
- Does your organisation use research-based competency models that define what specific non-technical behaviours distinguish successful from less successful performers in key functions ? Are they available on line for easy use in self and $360^0$ degree assessments ?
- Have these models been incorporated into practical tools that can be used as the basis for an integrated performance development program? Are they being used for such things as selection, self-assessment, performance appraisal, development of training objectives, and career/life planning?
- What behaviours tools have you in place to define and teach these behaviours to others?
- Are your HR programms focused too much on the "outward" needs of the organisation and not enough on the "inner" needs of individual employees ? Are you doing enough to liberate people's spirits and help them grow in jobs where their energies flow naturally?

The best available method for overcoming potential vulnerabilities in the interview process and for identifying specific behavioural criteria for excellence is a behaviourally anchored evaluation. In order to perform this type of interview, you should use a model that describes objective criteria of success for a specific job role (e.g., a success template). In addition, an excellent hiring intervention should focus on : traits and leadership skills that are critical for top performance in a specific job category.

The method of hiring and selection helps interviewers perform the most significant part of the screening by using objective scoring procedure. The final selection process relies on a scoring protocol (using specific evidence of competent behaviour generated during the interview) and subsequent dialogue of competency-based hiring and selection.

Succession planning is one of the most critical endeavours an organisation undertakes. In our experience, different companies apply succession planning for a variety of purposes. Most organisations, however, tend to focus on many of the goals simultaneously. No matter what the purposes, succession planning criteria and processes should stem from the clarification of key principles to guide the initiative.

At a more practical level, we have found that the criteria applied in succession planning should be multidimensional, simple to assess, and linked to "future" success.

This article illustrates how succession planning should be a purposeful initiative that focuses on developing critical leadership talent and how best in class companies structure and communicate clear principles, apply specific criteria, and implement a structured sustained process.

In the past, power and authority in organisations were perceived as a zero-sum game. For this reason, managers seldom empowered subordinates through delegation or communication of often-vital information. But for companies to survive in today's competitive global market, the power to make decisions must move as far down in the organisation as possible. This change from an authoritarian, hierarchical organisation to a delayered, downsized, participatory organisation has created a significant shift in the competencies required for excellent performance.

Although those who were best at various jobs always needed both leadership and management skills, today's employee requires much sophisticated leadership skills, particularly influence. The power equation has shifted from primarily formal, structural power, to informal, indirect, relationship-based methods for getting things done. This article looks at the dynamic intricacies of moving power down through the organisation.

**Return to top**

## Applying Technology to Maximize Human Assets

The past two decades have been a time of truly radical change. But, the next twenty years will encompass even more. In a recent edition of Business Week, the prospects for the future were described in the following way:

"All the ingredients are in place for a surge of innovation that could rival any in history. Over the next decade or so, the New Economy so far propelled mainly by information technology may turn out to be only the initial stage of a much broader flowering of technological, business, and financial creativity."

Business Week/August 31, 1998.

In a range of studies conducted globally with business leaders during the past ten years, we have seen the emergence of a consistent set of challenges stemming from technology-driven change.

These represent a true revolution in the dynamics of work driven by breakthroughs in information technology. In today's world, information is more freely shared across all global boundaries in ways that create new forms of value, new ways of working and new stresses and skill requirement for people. The impact on work prentices and productivity has been substantial.

# Session – 4

## Concept of Career Planning, HR Career Management and Career Stages

### Concept of Career Planning

While most people think the term career means "advancement" in an organisation, a broader view of career defines it as "individually perceived sequence of attitudes and behaviours associated with work-related activities and experiences over the Span of a person's life. In other words, the term career has an internal focus and refers to the way an individual views his or her career and it has an external or objective focus and refers to the actual series of job positions held by the individual; how individuals plan and implement their own career goals (career planning) and how organisations design and implement their career development programmes (career management). These processes are illustrated in Fig. As noted, career planning is a deliberate attempt by an individual to become more aware of his or her own skills, interests, values, opportunities, constraints, choices, and consequences. It involves identifying career–related goals and establishing plans for achieving those goals. Career management is considered to be an organisational process that involves preparing, implementing, and monitoring career plans undertaken by an individual alone or within the organisation's career systems.

A career development system is a formal, organised, planned effort to achieve a balance between individual career needs and organisation has certain needs to effectively utilize their personal skills. It is a mechanism for meeting the present and future human resource needs of the organisation. A career planning system co-ordinated with HR planning will foster a well–integrated HRM system. For instance, Coca-Cola implemented a career development system so it would be better able to develop its own employees to meet future staffing needs and to be able to promote employees internally.

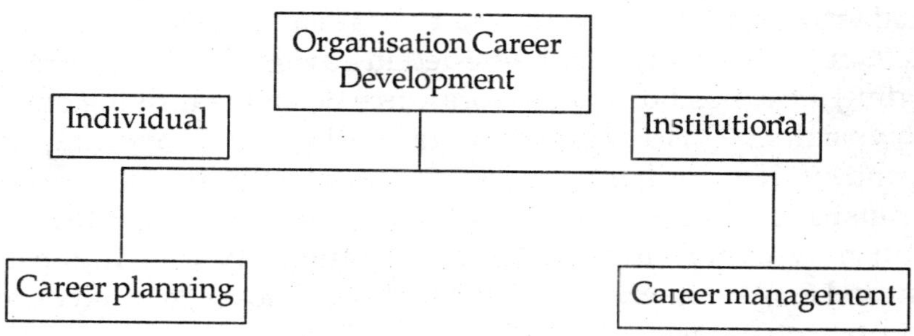

| Subprocesses: | Subprocesses: |
|---|---|
| • Occupational choice | • Recruitment and Selection |
| • Organisational choice | • Human Resource Allocation |
| • Choice of job assignment | • Appraisal and Evaluation |
| • Career sub-development | • Training and Development |

## Career

The sequence of person's work related activities and between and associated altitudes, values, and aspirations over the Span of one's life.

## Organisational Career Development

The outcomes emancipating from the interaction of individual career planning and institutional career management processes.

## Career Planning

A deliberate process for

1. becoming aware of self, opportunities, constraints, choices, and consequences.
2. identifying career related goals; and
3. programming of work, education, and related developmental experiences to provide the direction, timing, and sequence of steps to attain a specific career goal.

## Career Management

An ongoing process of preparing, implementing, and monitoring career plans undertaken by the individual alone or in concept with the organisation's career system. Basically, career development practices, are designed to enhance the career satisfaction of employees and to improve organisational effectiveness. It may, however be difficult to completely integrate individual and organisational career efforts because the rate at which an individual grows and develops may not at par an organisation's needs : For example, many of them in the workforce are interested in advancing in their present positions. Yet they are finding those positions to be morescarce given the thriving of management jobs through downsizing. This chapter in organisations by examining the interaction of individual and understanding of career processes of particular value is the role that managers must focus on a dynamic interaction of the individual will benefit. The organisation may experience increased productivity and highest organisational commitment and long range effectiveness, and the employee may have greater satisfaction, security, and personal development.

**Relationship Between Career Planning and HR Planning:**

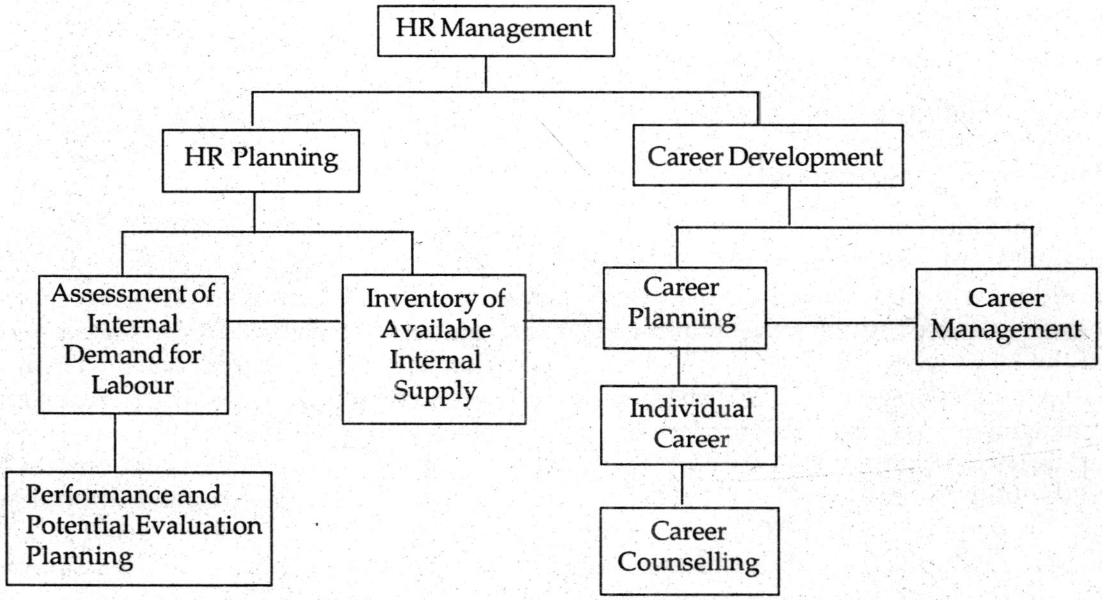


## Benefits of Career Management Planning

The benefits of career management planning includes: Attract, Grow and Retain Talent:

Career Management is a portfolio of services that enhances the ability of an organisation to attract, grow and retain talented and committed employees. These custom-designed programmes promote increasing performance by utilising a blend of the appropriate assessments, one-on-one interaction, online and targeted competency tools, competences based performance systems and succession planning.

## An Investment in Talent and the Organisation

The programme is to be designed for companies that want to grow their own talent and develop leadership. It is an investment the future of the organisation. Career management can also be used to move employees into more satisfying work and therefore generate more productive employees.

## Enhance Succession Planning

This is to enhance term functionality, retain potential leadership talent, and plan for succession.

Skills and issues addressed by Career Management Programme to encompass a wide range of topics, including but not limited to:

- Employee and Culture Surveys.
- Assessments.
- Competency modelling.
- High turnover.

## HR Career Management

Personnel activities like screening, training, and appraising serve two basic roles in organisations. First, their traditional role has been to staff the organisation – to fill its positions with employees who have the requisite interests, abilities, and skills. Increasingly, however, these activities are taking on a second role of ensuring that the long-run interests of the employees are protected by the organisation and that, in particular, the employee is encouraged to grow and realize his or her full potential. Referring to staffing or personnel management as human resource management reflects this second role. A basic assumption underlying this role is that the employer has an obligation to utilize its employees' abilities to the fullest and to give all employees chance to grow and to realize their full potential and to develop successful careers. One way this trend is manifesting itself is in the increased emphasis many firms are placing today on career planning and development.

Activities like personnel planning, screening, and training play a big role in the career development process. Personnel planning, for example, can be used not just to forecast open jobs but to identify potential internal candidates and the training they would need to fill these jobs. Similarly, an organisation can use its periodic employee appraisals not just for salary decisions but for identifying the development needs of individual employees and ensuring that these needs are met. All the staffing activities, in other words, can be used to satisfy the needs of both the organisation and the individual in such a way that they both gain : the organisation from improved performance from a more committed work force and the employee from a richer, more challenging career[2].

For example, performance appraisal's traditional focus has been on rating for the purpose of promotion, discipline, and rewards; using it to provide a career development focus means including development plans and individual goal setting. Similarly, HR planning traditionally focuses on job analysis and satisfying the organisation's staffing and adding a career development focus means including information about individual career interests and preferences as well as career path options.

Before proceeding, it would be useful to define some of the terms we'll be using throughout this chapter. A career is a series of work-related positions, paid or unpaid, that help a person grow in job skills, success, and fulfilment. Career development is the lifelong series of activities (such as workshops) that contributes to a person's career exploration, establishment, success, and fulfilment. Career planning is the deliberate process through which someone becomes aware of personal skills, interests, knowledge, motivations, and other characteristics; acquires information about opportunities and choices; identifies career-related goals; and establishes action plans to attain specific goals.

## Career Management Responsibilities of the Manager and the Employer

### Career Management Guidelines

Along with the employee, the person's manager and employer both have career management responsibilities. Guidelines here include.

**Avoid Reality Shock:** Perhaps at no other stage in the person's career is it more important for the employer to be career development-oriented than at the initial entry stage, when the person is recruited, hired, and given a first assignment and boss. For the employee this is a period during which he or she has to develop a sense of confidence, learn to get along with the first boss and with co-workers, learn how to accept responsibility, and, most important, gain an insight into his or her talents, needs, and values as they relate to initial career goals. For the new employee, in other words, this is (or should be a period of reality testing during which his or her initial hopes and goals first confront the reality of organisational life and of the person's talents and needs.

For many first-time workers, this turns out to be a disastrous period, one in which their often naïve expectations first confront the realities of organisational life. The young MBA or CPA, for example, might come to the first job seeking a challenging, exciting assignment in which to apply the new techniques learned in school and to prove his or her abilities and gain a promotion. In reality, however, the trainee is often turned off by being relegated to an unimportant low-risk job where he or she "can't cause any trouble while being tried out"; or by the harsh realities of interdepartmental conflict and politicking; or by a boss who is neither rewarded for nor trained in the unique mentoring tasks needed to properly supervise new employees. **Reality shock** refers to the results of a period that may occur at the initial career entry when the new employee's high job expectations confront the reality of a boring, unchallenging job.

**Provide Challenging Initial Jobs:** Most experts agree that one of the most important things you can do is provide new employees with challenging first jobs. In one study of young managers at AT&T, for example, the researchers found that the more challenging a person's job was in his or her first year with the company the more effective and successful the person was, even five or six years later. Based on his own research, Hall contends that challenging initial jobs provide "one of the most powerful yet uncomplicated means of aiding the career development of new employees." In most organisations, however, providing such jobs seems more the exception than the rule. In one survey of research and development organisations, for example, only 1 of 22 companies had a formal policy of giving challenging initial jobs, provide "one of the most powerful yet uncomplicated means of aiding the career development of new employees. This imbalance, as one expert has pointed out, is an example of "glaring mismanagement" when one considers the effort and money invested in recruiting, hiring, and training new employees.

Some firms "front-load" the job challenge by giving new employees considerable responsibility. At Saturn and Toyota even assembly workers are assigned at once to self-managing teams of highly skilled and motivated colleagues where they must quickly learn to be productive team members. At Goldman Sachs, young professionals are expected to contribute at once and immediately find themselves on teams involved in challenging projects. As one manger there said,

Even with fairly new employees, the partner in change will usually not be the first one to speak when a project team meets with a client often the newest member will; you take the responsibility and you're supported by the team. That's what attracts people to Goldman Sachs, the ability to make decisions early.

The merchandising manager trainee position at JC Penney's (their entry-level management position) is another good example. A trainee almost straight out of college might be assigned the job of supervising the jeans section in the menswear department. Fresh from college, in other words, he or she would be responsible (under the guidance of his or her manager) for the section's display, inventory management, customer service, and staffing. As one Penney's manager put it, "From my first day as a merchandising manager trainee-straight out of college I was running the 'store within a store'. JC Penney gives you guidance as you go along but won't hold your hand. You're kind of 'bracketed' in what you can do but you're basically running your own little shop.

The new merchandise manager trainees remain as trainees for about 12 months. During this time they are responsible for training themselves. To facilitate this process, they receive various training manuals, including "The Role of a First-Level Supervisor". This describes the trainee's responsibilities for activities including customer service, sales, gross profit, merchandising, visual merchandising, sales promotion, staffing, and time management. Each new trainee is also assigned a mentor – usually a merchandising manager or senior merchandising manager. The mentor provides guidance and weekly appraisals. The training program, however, is self-administered : Trainees are responsible for teaching themselves the merchandising job's details.

Trainees are appraised weekly by their mentors according to a schedule. At the end of week two, for instance, their personal selling skills are appraised. In week three, their visual merchandising skills are evaluated, in week four, their sales leadership, and so on.

At the end of eight weeks, the trainees get an extensive appraisal. At this point trainees meet with three people – the store manager, merchandising manager, and senior merchandising manager – and has what one manager referred to as a "very frank, outgoing discussion." A typical comment might be. "You're going to have to be much more assertive if you want a successful career here." They "lay it on the table" as one executive said, telling the trainees where they stand, what progress is being made, and what development is required.

After six months, trainees usually move into new assignments, where they assume more responsibility, often running large departments. At the end of a year they're generally ready for promotion to merchandising manager.

# Managing Promotion and Transfers

## Making Promotion Decisions

Employers must decide on what basis to promote employees, and the way these decisions are made will affect the employees' motivation, performance, and commitment.

### Decision 1: Is Seniority or Competence the Rule?

Probably the most important decision is whether promotion will be based on seniority or competence, or some combination of the two. From the point of view of motivation, promotion based on competence is best. However, your ability to use competence as a sole criterion depends on several things, most notably whether or not your firm is unionized or governed by civil service requirements. Union agreements often contain a clause that emphasizes seniority in promotions, such as: "In the advancement of employees to higher paid jobs when ability, merit, and capacity are equal, employees with the highest seniority will be given preference." Although this might seem to leave the door open for giving a person with less seniority but slightly better ability the inside track for a job, labour arbitrators have generally held that when clauses such as these are binding only substantial differences in abilities can be taken into account. In one case, for example, the arbitrator ruled that seniority should be disregarded only when an employees with less seniority stood "head and shoulders" above the employees with greater seniority. Similarly, many organisations in the public sector are governed by civil service regulations that emphasize seniority rather than competence as the basis for promotion.

### Decision 2: How Is Competence Measured?

If promotion is to be based on competence, how will competence be defined and measured ? Defining and measuring past performance is a fairly straightforward matter. The job is defined, standards are set, and one or more appraisal tools are used to record the employee's performance, but promotion also requires predicting the person's potential; thus, you must have a valid procedure for predicting a candidate's future performance.

Many employers simply use prior performance as a guide and extrapolate, or assume, that based on the person's prior performance he or she will perform well on the new job. This is the simplest procedure to use.

On the other hand, some employers use tests to evaluate promotable employees and to identify those employees with executive potential. Others use assessment centres to assess management potential.

### Decision 3: Is the Process Formal or Informal?

Next and particularly if you decide to promote based on competence, you have to decide whether the promotion process will be formal or informal. Many employers still depend on an informal system. Here the availability and requirements of open positions are kept secret. Promotion decisions are then made by key managers from among employees they know personally and also from among those who, for one reason or another, have impressed them. The problem is that when you don't make employees aware of the jobs that are available, the criteria for promotion, and how promotion decisions are made, the link between performance and promotion is cut. The effectiveness of promotion as a reward is thereby diminished.

Many employers therefore do establish formal, published promotion policies and procedures. Here employees are generally provided with a formal promotion policy statement that describes the criteria by which promotions are awarded. Formal systems often include a job-posting policy. This states that open positions and their requirements will be posted and circulated to all employees. As explained in Chapter 4, many employers also compile detailed information about the qualifications of employees, while others use work force replacement charts. Computerized information systems can be especially useful for maintaining qualification inventories on hundred or thousands of employees. The net effect of such actions is twofold: (1) An employer ensures that all qualified employees are considered for openings; and (2) promotion becomes more closely linked with performance in the minds of employees.

### Decision 4: Vertical, Horizontal or Other?

Finally, employers are increasingly having to deal with the question of how to "promote" employees in an era in which higher-level jobs are less available. On the one hand, lay offs due to mergers eliminated many of the higher-management positions that employees might normally aspire to, as has the flattening of most organisation charts. On the other hand, worker empowerment and a related emphasis on technicians, and first-line workers who aspire to higher-level positions but find their upward movement blocked by a dearth of openings

Several options are available here. Some firms, such as the exploration division of British Petroleum, have created two parallel career paths, one for managers and another for "individual contributors" such as engineers. In that way individual contributors, such as highly accomplished engineers, can move up to non-supervisory but still more senior positions such as "senior engineer". These jobs have most of the perks and financial rewards attached to management-track positions at that level.

Another option is to provide career development opportunities for an individual, either by moving the person horizontally or even within the same position he or she currently holds. Horizontally, for instance, a production employee might be moved to HR in order to give him or her an opportunity to develop new skills and test and challenge aptitudes. And, in a sense, "promotions" are possible even leaving the person in the same job: for example, some job enrichment is usually possible, and the firm can provide training that increases the opportunity for assuming increased responsibility.

The accompanying Diversity Counts feature addresses the question of why women sometimes fail to get to the top of the corporate ladder when it comes to promotions.

## Handling Transfer

### Reasons for Transfers

A transfer is a move from one job to another, usually with no change in salary or grade. Employees may seek transfers for personal enrichment, for more interesting jobs, for greater convenience - better hours, location of work, and so – or for jobs for greater comfort.

***

# 11 Innovation Management

## Innovation

Innovation is the initiation or adoption of new procducts, services, processes, procedures, or ideas by an organisation: The capacity to innovate is central to the ability of an organisation to adapt to changes in its environment. Many argue that its most serious shortcoming in the fact of increased global comptition is lack of innovation. The reasons given for an inability to generate sufficent innovation include:

(1) An overemplasis on short–term profits.

(2) An unwillingness to the high cost of capital.

(3) Government regulations.

(4) Resistance to change.

(5) Rigid organisation design and procedures that stifle new ideas, and

(6) Reward structures that control issues involve management philosophy, practices, and culture.

## Managing Creativity and Innovation

In today's world of liberalisation, privatisation and globalisation (LPG), it is more important than ever to be creative and innovative. That means thinking in seeing the world. Many management writers define creativity as the generation of a new idea and innovation as the translation of a new idea into a new company, a new product, a new service, a new process, or a new method of production. Economic historian Joseph Scheempeter viewed innovation as the source of success in the market economy, a view that is re-inforced by today's changing and competitive environment ment. The organisation that is not creative and innovative may not survive. Thus, managers at more and more organisations are looking for way to encourage and foster creativity and innovation on both the individual and the organisational level.

## Individual Creativity

Individuals differ in their ability to be creative. If asked to suggest possible uses for automobile tyres, noncreative people might say "buoys" and "tree swings", creative people might suggest such things as "eyeglass frames for an elephant" or "halos for big robots". Creative people also tend to be more flexible than noncreative people. They are able and willing to shift from one approach to another when tacking a problem. They prefer complexity to simplicity and tend to be more independent than less creative people sticking to their guns stubbornly when their ideas are challenged. Creative people also question authority quite readily and are apt to disobey orders that make no sense to them. For this reason, they may be somewhat difficult to manage in most organisations. Motivated more by an interesting problem than by material reward, they will work long and hard on something that intrigues them.

## Organisational Creativity and Innovation

Just as individuals differ in their ability to transfer their creative talents into results, organisations differ in their ability to translate the talents of their members into new products or services. To enable their organistions to use creativity most effectively, managers need to be aware of this process of innovation in organisations and to take steps to encourage this process. The creative process in organisations involves three steps:

- Idea generation.
- Problem solving or idea development, and
- Implementation.

### Generation of Ideas

The generation of ideas in an organisation depends (most) and foremost on the flow of people and information between the firm and its environment. For example, the vast majority of technological innovations have been made in-response to conditions in the market place. If organisation managers are unaware that there is potential demand for a new product or that there is disstisfaction with already existing products, they are not likely to seek innovations.

Outside consultants and experts are important source of information for managers, because they are frequently aware of new products, processes, or service developments in their field. New employees may have knowledge of alternative approaches or technologies used by suppliers and competitors. Among the organisation's regular members, those who are constantly exposed to information (out), their immediate work setting are valuable sources of new ideas. These people, called "technological gatekeepers" and they can play a particularly important role in stimulating creativity and innovation in research and development labs.

According to Rosabeth Moss Kanter, the generation of ideas is more likely to promote innovation when those ideas issue from the grassroots level of the organisation. She argues that empowering people on the lower levels of organisations to initiate new ideas within the context of a supportive environment is a valuable means of implementing successful innovations. In addition, although many new ideas challenge a company's cultural traditions, such innovative companies as Hewlett–Packard and Toyota nevertheless routinely encourage their employees to generate new ideas.

## Idea Development

Unlike idea generation, which is greatly stimulated by external contacts, idea development is dependent on the organisational culture and processes within the organisation. Organisational characterstics, values and processes can support or inhibit the development and use of creative ideas. The organisational structure also play an important role. Rigid organisational structure that inhibit communication between departments will often keep potentially helpful people from even knowing that a problem exists. By creating barriers to communication, rigidly structured organisations may also prevent problem solutions from reaching managers who need them. Management information systems (MIS), decision support systems (DSS), and expert systems store and retrieve generated ideas and aid managers in idea development. Recent advances in the networking of such systems are especially helpful for integrative problem solving.

## Implementation

The implementation stage of the creative process in organisations consists of those steps that bring a solution or invention to the marketplace. For manufactured goods, these steps include engineering, manufacturing, test marketing and promotion. While a high rate of innovation often short-term profitability, it is crucial for long-term growth. For example, the watch industry, which operates, by traditional practices, and old fastioned individual craftsmanship, has been in decline since the mid 1970s, when more innovative competitors introduced new products such as digital watches into the market. When Swiss watchmakers recently introduced new products such as popular, inexpensive Swiss wristwatch, they were able to regain part of the market that had appeared to be lost to them.

For innovation to be successful, a high degree of integration is required among the various units of the organisation. Technical specialists, responsible for the engineering side of a new product, must work with administrative and financial specialists responsible for keeping the cost of innovation within practical limits. Production managers, helping to refine the specifications of the new product, must work with marketing, advertising, and promoting it. Proper integration of all these groups is necessary for a quality innovation to be produced on time, on budget and for a viable market. Managers at organisations that are time integrating such activities in contrast, frequent and informal communication across an organisation has been shown to have positive effects on innovation. For this reason, task forces and matrix-type organisational structures, which encourage inter-departmental communication and integration, are particularly suited for generating, developing and implementing creative ideas and approaches.

## Establishing Climate for Organisational Creativity and Innovation

As we have seen above, creativity is best nurtured in a permissive climate, one that encourages the exploration of new ideas and new way of doing things. Many managers find it difficult to accept such a climate. They may be uncomfortable with a climate. They may be uncomfortable with a continuing process of change, which is the essential accompaniment of creativity. They may also be concerned that a permissive atmosphere encourages the break down of discipline of cost centres.

## Kanter's "Ten Rules for Stifling Innovation"

1. Regard any new idea from below with suspicion – because it's new and because it's from below:
2. Insist that people who need your approval to first go through several other levels of management to get their signatures.
3. Ask departments or individuals to challenge and criticize each other's proposals. (That saves you the job of deciding; you just pick the survivor.)
4. Express yor criticisms freely, and withhold your praise. (That keeps people on their toes.) Let them know they can be fired at any time.
5. Treat identification of problems as signs of failure, to discourage people from letting you know when something in their area isn't working.
6. Control everything careefully. Make sure people count anything that can be counted, frequently.
7. Make decisions to reorganise or change policies in secret, and spring them on people unexpectedly. (That also keeps people on their toes.)
8. Make sure that requests for information are fully justified, and make sure that it is not given out to managers freely. (You don't want data to fall into the wrong hands.)
9. Assign to lower-level managers, in the name of delegation and participation, responsibility for figuring out how to cut back, lay-off, move people around, or otherwise implement threatening decisions you have made. And get them to do it quickly.
10. And above all, never forget that you, the higher-ups, already know everything important about this business.

## Some Prescriptions for Fostering Organisational Creativity

### 1. Develop an acceptance of change

Organisation members must believe that change will benefit them and the organisation. This belief is more likely to arise if members participate with their managers in making decisions and if issues like job security are carefully handled when changes are planned and implemented (see our discussion on overcoming) resistance to change earlier in this chapter).

### 2. Encourage new ideas

Organisation managers, from the top to the lowest – level supervisors, must make it clear in word and deed that they welcome new approaches. To encourage creativity, managers must be willing to listen to subordinates' suggestions and to implement promising ones or convey them to higher–level managers.

### 3. Permit more interaction

A permissive, creative climate, is fostered by giving individuals the opportunity to interact with members of their own and other work groups. Such interaction encourages the exchanges of useful information, the free flow of ideas and fresh perspectives on problems.

### 4. Tolerate failure

Many new ideas prove impractical or useless. Effective managers accept and allow for the fact that time and resources will be invested in experimenting with new ideas that do not work out.

### 5. Provide clear objectives and the freedom to achieve them

Organisation members must have a purpose and direction for their creative behaviour.

### 6. Offer recognition

Creative individuals are motivated to work hard on tasks that interest them. But, like all individuals, they enjoy being rewarded for a task well done. By offering recognition in such tangible forms as bonus and salary increases, managers demonstrate that creative behaviour is valued in their organisations.

## Contemporary Change Issues for Today's Managers

Talk to managers. Read the popular business periodicals. What you'll find is that two issues have risen above the rest current change topics. They are stimulating organisational innovation and creating a learning organisation.

## Innovation

The relevant question is: How can organisation become innovative? The standard toward which many organisations strive is that achieved by the 3M Co. It has developed a reputation for being able to stimulate innovation over a long period of time. 3M has a stated objective that 30 per cent of its sales are to come from products less than four years old. In 1995, the figure was 32 per cent. In one recent year alone, 3M launched more than 200 new products.

What's the secret of 3M's success? What can other organisations do to clone 3M's track record for innovation? While there is no guaranteed formula, certain characteristics surface again and again when researchers study innovative organisations. We've grouped them into structural, cultural, and human resource categories. Our message to change agents is that they should consider introducing these characteristics into their organisation if they want to create an innovative climate. Before we look at these characteristics, however, let's clarify what we mean by innovation.

### Definition

Innovation is more specialised kind of change. Innovation is a new idea applied to initiating or improving a product, process, or service. So all innovations involve change, but not all changes necessarily involve new ideas or lead to significant improvements. Innovations in organisations can range from small incremental improvements, such as RJR Nabisco's extension of the Ore product line to include double stuffs and chocolate – covered Oreos, up to radical break-thoughts, such as the amazon.com bookstore on the Internet. Keep in mind that whey our example are mostly of product innovations, the concept of innovation also encompasses new production process technologies, new structures or administrative systems, and new plans or programme pertaining to organisational members.

### Sources of Innovation

Structural variable have been the most studied potential source of innovation. A comprehensive review of the structure-innovation relationship leads to the following conclusions. First, organic structures positively influence innovation. Because they're lower in vertical differentiation, formalisation, and centralisation, organic organisation facilitate the flexibility, adaptation, and cross-fertilisation that make the adoption of innovations easier. Second, long tenure in management is associated with innovation. Managerial tenure apparently provides legitimacy and knowledge of how to accomplish tasks and obtain desired outcomes. Third, innovation is nurtured where there are slack resources. Having an abundance of resources allows an organisation to afford to purchase innovations, bear the cost of instituting innovations, and absorb failures. Finally, inter unit communication is high in innovative organisations. These organisations are high users of committees, task forces, cross-functional teams, and other mechanisms that facilitate interaction across departmental lines.

## Innovative organisations tend to have similar cultures

They encourage experimentation. They reward both successes and failure. They celebrate mistakes. At Hewlett-Packard, for instance, CEO Lewis Platt has successfully built a corporate culture that supports people who try something that doesn't work out. Platt, himself, protects people who stick their neck out, fearful that to do otherwise would stifle the risk–taking culture he encourages among his managers. Unfortunately, in too many organisations, people are rewarded for the absence of failures rather then for the presence of successes. Such cultures extinguish risk-taking and innovation. People will suggest and try new ideas only where they feel such behaviours exact no penalties. Managers in innovative organisations recognize that failures are a natural by-product of venturing into the unknown. When Babe Ruth set his record for home runs in one season, he also led the league in strikeouts. And he is remembered for the former, not the latter!

Within the human resources category, we find that innovative organisations actively promote the training and development of their members so that they keep current, offer high job security so employees don't fear getting fired for making mistakes, and encourage individuals to become champions of change. Once a new idea is developed, idea champions actively and enthusiastically promote the idea, build support, overcome resistance, and ensure that the innovation is implemented. The evidence indicates that champions have common personality characteristics : extremely high self-confidence, persistence, energy, and a tendency to take risks. Idea champions also display characteristics associated with transformational leadership. They inspire and energize others with their vision of the potential of an innovation and through their strong personal conviction in their mission. They are also good at gaining the commitment of others to support their mission. In addition, idea champions have jobs that provide considerable decisionmaking discretion. This autonomy helps them introduce and implement innovations in organisations.

Given the status of 3M as a premier product innovator, we would expect it to have most of the properties we've identified. And it does. The company is so highly decentralised that it has many of the characteristics of small, organic organisations. The structure relies on extensive redundancy. For instance, every division, department, and product group has its own labs – many of which are deliberately duplicating the work of others. And consistent with the need for cross-fertilisation of ideas, the company holds internal trade shows where divisions will show their technologies to employees of other divisions. All of 3M's scientists and managers are challenged to "keep current".

Idea champions are created and encouraged by allowing scientists and engineers to spend up to 15 percent of their time on projects of their own choosing. And if a 3M scientist comes up with a new idea but finds resistance within the researcher's own division, he or she can apply for a $50,000 grant from an internal venture-capital fund to further develop the idea. The company encourages its employees to take risks and rewards the failures as well as the successes. And 3M's management has the patience to see ideas through to successful products. It invests nearly 7 percent of company sales revenue (more than $1 billion a year) in research and development, yet management tells its R&D people that not everything is going to work. It also fosters a culture that allows people to defy their supervisors. For instance, each new employee and his or her supervisor take a one-day orientation class where, among other things, stories are told of victories won by employees despite the opposition of their boss. Finally, while 3 M incurred its first lay-offs in decade during 1995, the company still continues to be a model of corporate stability. The average tenure for company officers is 31 years and the overall annual turnover rate within the company is a minuscule 3 per cent.

***

# 12 Employee Relations and Business Strategies

Employee Relationship Management (ERM) is a cutting–edge critical business process that enables your employees to do their job too better. It is a process used to better manage your relationship with, and the working practices and effectiveness of your workforce. Through integrated internal systems, ERM allows your employees to have the necessary information at their finger tips to meet your customer's needs, while at the same time working toward corporate objectives and meeting personal goals. In the same way, it appears, ERM bleeds into product lifecycle management (PLM). The value in people making and designing products to have more access to customer today. The good news is, if there is CRM, they can leverage and in the work environment. But today, identifiable ERM projects appear to be garden variety, aimed at ending the work brain. A small sampling of end users can be considered as various applications put to time and labour management, to check pay-check stubs, and for HR and employee and self-service. HR and people related processes including personal information updating, job change requests, vacation, equipment requisition requests etc. can be a core issue in ERM. ERM allows companies to optimize their business processes based on five principles i.e. -alignment management performance, continual communication, workforce development and straightening access to company resources. The real issues that are being faced by HR professionals today is how it manages the Human Capital Management solutions and how tangible benefits can be achieved in a cost-effective manner, embracing the best of the technology available today to deliver measurable value in a manageable changing environment.

It is likely that almost every aspect of change associated with the business strategy will have employee-relations implications. For example, mergers and acquisitions. Some idea of the scope of employee relation issues can perhaps be grasped from an analysis of the 'Head of Agreement' that can be reached with the trade unions of the organisations. Suppose the corporate Head and Head of Employee Relations, faced with the challenge of managing the employee-relation issues in a multi-union organisational environment, noted that HR was an integral part of the merger from the beginning. The Heads of Agreement reflected the wide scope of employee relations and this is a vital indicator for what should and should not be included in the employee-relations and this is an vital indicator for what should and should not be included in the employee-relations plan. The diagnostic plan is as under:

## Sample Heads of Agreement

### 1. Union Recognition

The Management could present the Union with a draft recognition and the required process which will protect the existing policy of recognition could be developed upon the following framework:

(a) **General Business:** The Management and the Union to have a shared commitment to accept the ongoing change in the organisation to face the competitive pressures and achieve organisational goals.

- To satisfy the stakeholders by fulfilling their needs.
- To enforce open communication and spirit of co-operation.
- To treat each recognised Union equally.
- To create positive working environment.
- To encourage employees join one of the recognised Union with participative attitude.
- To discuss the problems with each recognised Union open–heartedly.

(b) **Collective Bargaining:**

- To recognise the agreements.
- To finalise grading and wage fixation.
- To finalise declared holidays.
- To finalise number of Medical leaves with pay.
- To finalise the rate of wartime payment.
- To finalise other regular allowances.
- To finalise Transport facilities.
- To finalise Insurance Contribution Scheme.
- To finalise Equal Opportunities.
- To finalise Job securing.
- To finalise Transfer/Promotion policies.
- To finalise grievance handling machineries.

- To finalise Job Evaluation Methods.
- To finalise Working hours/Shifters etc.

It is the responsibilities of the Management to think over the above issues and consult with the Union regarding the terms and conditions for its implementations as below:

- Business results and upcoming changes.
- Restructuring employee after organisational change.
- Change in work practices.
- Performance Management/Potential Management.
- General Pension Schemes and other allowances.

**Employee – Relations Plan:**

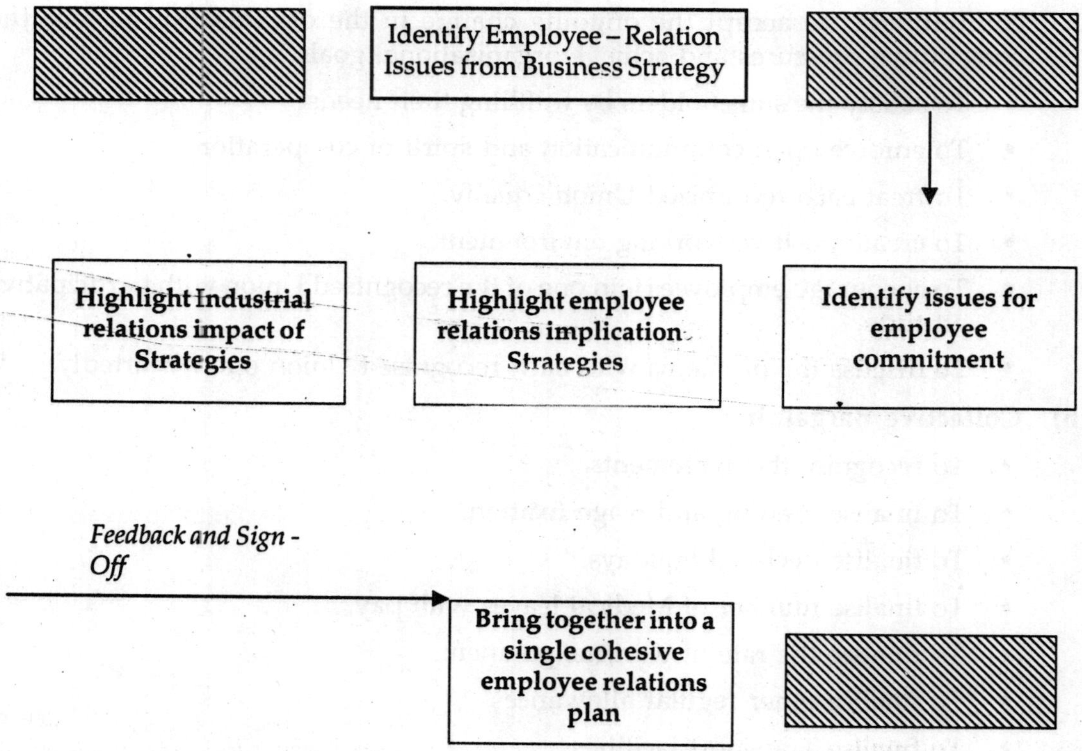


## The Modern Workforce – Understanding Diversity

The main issue is the nature of workforce diversity. It is rather a tough task to bring all the employee under one umbrella because this origin and background are different from each other. Hence the modern Human Resource Manager requirement set of competencies to dial with the modern complex workforce. These involve a level of understanding and sophistication so far not practiced. In non-unionized environment, the challenge is to gain agreement and commitment from every member of the workforce as individuals. In unionised environments, understanding the complexities of the diverse workforce is compounded by the need to satisfy the trade unions involved. And of course, there are not four very different groups of workers in generation X, generation Y. Baby formers and 'Matures'. One size does not fit all. This is a complex scenario requiring a multi–level employee relationship plan.

## Employee Relations

This is the broadest area and contains much that is general about the overall relationship an individual has with the organisation. A successful relationship could be established if there was employee trust, perceptions of fairness, and delivery of the deal.

- Key elements of good people management are job design, skills development and climate of a regular systematic involvement.
- Good people management practices are associated with a positive psychological contract based on trust, fairness, and delivery of the deal.
- An organisation culture in which employees believe their employer will look after their interests has positive outcomes for work performance.

The issue we face in dealing with employee relations/ER as part of wider HR plan is that it is possible to include almost every aspect of human resources practice as part of the employee–relations proposition. The ER aspect of the plan can thus, become too generalised. It is vertical to have objectives for the ER plan that are specific and unique to ER, otherwise a critical success factor within organisations – namely, how people are treated in their day-to-day relationship will be lost in a morass of generalisations. So the focus of the ER plan has to be & identify those aspects that are unique, and to present plans for their entertainment or delivery. Such plans might include:

- Proposals for employee involvement.
- Proposals for presenting the psychological contract in a way that is understood and accepted.
- A suggestion on how employees can have a voice in their employment conditions.

## Employee Involvement

It is necessary to finalise what creates or reinforces the 'need' for employees 'to want to act in a positive and motivated way. And yet so often business strategy is implemented in a way that does not take account of the needs or the views of employees. In the modern organisation the employee expects to be consulted about both the strategy and how it is implemented. This applies in both unionized and non-unionised environments. A key part of the employee-relations plan must be to outline exactly how it is to be achieved. Employee involvement can be achieved at least in two ways:

(i) By deciding how employees can become involved in the way work is organised

(ii) By deciding how they can have a greater influence on factors that affect the organisation as a whole.

## The Psychological Contract

It is accepted that a positive psychological contract based on trust and respect supported by progressive people management can contribute to higher levels of business performance. The psychological contract can be defined as the set of expectations held by the individual and specifying what the individual and the organisation expect to give in to and receive from one another in the course of their working relationship. The fact is that relationships have changed in organisations. This has caused problems for both employer and employee due to globalisation, downsizing, outsource, broadcasting, restricting, new rules, new workforce etc.

To overcome all the upcoming hurdles, we need a new psychological contact that fits those who see themselves as survivors of the massive change of the previous decades and those who have seen only opportunity because of these changes. The employee–relations plan is itself an opportunities to raise the level of understanding about the new contract that organisations must put in place to satisfy a diverse, discerning and educated workforce not prepared to believe in the tenet, 'your career is your responsibility'. They will want some clarification about how and why their employment relationship is important to the employer.

## Employee Voice

Employee voice is a way in which employees can actually participate in decision making. The following are the criteria.

- A two-way communication/exchange of views.
- Upward problem solving.
- Collective engagement.
- Having a say in the management policy making.
- Quality circle.
- Teamworking.

## Industrial Relations

The second aspect of the employee relations' plan concerns industrial relations and the associated implications. Those who have worked in HR for the past few years will be only too aware of the significant changes that have taken plan in this area. The overall thrust towards what might be seen a modernisation has continued apace. The current industrial relations environment is very different from the one that pitched IR professionals against the massed ranks of militant unionism. The sophistication of steward organisations has contributed to a more complex scenario on both sites.

For the purpose of the employee – relations plan then, it is necessary to understand both the organisation's experience and its definition of IR as well as external factors. Industrial relations tends to refer to the formal relationship between employer and employee. The objectives behind such a formal relationship might be:

- Minimising disruption at work and reducing the likelihood of overt conflict.
- Achieving greater stability in employee relations by channelling discontent through agreed procedures.
- Increasing co-operation and commitment so as to increase the likely acceptance of change.
- Increasing control over the labour process.

### Employee Commitment

The component parts of the employee commitment elements could be as under:

- An understanding of the current state of employee commitment through the use of staff attitude surveys – key questions are those such as 'would you recommend the company's products to a friend?' or 'How highly do you regard the company's position on social responsibility?'
- An understanding of the metrics that might at as a proxy for employee commitment, such as staff turnover, length of service, etc. – by segmenting the staff base it is possible to detect different attitudes of various types of employee that might be indicators of employee commitment.

## The Planning Process of Employee Relations

The factors that are critical to the preparation of the employee–relations plan are to be taken care of, the challenge is basically to prepare a plan that is not so general that it crosses other areas of HR and therefore becomes difficult to convert into specification.

### Identifying the Key Issues in the Business Strategy that are likely to Affect Employee Relations, Industrial Relations and/or Employee Commitment

The business strategy requires a focus on the core business and the outsourcing of some non–core function. The following needs to be taken care of during the employee – relations planning process:

- Legal issues and the Transfer of undertakings.
- Industrial relations and the need to brief trade union or other employee representatives.
- Morale issues for those being outsourced and the need to ensure an effective 'employee voice' in the process.
- Communications issues and the need to explain the rationale for the strategy.

## Highlighting the overall employee–relations implications of these strategies

Once the issues have been identified, it will be necessary to look at the implications for employee relations. For example, the business strategy calls for the increasing use of telephones for customer contact – which means the opening of a new call centre at a prospective plan. This is found to carry with it a range of changes in the employment relationship–changes that might include new ways of working, new terms and conditions of service, and/or a new mandatory training programme for which plans will have to be made, agreements with employees and their representatives reached, and a new contract, psychological as well as legal, implemental. The HR professional will have to work through the business strategies and identify, in each of them the core issue and appropriate HR action. The total process includes:

- For the overall organisational strategy to highlight the employee–relations implications.
- To identify these in three areas – employee involvement, the effect on the psychological contract, the implications of ensuring employee participation (employee voice).

## Identifying the Industrial Relations Implications for which Formal Agreement is required from Employee Representatives

The procedure for identifying industrial relations implication is as under:

- Identify how the organisational strategy will affect the fundamental of the formal employee relationship.
- Cross–refer these effects against the formal agreement with employee representatives.
- Cross–refer against any legal implications of moving to the new strategy.

## Engineering that the Issue of Employee Commitment is identified and a plan put in place to engage the workforce

No doubt, this is the most difficult part of the employee–relations plan. How to ensure employee commitment during times of strategic change is a challenge that most organisation faces today. If a new strategy is being proposed, how is it going to be communicated ? And once it has been communicated, how is the organisation going to get the buy-in and commitment of its employees ? The strategy in the world will fail if the employees are not engaged in its implementation. The process could be as follows:

- First and foremost make sure that employee commitment is actually seen as an issue. Too often the need to engage and eventually carry employees along with the strategy is not given enough air time. The employee–relations plan is a tested OK opportunities to do so.

- Identify the current status of employee commitment using staff attitudes measures. Where are the hot spots? If these are about resourcing, training to do the job, the performance of local management, they need to be identified.
- Then show how the implementation of a new strategy will impact on the current commitment. For example if a new customer relations management system is to be put in place will there be enough training to ensure its effectiveness ? Will employees take to the new processes, and the management is strong enough to pursue their teams of the merits of the new system?

### Articulating the new 'Contract' proposed and methods of obtaining buy–in from Employees

This is particularly important in that it embraces the problematic area of the fundamentals of the employment relationship. The psychological contract is a subject often talked about as critical. If so, then the employee relations plan should recognise it as such, and put in place actions for resolving issues and taking the employee to the point proposed by the strategy. Language is an important factor in this case. Referring to a 'psychological contract' probably will not get far in business–focused organisations looking for relevant solutions. The HR strategy could be as under:

- When outlining the plans, take account of employee expectations as well as the expectations of other stakeholders and try to think what would be the implication on job and career.
- How will the strategy change the working relationship? For example, terms and conditions of service are to be harmonised during a merger/acquisitions. Are there winners and losers ? If so, it will be essential to deal with this upfront in a natural way.
- Does the strategy demand more flexibility and change? If so, it will almost inevitably affect the 'contract' especially in organisations where stability has been the norm.

## Conclusion

It is critical that the employee representatives these days are engaged in and influence the business strategy. One way of gaining general buy-in is to ensure that there is a two – way process. In some countries, worker representatives on the Board have access to and participate in the strategy of the organisations in which they work at a very early stage. In others, works councils are used as sounding–boards and an opportunity to hear the organisation's plans. Where such ER mechanisms do not exist, the principles of two–way engagement of strategy must be fulfilled in a way appropriate to the organisation concerned. The employee relations plan should make provision in a way that it is achievable.

Finally, the joining-up of employee-relations equally important function of HR, and the human resource plan is an opportunity to do this. In this respect the three areas of employee relations, industrial relation and employee commitment should be presented within a holistic approach. These activities will being with them plans involving consultation, communication and engagement. It is important to ensure that three are co-oriented in an integrated way.

The employee-relations plan, there is the final part of the human resource plan. It is an appropriate concluding section in that it embodies a pervasive aspect of HR. Many areas of both business and HR strategy have an impact on the way the organisation interfaces with its employees. The ER plan is an opportunity to make sure that employees understand and are engaged in the strategy and that their representatives are able to support such strategies.

## References

1. Paul Turner (2002) *"HR Forecasting and Planning"*, Chartered Institute of Personnel and Development", UK.
2. H.John Bernardin *et. al.*, (1998) *"Human Resource Management – An Experimental Approach"*, Irwin McGraw – Hill, Singapore.
3. http://www. hrfolks.com/Articles/Career. asp.
4. http:// mmgindia.com/Competency mapping.html.
5. Atkinson, J. (1984) "Manpower Strategies for flexible organisations', *Personnel Management*, August, pp. 28 – 31.
6. Hyman, R. and Price, R (1983). *The New Working Class? White Collar workers and their organisations*, London: McMillan.
7. Friedman, A. (1997) *Capital and Labour*, London: McMillon.

***

# 13 Managerial Effectiveness in Organisations

Turnaround processes in organisations entail complex redefinition processes including redefining effectiveness. Modern management theories, such as the competing values approach, do acknowledge different effectiveness criteria but exclusively focus on the content of shifting managerial emphasis among these criteria, not on its how and why. The construction of managerial effectiveness in organisations from a structurationist perspective, emphasizing the multilevel character of organisations. From this perspective, managerial effectiveness loses its external and static properties and becomes a socially defined, possibly ambiguous, construct. The multiple definitions of effectiveness that arose in a large retail organisation as a consequence of substantial restructuring are described. It is shown that middle managers coped with and reworked partly conflicting norms of effectiveness that were espoused by higher echelons in different ways, some more proactively than others.

## Therotical Framework

The two central themes of this paper: 'managerial effectiveness' and 'organisational structuration'. The empirical question springs from the intersection of these two concepts.

## Managerial Effectiveness

To varying degrees, the aim of organisation and management theory has always been to gain practical knowledge, or to generate normative theories. This is also manifested in the effectiveness concept, which lies at the heart of many organisation theories (Lewin and Minton, 1987). At the same time the literature shows an uneasiness with the fact that, when scrutinized more closely, effectiveness keeps proving to be an elusive concept. Difficulties pertain to definitions, levels of analysis, criteria for measurement, and predictors for effectiveness (Goodman, Atkin and Schoorman, 1983; Shenhav, Shrum and Alon, 1994). The quest for universal theories of effectiveness seems doomed to failure in the face of the complexity of organisations. According to the principal agents theory (e.g., MacDonald, 1984) managers pursue value-maximizing ends in proportion to the buffers they can secure for themselves against the demands and pressures put on them. Here, managerial effectiveness is evaluated from an external, economic perspective. Managerial leadership theory stresses the competing values that are concurrently put forward. This approach (e.g. Quinn, Faerman, Thompson, and McGrath, 1990) does explicitly acknowledge different (competing) effectiveness criteria and specifies accompanying effective managerial roles, but exclusively focuses on shifting managerial emphasis among these roles. Neither theory generates insights into why or how the concept of managerial effectiveness changes. A social constructivist view approaches effectiveness from a different point of view. It helps to concentrate on the ways in which skilful practitioners make sense of their organisational situation, and how they come to define the content of effectiveness. From this perspective, the body of knowledge is to be seen as part of the institutionalized context in which managers operate . Effectiveness is no longer considered as a predetermined, externally defined construct, independent of the subject. Instead it is seen as emerging and developing within a specific social context through interaction processes (Maas, 1988). In the terms of Weick and Daft (1983), the content of effectiveness is socially negotiated. Nevertheless, while on the one hand the outcome of this negotiation is not predetermined, on the other the negotiation itself is not value and power-free, and existing practices will influence the interaction. In the appraisal of managerial effectiveness a great deal of attention is generally paid to the positive choices of managers, while in reality the individual, societal and institutional webs of relations they are embedded in influence, constrain, and even define their range of choices (Neu, 1992). An structurationist framework acknowledges both the socially constructed nature of 'effectiveness' and the institutional influences on this construction process.

## Multidimensional Structuration of Organisational Reality

'Duality of structure' means that the structural properties of the organisation are to be seen as both the medium and the outcome of human interaction processes. Social practices reflect the ability of humans to modify the circumstances in which they find themselves, while simultaneously recreating the social conditions (rules, knowledge, resources) which they inherit from the past. People recreate the social conditions because they endorse the value of existing cognitions, norms, and resources by using them in their actions, *the institutional context and managerial agency* because of the duality of structure, the broader institutional contexts in which interaction takes place are important. Institutions refer to reproduced rules and resources, the latter also encompassing a vast range of knowledge and skills. The stress on knowledge and reflexivity is important because it suggests that organisations can be moved in some coherent and explicit direction. Here lies the possibility of deliberate strategy . The dominance of institutionalized structure is compatible with managerial agency when we take into account that Giddens stresses the availability of alternative structural principles. These alternatives derive from the overlapping social systems (e.g., professional, economic, religious, communal) that constitute our complex organisational world. This complexity, together with the dialectic of control, enables managerial agency.

***Dialectic of control:*** All organisations involve a tendency towards hierarchy, but these tendencies are always accompanied by countervailing tendencies towards the recapture of power by those on the lower levels. The settings of interaction in time and space allow various forms of concealment (to sub and super-ordinates) which 'balance other forms of exposure. The activities of those in an office setting are often monitored by the 'results' of their activities, not by direct supervision. However, such results, even if deemed satisfactory, may be reached by methods actually in some part subversive of formal patterns of authority within the organisation *complexity of the multidimensional, open organisational world* How does this complexity enable managerial agency? Organisational actors may draw on rules of conduct that originate from different social systems. Or, put differently, organisations consist of overlapping social systems, a number of them stretching beyond the time-space boundaries of 'the' organisation itself. Because actors thus have access to a diversity of social systems, they have some choice over the structural principles they enlist in their organisational activities. Thus, two forms of managerial agency may be distinguished the first stems from the internal ambiguity and plurality of the rules governing the reproduction of particular sets of social structures. In complex systems, actors must exercise discretion in interpreting their immediate roles. The second form stems from the contradictions between a system's intrinsic structural properties and the alien rules and resources of other activity systems in which organisational members also participate, and/or that cross-cut and overlies the boundaries of the organisation. For example, in recruitment activities a personnel manager may try to adhere to the written ethical codes of the professional association of which he/she is a member, rather than to the existing policies in the organisation. Managerial agency in the second, stronger, sense is possible because managers have a range of structural rules and resources which inspire and empower their actions, at least in so far as they are able to access these alternative structural principles. It is equally important that those they wish to influence actually acknowledge the legitimacy of these alternative principles. In the case of the personnel manager it may well be that when he/she applied for his/her present job, one of the selection criteria was membership of this association. By referring to this fact, he/she can legitimize her actions. The social identity of both the influencer and the influenced constrain the agent's actions These theoretical concepts led to the following **research question**: *In what way is the management of the meaning of 'managerial effectiveness' for middle managers in a multi-level organisation enabled and constrained by the structural properties of the social systems in which the managers participate?*

## Managerial Effectiveness

The main job of management is not producing results. Workers are to produce results. Managers produce performers. The top management is visionary. They plan for 2, 5 or 10 years from now and the manager has two duties:

1. to translate the vision or dream in-terms of projects

2. to produce performers who are self-motivated.

Worker's job is to produce results by executing the projects. The results will be extraordinary with superb quality. The technique of effective leadership gives a leader a healthy philosophy of life along with insight and foresight.

## Intellectual Capital: History and Approaches

### Introduction

Management theorists and practising managers have been long conversant with the fact that hidden and intangible assets are as important to the long term profit position of a company as are the traditionally established traditional assets. The interest in intangible resources of a firm Hall (1992), and the learning perspectives of an organisation Nevis *et. al.*, was prevalent in the research realms from as early as 1970s. Handy suggests that businesses will need to become more like universities with respect to the emphasis which is placed on being information/knowledge positive as well as being cash positive.

The realisation that management today is increasingly about managing intangible resources is beginning to dawn on business managers and academics alike (Itami, 1987). Intellectual capital (IC) has been identified as the key intangible resource in firms. Consequently, ensuring that managers understand this, and that organisational structures and cultures reflect this, as fast becoming a matter of organisational survival. Therefore organisations will need practical methods that can be used to quickly increase understanding and commitment to managing intangible resources.

Organisations, depending on the industry they operate in; have attempted to account for some form of intangibles in one way or the other. People intensive organisations like labor intensive manufacturing units and consultancies attempt to account and put a value to their manpower. A firm involved in interfacing with the external environment (customers, suppliers, vendors, competitors) is interested in the goodwill and the customer satisfaction while a marketing intensive firm attempts to promote its brand name. Such exercises however were isolated and not integrated until Skandia's attempt to measure and manage the entire spectrum of its intellectual capital. And since then the act has been enthusiastically followed by many other firms.

This should not be surprising since in many instances the hidden assets have overtaken financial holdings, real estate, inventories, and other tangible assets in reflecting the most valuable part of many companies. The difference between a company symbolising the information era, Microsoft shows this difference. The market capitalisation of GM in 1996, which has considerable traditional assets, is approximately $ 40 billion. Microsoft, which has few such assets apart from its headquarters building in Seattle, has a market capitalization of some $ 70 billion! The ratio between a company's market value and the cost of replacing its assets (Tobin's Q) is getting larger in most industries, not only in service industries, but in all businesses where companies integrate smart technologies, software, electronics and total solutions into their existing products. Hence currently intellectual capital management is a favourite management jargon well set to make its presence felt in the 21st century in much the same way as scientific management did in the 1960s, and BPR and value chain integration in the 1990s.

Concepts like hidden assets, intangible resources, or most recently "intellectual capital" often say more about the future earning capabilities of a company than any of the conventional performance measures we currently use. If the top-fifty programmes suddenly left Microsoft, the share price of the company is likely to drop dramatically. The absurdity is that while a company may just have gone into "intellectual bankruptcy", the short-term profits may very well rise since costs have been lowered! Thus, it should not be surprising that the Securities and Exchange Commission in the US have recently indicated they will soon require an intellectual capital supplement to companies' annual reports.

## Resource Based Perspective of Management – A Precursor to Intellectual Capital

Neo classical economics presumes resources to be homogeneously distributed within industries and in addition easily accessible by competing firms. Hence a firm had to ingeniously exploit these resources in order to become successful and profitable. Competitive advantage was derived from the management's ability to realign the industry structure to suit the firms' advantage. Thus, the role of management was to figure out smart ways to combine products and markets given the bargaining power of suppliers and customers, entry barriers and potential substitute technologies and/or products.

The analysis of resources endowments had been typically confined within economic boundaries such as labor, capital and perhaps land. However, a seminal work by Penrose questioned this classification and proposed a broader set of resources way back in 1959 itself. This was probably the beginning of the resource based school in management science. Though this viewpoint did not receive much formal attention apart from Rubin, by 1980s followers of this school of thought suggested that competitive advantage was derived not only via various product-market combinations in a given industry but was due to differences in organisational resources of difference kinds. Because resources cannot always be transferred or imitated we must look inside the firm to find the real sources for sustainable differences in the resources.

Aaker had identified the route to sustainable competitive advantage as being a process of managing assets (tangible and intangible) and skills which involves the following three stages: firstly, the identification of the relevant assets and skills by observing successes and failures; secondly, the selection of those assets and skills which will be relevant to the future needs of the market and thirdly the implementation of programs which will develop enhance and or protect these assets and skills.

Pushing these ideas further ahead Barney developed four criteria for assessing what kinds of resources would be competitively advantageous: (1) value creation for the customer, (2) rarity compared to the competition, (3) imitability and (4) substitutability. The only resource that seems to pass this acid test is "knowledge" regardless of whether you call it invisible assets, absorptive capacity, core competencies, strategic assets, core capabilities, intangible resources, organisational memory, or other concepts carrying similar meaning.

Intangibles could be either assets or skills. Richard Hall provided a framework of classifying these knowledge sources which is especially relevant in the present discussion which may enjoy legal protection. These are trademarks, Patents, Copyright, Registered Designs, Contracts, Trade secrets, Reputation and Networks. Intangible skills are those that do not have legal protection but complement the assets and are crucial to survival and prosperity of a firm. These are the know-how of the employees (and suppliers, distributors etc.) and culture of the organisation.

Itami and Roehl claim that intellectual assets are based on information. They can include anything from brand loyalty (the result of information from the company to the environment), to technological or technical skills (with information flowing from the environment to the company), to internal goodwill (presumably helped by free flow of information inside the company).

Likewise, the well-known and widely applied concept of core competencies is another example of a source of sustainable competitive advantages from this perspective. To identify core competencies and distinguish them from "non-core" competencies, the authors suggest three tests : core competencies should be suitable for application in many different markets; they should create a significant contribution to customer value; and, in line with Barney, competitors should have problems imitating the core competencies of a company. They adopt the narrow economic perspective : that difficulty in duplicity is the basis for defining the leading edge of a company. Hence they focused on the factors within the firm and not the outside to derive sources of these core competencies. Intangible knowledge is one of the most difficult attributes to duplicate and hence can be safely assumed to be a source of competitive advantage.

## Knowledge Management and Intellectual Capital Management

The emerging concept of Organisational Learning also integrated with the resource based theory to highlight the importance of intangibles. Together the two streams of management thought from the background of research interests in knowledge management that was to later help establish the importance of intellectual capital.

Argyris (1977) defines organisational learning as the process of "detection and correction of errors". In his view organisations learn through individuals acting as agents for them: "The individuals' learning activities, in turn , are facilitated or inhibited by an ecological system of factors that may be called an organisational learning system". Nevis, DiBella and Gould have defined organisational learning as the "the capacity or processes within an organisation to maintain or those advanced by Argyris and Schon (1978), Dodgson (1993) and (1990).

Huber considers four constructs as integrally linked to organisational learning: knowledge acquisition, information distribution, information interpretation, and organisational memory. Weick argues that the defining property of learning is the combination of same stimulus and different responses, however it is rare in organisations meaning either organisations don't learn or that organisations learn but in nontraditional ways. In this view, "a more radical approach would take the position that individual learning occurs when people give a different response to the same stimulus, but organisational learning occurs when groups of people give the same response to different stimuli."

The current view of organisations is based on adaptive learning, which is about coping. Senge notes that increasing adaptiveness is only the first stage, companies need to focus on Generative Learning or "double-loop learning" (Argyris,1977). Generative learning emphasizes continuous experimentation and feedback in an ongoing examination of the very way organisations go about defining and solving problems. In Senge's view, Generative learning is about creating it requires "systemic thinking ," "shared vision," "personal mastery," "team learning," and "creative tension," [between the vision and the current reality]. Generative learning unlike adaptive learning, requires new ways of looking at the world.

In contrast, adaptive learning or single-loop learning focuses on solving problems in the present without examining the appropriateness of current learning behaviours. Adaptive organisations focus on incremental improvements, often based upon the past track record of success. Essentially, they don't question the fundamental assumptions underlying the existing ways of doing work. The essential difference is between being adaptive and having adaptability.

To maintain adaptability, organisations need to operate themselves as "experimenting" or "self-designing" organisations, i.e. , should maintain themselves in a state of frequent, nearly-continuous change in structures, processes, domains, goals, etc., even in the face of apparently optimal adaption (Nystrom *et. al.*, 1976; Hedberg *et. al.*, 1976; Starbuck 1983). Hedberg *et. al.*, argue that operating in this mode is efficacious, perhaps even required, for survival in fast changing and unpredictable environments. They reason that probable and desirable consequences of an ongoing state of experimentation are that organisations learn about a variety of design features and remain flexible.

The strategy an organisation adopts for learning is important. As Mintzberg stated: the key is not getting the right strategy but fostering strategic thinking in the organisation. Or as the oil giant Shell has leveraged the concept in its credo "planning as learning". Faced with dramatic changes and unpredictability in the world oil markets, Shell's planners realized a shift of their basic task: "We no longer saw our task as producing a documented view of the future business environment five or ten years ahead. Our real target was the microcosm (the 'mental model') of our decision makers. "They reconceptualized their basic task as fostering learning rather then devising plans and engaged the managers in ferreting out the implications of possible scenarios. This conditioned the managers to be mentally prepared for the uncertainties in the task environment. Thus, they institutionalized the learning process at Shell. To sum up, strategic management research seems to have shifted its focus from looking outside at the industry structure to uncover the "true" basis for sustainable competitive advantage to a realisation that heterogeneously distributed resources provide more fertile soil for such advantages. The acid test of imitability led to realisation that knowledge, often in the guise of "core competencies" should be the real nexus of attention in companies. Finally, in a Newtonian-inspired reductionism, scholars have tried to slice knowledge into its finest elements, seemingly hitting the wall at the old distinction between a tacit and an explicit knowledge component.

## Intellectual Capital – Its Need and History

All healthy organisations generate and use knowledge. As organisations interact with their environments, they absorb information, turn it into knowledge and take action based on it in combination with their experiences, values and internal rules. Without knowledge, an organisation could not organize itself; it would be unable to maintain itself as a functioning enterprise.

In 1991, the American Institute of Certified Public Accountants (AICPA) formed a Special Committee on Financial Reporting to address a growing concern about the relevance of orthodox financial reporting and disclosure to the modern economy. According to the committee report there were a number of substantial areas for improvements. These according to Mavrinac and Boyle could be realized with "The provision of information about corporate plans, opportunities, risks and uncertainties. Better alignment of external reporting systems with internal management control and information systems and enhanced discussion of the non-financial performance factors that create longer-term value." Underlying these recommendations is the assumption that non-financial performance data have value relevance and can be effectively used by investors as leading indicators of future financial performance.

Also, a lack of common practices for disclosing and visualizing intellectual Capital hurts all stakeholders and investors. They too can miss subtle change in tenor or the loss of a key knowledge carrying employee that signals the coming eclipse of a corporate star. And it is not rare that many deserving companies are underoptimized and undercapitalized and thus sometimes are unable to complete their destiny. Meanwhile other, troubled firms are artificially propped up until they collapse, pulling down shareholders and investors with them.

Some of the intellectual property and intangible assets that are being exploited abroad include:

Proprietary Product Technology, Proprietary Process Technology, Trademarks and Brands, Large Scale Manufacturing Economics, Large Scale Purchasing Economics, Favorable Financing, Distribution Networks, Management Information Systems and Assembled Workforces. These can go a long way to increasing the market value of any enterprise. The most powerful of these assets contribute to the above-average profits of their owners and can also represent entry barriers against competition. Direct intangible assets contributions can take the form of premium pricing. The premium can be the result of enhanced product performance, derived from proprietary technology or can be derived from the consumer perceptions that come from keystone brand names. Above-average profits can also be derived from production cost savings techniques associated with proprietary process technology.

Internationally, intangible assets are a major force behind direct foreign investment. New market opportunities may the motivation, but intangible assets are the basis for success abroad. Intangibles allow multi-national corporations to successfully venture abroad and fully exploit inherent profit advantages. Rarely do licensing deals allow the licencer to extract all of the superior profits associated with a proprietary intangible asset. Joint ventures also force a sharing of the excess profits derived from intangibles. Direct foreign investment, where a multi-national corporation controls a foreign operation, is one of the best methods for fully enjoying the value of proprietary intangible assets.

The first use of the term "Intellectual Capital" attributed to John Kenneth Galbraith, who in a letter to economist Michael Kalecki in 1969 wrote: "I wonder if you realize how much those of us in the world around have owed to the intellectual capital you have provided over these past decades".

As the previous documentation shows, the idea of intangible assets and intellectual property is a very old one. However, attempts by the industry to integrate the intangible asset in everyday functioning is relatively recent. The first such attempt was made by Skandia, a Swedish financial and insurance services multinational. What Skandia did was not merely to categorise its hidden resources but also to account it and measure it as a part of its 1994 annual report.

By October 1994, Fortune magazine carried a cover story entitled " Your Company's most Valuable Asset: Intellectual Capital," by Thomas Stewart. This was followed up with several other articles in this as well as other business magazines addressing the issue of intangible asset and how they are undermined in corporate functioning.

## Defining Intellectual Capital

Accounting theory defines intangibles as assets that do not have physical substance, that grant rights and privileges to a business owner and that are inseparable from the enterprise. Accounting theory also defines them as assets for which the determination and timing of future benefits is very difficult. Their existence is dependent on the presence, or expectation, of earnings. They typically appear last in the development of a business and disappear first in its demise.

Thomas Stewart has defined IC as: "the sum of everything the people of the company know which gives a competitive advantage in the market".

The early use of the term thus describes the dynamic effects of individual's intellect. When managers and consultants use the term, it becomes more organisational:

Edvinsson and Sullivan defines it as: "Knowledge that can be converted into value".

Laurence Prusak of Ernst & Young defines it as: "Intellectual material that has been formalized, captured and leveraged to produce a higher-valued asset".

Both Skandia and Ernst & Young emphasize the static properties of knowledge, that is: inventions, ideas, computer programs, patents, etc., as Intellectual capital.

Edvinsson & Sullivan also include human resource, Human Capital, but emphasize that: "it is clearly to the advantage of the knowledge firm to transform the innovations produced by its human resource into intellectual assets, to which the firm can assert rights of ownership. One major task of IC managers is to transform human resource into intellectual assets".

According to Edvinsson, IC is very important as it is "the study of the roots of the company's value, the measurement of the hidden dynamic factors that underlie the visible company of buildings and products." Under his direction Skandia a Swedish insurance firm defined intellectual capital as " the possession of the knowledge., applied experience, organisational technology, customer relationships and professional skills that provide .......a competitive edge in the market".

SEC commissioner Wallman includes in IC "not just human brainpower but also brand names and trademarks, .....even assets booked at historic costs that have transformed through time into something of greater value". Factors like employee training (both past and present), technical leadership, client servicing are some of the factors included as a part of IC by researchers.

Smith and Parr provide a more objective definition of intangible assets. These are "all the elements of a business enterprise that exist in addition to monetary and tangible assets." They are the elements, after working capital and fixed assets, that "make the business work and often are the primary contributors to the earning power of the enterprise."

H.T. Johnson, professor of business administration at Portland State University, holds that Intellectual Capital hides within that most mysterious traditional accounting entry, "goodwill". The difference is that traditionally goodwill emphasized unusual, but real, assets such as trademarks. By comparison, Intellectual Capital looks beyond to more ineffable assets such as the ability of a company to learn and adapt.

Gary Hamel and some other theorists have suggested that intellectual capital actually subsumes what we usually think of as fixed assets, which on closer inspection prove to be less fixed than we thought. He argues that an asset is really only a perception of an opportunity about which a majority of people have agreed. Charles Handy has estimated that these intellectual assets may typically be worth three or four times a company's tangible book value. According to Morgan Stanley's World Index, the average value of companies on the world's stock exchanges is two times book value.

All corporations possess a portfolio of assets that are used to carry out operations aimed at earning a profit that represents a reasonable return on investment. Corporate assets fall into three categories: monetary, fixed and intangible. Monetary assets are primarily comprised of cash, investment securities, inventories and accounts receivable. Examples of fixed assets include machinery, buildings, trucks, and anything else that you can touch. Intangible assets are "everything else".

On a more concrete vein, Eisen states that assets are four types. Three precise and measurable and the fourth imprecise and essentially unmeasurable until it is sold. The first two of these assets are current that are likely to be consumed or sold within a year and fixed, which have a useful life of more than one year. The third type is investment such as a company's holdings in stocks and bonds. The fourth asset type is the intangible assets that have no physical existence but are still of value to the company. Typically they are long term, and just as typically they cannot accurately be valued until the company is sold. These arose in response to a growing recognition that non-bookkeeping type factors can have an important role to play in a company's real value. Some of these are pretty obvious: Patents, trademarks, copyrights, exclusive market rights – all conferring on their owners a competitive advantage that has an impact on the bottom line.

## Classifying Intellectual Capital

Intellectual capital has existed for as long as humans have. Its organisational significance has been documented and exploited only in the recent past. Intellectual Property Rights, Patents are some examples of intellectual assets acknowledged by the laws of may countries.

An attempt has been made by many researchers and consultants to classify and codify the areas in intellectual capital. This helps a great deal in managing the intellectual capital of the firm. Many working models of IC classification are available. Skandia's IC Navigator, Sveiby's Intangible Assets Monitor, and Norton and Kaplan's Balanced Scorecard to name a few. While it is true that a firm's intellectual capital can be best classified and assessed by its own members, some wide guidelines are available which are common to all enterprises irrespective of the industry they operate in. The various classifications discussed here provide such wide guidelines.

Annie Brooking has provided an exhaustive classification of intellectual capital. She classifies all intellectual assets into four parts: Market Assets, Human Centered Assets, Intellectual Property Assets and Infra Structural Assets.

*Market Assets* include factors in the external environment in the firm involving its interaction with the customer, competitor, suppliers and other external agents. These are : service brands, product brands, corporate brands, customer loyalty, repeat business, company name, backlog, distribution channels, business collaborations, franchise agreements, licensing agreements, favourable contracts as well as the three categories of customers proposed by Brooking champions, customers and evangelists.

*Human Centered Assets* include employee related attributes. These are : Education of the workforce, their vocational qualifications, work related knowledge, occupational assessments, psychometrics and work related competencies.

*Intellectual Property Assets* include the technological and research bases of a firm. These are: Patents, copyright, design rights, trade secrets, know-how, trademarks and service marks.

*The Infrastructural Assets* includes such organisational parameters as management philosophy, corporate culture, management processes, information technology systems, networking systems and financial relations.

Following a similar approach Smith and Parr have categorized intangible assets as rights, relationships, grouped intangible and intellectual property.

***Rights*** are acquired through establishing contractual agreements with other businesses, individuals, or governmental bodies. They exist according to the terms of a written contract that defines the parties to the agreement; the nature of the rights, goods, or services transferred; the transfer consideration; and the duration of the agreement. They can be in the form of *Receiving Contracts* (that enable an enterprise to obtain goods or services at an advantageous price). *Franchises* and *Providing Contracts* (that afford the business the opportunity to provide goods or services to others at a profit.

***Relationships*** are those established with outside agencies, other companies and other individuals. These are non-contractual and can, at the same time be both ephemeral and extremely important to the enterprise. These encompass the *assembled workforce, the customer relationships and the distributor relationships.* ***The Grouped Intangibles*** are those intangibles that escape the analysis of appraisers and remain as a residual. They are commonly referred to as *goodwill* and *going concern* value. Intellectual Property includes proprietary technology, patents, copyrights, trademarks and even computer software as it is subject to patent and copyright.

Practising consultants and organisations have also forwarded a scheme of classification and assessment of intellectual capital. Skandia, under the direction of Edvinsson proposed the IC Navigator as a tool for classifying and measuring the components of intellectual capital. A discussion of the navigator shall follow in the subsequent section. For Edvinsson the most important distinction is between the intellectual capital that goes home at night, i.e., the Human Capital and that which is left behind, i.e., the Structural Capital. The latter can be further classified as Organisational Capital consisting of Innovation and Process Capital resting in the technology and research at the organisation and Customer Capital reflecting the value derived by a customer from the organisation. Saint Onge provides a different perspective by giving customer capital the same importance as human and structural capital. According to him customer capital is not a sub-set of structural capital as Edvinsson assumes it to be.

Sullivan and Teece provide a simplified outlook that gives importance to the human resources of the firm. According to them "Intellectual capital has two major components: intellectual resources and intellectual assets. The intellectual resources of the firm reside within the minds of the employees... This resource includes the collective experience, skills and general know-how of all of the firm's employees. We call it a resource because it is available to the company to use for profit generation, yet it would be difficult for the company to sell these assets in disembodied form. ... Intellectual assets, the second component of IC are the codified tangible or physical descriptions of specific knowledge to which the company can assert ownership rights and they can readily trade these assets in disembodied form.

***

# Part – II

# 14 Organisational Development

The organisations of today are producing products and services which were unknown in the past and thus giving in a new life to every individual with much higher material comforts than ever before. We know that elements are made of different molecules and atoms which can be polymerised. Similarly, individuals and the groups working in an organisation resulting in a cohesive but enormous force. This process of polymerisation can be achieved in modern industrial system where individuals and groups in the organisation are polymerised, resulting in "organisational development". Human polymerisation needs the following three catalysts: (1) Individuals; (2) Ideas and Desires; (3) Organisational System.

An individual can establish a bond with other individuals which multiply and generate power to create, to build and to produce organisational development represents the way of leading man at work and managing their multi-relations in such a way as to make them happy, productive and strong.

Organisational development is a complex educational strategy to bring in change of beliefs, attitudes, values and structure of an organisation so that it may adopt changing environment. This is a technique for facilitating change and development among people, technology and organisational structural. Organisational development consists of the following elements:

(1) Organisational Development

(2) Organisational Planning

(3) Management Development

It is an attempt to integrate individual needs for growth and development with organisational goals and objectives in order to make a more effective organisation. In order to be strong and effective, an organisation must satisfy the following conditions:

- It must be able to both protect and react with flexibility to changing environmental demands.
- Its members must continually increase their competence in a climate of support and freedom from threat;
- Both organisation and its members must separate in an action research way collaboratory with each other in trying out new ideas and barring from their own experience.

Traditional training and development programmes do not produce the above benefits. The reasons are that these programmes:

(i) Are commonly undertaken on a piecemeal basis in artificial settings as a reactive measure to meet some situational crisis.

(ii) Are commonly content-based emphasizing transmission of theoretical information and concepts.

(iii) Frequently aim at improving one or another part of the organisation with disregard of the whole; and

(iv) Are not collaborative enough to stimulate action.

This has made people realise in recent years the importance of altering the culture of the organisation as a whole through an organisation development programme. Several writers have defined OD in different ways. Simply apart, OD is an educational strategy, using behavioural science knowledge, to bring about a planned, long-term, system-wide change in the culture and social processes of an organisation in order to improve its capabilities in solving its present problems and in coping with the future changes in its external environment. OD has been defined by Wendell and Ecil Bell as: a top management supported, long-range effort to improve an organisation's problem-solving and renewal processes, and management of organisation culture – with special emphasis on formal work-term, temporary team, and inter-group culture with the assistance of a consultant facilitator and the use of the theory and technology of applied behavioural science, including action research.

## Characteristics of OD

Important characteristics of OD which emerge from the above definition are as follows:

- Fluid internal structure
- Built in provisions for self-criticism
- Hospitable environment
- Effective programme for the recruitment and development of employees so that their personal dispositions fit with role demands, and
- Some means of combating the process by which men become prisoners of their procedures.

Reddin defines an effective organisation as one which prefers:

(i) To do right things rather than doing things right

(ii) To produce creative alternative solutions rather than merely solving them

(iii) To optimize resources utilization rather than safeguarding them

(iv) To obtain results rather than following duties; and

(v) To increase profits rather than lowering costs.

1. OD aims at developing OCTAPACE culture in an organisation which is the pre-requisite of an effective organisation. This acronym stands for eight important values, *viz.*,

O: Openness, i.e., complete disclosure of one's feelings

C: Confrontation, i.e., facing problems and findings their solutions

T: Trust, i.e. mutual confidence

A: Authenticity, i.e., willingness to acknowledge one's feelings

P: Proaction, i.e., willingness of the organisation to take initiative in influencing a situation instead of merely reacting to it.

A: Autonomy, i.e., the quality of an individual to seek help from others without feeling inferior.

C: Collaboration, i.e., members working in teams, and

E: Experimentation, i.e., taking action on a limited trial basis.

## 2. OD is a Planned Long term effort

In other words, OD is not an *ad hoc* one-shot activity. An OD programme usually consists of a series of techniques (called interventions) which follow one another in a planned way for a number of years. It is then only that the culture of an organisation is changed. Thus a 3-days or a week-long T-group experience does not constitute OD.

## 3. OD is a System wide change

The emphasis of OD is on changing the system as a whole rather than on changing a few individuals. In this respect, the approach differs from many other training programmes where the target of change is the individual and not the total system.

In OD the change is primarily directed toward the important social processes of the organisation such as planning, decisionmaking, communication, etc. An OD consultant believes that these process are the important leverage points for changing the organisation's culture. However, as OD programme proceeds it may trigger changes in many other areas also. Thus, when the work-related attitudes, beliefs, sentiments, and values of people change, a change may also become necessary in the organisation's design, structure, technology, etc. This is known as the domino effect where one change touches off a sequence of related and supporting changes throughout the organisation.

## 4. OD is an Educational Strategy

Since OD is directed towards the human and social processes of an organisation, the desired change can be brought about through education only. There can be three ways to educate people depending upon the assumptions, which one makes about them. If it is assumed that all people are rational beings and they accept a change if they are convinced about its advantage, then simple dissemination of knowledge about the benefits may be enough. This type of educational strategy is known as empirical rational strategy. If the assumption is that people accept only that change which matches their attitudes, values and norms then they may be need to be educated twice-first, for discarding their current values and second, for replacing them by the desired values. This type of educational strategy is called normative re-educative strategy. Finally, if the assumption is that people accept only those changes which are dictated to them by some superior authority then they may need to be ordered. This type of strategy is called power-coercive strategy. In OD normative re-educative strategy is generally followed.

## 5. OD Uses Behavioural Science Knowledge

OD experts draw on the knowledge and technology of various behavioural sciences such as psychology, sociology, anthropology, etc. Some examples of the practical uses to which the knowledge of these sciences has been put are as follows:

- Maslow's, Herzberg's and Mcgregor's views for motivating people.
- Homan's views (interaction, activity and sentiments) for moulding social activity.
- Lewin's views (force field theory) for introducing change.
- Sturib's views (importance of social norms) for determining perceptions, motivation, behaviour, and
- Homan's views (exchanged theory of behaviour) for that people who tend to maintain a balance between what they give to and receive from the organisation.

## 6. OD Focuses on Practice

The reason for this is that if a goal is to change organisation culture (by changing people's attitudes and behaviours), practice is required for such change to occur. One does not born to play cricket or drive a car by getting increased knowledge about how to play cricket or drive a car. Nor can one change one's managerial style or strategy through receiving inputs of new knowledge alone. It is necessary to examine present behaviour, experiment with alternatives and begin to practise modified ways, if change is to occur. OD techniques rely heavily on experience as their main method of influence. Thus, is T-group or sensitivity training a participant learns new skills, attitudes, and values by observing gestures and postures of others, listening to variations in their tones and interpreting words for their ulterior meanings rather than looking for theoretical information and concepts only. These techniques make greater use of the readily observable 'have-and-now' data than of the less observable 'there-and-then' data (e.g., data related to roles and structures).

## Nature of OD

OD is very much similar to action research. Both OD and action research are data based problem solving techniques which call for collaboration between the consultant and the client from the beginning. This facilitates putting into effect the remedies decided upon. In both the techniques the practical implications of expert recommendations are simultaneously tested during the course of research or OD programme. This makes recommendations feasible and practical. Both the techniques involve identical steps, namely: (a) data collection and problem identification, (b) formulation of action plan on the basis of certain hypothesis, and (c) continuous testing of action plan. An example will move this point clear. Say, an organisation is facing the problem of unproductive staff meetings: people do not come, do not take interest, do not interact, and do not show involvement and so on. The management wants to make the meetings productive. Here, both in OD and action research the first step would be to collect data about the *status quo* and to identify the problem. If the data suggest that people dislike meetings and consider them as unproductive then the consultant may as his second step begin search for causes of the problem. He may generate a number of hypothesis for being tested. For example, he may assume that the meetings will be made productivity if :

(a) The management solicits and uses agenda topic from members;

(b) The chairmanship of the meeting is rotated

(c) The meetings are held only fortnightly (and not weekly).

(d) The management allows greater freedom to members during meetings.

In the third step each one of these hypothesis will be tested one by one to react a final conclusion. This action research nature of OD suggests the necessity of effective feedback and monitoring so that as and when new problems emerge new directions may be taken.

Sometimes, however, an OD programme may not follow the action research model. This may happen where the OD consultant decides to apply some free-planned package of techniques straightaway (without formulating and testing the hypothesis) for the following reasons:

(a) He has developed a liking for certain OD techniques, or

(b) He wants to specialize in certain OD techniques, or

(c) The client is pressing him to apply certain OD techniques only.

## Need for Organisational Development

When an individual gains some new insights into his behaviour, he may find it difficult to use new behaviour on the job. He may bear that the other members of his group won't understand so he prefers to continue in old basis. There is a little evidence that the training facilities bring organisational change. For an individual to make personal changes on the job, an organisational climate should exist to support these changes. Otherwise, training the individual will have little or no impact on the organisation. Developing the system, to support the desired change, is a basic part of the organisational development. Developing the system involves building more effective interpersonal relationship among the members of the working group. For example, the team may become more efficient, responsive, flexible and creative from the point of view of the organisation. The concept of team-building lies in the art of organisation development but organisation effectiveness requires more than effective teams.

Organisational development is not a programme or a project rather it is a continuing process. This process may involve certain projects, planning and implementation of a changed specific programme such as seminars, conferences, appraisal, interviews with an object to develop better procedures and supporting climate for dealing with organisation problems.

Technological change in industries are well-planned and implemented with considerable care but organisational change that is modifying some part of organisation structure or implement of new process of work is often not a deliberately planned but a haphazard activity. Planning, implementing and evaluating these organisation changes are part of organisational development.

## Concept of Organisational Development

Organisational development believes that organisational members can learn to describe its culture and can be helped to plan what it should be and what it is to do? The essential characteristic of organisational development is the involvement of the people in the organisation to carry out various activities. Those activities are designed to meet the organisational objectives with and around the interaction of groups within the organisation. The organisational development feels that it aims to develop, increase understanding between and within groups in order to reduce tensions and introduce team management. Organisational Development objectives are to improve organisational effectiveness and organisational health.

## Objectives of OD

Following are the main objectives of OD:

1. To develop the organisation's capacity to effectively diagnose and solve its current problems.
2. To enable the organisation to successfully adapt itself to a new environment.
3. To increase the level of trust and openness of communication among organisational members.
4. To increase member's identification and commitment with the organisation.
5. To improve the planning and great setting skills of members and teams.

6. To create conditions where conflict between members or groups is brought out in the open and managed rather than swept under the rug.
7. To move forward high collaboration and low competition between interdependent units.
8. To reorganize work e.g., by reducing the layers of supervision or by relocating decision making and problem-solving as close to the sources of information as possible. This means moving towards a norm of the authority of knowledge and the authority of role.

## Introducing Organisational Development

Organisational development is an action-programme based on valid information about the current opportunities. Organisational development instrument is similar to questionnaire constructed around the concept of management. To introduce organisational development, one should start with management training programmes and go over to management development work and step by step to organisation development.

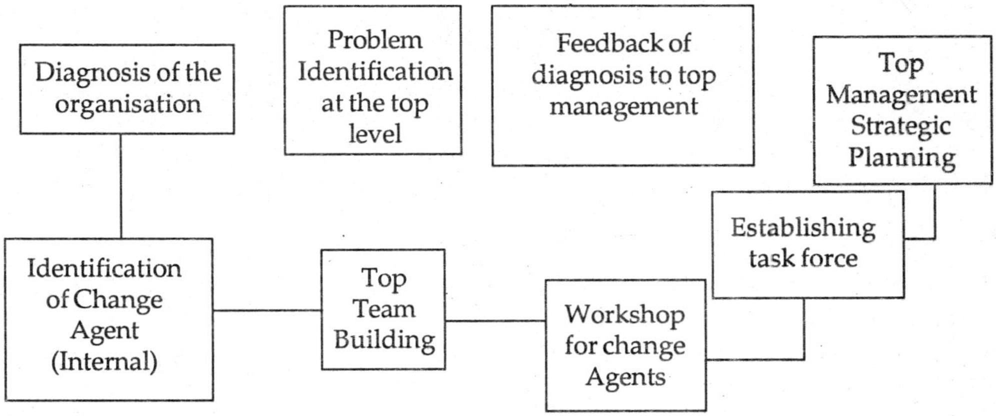


Organisational Development requires: (a) Collection of data; (b) Action component, and (c) Process Maintenance development activities need to be planned from the beginning – initial diagnosis.

Organisational development can be termed as human development. Organisational development is a simplified model of man and organisation. It is based on he concept of theory 'Y' of McGregor. It employs wide range of methods extending from less-structured and goal-orienting technologies like managerial grid, role building, role of negotiation, motivation, development, management by objectives, etc., to bring about the desired change. Grid training and laboratory training methods of organisational development helps in problem-solving knowledge and skills. Management of objectives helps in goal setting both for individuals and teams.

## OD Expert (Change Agent)

An OD expert is known by various names such as a consultant, a change agent, an interventionist, a catalyst, a facilitator and so on. He is called catalyst because he produces change in other without himself undergoing a change. The name facilitator is also given to him because his job is only to help or facilitate the process of OD, i.e., to help the organisation identify, clarify and confront its problems and not solve the problems himself. An OD expert may either be invited from outside the organisation or may be from inside the organisation, e.g., a personnel manager or a union representative. There are certain advantages in having an outside expert:

(a) He has greater expertise and knowledge to diagnose the problem.

(b) He has wider experience of having worked in other organisations

(c) He is able to devote full time.

(d) He has better infrastructure in terms of Library and Office.

(e) He can look at the problems more objectively and can present a fresh point of view.

The disadvantage of an outside expert is that his knowledge of the organisation in-respect of its technology, products, markets, financial and human resources, competition, culture, power equations, etc., is limited. In most situations he needs considerable time to familiarize himself with these details before he can launch an OD programme effectively. This disadvantage can be overcome by associating few inside experts can help the outsider in 3 ways:

- They can build a close liaison between him and the organisation.
- They can act as reference persons with whom the outside expert can check the practicability of his suggestions.
- They can mitigate fear and suspicion which often arouse in people's mind following an outsider's entry in the organisation.

### Qualities of a Change Agent

Following are some important qualities of a good change agent:

(i) Environmental Sensitivity: i.e. intimate knowledge about the formal and informal aspects of the social system especially its power structure and the opportunities and threats present in its operating environment, sensitivity to the situation and to the way one is being perceived by others.

(ii) Problem–sensing and problem solving skills.

(iii) Implementation skills, i.e., the ability to plan, organize, coordinate and control the change efforts.

(iv) High Stress Threshold, i.e., the ability to face criticism and failures.

(v) Interpersonal competence, i.e., the ability to listen with empathy, communicate clearly with openness and give factual feedback.

(vi) Achievement motivation, i.e., a strong desire to achieve results in-terms of the desired changes and innovations.

(vii) Motivation skill; i.e., the ability to rope in influential people in the change effort.

(viii) Role flexibility, i.e., the ability to play many roles simultaneously.

## Phases of an OD Programme

Following is the typical sequence of various phases involved in the introduction of an OD programme:

### 1. Motivation for introducing an OD Programme

This may come about as a result of various internal and external pressures felt by the top management. It may also be the result of the initiative taken by a new Chief Executive or a personnel manager or the recommendations of some high-powered committee. The management then seeks help of some OD expert. It tells him about its problems, the changes which it would like to observe happening inorder to be sure that the desired outcomes are taking place and so on. The expert on his part tells the management what OD is and what it involves. He tells the management that OD is like playing the market. Every OD technique is a calculated risk which may click or may not click. There are no guarantees. The management will continue to have problems no matter what it does. The question which the expert poses before management is, "which problems would you rather have? The ones you have now? Often this leads to greater clarity and commitment on the part of management. It helps in reducing the level of fantasy around OD and what it can do. The expert also explains to the management the financial implications of the proposed OD programme. As a result of this meeting the expert is either invited to the organisation for further talks or the management gives up the idea of introducing OD programmes.

### 2. Signing the Contract

If at the end of the first phase the expert is invited to work for introducing OD in the organisation he may be asked to sign a written agreement defining his relationship with the organisation. The expert may have the following 8 types of relationship with the organisation:

#### Continuous Arrangement

Here the expert works as a retainer for the organisation, working on the ongoing problems for 2 or 3 days in a month.

### Periodic Review

Here the expert helps the organisation in reviewing its effectiveness periodically. He collects the necessary information and helps in diagnosis and action planning.

### Project Arrangement

Here the expert helps the organisation in reviewing its effectiveness periodically. He collects the necessary information and helps in diagnosis and action planning.

### Project Arrangement

Here the expert helps the organisation in introducing a particular programme or project such as MBO or Computer or merger with some other organisation and so on.

### Educational Consultation

Here the expert provides to the client information on the state-of-the-art. For example, he may explain what OD is, what are the latest trends and techniques and so on. This arrangement is often used by staff people to soften the attitudes of line people to accept change.

### Trainer Arrangement

In this arrangement the expert imports specific training (e.g., sensitivity training) to the people.

### Package Programme

Here the expert introduces some pre-decided OD techniques in the organisation.

### Consulting Team

In this arrangement there are a number of consultants back one assigned to a particular sub-system of the organisation and preferably paired with an inside consultant. This pattern is used in a relatively complex organisation.

### Organisation-wide Evaluation

In this arrangement the expert makes a comprehensive study of the total organisation in terms of its norms, culture, employee commitment, effectiveness, etc.

## 3. Diagnosis, Data Collection and Deliberation

In this phase the outside expert and his internal counterpart jointly diagnose the problem and collect the necessary data. In OD the data are needed mostly about the organisation's financial, technical or marketing aspects. Data about the human social processes are collected by interviewing some key individuals at the top because it is they who determine these processes. Some people at lower levels may also be interviewed. The outside expert may also attend meetings to observe how people voice their differences and resolve them. He may note down important events which are likely to give him clues about the areas towards which he must direct his probe. One point to be remembered here is that the data to be collected by the expert can never be precisely decided by him in advance. He decides according to the leads which he receives. Quite often well thought out data collection plans have to be given up because something else emerges as more meaningful for the expert.

The expert finally sits with the key persons to analyse the data and decide:

- What is the specific change problem?
- What sub-system or parts are particularly affected?
- What is the present state of these affected parts?
- How far are these parts ready and capable for change?

## 4. Planning the Strategy for Change and Working out Specific Interventions

In this phase the external and the internal experts jointly workout the strategy for change. They discuss with each other the various types of OD techniques (called interventions) for dealing with the problem and finally plan their phasing, sequencing and linkages. It should be stressed here that there is no one best strategy suitable for all organisations. Every strategy must be tailor-made in the light of the organisation's problems, the amount of time and money available, readiness and receptiveness of different sections to the OD programme and the expert's own experience.

## 5. Monitoring and Evaluation

As the OD programme progresses the measurement of its impact becomes essential. Answers are, therefore, sought to the following questions:

- Are OD techniques producing the desired effects?
- Is the problem solved?
- Is there continued involvement of top management in the programme?
- What are the undesirable ramification of the programme? What needs to be done about them?
- What is the culture of the outside expert's own group? Are his men setting right type of example before others? (who will follow the teachings of the expert about the desirability of resolving inter-personal conflict if members of his own team are fighting among themselves? Who will follow the expert's teachings to measure performance against objectives if his own OD team is unaware where it is going?

### 6. Institutionalisation and Internalisation

This is the last phase of OD programme. By institutionalisation means making the change a permanent part of organisation and by internalization is meant stabilization of change so that it becomes a natural part of people's workstyle best they may slip back to the old style.

The desired change that has taken place in the attitudes and behaviours of individuals and groups is reinforced by making appropriate changes in the appraisal, compensation, training and communication subsystems. OD programme is institutionalized by creating a separate department to take care of the programme on the outside expert's withdrawal.

## OD Interventions

The term 'OD intervention' refers to a very wide range of diagnostic and problem-solving techniques which are employed usually with the assistance of an outside consultant (called the change agent) during the course of an organisation development programme.

OD Techniques can be divided into three categories:

1. Techniques for changing and developing individuals' behaviour. These include achievement, motivation, training, behaviour modification, job enrichment and management by objectives.
2. Techniques for changing and developing group behaviour these include sensibility training, team building and related techniques.
3. Techniques for changing organisational structure and control systems. These include decentralization, participation, human resource accounting, survey feedback, etc. Usually this category of intervention is not referred to as OD. A new term, organisation design, is used increasingly to describe these changes 'Nevertheless, these methods are intended to improve organisations and can be considered development techniques in a broad sense.

While using any one or more of the above techniques, the change agent must remember that he is not a problem solver – he is merely to help the organisation identify, clarify and confront its problems. There is sufficient evidence to show that where an agent – especially an external consultant – has intervened to the extent of actually solving organisational problems himself, without developing internal awareness of, and skills in problem solving, the result is that:

- The problem is more likely to recur.
- The organisation is still dependant on the consultant.
- The internal staff do not learn, grow or develop, and self-motivation is reduced.

The objective of the change agent is to help people help themselves – to help the organisation become a self-reviewing and sub-sufficient entity. He helps the organisation in bringing about socio-technical changes so that the organisational climate becomes more conducive to improved co-operation and collaboration. Solutions must evolve willingly.

## OD in Indian Industry

OD has been successfully implemented in a number of companies in India. Some probable examples are Kamani Enterprise, Tata Iron & Steel Co., Hindustan Machine Tools, Hindustan Aeronautics, State Bank of India, Bokaro Steel, Orient Paper Mills etc. Experience in these and other organisations has, however, shown that the following conditions must exist for the success of an OD programme:

### 1. Support from the Top

The programme must be supported by the top management. Its behaviour must communicate to the people that they will be rewarded for engaging in improvement activities.

### 2. Match between the Professed Values and Behaviour

The actual behaviour of top management must match with its professed values. If the top management preaches theory 'Y' and practices theory 'X' subordinates lose trust in it and become cautious, conservative and self-protective.

### 3. Definite Goal

Some organisations promote OD programmes without first determining the purpose which these programmes are intended to achieve.

### 4. Domino Effect

It should be remembered that change in any one part of the organisation calls for a sequence of related and supporting changes in many other parts. If this is not done the change effort may not succeed. This is called 'Domino effect', thus a change in the technology of a task may require a change in the communication pattern or a change in the organisation structure or a change in the reward system.

### 5. Strong Linkpins

OD can succeed if what like describes as 'linkpins' are present in the organisation. These are the roles which connect various levels and various parts of the organisation. They thus help in spreading out the change in all directions.

### 6. Tailor-made Programme

Sometimes an OD programme used elsewhere is forwarded and applied without examining its appropriateness for the present organisation. This adversely affects the success of the programme which needs to be tailor-made. A cook-book approach in such cases seldom succeeds.

### 7. Difference between Training and OD

The OD programme must not be confused with the usual training activities such as sensitivity training or MBD. These activities, no doubt, may form part of an OD programme but they are not OD in themselves. Further, OD programme should not be expected to yield quick results. An OD effort may be expected to show meaningful results only after 3 to 3 years.

### 8. Correct Understanding of the Role of External Consultant

The role of the external consultant should be clearly understood. Very often the top management thinks that thereafter it is the consultant's entire responsibility to handle the change effort. This is not correct. It is only through the joint effort of both that the synergy effect can be produced.

## Criticism of OD

Though OD is a best tool for overall development of the organisations, it is not defectless. Some important grounds on which OD is criticized are as follows:

### 1. There is not enough evidence to scientifically prove the effectiveness of OD Techniques

Most of the documentation is in the form of case studies which do not establish a clear linkage between OD effort and organisational performance. Hence, the charge that OD successes are nothing more than "Hawthorne Effects" can seldom be refused. But lack of "Scientific Proof" also does not imply that we conclude the opposite – that OD efforts do not lead to improved performance. There, is, in fact, more than enough "anecdotal" evidence to warrant the belief that such efforts may, under favourable circumstances, result in major benefits.

### 2. OD concepts are little more than "advanced human relations"

This, however, is not correct. OD goes well beyond the human relations efforts in scope focusing on the entire socio-technical system rather than on limited aspects of either one or the other. It rejects simplistic human relations notions of "one best way" and "happiness leads to performance". And most important, it believes that development occurs as members learn experientially rather than by following dictums of engineers or personal specialists.

### 3. OD despite its proponents claims is not a total systems approach dealing with all facets of the system

Many OD efforts result in only a few policy and role changes and in only few instances are major structural changes or redesigns of technical systems associated with an OD effort.

So far OD has been focused on the internal dynamics of organisations and remarkably little attention has been given to the cultivation of theories and intervention practices that are centered on organisational/environmental relationships. Moreover, almost nothing has been done with complex problem of theories and strategies for developing relationships between a number of organisations (what technically could be called an organisational set) in an environment.

## Organisational Development and Management Development

Organisational development is the addition of organisational planning and management is the addition of organisational planning and management development. Organisational planning deals with structural aspects, levels of hierarchy, span of control and job description. Management development deals with human aspects of career planning. Development deals with deliberate changing of the instrumentation through the utilization and application of valid knowledge, success planning, appraisal systems and training.

The need for starting organisational development goes beyond the need for Management Development. The need of organisational development obviously goes beyond the development of the individual manager. It requires a trial system involvement and commitment to a long-term renewal of the organisation. The commitment needed in organisational development is for greater than for management development. In the latter, it is for more difficult to arrive at conditions similar to those faced on the job. Quite often, the manager trained for a management technique learns new concepts but when he refers to job and starts implementing them, he is frequently faced with the problem of lack of support from his superiors and his subordinates.

Normally, management development is given a lip service with little or no support from top management. Management Development and Organisational Development are not only compatible but are also complementary to each other. The former is an arm of the latter. Organisational development process perceives various problems which management development process can handle. Management development and organisational development efforts are concerned with issues such as communication, planning, motivation, and the coordination of goals. Management development aims at improving the skills in problem-solving and decisionmaking and it strikes to develop management to contribute for the growth of the organisation. Organisational development attempts to make this possible by creating conditions in which managers can make these contributions. In fact, the objectives of organisational development and management development are to improve the effectiveness of an organisation. The strategies for both are concentration on change and on change agents. The relationship of Management Development and Organisational Development is summarized as under:

| Management Development | Organisational Development |
|---|---|
| Teach Manager new skills | Facilitate problem-solving on the job |
| Expand manager's conceptual understanding | Plan and implement changes |
| Change managerial attitudes | Increase sense of "ownership" – belonging of organisational objectives among employees |
| Upgrade manager's present knowledge and skills in areas like problem-solving and decision making | Create conditions so that decisions are made on the basis of competence. |
| To be initiated when something is wrong with the manager | To be initiated when something is wrong with the system |
| To initiate when managers do not know the company policy, management philosophy and needed skill | To initiate when problems are with a manager, technological change and organisation structure |

It is important that the top management gives full leadership and active support to Organisational Development efforts in order to make it successful and operative in the organisation. If the top management is giving a lip service only then it is quite critical to succeed on Organisational Development programme. It is vital that all level of management are involved in any change process.

***

# 15 Organisational Change

## Management of Change and Organisation Development

Change is one of the most important characteristic features of modern organisations. Every organisation must develop adaptability to change lest it may be swept away by the forces of change. There are many forces which act on the organisation and make change not only desirable but also inevitable. These forces include technology, market forces and general socio-economic environment. These are the external forces which necessitate change in internal organisational variable like machinery, equipment and processes, policies and procedures, structural relationships etc. Any factor in the internal environment that affects the way the organisation carries out its activities is also a force of change. Management policies and practices and employees' attitudes and behaviour are the most important forces which pressurize the organisation for change.

## Meaning and Nature of Change

The term 'organisational change' implies the creation of imbalances in the existing pattern of situation. When an organisation operates and functions for a long time, an adjustment between its technical, human and structural set-up is established. It tends to approximate equilibrium in relation to its environment. In other words, organisation members evolve a tentative set of relations with the environment. They have to adjust with their jobs, working conditions, friends and colleagues etc. Change requires individuals to make new adjustments and the fear of adjustment gives rise to the problem of resistance to change.

Organisational change denotes any alteration which occurs in the overall work environment of an organisation. It has following characteristics:

(i) Change results from the pressure of forces which are both outside and inside the organisation.

(ii) The whole organisation tends to be affected by change in any part of it.

(iii) Change takes place in all parts of organisation, but at varying rates of speed and degrees of significance.

Keith Davis has explained the effect of work change with the help of an experiment using an air-filled balloon. When finger (which represents change) is pressed against the exterior of the balloon (which represents the organisation) the contour visibly changes at the point of impact. Thus, a pressure representing change produces an obvious deviation at the point of pressure. But simultaneously, the entire balloon (organisation) is affected and stretched slightly. So it may be generalized that **the whole organisation tends to the affected by change in any part of it.**

Change is a continuous phenomenon of organisational life. The survival of growth of an organisation depends to a great extent on its ability to cope with change required by forces operating within it boundaries and in its external environment. An organisation is an open system, which means that it has a constant interactional and interdependent relationship with its environment. Any change in its environment, such as changes in consumer tastes and preferences, competition, economic policies of the government, etc., make it imperative for the organisation to make changes in its internal system. Further organisation is composed of a number of subsystems which are also in a dynamic relationship of interaction and interdependence with one another. Any change in a subsystem creates a chain of changes throughout the entire system as illustrated earlier.

## Forces for Change

An organisation depends on and must interact with their external environment in order to survive and grow. They get inputs from their environment, transform them through various processes and export outputs to the environment. They take what environment gives and give what environment wants. Thus organisations are constantly responding to their external environment by making necessary changes in the internal forces. For example, marketing department wants new products which will require changes in production, purchase and other departments. Thus pressures for change are created both by external and internal forces.

### External Forces

(i) **Technology:** It is the major external force which calls for change. The rate of technological changes is greater today that any time in the past and technological changes are responsible for changing the nature of jobs performed at all levels in the organisations. The computer technology and automation have made a remarkable impact on the functioning of organisations in the recent times. Technological advancement is thus a permanent fixture in the business worked and it continues to demand the manager's attention as a pressure for change. Japanese firms have progressed rapidly because they are very fast in adopting new technological innovations.

(ii) **Marketing Conditions:** Marketing conditions are no more static. They are in the process of rapid change as the needs, desires and expectations of the customers change frequently. Moreover, these is tough competition between manufacturers and suppliers in the market. The market is flooded with new products and innovations everyday. New media of advertisement and publicity are being evolved for influencing the customer. All these factors put great pressure on the modern organisations to change their technologies and marketing strategies.

(iii) **Social Changes:** Because of spread of education, knowledge explosion and Government's efforts, social changes are taking place at a fast pace. The drive for social equality (e.g., equal opportunity to women, equal pay for equal work etc.) has posed new challenges for the management. The management has to follow social norms in shaping its employment, marketing and other policies.

(iv) **Political Forces:** Political forces outside the country have an important influence on large business houses, particularly the transnational corporations. The relation between government and business houses has become very complex in modern times. The interference of government in business has increased tremendously in most of the countries. Many laws have been passed to regulate the activities of the corporate sector. The organisations have no control over the political and legal forces, but they have to adapt to meet the pressures of these forces.

## Internal Forces

(i) **Change in Managerial Personnel**: Old managers are replaced by new managers which is necessitated because of retirement, promotion, transfer or dismissal. Each manager brings his own ideas and way of working in the organisation. The relationships, more particularly informal ones, change because of changes in managerial personnel. Moreover, attitudes of the personnel change even though there is no change in them. The result is that an organisation has to change accordingly.

Changes in the organisation are quite fast when executives at the top change. No two executives have the same philosophy and style. The new executive will follow his own style and will like to put into practice his own ideas and philosophy. This may lead to important changes in the organisation in terms of organisation design, allocation of work to individual, delegation of authority, installation of controls etc.

(ii) **Change in Operative Personnel**: The make up of the workforce is changing fast. The new workers have better educational qualification, place greater emphasis on human values and question authority of managers. Their behaviour is very complex and leading them for the attainment of organisational goals is really a challenge. The changing expectations of personnel certainly acts as a pressure that has to be handled properly by the organisations.

(iii) **Deficiencies in Existing Structure:** Changes may be needed to rectify deficiencies in the present organisational set up. These deficiencies may be in the form of unmanageable span of management, larger number of managerial levels, lack of coordination between various departments, obstacles in communication, multiplicity of committees, lack of uniformity in policy decisions, lack of co-operation between line and staff, and so on. However, the need for change in such cases goes unrecognized until some major crisis occurs.

(iv) **Chain Effect of Change:** Quite often, a change sets off a sequence of related and supporting changes. This is known as Domino effect. For instance, creation of a new department may lead to creation of new managerial posts and reallocation of work in some other departments. If this aspect is not considered, there will be adverse effects on other parts of the organisation and problems of coordination and control in future as shown in Exhibit 1. Therefore, repercussions of any change must be studied and analyzed adequately before it is introduced.

## Exhibit – 1

**Impact of Change in one sub-system on other sub-systems**

| Subsystem | Organisational | Possible adverse Impact on Other sub systems |
|---|---|---|
| Technology | Change in process technology<br>Introduction of robotics | Retraining of personnel<br>Displacement of workers |
| Structural | Job Modification Addition of New department | Loss of status<br>Reallocation of resources<br>Reassignment of personnel |
| Human | Transfer of key executive | Change in reporting relationship<br>Loss of technical expertise |

(v) **Fear of Inflexibility:** Dynamic Managers also bring about changes to avoid developing inflexibility in the organisation. The rationale behind is that organisational members develop liking for change and they do not resist changes unnecessarily whenever need arises in the future.

## Types of Changes

Joseph L. Massie has identified the following types of changes in the manager's world:

1. **Changes in the Knowledge, Information and Techniques:** The profession of management has its deep roots in the engineering field is advancing greatly. New techniques of production are being invented. Now a great deal of research is also being conducted in various institutions of the world on behavioral science.

It is recognized that whenever a manager must deal with other persons, some aspect of behavioral science comes into play. Therefore, the application of behavioral science to the management field is getting top priority.

2. **Changes in scope of Management:** The writings of early management thinkers were primarily concerned with technical problems and their solutions. But with the pressure of time, it was found that the process of management has universal application. Many problems in different types of organisations like industrial, educational, religious, hospital, etc., are common and they call for the application of certain management principles. This has broadened the scope of management and given birth to the demand for specialization of the application of management knowledge.
3. **Change in the Issues and Problems before Managers:** There has been a great change, both in magnitude and number, in the problem before present day managers. These changes are caused by the emergence of large scale organisations and the separation of management from ownership. Moreover, there has been an awakening of the working class. Trade unionism has spread throughout the world. Consumers have also become conscious about their power over the organisations.
4. **Changes in the Environment:** The world is changing fast, population changes are becoming extremely significant to managers. Other changes can be viewed as changes in consumers, factors of production, social conditions, political conditions and economic trends. The increase in the size of consumer markets and the segmentation of markets into strata has created new problems. Consumption patterns are changing widely and managers continually search for market information to help them make sound decisions. Values, expectations and aspirations of the customers are continually undergoing transformation.
5. **Change in the Pace of Change:** The changes facing the managers today are made even more significant by the increased rate of change in various dimensions such as speed of data handling, use of energy resources, etc. The types of changes and the differences in the rate of change will create an organisational world filled with uncertainty and problems. The manager facing the possibility of change must be prepared and willing to accept the conditions to uncertainty.

## Reactive vs. Proactive Change

Very few organisations adapt and change in a smooth and orderly way. Most of the organisations attempt to stick to old practices and procedures rather than planning change. For instance, workers in a factory have a long standing demand of profit sharing and they go on strike to press their demand. The change would be reactive if a profit-sharing plan is introduced because of pressure of the trade unions. Reactive change is brought by the management grudgingly since the survival of the organisation is in danger. But, if on the other hand, the management introduces on its own a profit-sharing plan to enhance productivity and motivation of employees, such change would be called proactive or planning change.

Proactive change is a change that is initiated by an organisation because it is identified as desirable whereas reactive change is the change implemented by an organisation under pressure from environmental factors. Planned change is a proactive approach. Proactive management tries to anticipate the future and to see the organisation as it should be if it is to be effective in the future. Management will never be able to anticipate the future with total accuracy, but proactive planning can reduce those out-of-step periods that characterize reactive organisations.

### Evolutionary, Revolutionary and Planned Changes

Evolutionary changes are slow and there is a fear that organisation may not cope with the future. Revolutionary changes result in totally changing the *status quo* and these are dangerous except where situation becomes highly intolerable. Planned changes are systematically introduced by the management.

### Planned Change

A planned change is brought by an organisation with the purpose of achieving something that might otherwise be unattainable or attainable with great difficulty. This approach represents the planned alteration in the existing organisational system. It is a means of dealing with those changes that may be crucial for survival. It involves a greater commitment of time and resources, requires more skills and knowledge for successful implementation; and can lead to more problems if implementation is unsuccessful.

## Levels of Change

In the context of organisation, changes may occur at three levels, i.e., individual level, group level and organisational level.

### Individual Level Change

Individual level changes may take place due to changes in job assignment, transfer of an employee to a different location or the change in the maturity level of a person which occurs over a period of time. The general opinion is that change at the individual level will have impact on the group which in turn will influence the whole organisation. Therefore, a manager should never treat the employees in isolation; he must understand that the individual level change will have repercussions beyond the individual.

### Group Level Change

Many of the organisational changes have their major effects at the group level. The groups can resist change, as for example, the trade unions can strongly resist the changes proposed by the management. Informal groups can pose a major barrier to change because of the inherent strength they contain. Changes at the group level can affect the work flows, job design, social organisation, influence and status systems and communication patterns.

The groups, particularly the informal groups, have a lot of influence on their individual members. As such by effectively implementing change at the group level, resistance at the individual level can be frequently overcome.

## Organisational Level Change

The changes at the organisational level may take the following forms:

(i) **Strategic Change:** It involves changes in the basic objectives and policies of the organisation. For example, joint venture with another firm globalization of operation, divestment of a loss-making unit, etc., have far reaching consequences for organisation and the individuals and groups working in the organisation.

(ii) **Structural Change:** It involves changing the internal structure of the organisation. This change may be in the whole set of relationships, work assignment and authority structure. Change in organisation structure is required because old relationships and interactions no longer remain valid and useful in the changed circumstances.

(iii) **Process Oriented Change:** Such changes relate to the technological developments, information processing and automation. They involve replacing or retraining personnel, heavy capital equipment investment and operational changes. All this will affect the organisational culture and as a result the behaviour pattern of the individuals and groups.

(iv) **People Oriented Change:** People oriented changes are directed towards performance improvement, group cohesion, dedication and loyalty to the organisation. This calls for closer interaction among the employees and special behavioral training to them.

## Causes of Resistance to Change

People resist changes to protect themselves from the real or perceived effects of change. Man by nature resists what is unfamiliar to him. This is partly because he fears the new and unknown and partly because adopting of new ideas is a painstaking process. The resistance to change or opposition to change may be logical and justified in some cases. Sometimes, people do not resist change. They may oppose the change agent or mode of implementing the change.

Human resistance to change may take the form of passive acceptance, subtle sabotage, aggressive refusal, complete breakdown of work and so on depending upon the situation. Resistance in any from is not a good sign of industrial relations in any undertaking. It is the duty of the management to restore and maintain the group equilibrium and personal adjustment which change upsets. Change requires individuals to make new adjustments for which they are not prepared. This causes resistance on their part.

Resistance to change may be caused by (i) economics (ii) psychological, and (iii) social factors.

The economic factors causing resistance are as under:

(i) workers apprehend technological unemployment

(ii) workers fear that they will be idle for a major portion of their time due to higher efficiency of new technology.

(iii) Workers are afraid of demotion as they do not have the new skills required for the performance of new jobs.

The psychological factors of resistance are listed below:

(i) It is the human psychology to maintain *status quo*. Human beings resist change by nature.

(ii) Workers may apprehend boredom in new jobs because of increased automation.

(iii) Workers may lazy and reluctant to learn new things.

(iv) Workers do not have complete knowledge about the change. They may make their own assumptions about change. The assumptions may be totally illogical.

The workers may resist change because of the following social reasons:

(i) It may be felt by the workers that their status will go down as a result of introduction of new technology.

(ii) Changes may require new social adjustments which are not liked by the workers.

(iii) Workers as a group oppose change as they are unfamiliar with the change.

(iv) Workers resist changes which are brought about without consulting them.

## Causes of Organisational Resistance to Change

At the organisational level also, change may be resisted. The main reasons for this are as under.

1. **Organisational Structure**: Some organisational structure have inbuilt mechanism for resisting change. Consider, for instance, a typically bureaucratic structure wherein jobs are narrowly defined, lines of authority is clearly spelt out and the flow of information is stressed from top to bottom. In such an organisations structure, new ideas rarely travel down the hierarchy because these are screened out. Innovations are not suitable for such an organisation.

2. **Resource Constraints:** Some organisations resist change due to scarcity of resources. Greater the scarcity of resources, greater is likely to be the resistance to change. An organisation may not like to incorporate change because it requires huge investment.

3. **Threat to Power:** When people at the top consider change as a potential threat to their position and influence, they resist it. Change may disrupt the power relationships and produce new power equilibrium. This new equilibrium may reduce the power and prestige for some of the senior executives. Therefore, they would oppose the change.

4. **Sunk Costs:** An organisation may also resist change because it has invested in fixed assets and human resources. This cost cannot be recovered unless the assets and resources are put to productive use. When change is introduced, many of these cost become useless. That is why, existing machines may not be replaced with change in technology. Similarly, some executives may be retained despite their outdated skills and experience. Their pay and other benefits represent sunk costs.

## Strategies to Overcome Resistance to Change

Since it is natural for human beings to resist change, the main problem in introducing and implementing change is to overcome resistance to change. Efforts for overcoming resistance to change can be made both at the individual level and the group level. The main techniques that can be used to overcome resistance to change are given below:

1. **Education and Communication**: One of the simplest techniques to overcome resistance to change is to inform people about the change. People can be educated to become familiar with the nature and process of change. Counseling and training can be used to change the basic values and attitudes of people. Communication is very useful because many people resist change due to lack of information or misunderstanding. While communicating change, a manager should explain:

   (a) What the change is?

   (b) Why the change is needed?

   (c) When it is to be introduced?

   (d) How it will be implemented?

   (e) How the change will be beneficial to all?

   This would help people to visualize the need for and logic of change. They would appreciate the change much better and will accept it easily. The main advantage of this method is that once convinced people themselves would help in the implementation of change. However, it is a time-consuming method and requires continuous education of those affected by the change.

2. **Participation and Involvement**: The management should discuss the change with the subordinates because people who have an opportunity to participate in planning for change will have some feeling of commanding their own destiny and not of being pushed around like so many pawns on a chessboard. Participation will give the people involved a feeling of importance. They are likely to be more committed to the change if they are convinced about the rationale of change. On the other hand, a change imposed from above is likely to make people feel that their knowledge and skills are being ignored.

3. **Education and Training:** In order to successfully implement the change, subordinates must be indoctrinated in new relationships, taught new skills,

helped to change attitudes, given the information they need to understand where they fit into the picture and how they will be expected to operate under the new set-up. The educational process can be aided by training classes, meetings and conferences.

4. **Facilitation and Support:** Easing the change process and providing support for those caught up in it is another way managers can deal with resistance to change. These include listening, providing guidance, allowing time off after a difficult period, and offering facilitative and emotional support. Facilitative support means removing physical barriers in implementing change by providing appropriate training, tools, materials, etc. Emotional support is provided by showing personal concerns to the subordinates during periods of stress and strains.

5. **Negotiation and Agreement:** Negotiation with resistors and offering them incentives may be a useful technique for overcoming resistance. Examples are union agreements, promotion of nominees of the union, increased economic benefits to employees, etc. It may become relatively easy to avoid major resistance through negotiation.

6. **Manipulation and co-optation:** Sometimes, managers covertly steer individuals or groups away from resistance to change. They may manipulate workers by releasing information selectively or by consciously structuring the sequence of events. Or they may co-opt an individual, perhaps a key person within a group, by giving him or her a desirable role in designing or carrying out the change process. Aside from the doubtful ethics of such techniques, they may also backfire.

7. **Explicit and Implicit Coercion:** Managers may force people to go along with a change by explicit or implicit threats involving loss of jobs, lack of promotion and the like. Managers may dismiss or transfer employees who stand in the way of change. As with manipulation and co-option, such methods, though not uncommon, are risky and make it more difficult to gain support for future change efforts.

Overcoming resistance to change will involve pursuing more than one of the above techniques. Which techniques to employ, and how to translate them into effective actions, will depend on the specifics of the situation as shown in Exhibit-2.

## Exhibit – 2

**Strategies of Managing Change**

| Approach | Commonly used in situations | Advantages | Drawbacks |
|---|---|---|---|
| 1. Education + Communication | When there is a lack of information or inaccurate information and analysis | Once persuaded people will often help with the implementation of the change | Can be very time consuming if lots of people are involved |

| | | | |
|---|---|---|---|
| 2. Participation + Involvement | Where the initiators do not have all the information, they need to design the change and where others have considerable power to resist | People who participate will be committed to implement change and any relevant information they provide will be integrated into the change plan | Can be very time consuming if participators design an inappropriate change |
| 3. Facilitation + Support | Where people are resisting because of adjustment problems | No other approach works as well with adjustment problems | Can be time consuming expensive and still fail |
| 4. Negotiation + Agreement | Where someone or some group will clearly lose out in a change and where the group has considerable power to resist | Sometimes it is a relatively easy way to avoid major resistance | Can be too expensive in any case if it alerts other to negotiate for compliance |
| 5. Manipulation + Co-optation | Where other tactics will not work or are too expensive | It can be a relatively quick and expensive solution to resistance problems. | Can lead to future problems if people feel manipulated |
| 6. Explicit + Implicit Coercion | Where speed is essential and the change initiations possess considerable power | It is speedy and can overcome any kind of resistance | Can be risky if it leaves people mad at the initiators. |

## Role of Communication in Introduction of Change

Adaptation to change is the antithesis of resistance to change. Management of an enterprise should plan changes in such a way that it is easy to implement them. The planned changes should strike a balance between the needs of the organisation and those of the individuals. They should focus upon making the transaction smoother and less disruptive. For this, management must take the worker's representatives into confidence. If it can do so, there will be the least problem in implementing any change. The management should properly emphasize the need and significance of change. If the management implements change by properly informing those who are affected by it and by explaining to them the logic of change, there will be less resistance. This may not be true in all the cases because in some cases people may not accept change even if they have been logically convinced about the change. Hence, attempts to educate people about the change certainly helps in acceptance, but it does not always ensure that there will be no resistance to change.

Change should first be implemented in a selected part of the enterprise to study the reactions of people there. The reactions of the people should be analyzed properly and modifications may be introduced wherever management thinks fit. Management should also see that there is two way communication between the management and the workers so that the former comes to know the reactions of the latter directly without any delay. Two way communications will go a long way towards removing fears and apprehensions of the workers and bringing understanding between the management and the workers.

## Role of Groups in Introduction of Change

Management should understand group dynamics to bring about change. A group is a cluster of persons related in some way by common interests over a period of time. Members of the group interact with each other and develop group cohesiveness among themselves. Therefore, management should consider the group and not the individual as the basic unit of change. Group interactions are one of the social situations which facilitate adaptation to change. This was very well shown by the Hawthorne Studies. Each individual did not feel free to set up for himself a production quota; it was set and enforced by the group. Workers who deviated significantly in either direction from the group norms were penalized by their co-workers. It was found that a person who resists pressure to change his behaviour as an individual will often change it quite readily if the group of which he is a member changes its behaviour. "As long as group standards are unchanged, the individual will resist changes more strongly the further he is to depart from group standards. If group stands itself is changed, the resistance which is due to the relation between individual and group standard is eliminated.

Experiments conducted by Kurt Lewin on changing habits showed the power of the group to produce changes in the behaviour of group members and thus overcoming resistance to change. An experiment studying how to get mothers to give their children orange juice and codliver oil is discussed below.

The objective of the experiment was to convince mothers with newly born children to feed codliver oil and orange juice to their babies immediately following their departure from the hospital. The investigators divided the mothers into two groups. In the first a doctor talked to each mother singly for about 25 minutes, telling her the virtues of new types of food for her child. In the second, group of six mothers discussed with the doctor and among themselves the values of the use of the new food items for their children for about 25 minutes.

The results were conclusive. Checking the two groups after two weeks and again after four weeks, the investigators found that the mothers who participated in the discussion group gave their children oranges juice and codliver oil more frequently than the other mothers, although both the groups were major inclined to feed their children orange juice than codliver oil. After four weeks, 90% of the mothers who received group instruction were feeding their children cordliver oil as compared with about 50% of the mother who were instructed individually. In the case of orange juice, the comparable figures were 100% and about 58%. Other experiments on changing people's eating habits consistently revealed the same phenomenon. Group discussions were much more effective in changing attitudes than other methods such as two persons discussion or lecture groups.

## Roethlisberger's Experiments

Works change operates through each employee's attitudes to produce a response that is conditioned by feelings towards the change. This relationship was illustrated in a series of classic experiments by Roethlisberger and his associates. In one instance, lighting was improved regularly according to the theory that better lighting would lead to greater productivity. As was expected, productivity did increase. Then lighting was decreased to illustrate the reverse effect, ie., reduced productivity. Instead, productivity increased further. Lighting was again decreased. The result was still greater productivity. Finally, lighting was decreased to 0.06 of a foot-candle, which is approximately equivalent to moonlight. According to Roethlisberger, "Not unit this point was reached was there any appreciable decline in the output rate."

In the above experiment, lighting was in no way causing any change in output. In other words, there was no direct connection between the change and the response. Some other intervening variable, later diagnosed as employee attitudes, had crept in to upset the expected pattern. Roethlisberger illustrated the new patter by means of a model of response to change known as the "X" chart. It is shown in Fig. 1, each change is interpreted by individuals according to their attitudes. The way that people feel about a change then determines how they will respond to it. These feelings are not the result of change; they are caused. Once cause is personal history, which refers to people's biological processes, their backgrounds and all their social experience away from work. This is what they bring to the workplace. A second cause is the work environment itself. It reflects the fact that workers are members of a group and are influenced by its codes, patterns, and norms.

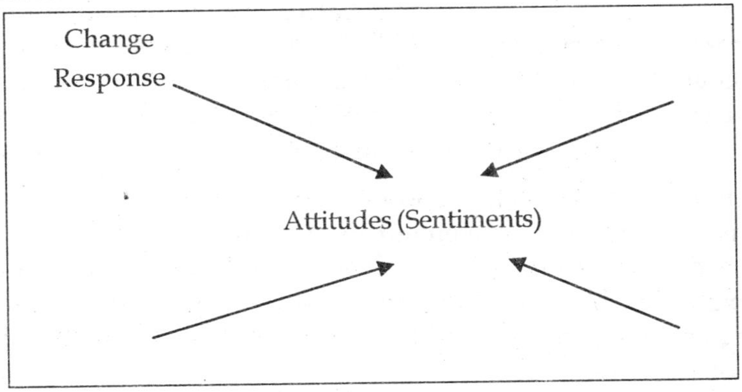


**Fig. 1: X Chart**

## Planned Change

Change may be either necessitated by the pressure of external forces or brought by deliberate and conscious efforts of the management. The latter type of change is called the volitional or planned change. According to Warren Bennis, "Planned change encompasses the applications of systematic and appropriate knowledge to human affairs for the purpose of creating intelligent action and choices. Planned change aims to relate to the basic disciplines of the behavioral sciences as engineering does to the physical sciences or as medicine relates to the biological sciences. The management may decide to go in for planned change to cope with complex problems of modern society and the growth of behavioral sciences.

Planned change may be defined as a conscious and concerted attempt of management of an organisation to monitor the environment, to assess their impact on the organisation and to evolve appropriate alternatives so as to utilize the environmental forces to the advantage of the organisation. Planned change is thus the international attempt by an organisation to influence the *status quo*. It is through planned change that an organisation can plan to bring changes for growth and development.

## Lewin's Change Model

Resistance to change could be overcome on an enduring basis by systematically planning and implementing the process of change. Kurt Lewin identified the following phases in the process of planned change: (1) unfreezing the *status quo*, (2) moving to a new level, and (3) refreezing at the new level. These are discussed below:

(1) **Unfreezing:** It refers to making individual aware that the present behaviour is inappropriate, irrelevant, inadequate and hence unsuitable to the changing demands of the present situation. Edgar Sachein outlines the following elements which are vitally necessary during this unfreezing phase:

   (i) Support for the old way of doing things must be removed by recognizing its inadequacies. The first stage is basically a fact-finding process. It is most effective when employees are fully involved, not merely told by management that changes will take place. For instance, an office wants to investigate replacing its typewriters with computers. The office manager would be wise to ask typists for their problems in using the old typewriters.

   (ii) Alternative plans of action should be evaluated and the best plan - chosen. Again, employees' involvement in evaluation can be valuable in gaining their acceptance of the plan finally chosen. In the office we just mentioned, for example, the typists might be asked to try out computers and then report on their efficiency, filing space, convenience with floppy disks and ease of correction.

   (iii) Attempt should be made to gain commitment to change. To do this, the manager must overcome the natural resistance to change of those who are affected by it.

   (iv) If necessary, willingness to change should be linked with rewards and unwillingness to change with punishments.

(2) **Implementing Change:** Once the subordinates become receptive to change, the manager as a change agent, should introduce the proposed changes in a

systematic manner with the full cooperation of the subordinates. They should be given intensive orientation as to the behavioral changes necessary for successful introduction of the proposed change so that adaptation to the new environment takes shape as desired.

(3) **Refreezing:** It is a phase of stabilization, assimilation and institutionalization of the changes that are successfully implemented. Such changes should remain as a stable and permanent characteristic of the system until another need arises for change. The new roles, relationships and behavioral patterns should be allowed to take on the characteristics of habits. The subordinates should get a genuine feeling that the benefits generated by the change are worthwhile.

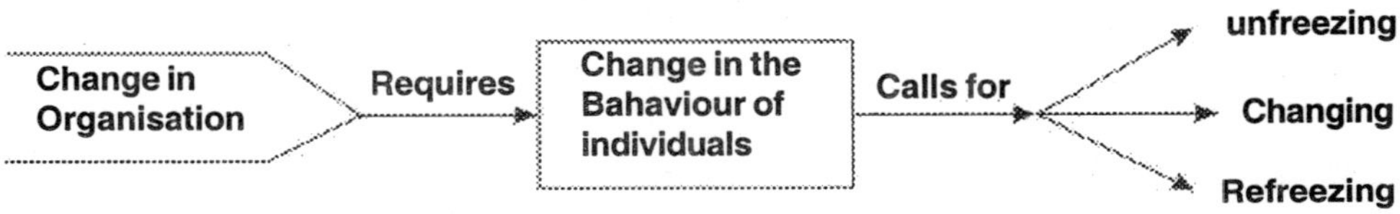


**Fig. 2: The Change Process**

Although the success of a change attempt depends on completion of the latter two steps (moving and refreezing), an organisation's ability to adapt must first be determined by whether or not its current level of functioning can be unfrozen. That is if the organisation neither perceives a need to change even if one actually exists nor possesses the desire or ability to alter the *status quo,* voluntary changes will presumably not be initiated, thus ending possible organisational adaptation before it begins. Identification of the sources of organisational resistance to change, and the sources of impetus for change and the organisational characteristics that accommodate imbalance between these forces should be dealt with since obviously the balance between these forces cannot be systematically upset (unfrozen) until the sources are identified.

## Force Field Analysis

Kurt Lewin introduced Force Field Analysis for implementing change. Force Field Analysis identifies (i) What forces are likely to push the change (i.e., driving forces) and (ii) What forces are likely to restrain it (i.e., restraining forces). The number and the strength of the driving and restraining forces must be identified. According to force field theory, the present situation in which change is to be attempted is a quasi-static equilibrium of driving forces and restraining forces as shown in Fig. 3. Organisational stability, or quasi-static equilibrium occurs when the driving and restraining forces balance each other in such a way as to maintain a constant level of functioning for a while.

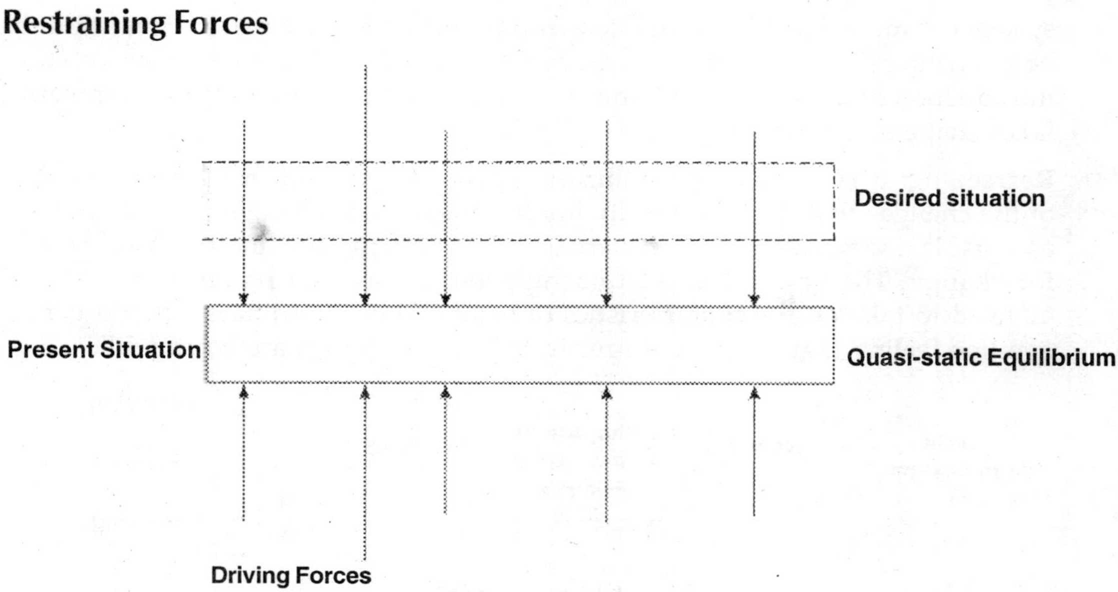


**Fig. 3: Lewin's Change Model (Force Field Analysis)**

The present equilibrium can be changed by strengthening the driving forces or by weakening the restraining forces. All these forces reside in the group. Lewin propounded that it is usually easier to change individuals formed into a group than to change any of them separately. As long as group standards are unchanged, the individual will resist changes more strongly the farther he is to depart from group standards. If the group standards are changed, the resistance which is due to the relation between individual and group standards would be eliminated.

The implication of Force "Field Analysis for the manager is that 'before embarking on a change strategy, he must properly identify and evaluate the forces favoring change (driving forces) and those opposing ( restraining forces). This will enable him to remove the hindrances that block change efforts. He will not waste his time and energy on those forces over which he has no control. Under the framework of forcefield analysis, a manager should take the following steps:

(a) **Recognize the driving forces**—The first step toward organisational change involves reorganizing major changes in the environment and problem within the organisation. In order to recognize the pressures to change, managers need to develop a keen sensitivity towards the external and internal environment.

(b) **Increase the driving forces**— Once the need for change is identified, it needs to be communicated to the people concerned. If members know why the change is needed, they are more likely to adopt it.

(c) **Manage the resisting forces**— People resist change because they perceive it to be harmful to them. It is, therefore, essential that they are made aware of its benefits. Rewards many be linked to willingness to change and resistance to change may be punished.

Unfreezing may be affected by encouraging the driving forces which take the behaviour away from the *status quo*. Alternatively steps may be taken to overcome the restraining forces which tend to perpetuate the *status quo*. Several techniques are available for unfreezing, e.g., education, communication, participation in decision making, negotiation offer of rewards manipulation, coercion or punishment etc.

## Driving Forces (Forces for Change)

Organisations managing to survive in the long-run adapt to new external and internal environmental conditions (sometimes whether the participants and power holders want or not). This suggests that change can come in two ways: involuntarily or voluntarily.

Involuntary changes arise for many reasons, but quite commonly as a result of personnel turnover. As Kaufman explains, "Replacement personnel in organisations are all a little bit different than their predecessors (and from each other), particularly if they are of different generations. They produce changes. The process may be very gradual and consequently almost imperceptible.... Nevertheless, it goes on relentlessly." Thus, "The regeneration of organisation" comes about quite naturally.

Another need for change is experienced by organisational participants in the form of pressures of anxieties, which are created by discrepancies between the desired or potential level of organisation functioning (formal or informal) and the actual or predicted level. That is, "a motive force for change occurs in 'discrepant situations', in cases of a difference between stimulus and a person's 'internal anchors' of attitudes, perceptions, or whatever."

The examples of driving forces are:

(i) Dissatisfaction with the present equilibrium, i.e., need for changes are felt.

(ii) Conflicts in the organisation.

(iii) Changes in organisational goals.

(iv) Difference in personal and organisational goals.

(v) Desire for innovation.

(vi) Low productivity and rising costs.

## Restraining Forces (Forces for Stability)

The literature that addresses the organisational tendency to resist change forces on resistances that arises from a pair of sources; personal and organisational. Resistance from either sector can be fully intentional, in which case the change agent may find a rational model of the change process useful or the resistance can be somewhat unintentional and require additional measures to bring it to the surface.

### Personal Sources of Resistance

Individuals may resist change in general for various reasons of which they may or may not be aware. Conscious resistance presumably arises when an individual perceives a change as a threat to the security of personal advantages associated with the *status quo*. Conversely, resistance may arise as a result of anticipated disadvantages that accompany change. Suffice it to say that there are a number of sources of personal resistance to change and that personal resistance can result in unsuccessful change attempts and often does if not dealt with properly.

### Organisational Sources of Resistance

There are several obstacles to change inherent in the organisation. Such barriers to change include resource limitations, sunk costs, accumulation of official constraints, unofficial and unplanned constraints on behaviour and inter-organisational agreements.

## Concept of Organisation Development

The term 'Organisation Development' (OD) came into prominence in the 1960s. It seeks to use behavioral science knowledge to help organisations adjust rapidly to change. The underlying principle of OD is that the ideals way to achieve change in organisations is to alter each person's entire formal or informal role set to support the change. It is more difficult to Chang an individual alone because he is placed into role conflict as his peers, superiors and subordinates retain the same role expectations of him. In such circumstances, it would be worthwhile to revise the entire role set to support the change.

Two important factors have caused the use of OD as a technique of planned change. Firstly, training for change does not work properly only through reward structure on the job unless there is a proper change in the environment of the organisation in which people work. Secondly, in a dynamic environment, the change is extremely rapid. This requires a highly receptive and effective organisation so that changes are implemented and absorbed to make the organisation survive and grow. OD helps a lot in this direction. "It (OD) tries to free up communication tightness by increasing the amount, trust and candour of communication. It seeks to build problem-solving capability of communication by improving group dynamics and problem confrontation. In short, it reaches into all aspects of organisation culture in order to make it more humanely responsive."

## What is Organisation Development?

OD is an educational strategy which focuses on the whole culture of the organisation in order to bring about planned change. It seeks to change beliefs, attitudes, values and structures, in fact, the entire culture of the organisation, so that the organisation can better adapt to technology and live with the pace of change." Thus, organisation development may be defined as a technique for bringing change in all the aspects of the organisation so that change is easily absorbed.

Definitions of OD given by eminent behavioural scientists are as under: "Organisation Development is a long-range effort to improve an organisation's problem-solving and renewal processes, particularly through a more effective and collaborative management culture, with special emphasis on culture of formal work teams, with the assistance of a change agent, or catalyst and the use of the theory and technology of applied behavioural science including action research."

—French and Bell

"Organisation Development is an educational strategy intended to change the beliefs, attitudes and structure of organisation so that they can better adapt to new technologies, markets and challenges."

—Warren Bernies

"Organisation Development is an effort (1) planned (2) organisation-wide, (3) managed from the top (4) to increase organisational effectiveness and health through (5) planned interventions in the organisation's process', using behavioural science knowledge.

—R. Beckhad

## Characteristics of OD

*(i)* *System Orientation:* Organisation development is system oriented. It is concerned with the interactions of the various parts of the organisation which affect each other. It lays stress on inter-group and inter-personal relationships. It is concerned with structure and process as well as attitudes. The basic issues to which it is directed is: How do all of these parts work together to be effective? Emphasis is on how the parts relate, not on the parts themselves.

*(ii)* *Use of Change Agent:* Organisation development is generally implemented with the help of one or more change agents, whose role is to stimulate, facilitate and co-ordinate change. The change agent usually acts as a catalyst, sparking change within the system while remaining somewhat independent of it. Although change agents may be either external or internal, they are usually consultants from outside the company. Advantages of using external change agents are that they are more objective and have diverse experiences. They are also able to operate independently without ties to the hierarchy and politics of the firm.

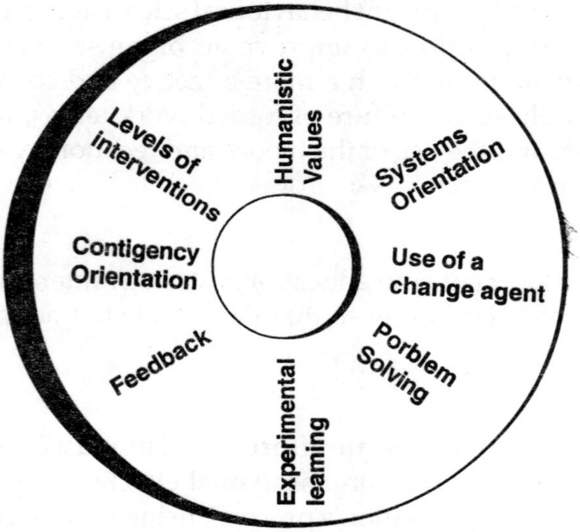


**Fig. 3: Characteristics of Organisation Development**

(iii) *Problem Solving:* Organisation development is concerned with problem solving. It seeks to solve the problems through practical experiences gained on the work and not merely through theoretical discussions as in a class room. These problems mainly occur at the time when working on the job; hence the problems are real. Thus, it develops an attitude of problem solving among the organisational members. This focus on improving problem solving skills by discussing data-based system problems is called action research. In other words, employees are "learning how to learn" from their experiences, so they would solve new problems in the future.

(iv) *Experimental Learning:* Organisation development provides experimental learning to help the participants learn new behaviour patterns. Through experience, they can discuss and analyze their own immediate experience and learn from it, This approach tends to produce more changed behaviour than the traditional lecture and discussion, in which people talk about abstract idea. Theory is necessary and desirable, but the ultimate test is how it applies in a real situation.

(v) *Human Values:* OD programmes are often based on humanistic values. The values are positive beliefs about the potential and desire for growth among employees. To be effective and self-renewing, an organisation needs employees who want to increase their skills and contributions. The best climate for this to happen is one that creates opportunities for growth by stressing collaboration, open communications, inter-personal trust, shared power and constructive confrontation. They all provide a value base for OD efforts and help ensure that the organisation will be responsive to human needs.

(vi) *Contingency Oriented:* Organisation development is situational and contingency oriented. As people learn to develop their behavioural concepts through experience, they can suggest various ways to solve a particular problem and to adapt any of them most suited in the present circumstances. Thus, OD is flexible and pragmatic, adapting actions to fit particular needs.

(vii) *Levels of Interventions:* OD programmes are aimed at solving problems that may occur at the individual, inter-personal group, inter-group and total organisational level. OD interventions are designed for each level as for instance career planning at the individual level, team building at the group level.

(viii) *Feedback:* Organisation development provides feedback to participants so that they may be able to collect the data on which decisions are based. For this purpose, participants may be divided into several groups according to the functions. Each such group takes its own decision on the subjects referred to it, and then, the decisions are forwarded to the other group for feedback. Each group comes to know the impression of other groups about it and then groups meet together to thrash out any misunderstanding developed among them. In this way, decisions of each group are checked by other and the final decision is reached.

## Exhibit – 3

**Organisation Development vs. Management Development**

| Basis | Management Development | Organisation Development |
|---|---|---|
| 1. Objective | Improving manager's performance | Increase the effectiveness of the organisation |
| 2. Approach | Train and equip employees and managers to perform better | Focus on design, not on the managers to perform better |
| 3. Approach | Education and Training | Problem-solving approach |
| 4. Perspective | Development of individual executives | Long-term strategy for organisational innovation and renewal |
| 5. Specialist or change agents | Not required | Trained specialists or change agents required. |

## Goals of OD

Organisation Development (OD) seeks to change the organisational environment in which people work. It aims at the improvement of the total system to ensure that there is a sustained change in the behaviour of people which is conducive to a better organisational performance. Some of the common goals of OD programmes are to:

(i) develop a self-renewing, viable system which can be reorganized in a variety of ways, depending on the tasks that are to be performed;

(ii) increase the level of trust and support among the organisation's members;

(iii) create an environment in which authority-assigned role is augmented by authority based on knowledge and skill.

(iv) increase openness and authenticity of communications laterally, vertically, and diagonally;

(v) increase the level of group responsibility in planning and implementation;

(vi) optimize the effectiveness of both the static (the basic organisation chart) and the temporary systems (the projects, committees, etc.) through which much of an organisation's work is accomplished by built-in continuous improvement mechanisms;

(vii) move towards high collaboration and low competition between inter-dependent units;

(viii) reach the point where decisions are taken on the basis of an information source rather than an organisational role; and

(ix) enhance the identification of members and groups with the organisation as a whole; and thus increasing loyalty and commitment among the members.

## Benefits of OD

Margulies and Raia have given the following benefits of Organisation Development:

1. Provides opportunities for people to function as human beings rather than mere resources in the productive process.
2. Gives each member of the organisation opportunities to develop to his full potential.
3. Seeks to make the organisation more effective in meeting all its goals.
4. Tries to create an environment in which exciting and challenging work can be found.
5. Gives people in organisations the change to influence how they relate to work, the organisation, and the work environment.
6. Treats each human being as a person with a complex set of needs, all of which are important in his or her work-life.

## Limitations of Organisation Development

Organisation development has certain limitations also which are listed below:

1. OD can be no more powerful than the behavioural science concepts on which it is based. Behavioural science has many limitations which are applicable to organisation development also.

2. OD requires use of certain persons (change agents) who can take initiative to bring about change. Complacent people cannot be helpful in implementing organisation development.
3. OD cannot be applied without giving due consideration to the local circumstances existing within each sub-system of the organisation. The local circumstances may pose a problem in adapting to change.

## Assumptions of OD

Organisation development is based on certain assumptions which are as follows:

1. Most individuals have drives towards personal growth and development. However, the work habits are a response to work environment rather than personality traits. Accordingly, efforts to change work-habits should be directed towards changing how the person is treated than towards attempting to change the person.
2. Highest productivity can be achieved when the individual goals are integrated with the organisational goals.
3. Co-operation is more effective than conflict. Conflict tends to erode trust, restricts collaboration and eventually limit the effectiveness of the organisation. In healthy organisations, efforts are made at all levels to treat conflict as a problem subject to problem-solving methods.
4. Suppression of feelings adversely affects problem solving, personal growth and satisfaction with one's work. Accordingly, free expression of feelings is an important ingredient for commitment to work.
5. Growth of individuals is facilitated by relationships which are open supportive and trusting. Accordingly, the level of inter-personal trust, support and cooperation should be as high as possible.
6. The difference between commitment and agreement must be fully understood. Agreeing to do something is totally different from being committed to do something. Sense of commitment makes it easier when this commitment is based upon participation in the process.
7. Organisation development must be reinforced by the organisation's total human-resources system.

## Steps in Organisation Development

The steps in OD are explained below:

1. **Identification of Problem.** The process of Organisation Development starts with the identification of the problem in the organisation. Analysis of various symptoms—both overt and covert—may help in identifying the problem. Diagnosis gives identification of the problem and its causes and determines the

scope of future course of action. It involves a number of techniques concerned with identifying concerns and issues, establishing priorities and translating them into aims and objectives. At this stage itself, the collection and analysis of data are undertaken. Major consideration is given to the techniques of identifying major problems and issues.

2. **Preparation Change Agents**. Many firms employ management consultants to suggest strategy for change. The management consultants or OD practitioners should attempt to transform diagnosis of the problem into a proper action plan involving the overall goals for change, determination of basic approach for attaining these goals and the sequence of detailed scheme for implementing the approach.

3. **Collection of Data.** Surveys may be made to determine organisational climate and behavioural problems. The consultant usually meets with individuals and groups away from work to develop information from questions such as these
   (a) What kinds of conditions contribute most to your job effectiveness?
   (b) What kinds of conditions interfere with your job effectiveness?
   (c) What would you like to change in the way this organisation operates?

4. **Data Feedback and Confrontation**. The data which has been collected in the third step will be given to the work groups, who will be assigned the job of reviewing the data. Any areas of disagreement will be mediated among themselves only and priorities will be established for change. The focus of all discussions at this stage is to identify real problems in the organisation.

5. **Intervening and Implementing the Change.** Intervening in the system refers to all the planned programme activities during the course of an OD programme. OD interventions are "sets of structured activities in which selected organisation units (target groups) engage with a task or a sequence of tasks where the task goals are related directly or indirectly to organisational improvement. Interventions constitute the action thrust of organisation development; they make things happen." OD interventions include team development, laboratory training, managerial grid training, brainstorming and intergroup team building. The intervention should take place at all the three levels, namely, individual, group and organisation.

6. **Evaluation and Feedback**. Organisation Development is generally a long-term process. Therefore, it is essential to carefully monitor the programme and get feedback regarding what is going on after the initiation of the OD programme. This will help in introducing modification, wherever necessary. For effective appraisal of OD programme, the use of critique sessions, systematic appraisal of change efforts, and the comparison of pre and post training behavioural pattern is very effective.

## Change Agents

Change agents are the persons who initiate change in the organisation. Management as a whole can be called the change agent as it is continuously engaged with managing change in the organisation. They are known as internal change agents. Besides, external change agents may also be engaged. These are the persons who are experts in their respective fields and offer their expertise to the organisation by charging consultancy fee. Generally, the consultation is for a limited period and on part-time basis.

An external change agent is a professional who moulds the behaviour of organisational members in the direction deemed desirable. He helps the organisation adjust to variations in its external or internal environment. The change agent develops a need for change on the part of his clients. The client system is made to realise the importance and benefits of intended change. He is able to anticipate problems likely to be faced by the client system during and after the change process and think of ways and means of minimizing and remedying them.

An internal change agent is a member of the organisation who is entrusted with the responsibility of facilitating change in the organisation. The internal change agents may be from any level and any department. Their selection as change agents will depend on the nature of change and overall suitability of the people for change. Both internal and external change agents work in harmony a good deal of interaction through early contacts between them is require to develop relationship of mutual trust and understanding.

The functions of change agents are as follows:

(i) To help the organisation to adapt to internal and external change;

(ii) To organize and conduct team building programmes.

(iii) To facilitate planned organisational changes to take place.

(iv) To undertake organisation diagnosis and to bring the diagnosis to the top management's notice.

(v) To motivate organisational members to accept changes willingly.

### Role of Change Agent

The role of change agent would depend upon the people involved, the organisation culture and the problem or crisis at hand. Simply stated, he plays the following roles:

(1) *He establishes a change relationship with the client system*. The clients feel that the change can be effectively brought about with the help and support of change agent. The change agent is able to identify the problem faced by the client after the diagnoses its problems.

(2) *He identifies the need for change*. The client is made to feel the need for change. The change is not thrust on the organisation. Its management understands the relevance and necessity of change and is willing and supportive of the change.

(3) *He prepares a blueprint of action for implementing the change in the organisation.* The support of the client system is enlisted in translating the planned change into action process. Thereby resistance to change effort is minimized.

(4) *He stabilizes change and prevents discontinuance.* Any change is moving the organisation towards a newer equilibrium from the earlier one. If the new equilibrium is not maintained, the organisation is likely to revert to the earlier equilibrium and the change effort will be failure. The client system should be made to realize the importance of this and the new patterns of behaviour have to be stabilized.

(5) *He achieves a terminal relationship with his client.* No change agent can continue to be associated with a change effort too long. At some time, during the change process, the client should feel confident to take over and maintain the change effort. That would be opportune time for change agent to terminate relations with client system. There should be no undue dependence on the change agent and the client system should carry on the on-going activity with confidence.

## OD Interventions

### Techniques of Organisation Development

Intervening in the system refers to all the planned efforts or activities during the course of an OD programme. OD interventions are "sets of structured activities in which selected organisation units (target groups) engage with a task or a sequence of tasks where the task goals are related directly or indirectly to organisational improvement. Interventions constitute the action thrust of organisation development; they make things happen." OD interventions include team development, laboratory training, managerial grid training, brainstorming and inter group team building. The intervention should take place at all the three levels, namely, individual, group and organisation.

Some of the prominent OD interventions are:

1. Sensitivity Training
2. Team Building
3. Process Consultation
4. Role Playing
5. Management by Objectives
6. Grid Development
7. Restructuring
8. Job Redesigning
9. Job Enrichment
10. Survey Feedback

## 1. Sensitivity Training

It is the method of changing behaviour of the personnel in the organisation relying on unstructured group interaction to smoothen interpersonal relationships. In this process, the actual technique employed is termed as T-group. 'Sensitivity' in this context means sensitivity to self and self-other relationships. In this training, 10-12 persons are involved, who are assisted by a professional who is a behavioural scientist.

Sensitivity or T-group training provides a free atmosphere which breaks through the barrier of intellectualization and verbalization. It emphasizes "open your eyes, look at yourself, and see how you look to others. Then decide what changes, if any, you want to make and in which direction you want do." Thus, the emphasis of T-group is on self-improvement based on the analysis of one's behaviour *vis-a-vis* the other members of the organisation ensure individual and organisational goal achievement.

The benefits of sensitivity training are:

(i) It makes trainees sensitive to emotional reactions and expressions in themselves and others.

(ii) The participants sharpen their ability to perceive and to learn the implications of their actions in the process of drawing their attention to their own or other's feelings.

(iii) It stimulates and develop personal value and goals which an commensurate to social goals and scientific methods of persona decision-making.

(iv) It develops a scientific attitude to tackling future situations.

(v) It helps achieving behavioural effectiveness in transactions in environments prevailing around the participants.

Sensitivity training is criticized on the following grounds:

(i) It forces many individuals to undergo a personality change — humiliating and anxiety provoking experience from which they might not recover.

(ii) It strips some people of defenses which they badly need and provides them with nothing to replace these defenses.

(iii) It encourages behavioural modes that are acceptable in the laboratory but unacceptable in most organisational settings.

(iv) It encourages and coerces individuals to reveal aspects about themselves that constitute an invasion of privacy, thus harboring later resentment in participants.

To sum up, sensitivity training has both strong and weak points. It is essential for the management to take adequate steps to remove the deficiencies of sensitivity training. If used with care, it can be of great value in overcoming resistance and introducing change in the organisation.

## 2. Team Building

The emphasis in team building is on improving the effectiveness and efficiency of the group and not of the individuals alone as is the case in T-group. It is a technique which is used at the group level. Its purpose is to increase trust among members because people work better together when there is open and honest sharing of the problems. At the initial level, attempts are made to develop such as environment where mutual trusty can be developed among the team members.

Team development consists of problem identification, examination of effect of differences in perception, giving and receiving feedback about adverse feelings of members to overcome these feelings, developing interactive skills, personal contact with team members to solve differences and follow-up actions to review what has been learned and what the next step in team development should be. These steps bring about cooperative and supportive feelings among members of the team.

## 3. Process Consultation

Process consultation is the process that exists within a group or between groups. It is affected by the process consultant. He helps "the client to perceive, understand and act upon process events which occur in the client's environments." Schein felt that the consultant is vitally concerned with such process as human actions which will come up in the work-flow, meetings and the formal and informal interactions among people within the organisation. The process consultation lays emphasis on the processes of communication, functional roles of group members, problem-solving and decision making in group, growth of the group, leadership and authority and inter-group relationship.

The process consultation technique as advocated by Schein includes six steps. They are: (i) contact with the client, (ii) define relationship between the client and the consultant in terms of the expectations of the client and the expectations of the consultant in the form of fee, etc., (iii) selecting a setting and the method of work by the client, (iv) gathering data to make a diagnostic study, (v) suitable intervention, and (vi) termination of formal relationship between the client and the consultant after the completion of the specified task.

## 4. Role Playing

Role playing is a technique of creating a life situation, usually involving conflict between people, and then having persons in a group play the roles of specific personalities. In industry, it is used primarily as a technique for modifying attitudes and inter-personal skills. Typically, the situation is structured by setting forth the facts of the situation, the event that led up to present situation and other relevant information described. For instance, two trainees may play the roles of a superior and a subordinate to discuss the latter's grievances. The purpose of role playing is to aid trainees to understand certain problems. Role playing is generally used for human relations and sales training. This technique makes trainees self-conscious and imaginative and analytical of their own behaviour.

The merits of role playing are as under:

(i) When one is asked to put oneself in someone else's place and play the role of that person, it generally increases awareness of the other's problems.

(ii) Role playing helps the participants to appreciate that the behaviour often is a consequence not only of their personalities but also of the situation and helps them to identify and recognize some of their own faults.

(iii) The trainee can broaden his experience by trying different approaches, while in a real situation, he has only one chance. By evaluating the different ways of handling the same situation, he able to see the strengths and weaknesses of these approaches.

(iv) In a sense, role playing in more than an experience because it permits observation, discussion and emphasis that are not customarily part of experience.

Alongwith these merits, role playing has certain weaknesses, which partly offset its utility. These are listed below:

(i) Some individuals become too involved in the "acting" and lose sight of the purpose of the exercise.

(ii) Some trainees may place more emphasis on show-off and acting than on the problem involved.

### 5. Management by Objectives

Managing by objectives is a behavioural technique which integrates the company's need to achieve its goals for profit and growth with the manager's need to contribute and develop himself. According to George S. Ordiorne, the System of Management by Objectives can be described as a process whereby the superior and subordinate managers of an organisation jointly identify its common goals, define each individual's major areas of responsibility in terms of results expected of him and use these measures as guides for operating the unit and assessing the contribution of each of its members. Ordiorne also stressed that MBO is not merely a set of rules, a series of procedures or even a set method of managing, but it is a way of thinking about management.

Management by objectives is a comprehensive philosophy of management. It is bound to affect the entire organisational structure, culture style. Management by objectives calls for regulating the entire process of managing in terms of meaningful, specific and variable objectives at different levels of management hierarchy. Management by objectives moulds planning, organizing, directing and controlling in a number of ways. It stimulates meaningful action for better performance and higher accomplishment. It is closely associated with the concept of decentralization because decentralization cannot work without the support of management by objectives.

### 6. Grid Development

Grid development is based on Blake and Mouton's model of leadership called the Managerial Grid. Their model depicts two prevailing concerns found in all organisations, i.e. concern for productivity and concern for people.

Some managers are high in concern for productivity but low in concern for people; others are high in concern for people but low in concern for productivity. Besides helping, managers evaluate their concern for people and productivity, the Managerial Grid stresses the importance of developing a team-management leadership style.

In grid OD, change agents use a questionnaire to determine the existing styles of managers, help them to re-examine their own styles and work towards maximum effectiveness. A grid OD programme generally has six phases:

1. **Training**. Key managers learn about grid concepts and how they are applied in a week-long seminar. They assess their own managerial styles and work on improving such skills as team development, group problem-solving and communication. After appropriate instruction, the key managers will work to implement the grid programme throughout the organisation.
2. **Team Development**. The trained managers bring their new understanding of Managerial Grid concepts to the work situation. Emphasis is placed on improving both manager-subordinate relationships and team effectiveness, so the team will operate on the 9 grid level.
3. **Inter-group Development**. This phase focuses on the relationship between the organisation's work groups to improve coordination and cooperation. Inter-group tensions are dealt with openly and joint problem solving procedures are developed.
4. **Organisational Goal Setting**. Top managers together create an ideal model of the organisation. They set goals to be tested, evaluated and refined by managers and subordinates working together throughout the organisation.
5. **Goal Attainment**. Organisation members seek to make the ideal model a reality. Each sub-unit examines how its activities should be carried out in order to achieve excellence and it proceeds to take whatever corrective actions are necessary.
6. **Stabilisation.** Eventually, the results of all the phases are evaluated to determine which areas of the organisation still need improvement or alteration. Efforts are made to stabilize positive changes and to identify new areas of opportunity for the organisation.
7. **Re-structuring.** The organisation's structure may be changed to make it more efficient by re-defining the flow of authority. There can also be changes in functional responsibility, such as a move from product to matrix organisational structure.

   Organisational structure often reflects the personal desires, needs and values of the chief executive. Changing structure, therefore, may create resistance and concern because people are worried about their power or status, or how the change will affect their work-group.
8. **Job Redesigning.** Work design is a broad term meaning the process of defining tasks and jobs to achieve both organisational and employee goals. It must,

therefore take into account the nature of the organisational interest, the organisationl structure, the information flow and decision processes, the differences among employees and the reward system. Within the broad scope of work design is the design of individual jobs, that is, job design. Job analysis is the process of obtaining information about jobs. Job redesign makes use of job analysis to redefine the job in terms of tasks, behaviour, education, skills, relationship and responsibilities required.

When job designing is the objective, job analysis is indispensable. Fortunately, job designers hardly ever have to start from scratch because few functions are entirely new. Much of job design, therefore, consists of redistributing activities and re-configuring existing jobs. Even under circumstances where jobs are entirely new, imaginative job designers have been able to design future activities accurately.

9. **Job Enrichment.** Job enrichment implies increasing the contents of a job or the deliberate upgrading of responsibility, scope and challenge in work. Job enrichment is a motivational technique which emphasises the need for challenging and interesting work. It suggests that jobs be re-designed so that intrinsic satisfaction is derived from doing the job. In its best application, it leads to vertically enhanced job by adding functions from other organisational levels making it contain more variety and challenge and offer autonomy and pride to the job-holder." The job-holder is given a measure of discretion in making operational decisions concerning his job. In this sense, he gains a feeling of higher status, influence and power.

   The term 'job enlargement' connotes something different from 'job enrichment'. Job enlargement attempts to make a job more varied by removing the dullness associated with performing repetitive operations. It involves a horizontal loading or expansion, i.e., the addition of more tasks of the same nature. But in job enrichment, the attempt is to build into the job a higher sense of challenge and importance of achievement. Job enrichment involves vertical loading of functions and responsibilities which require higher level of skills and competence.

10. **Survey Feedback.** A major difficulty in relying solely on sensitivity training is that it neglects the important procedural aspects of the functioning of teams. While the team members may get along with each other better as a result of the sensitivity training, in most cases, they will not become more effective unless there is an improvement in their actual procedure, the way they go about solving their problem.

To restore the balance, another approach to team development has emerged, that of survey feedback. This approach, first developed at the Institute of Social Research of the University of Michigan, aims to get teams in organisations to devise better processes for handling the issues facing them. Although consultants differ in how they apply survey feedback approach They usually require the team to spend some time in highly concentrated activity, usually from two to three days, away from the working situation, in examining how it goes about its tasks of setting objectives, making decisions, tackling problems and relating to each other.

As its title suggests, the method used by the consultant is to "survey" the situation as it currently is and "feedback" his analysis to the group. The feedback information is then discussed and worked on by the team members, who gradually learn to take over from the consultant the process of surveying what they are doing and feeding this back to themselves as an essential aid to their long-term development as a team. The concentrated 2-3 days' feedback survey activity has the objective of creating an awareness among team members of what processes are going on within the group situation and then training them to build on the positive elements in those processes and to reduce the negative elements. In order to do this, the consultant may use a number of structured exercises and survey instruments and also encourage the team members to use sensing, critiquing, and other feedback methods.

Survey feedback approach is most effective at improving teams whose members already possess higher degree of conceptual skills and are dealing with long-term issues. This approach is less useful with teams which are concerned essentially with day-to-day activities and short-term results.

## Case Incident 1

Narmada Chemicals is a large chemicals manufacturing firm located in the Western ghats. It is involved with both research and the production of various product sold to wholesale customers as well as over-the-counter pharmaceutical. Recently Ram Moorthi was appointed as the new director of the company's research & development function. He took over at a time when this part of Narmada Chemicals seemed to be in some turmoil. The previous director resigned suddenly, leaving an administrative vacuum. In addition, executives of some of the other department had been complaining that the R&D people were not pulling their weight. Several had wondered out loud where the new products were that the company needed in order to remain competitive? Why were not those high-priced professionals working harder to achieve a new breakthroughs?

The firm's CEO seemed to be on the side of the other departmental heads in believing that major changes in the R&D function were needed and quickly. He frequently stated, "This is a fast-moving industry and those firms that do not remain novel will simply be left behind." At any rate, he instructed Ram Moorthi to get things moving as rapidly as possible.

Ram Moorthi's appointed was approved by the Board of Directors over the expressed opposition of several of the senior research people. They did not feel that his background or previous experience made him sufficiently qualified to take over the complex task of supervising a diverse group of research scientists. There were twenty-five highly trained professionals in this group, twenty of whom possessed Ph.D. in Physics, Chemistry or Microbiology. The other five had Master's Degrees but had worked in R&D for over fifteen years. There was relatively little agreement within this large group about the major problems facing the group or how they could be solved. In fact, several of the scientists believed that everything was fine the way it was.

Even though Ram Moorthi had no direct experience with R&D, he did have a track record as manager in other areas and he had Master's degrees in both finance and chemical engineering. He did not believe that he would have problems relating to the R&D group. In fact, he felt quite confident that he could turn things around in relatively short period.

Upon assuming his new duties, Ram Moorthi moved quickly to bring changes in the R&D department. He began by conducting interviews with several of the senior scientists in order to learn about the operations and how the employees perceived the situation. He followed up with several open meetings attended by most of the department members.

For the first few months, everything was smooth. The department members appeared satisfied with Ram Moorthi and morale actually improved However, it soon became apparent that things were not as rosy as they seemed at first. Several of the senior researchers began to complain that changes were taking place and that they had never been consulted. In additions a number of people had received long critical letters from Ram Moorthi suggesting that they were no longer making positive contributions to the company or the department.

By the end of the first year, top management had begun to realize that all was not well. Morale in the R&D department was very bad. There seemed to be a movement afoot to request Ram Moorthi's resignation. Two of the more promising younger scientists submitted their resignations citing intolerable working conditions and a number of others were threatening to do the same. To make matters worse, the firm was not successful in recruiting the replacements it needed. Whether or not this was due to Ram Moorthi was not really clear.

When asked, the senior researchers complained that Ram Moorthi was an autocrat. He did not carefully think through problems and appeared not to systematically analyse situations. Also, he was impatient. He wanted everything to happen immediately. For example, for sometime, top management had been considering the use of robots in several department. Without consulting anyone in R&D, Ram Moorthi volunteered his department as a test site. One morning a memo arrived announcing the change, nobody in the department was even aware of the possibility of such a change.

At the moment, top management is faced with a serious dilemma. Ram Moorthi had a record of competent management and he was hired with a mandate to get things moving. However, rather than improving, this situation seems to have gone worse. Should they fire Ram Moorthi, move him to another.

## Case Incident 2

A business school is being run very successfully and is known for providing value based education with a very high degree of transparency and professionalism located in the National Capital Territory (NCT) of Delhi. It has been established under the self-financing scheme and is affiliated to the University established by the Government of NCT of Delhi.

On Feb. 15, 2003, there was a cricket match between Australia and India from 1330 hrs. IST under the World Cup series. There was lot of curiosity amongst Indians in general about the outcome of the match. The students of a particular class in the Institute decided to go for mass bunking mainly because of two reasons. First being the cricket match and the second being a class that was not very interesting. The scheduled teacher could not reach by 1320 hrs., the scheduled time for the class due to some miscommunication and the students did not wait for the other teacher to start which takes about ten minutes. The general practice, since inception, being followed by the Institute was that if the scheduled teacher is not able to make it in time then the class is given to some other teacher of the same class. The students were well aware of this practice and that is why they left the premises very quickly to have the opportunity to watch the cricket match. The attendance was thin in the subsequent classes also, say about fifty percent.

The day was historic for both the cricket match as India scored the lowest score of 125 all out in the World Cup cricket and the Institute as such an incident occurred for the first time in the history of the Institute.

A high powered committee of the Institute was called immediately to take stock of the situation. A very serious note was taken about the situation involving a case of indiscipline by the students and various alternatives were discussed apart from ensuring that there is no communication gap regarding the time table.

One of the alternatives that came forward was that all the classes for that particular section should be suspended till further orders. The other alternative proposed was that five students who were leaders of this move should be suspended from attending classes till further orders. Another view was about the role of Class Representatives and their responsibility in such situations and as to why they should not be suspended from attending classes.

The Director referred a real life story that transformed the life of one of the students who is currently a team leader of the consulting wing of the Institute. The incident that he shared pertains to the year 1998 when some students were supposed to make a presentation in the class and the attendance in the class was very thin. The teacher who is currently the President of the Governing Body, asked about the reason for low attendance and he was informed about the cricket match that was going on simultaneously. The teacher laughed and asked a few questions:

(a) Do you know that how many people in India would be watching this cricket match and how many are playing?

(b) What these players are likely to get if they come out as winners or losers?

(c) What the viewers are likely to get while watching the match and after the match is over?

(d) How much is the productivity loss in terms of man-hours in one-day match and in five-days match?

(e) Where does India stand today in terms of productivity and work culture as compared to Japan, USA, etc.?

The responses to these questions were discussed in the class and the figures that came out were mind boggling. The result of that discussion has not been studied on other students but one of the students who is currently the team leader and heading a consulting wing of the institute says that he has not been able to watch cricket match after that incident. He further says that the transformation is not only regarding watching one event but in all the activities that he undertakes. He now does an analysis about the various aspects including the cost-benefit analysis before undertaking any such activity. He still keeps track of the news about the outcome of the cricket match from the newspaper to satisfy his need for sense of pride in case India wins a match. He says that beyond this sense of pride there was nothing more that he used to get earlier for which he now invests only two to five minutes.

The President remarked that it would be wonderful if everyone who has something to contribute in the productive hours does that first because no productive hour lost can be regained by any means. But that seems to be an ideal situation and continued the discussion to help evolve some permanent solution.

A thought came that let us do something where again we would be number one in the country. The thought was that let us put the profile of each student on the internet and let us put a line in the character certificate about the detailed report on the web-site about the student. The profile would contain both the deeds and misdeeds done by the students during the time that he invested or spent with the Institute. This would make the system more transparent to the society at large. Anybody who wants to know the details about any pass out or drop out from the Institute would have access to that information without any manual help. Video camera monitoring system and smart campus card access control system would ensure the tracking about each activity in the Institute. The remarks given by each faculty for each subject would also speak volumes about the student. This would help the prospective employers of the students passing out from this Institute to have a better picture about the overall development and holistic perspective about the candidate in question. Earlier, they used to get a mark-sheet and a character certificate of each candidate to know about the performance.

The meeting continued for about four hours discussing the pros and cons of each alternative and the behavioural issues involved. The meeting was adjourned for the day and it was decided to take a decision in the next meeting.

## Questions

1. What is the real problem in this case? Is it possible to transform all the students? Justify your answer.
2. What decision would you have taken if you were the Director of the Institute?

3. What recommendations would you make if you were the Consultant Organisational Behaviour?

## Case Incident 3

Mr. Kulkarni got promotion last year and has been posted as Foreman in a production shop. Before his promotion to the management cadre, he had been a supervisor for four years. His work on that job had considerably been outstanding it may be recalled that Kulkarni joined the company as a Trade Apprentice. He did well in his subsequent jobs. He rose to the job of a supervisor in about six years. His human relations were generally good. His colleagues had wished him well on his promotion.

To improve the working of his shop, Kulkarni introduced some changes in his shop. He re-allocated the responsibilities of the supervisors and changed the shifts and machines of some operators. He thought that this change would improve the working of his shop. However, from that time onwards Kulkarni began to have trouble as a foreman. The supervisors in his shop gave him the silent treatment. The operators seemed to make mistakes even in doing simple things. Everyday there was a machine shutdown. By the end of the quarter, Kulkarni's workshop was showing the poorest production record in the whole of plant.

### Questions

1. What do you think has gone wrong?
2. Did Kulkarni make a mistake in introducing the changes? Justify your answer.
3. If you were Kulkarni, what would you do to get the things right?

***

# 16 Organisational Conflict

It is a comprehensive term covering misunderstanding to irritation, structure breakdown and non-cooperation. The symptoms of conflict are confrontation strikes, lock-outs, donors agitation, destruction, obstruction and breakdown etc.

Conflict means breakdown in the standard mechanism of decision making and if occurs when an individual or a group experiences difficulty in selecting an alternative. The conflict is multi-dimensional and the four dimensions of conflict are:

1. Conflict within the individual
2. Interpersonal conflict
3. Intergroup conflict
4. Inter-organisational conflict

## 1. Conflict within the individual

Management should keep in mind that all men have conflicts within themselves. The conflict within the individual can display in itself number of alternatives. Conflict occurs because of discrepancy between the individual's real ability and the ability needed to hold his present position. Individual conflict can also occur because of his different positions and roles within the organisation. The individual can also occur because of his different positions and roles within the organisation. The individual can also create conflict within himself if there are too many ambiguities contained in his position. Therefore, there are several reasons for conflicts which can individual experiences within the confinement of his job duties.

## 2. Inter-personal Conflicts

All conflicts are basically interpersonal conflicts because most of the conflicts involve conflict between a person in one group and another in the same or different group. It can be presented in-terms of different levels of obstruction. It may lead to delay in decisionmaking or may arise either due to distortion in the structural form or because of the complexity of individual needs. Interpersonal conflict has the tendency to resolve itself because of the conflict has the tendency to resolve itself because of the conflicting parties of able to continue in a tense situation for a very long time. Time is the healing factor for it. It is the time factor which normally helps to resolve interpersonal conflicts.

### 3. Intergroup Conflicts

Most of the intergroup conflicts are because of their rational goals of individuals and groups. The conventional method of managing group conflicts are:

(a) Use of authority for the suppression of conflicts

(b) Blaming the other party

(c) Finding a scapegoat

The managing of conflict will vary because of the circumstances and external environment, case history, assumptions and belief about the groups. The new techniques of inter group conflict are:

(a) Decentralisation of power and authority

(b) Development of subordinates

(c) Participation style of management

(d) Job enrichment and job enlargement

### 4. Inter-organisational Conflicts

In inter-organisational conflicts, the external environment like social institutions, group dynamism, culture of the group and government policies play an important role. Conflicts are not evil but part of the natural order. Conflicts are because of the generational gap. Managers must try to live with the conflict. In the conflict is properly handled, it can be constructive in achieving the results. It can act as a stimulus, it may be a challenge and motivational force to keep the organisation going.

## Conflict

Traditional management considers conflict as harmful and recommends suppression. But this view no longer holds good. Conflict can never be wiped off completely. Moreover, conflicts are not all together bad. It has creative elements as well. Therefore, the emphasis should be on harnessing it for improvement rather than fighting, considering it harmful. The conflicting parties should approach the conflict in-terms of "problem-solving" rather than in-terms of "win-loss". The "win-loss" tendency generates hostilities, rules out constructive solutions and the parties think in-terms of sectional gains and concessions rather than mutual benefits.

If conflicts are skilfully handled, they can resolve the problems and improve the human relations in the organisation. They can generate challenging spirit and make the management pool resources to accelerate the pace of progress overcoming the speed-breakers conflict and problems are the price of progress. Conflicts, therefore, are not discouraging but the attitude towards them can be. If handled properly, they produce creative problem-solving situation to help the organisation to achieve its goals.

Conflicts continually occur in our social life. They occur at various levels within the individuals in a group and between groups and may have important implication on the work and effectiveness of the persons and groups involved.

The nature and intensity of conflict varies from individual to individual, and from group to group and it puts a manager in a very difficult situation. A manager often experiences his most uncomfortable moments when he has to deal with conflicts or differences among people or groups of people of work. Presence of conflict complicates his job in so many ways and therefore, it is of great importance that the manager should understand the conflict and try to handle it effectively.

## Management of Conflict

The management job within the business organisation calls for the manager to function in such a way as to maximise the coordination of human and work system and to minimise the conflict of the individuals within the formal organisation. Management is a dynamic process which is charged with the responsibility for optimising the utilisation of internal resources for the accomplishment of external purposes. Thus, the managerial environment may be characterised as elements of conflict and change.

Conflict is represented as the multi-faced dimensions of management practice: Internal-external animate-inanimate and national-international. Conflict has been referred to broadly as the totality of differences arising in the various value-orientation of the environmental systems. Conflict of the individual within the formal organisátion can be handled through a system of authority, organisation structure and work flow. There is a need of managing a business organisation within an internal and external environment of change and conflict.

Management of conflicts has assumed great significance because it influences the human relations at work. Lakhs of people, almost everyday, return home from work in despair, depressed and disgusted with their job problems. Because of differences in their minds and with other people, they feel uneasy and unhappy. Though they spend about one third of each day (only five or six days a week) at work place, the psychological handover of the tension and conflict generated at the place of work continues even beyond the hours of work. He has also to face conflicts in his social life, this means that a major portion of the employees life goes in conflicts. These prolonged conflicts and tensions tell upon employee's mental and physical health and set at the basic roofs of his efficiency and productivity.

## Conflicts in an Organisation

The conflict free company has never existed and will never exist. Antagonism, tensions, aggressions, stored types, negative attitudes and the frustration and perceived conflicting needs will always be present, whenever men are forced to live and work together. Thus, the reality of conflict in organisations cannot be denied. As a matter of fact, conflict can be viewed as a necessary condition for bringing about change in any system.

Organisations, therefore, use a number of conflict resolution mechanisms to solve these problems as and when they arise. Bargaining in the case of limited resources conditions, minimising the need for interdependence by reallocation of resources etc. In case of superior – subordinate problems, some of the common strategies used by organisations are to resolve conflicts. Even if the conditions of conflict are present, the organisation tends to limit the perception of these conflict which are of immediate consequence. As a result, organisation tends to become highly selective in attending primarily to short-term conflicts, the symptoms of which have become visible and thus can easily be detected.

Thus, interest in the nature of organisation and its multiple goals are the conditions of conflict. Thus in order to reduce dysfunctionality of conflict leading to subsequent increase in its constructive resolution. It will be necessary to create an open confirmation and problem-solving climate in the organisation that can sustain, encourage and strengthen the conflict resolution mechanisms.

### Stages of Conflict

Five stages of conflict episode may be identified as :

1. Latent conflict
2. Perceived conflict
3. Felt Conflict
4. Manifest Conflict
5. Conflict aftermath

### 1. Latent Conflict

Four basic types of latent conflicts are:

(a) Competition for scarce resources

(b) Drive for autonomy

(c) Divergence of goals

(d) Role conflict

Competition forms the basis for conflict, when the aggregate demands of participants for resources exceed the resources available to the organisation. Autonomy needs form the basis of conflict when only party either seeks to exercise control over some activity that another party regards as its own province or seeks to insulate itself from such control: goal divergence is the source of conflict when two parties which must cooperate on some joint activity are unable to reach a consensus on concerted action. Two or more types of latent conflicts may also be present at the same time. The role conflict model trades the organisation as a collection of role sets, each compound of the focal persons having different roles. Conflict is said to occur when the focal person receives incompatible role demands or expectations from the persons in his role set. The difficulty in this is that it treats the focal person as merely a passive receiver rather than as an active participant in the relationship.

### 2. Perceived Conflict

Conflicts may sometimes be perceived when no conditions of latent conflict exist and latent conditions may be present in a relationship without any of the participants perceiving the conflict. The case in which conflict is perceived when no latent conflict arises is said to result from the parties misunderstanding of each other's true position. Such conflict can be resolved by improving communication between the parties.

### 3. Felt Conflict

There is an important distinction between perceived conflict, and felt conflict. We may be aware that "B" and "A" are in serious disagreement over some policy, but it may have no effect whatsoever on "A"s affection towards "B". The personalisation of conflict is the mechanism which causes many people to be concerned with dysfunction of conflict. There are two explanations for the personalisation of conflict. First, the inconsistent demands on efficient organisation and individual growth which is created within the individual. Conflicts may also result from crisis or from extra-organisational pressures. Individuals need to vent these antics in order to maintain internal equilibrium. Secondly, conflict becomes personalised when whole personality of the individual is involved in the relationship. Hostile feelings are most common in the intimate relations that characterise various institutions and residential colleagues.

### 4. Manifest Conflict

By manifest conflict, it is meant any of the several varieties of conflicting behaviour. The most obvious of thesse is open aggression, but such physical and verbal violence is usually strongly prescribed by organisational norms. Except for prison, riots, political revolutions and extreme labour unrest, violence as a form of manifest conflict is rare. The motivation towards violence may remain, but they tend to be expressed in less violent form.

### 5. Conflict Aftermath

Each conflict episode is but one of the sequence of such episodes that constitute the relationships among organisation members. If the conflict is genuinely resolved to the satisfaction of all participants, the basis for a more cooperative relationship may be laid, or the participants in latent conflicts not previously perceived and dealt. On the otherhand, if the conflict is merely suppressed but not resolved, the latent conditions of conflict may be aggravated and explored in more serious form until they are rectified or until the relationship dissolves. This conflict episode is called "conflict aftermath".

## Source of Conflict

The source of conflict is found in some degrees of actual or perceived divergence of interests. At one extreme, conflict is rooted in a sharp incompatibility or collusion of interests. Any satisfaction or victory, for one side means dissatisfaction or defeat for the other. In game theory, this limiting case is described as a zero sum game. At the other extreme, conflict may be rooted in the interests that are different but not necessarily incomparable. People disagree over facts, goals, methods and values because they have different interests and perceptions.

Decision making itself is a fundamental source of conflict because it invariably involves conflicting considerations or pressures. But most conflicts are embedded in a multi-dimensional matrix of interests. Each conflict usually involves a complete set of interests. It can be properly identified only by a profile or vector or different points. The factors affecting the sources of conflict are:

### 1. Informational Factors

These exert their influence when various points of view have been developed on the basis of different part or have a limited knowledge and they disagree.

### 2. Perceptual Factors

These exert their influence when the persons have different images of the same stimulus. Because of perception, each will attend to and select from the information available, those items which he thinks important. Each will interpret the information in a somewhat different manner. The picture which he gets from his own experience, is unique to him. Thus, it is not surprising that the same basic facts may produce distinctive perceptual pictures in the minds of different individuals.

### 3. Role Factors

Role factors influence the source of conflict because each individual occupies a certain position or status in the society or in the organisation. The fact that he occupies such a position or status may put certain constraints on him if the discussion is related to this role.

## Negative and Positive Aspects of Conflict

The negative potentials of conflict are quite obvious. Just as internal conflict within an individual can destroy his ability to function, similarly internal conflict within an organisation may result in some sort of blocks in decisionmaking. For those who want to destroy an organisation or its effectiveness, there is probably no more effective method then the promotion of internal conflict. The destructive possibilities or inter-organisational conflicts are even more apparent. It may result in unnecessary competition and may put the existence of a small organisation in danger.

Conflicts do not constitute always a bad thing. Whether conflict is desirable or not, depends upon what purpose is served by conflict. For instance conflict may provide an opportunity for releasing tension which otherwise would remain suppressed. Conflicts also provide opportunity for review of existing positions and making better alternative acceptable to the parties concerned. Though a conflict may threaten the emotional well-being of individual persons; it may also be a positive factor in personal character development. Therefore, it is difficult to say whether conflict is functional or dysfunctional.

## Why Conflicts Arise?

Tensions and Conflicts arise due to many factors such as economic, social and psychological. Psychological factors no doubt contribute predominantly. For instance, feeling of insecurity is a patent cause of tension and conflict. It is generally the case that fear of security is 20% financial and 80% emotional. Personal earning is not solely the answer to present days growing search for security. Self-knowledge and recognition, besides a source of livelihood will probably ensure better security.

Conflicts may arise due to lack of consideration, lack of appreciation, misunderstanding or bad handling of situations and problems. Though the 21st century has been credited for having more unprecedented advances in science and technology, the vast field of human relations still remain unexplored to a great extent. Nevertheless, some industrial enterprises with a view to improve efficiency, and effectiveness and to reduce conflict, are becoming increasingly conscious of it and want to promote harmonious work relationships. As a result of this consciousness and search, we find today greater emphasis on human relations than ever before.

## Approaches to Conflict Resolution

Since the conflicts in organisations may have serious consequences, so the question is how to approach to the resolution of conflict. R. Blake has suggested three alternative approaches to the problem of dealing with conflict:

1. "Conflict is inevitable, agreement is possible". On this view, one may decide to fight it out. This would result in "win-lose" power struggle. Such a struggle may appear beneficial to the winner immediately following the struggle, but the main issues of conflicts can hardly be solved this way. Alternatively, the parties may depend on third party judgment or on fate. But still the main issues are likely to remain unresolved.
2. "Conflict may not be inevitable: agreement is not possible", on this assumption, the parties may decide to withdraw from interaction or become indifferent to

the problems they face. This approach may also provide satisfaction and benefits to some, but may not lead to any meaningful resolution of conflict.

3. "Although conflicts may arise in various situations, agreement is possible". This is regarded as the most satisfactory approach to deal with conflicts. Here both parties would recognise that there is a need for solving the problem that has arisen. On this premise, the parties may begin interacting with each other. The problem may first be identified and then ways and means devised to solve it. A typical example of this method is collective bargaining. By negotiating and from bargaining, it may be possible for the parties to arrive at solutions which are less temporary and more widely acceptable to all the other solutions. Morever, negotiations provide opportunities to groups and persons to understand each others strength and weakness, abilities and constraints. Such understanding may be useful in dontaining or solving future conflicts more easily and efficiently. Schmidt and Tannenbum have suggested fair approaches which may be used by a manager at different times to deal with the conflicts. These are: (1) Avoidance (2) Repression (3) Sharpening into conflict (4) Transformation into problem-solving.

## Avoidance of Differences

A manager can avoid the occurrence of many differences among his different subordinates. For example, he can place people in groups whose experiences are similar, who have had similar training and who come from a similar level of society. Because of something in common, these people tend to see things similarly to have common interests and objectives, to approach problems in much the same way. The behaviour of such persons/groups is more predictable and it is easy for the manager to avoid conflict. Another way of avoiding differences is the controlling of inter-personal contacts of the people. He can place two conflicting individuals in different groups or physical locations.

The important question arises here is whether the conflicts showed be suppressed in the beginning or not. Most of the people view conflict as something very low and so according to them it should always be avoided. This approach may work well in certain specific situations only. The manager who uses this approach continuously runs the risk of reducing the total creativity of his staff. In an atmosphere where differences are avoided, no new idea will come into surface and the old ideas are likely to go unexamined. There is genuine danger of the organisation's slipping unknowingly into a rut of complacency.

## Transformation of Conflicts into Problem-solving

The persons involved in the conflict can bring to bear on the problem a greater variety of insights. If the differences are such as enriching, the individuals involved are likely to come up with a better solution because many problems can be seen clearly only if the individuals who see different aspects may come together and pool their information. When it comes to choosing courses of action for a given problem, differences among the individuals in an organisation can help to increase the range and variety of alternatives suggested.

The transformation of conflict into problem solving situation may also help to deal with some of the feelings which often accompany disagreement, frustration, resentment and hostility. The manager using this approach may help to channelise the energy generated by feelings into creative, rather than into destructive activities. For this, he should clarify the nature of conflict and give recognition to the feelings of individuals involved. He should also give attention to maintaining relationships between the disputing parties and should create appropriate vehicles for communication among the disputing parties.

When the disputing parties negotiate, discuss and communicate with each other, at least they would agree to differ in certain areas, in certain aspects and on certain matters and this initial area of agreement can be improved by means of clarity, consistency and continuity of communication. One is made to see the other man's point of view when one could transmit his views. Lippitt and Schmidt, while writing on "crisis in a developing organisation", noted the many types of crises organisations face. They identify five stages with crisis described as:

1. At the start, to create a new organisational system
2. To survive
3. To stabilise
4. To earn a good reputation
5. To achieve uniqueness, and
6. To earn respect and appreciation

## Internal Change

It is possible to identify several common categories of problems that frequently precipitate crisis. It can be noted, for example, that some of them are essentially internal in their origin. They arise out of changes in the variables within the system. The organisation's people may change in-terms of their attitudes and values, their knowledge and sophistication, their average age and experience.

Such changes may and do create difficult problems for organisations and their leaders. They may result in individuals and groups may feel that their goals and interests are in conflict with those of the organisation. They may resist its leadership and control.

## Exogenous Factors

At the same time, organisations may encounter problems generated outside the system but in its environment. Political change, for example, may make the organisatilon's mission less acceptable or more difficult. Organisations established to sell alcoholic liquors faced such a crisis in the historic or era of prohibition. Social change may create new problems: emphasis on disagreement and equal opportunity in recent years provide an example.

## Organisation vs People.

Within an organisation, one major problem area involves relationships between the organisational and the individuals who compose it. Another is concerned with conflicts (1) among and between organisations, and (2) involving the sub-organisation within an organisation.

Traditional theory saw little need for concern about the interface between the organisation and its people. However, Bennis has provided a succicnt summary:

"In classical theory, then, the conflict between the man and the organisation was neatly settled in favour of the organisation. The only road to efficiency and productivity was to surrender man's needs to the service of the bloodless machine".

Much of the more recent theory presents a different view. It is concerned with the efforts of organisational climate on individual contributions and assumes that an organisation must promise its members significant satisfactions. Rising interest in the "individual-centered" approach to management turned the spotlight on the organisation – person interface.

Five major human problems confronting contemporary working organisations include:

1. How to integrate personal needs with organisational goals.
2. How to distribute power and authority
3. How to develop mechanisms capable of reducing intraorganisational conflict
4. How to ensure effective adaptation to changes in the environment, and
5. How to assure vitality and growth and prevent decay.

Among the above, allocation of authority and power deserves detailed treatment while the others have been dealt with in the desired degree of detail.

***

# 17 Compensation Management

## Introduction

The term 'Compensation' refers to all forms of financial returns and tangible benefits that employees receive as part of an employment relationship. Beyond this pure economic exchange model, compensation may also be viewed as (a) a system of rewards that motivates employees to perform; (b) a critical communication device through which organisations convey and reinforce the values, culture, and the behaviours they require; and (c) an important mechanism that enables organisations to achieve their business objectives.

As the business environment becomes increasingly complex and global, the challenge to create and maintain effective compensation programmes, given cost constraints, also requires greater professional expertise, organisational understanding, creativity, and vision than ever before.

Compensation practices have important implications for organisations, for individuals, and for society as a whole. Harvard Professor Rosabeth Moss Kanter considers compensation a key to competitive advantage (or disadvantages). She asserts, "Innovations in compensation are necessary to succeed at the doing-more-with-less balancing act: simultaneously reducing obligations and stretching capacities, lowering fixed costs and encouraging new ideas. In the post entrepreneurial corporation, pay must more nearly match contribution.

From the organisation's perspective, compensation represents a major investment. In labour-intensive organisations, labour costs typically constitute the single largest proportion of the organisation's operating budget. In some organisations, employee remuneration costs may be 70 to 80 percent of operating budget.

Organisations that have higher labour costs than their main competitors might have to charge higher prices to make up the difference, and price is a major source of competitive advantage (or disadvantage). But these organisations may also be competing against each other in the labour market for scarce skills. Microsoft has been able to recruit the very best computer engineers to some extent, because of its superior compensation packages. Thus, while labour costs may be higher, at least for certain jobs, Microsoft takes the position that winning in the labour market is worth it. If higher labour costs translate into higher productivity, new products, and higher quality, the cost may be worth it. Effective compensation systems should constantly monitor the trade-off between labour costs and personnel requirements.

Many downsizing/reengineering efforts are directed at shrinking payrolls and reducing labour costs to stay competitive. Some experts maintain that this recent vigilance has paid off in the form of higher productivity, higher profits, and simultaneously the wages and benefits has declined as a percentage of output to their lowest level. The vigilance comes in many forms such as – outsourcing, the use of temporary and part time employees, and the expansion of labour markets into lower wage countries have all contributed to the control of employee wages. With the increased globalisation of the world economy, fostered by improvements in technology, communications, logistics, and distribution even the service sector of the economy, fostered by improvements in technology, communications, logistics, and distribution even the service sector of the economy is taking advantage of labour wages in other countries to get work done. The high-tech industry, for example, now routinely contracts with operations in India for computer programming previously done by V. S. workers. This results in a substantial reduction in labour costs.

Other countries of the world now look outside their borders to produce products and services. Mercedes-Benz and BMW cars are now built in the United States instead of in Germany, partly because of reduced labour costs (german workers have the highest pay and the shortest working hours in the world). But why didn't BMW build a plant in Mexico (instead of South Carolina) to reduce labour costs even further. The cost of labour can be assessed only in the context of other variables such as access to markets, distribution, and workforce quality. Labour costs must always be assessed in context with a focus on corporate strategy, corporate performance, and the critical relationship between what a company pays and its ability to attract and retain valuable employees.

The influence of trade unions in Indian economy has been considerably decreasing and the Indian companies now have more flexibility to reduce their labour costs. For example, the Supreme Court in a landmark judgement has announced strike in industries as illegal and not as a right. On the other hand, lots of PSU's are facing the action of dis-investment and privatisation. Compensation practices are a key factor that influences the type and level of talent an organisation can attract and retain. They also represent an important opportunity to align, focus, and direct worker's attention to critical projects and priorities. Thus, compensation practices can directly influence an organisation's survival, profitability, long-term growth potential and competitive advantage.

From the individual perspective, compensation plays a major role in influencing one's lifestyle, status and self-esteem. Compensation affects where people live, how much disposable income they have, how they spend vacations and where their children will be educated. Compensation influences people's choices of which jobs to accept, how long they will stay, and the degree of effort they will apply. From a societal viewpoint, the general compensation practices of organisations have long been viewed as a platform for social change. Legislation like Industrial Disputes Act 1947, Trade union Act 1926, Payment of Wage Act...., Minimum Wage Act...., Equal Remuneration Act ...., Workmen Compensation Act, Maturity Act, Employees State Insurance Act, Provident Fund Act, Employees Pension Act, Gratuity Act directly regulate compensation practices within the employer-employees relationship in a direction that society believes to be desirable. Some argue that excessive compensation practices are the principal reason the Indian Industries (PSUs) are incurring more in non-momentary incentives than monetary benefits. Some assert that industry setbacks can be traced to product price increases necessitated by the unreasonable wage and benefits demands of its workers.

## A Historical Survey

The low of workmen's compensation or as introduced in India in 1923, twenty-six years after it has been introduced in England. To England it had come from Germany where it had been introduced in 1884 by the Iron Chancellor, Bismark, who was the first among the European statesmen to understand fully the implications of the Marxist challenge and to take some steps towards forestalling the threatened revolution of workers by providing for their security in various forms. One of the benefits secured to the workers by a new law was a right to receive compensation from their employer for injuries suffered in the course of employment, irrespectively of any fault or breach of duty on the part of the employers. It has been rightly remarked by Hon'ble Mr. Justice Phanibhushan Chakravarty, Ex. Chief Justice Calcutta High Court that in England, however, the movement towards a law of workmen's compensation sums to have been caused by broad consideration of justice and humanity rather than a motive of neutralising the revolutionary potentialities of the working class by seeking actively to their contentment. In its scope too, the British Act of 1897 fell short of the German precedent in one respect while the German Act required employers to indemnify injured workmen, or in the case of fatal accidents, their families and it also set up an increase system under which the employers were obliged to insure the risk, the British Act only made indemnification at prescribed rates obligatory, but left insurance of the risk to remain optional.

What the Indian Act was enacted, the law in force in England, on which it is modelled was the Act of 1906, at last amended by the Act of 1923 in order to understand what exactly that law amounted to, towards the middle of the 19th Century, it began to be felt that there was too much of government which was destroying individual initiative and affecting the prosperity of the nation. The feeling led to the evolution of the doctrine of the *Laissez faire* which means let things alone. After it had been formulated the doctrine of *laissez faire* found a rapid and wide acceptance particularly in England, and it ushered in a period during which the agencies of production operated under condition, of complete economic freedom. The experiment with a policy of complete economic freedom was carried on for a considerable period but in the end, *laissez faire*, in its turn, began to reveal its own defects. Taking again the sphere of employment alone, it was found that not only were the employers imposing, in the name of freedom of contract, cruelty, harsh terms on the employee who had no equal for gaining power and forcing them to work for unconsciously long hours and under appalling conditions but the employees had even no adequate means of relief against the employers for injuries sustained in their service.

Although the workmen's Compensation Act was enacted to make it easier and cheaper for the workmen to obtain at least some compensation, it did not rid his chance of getting compensation altogether of uncertainty and difficulty. He had still to prove that the accident, causing the injury had not only arisen in the course of his employment but had also arisen out of it and his claim could be defeated if it could be shown, except in cases of death or serious and permanent disablement, that he himself had been guilty of wilful misconduct which had led to the accident.

It will thus be seen that, in England, workmen's compensation has ceased to be a matter of decree by the courts against the employer on proof of the necessary facts and has become an insured benefit obtainable from the state of special fund maintained for the purpose. This is the short story of the history and development of workmen's compensation payable to the workers in England beautifully and critically traced by Hon'ble Mr. Justice Chakravarty. Similar dissatisfaction in the United States with the operation of employer's liability laws resulted investigations by various government commissions. In 1910, New York became the first state to enact a workmen's compensation law sufficiently comprehensive to meet the problem effectively. By the end of 19th century the coincidence of increasing industrial injuries and decreasing remedies had produced in the United States a situation ripe for radical change, and when, in 1893, a full account of the German system written by John Graham Brooks was published as the fourth special Report of the Commissioner of Labour, legislators all over the country seized up on it as a clue to the direction which efforts of reform might take. Another stimulus was provided by the enactment of the first British Compensation Act, in 1897, which later became the model of state Acts in many respects.

It would be desirable to mention the brief historical note as to how the workmen's compensation law has been developed and enacted in our country. The question of granting compensation to workmen for fatal or serious accidents was first raised in India in 1884 and the need for proper legislation was emphasised by factory and mining inspectors. But the question of framing legislation was taken up by the government of India only in the end of 1920 and in 1921 public opinion on the subject was invited. In order to examine the question in some detail it was referred to a small committee composed of Legislative Assembly members, Employer's and worker's representatives and medical and insurance experts, which met in 1922.

The committee's detailed recommendations for framing legislation were accepted and a Workmen's Compensation Act was passed in 1923. The measure followed the British Act in its main principles and in some of its details, but it contained a large number of provision designed to meet the special conditions in India. This act was the first step towards social security in India. This was followed by legislation enacted in several states for the protection of workers. Under these enactments the responsibility for payment of compensation rested with employer, a system which led to certain hardships. The Royal commission on labour reviewed the subject and made a number of recommendations as regards workmen's compensation. The commission's recommendations involved the substantial extension and enlargement of the rights the Act conferred and its revision in number of matters of detail.

The general scheme of the Act is that the compensation should ordinarily be given to workmen who sustain personal injury by accidents arising out of and in the cause of their employment. Compensation is also given in certain cases for occupational diseases as listed in the IIIrd schedule. It may not be irrelevant to point it out that the International Labour Organisation has also influenced the codification of workmen's compensation law as it has been remarked that the restrictions on import during the World War-I gave rise to a considerable expansion of industries in the countries. The expansion was augmented by the victories, emergence of the allies as a result of which a good deal of capital was invested in the country. The treaty of Versailles emphasised the fact that the failure of any nation to adopt human conditions is an obstacle in the way of other nations, which desires to improve the conditions in their own countries. It was felt that universal peace based on social justice was essential. In order to achieve this end, the International Labour Organisation was formed. The first session of the ILO met at Washington in 1919 and India as an original member of the League of Nations also participated. It was due to the influence of the International Labour Organisation that the Workmen's Compensation Act was passed.

Prior to the passing of the Act, compensation was payable in case of fatal accident. The Indian Fatal Accidents Act, 1855 is based on the English Act and enables certain heirs of the deceased person to sue for damages when death is caused by an actionable wrong. This Act overrides the dictum that a personal action dies with the person injured *"personalis motiureim persona"*. The defence under the doctrine of common employment, by which the employer is not normally liable to pay damage to a workman, or the doctrine of assumed risk, by which an employee is presumed to have accepted a risk if it is such that he ought to have known it to be the part of the risks of his occupation were, however, open to the employer. The Royal Commission on labour regarded both these doctrines as inequitable and recommended that measure should be enacted abrogating these defences. The result was the enactment of the Employer's Liability Act, 1938. The Act was amended by the Employers Liability (Amendment) Act, 1951, as it was found that the defence of common employment was still available to the employer due to the limited scope of section 3(d). The defect was removed by the Amending Act of 1951.

Freedom from want and security against economic fear is one of the fundamental needs of our country. The constitution affirms to all people of India, *inter alia*, social and economic justice, but this has yet to be secured by a peaceful, social and legislative steps. It has been aptly said that, "it is the function of an ideal welfare state to give to every citizen the opportunity of earning his living and freedom from fear —fear specially of economic ruin which can involve physical and even moral ruin.

In order to provide social security to the working people various legislative steps have been taken in our country like other countries of the world. It may not be incorrect to say that the Workmen's Compensation Act, 1923 has been the first step towards social security in our country. The basic principle of this legislation is social justice. Under these circumstances, the Act was passed to provide social justice and security to the workers who are working under dangerous and risky conditions of work in the factories.

Compensation is typically divided into direct and indirect component. The term *direct compensation* is used to describe financial remuneration, usually cash, and includes such elements as basic pay, overtime pay, shift differentials, bonuses, sales commissions, and so on. *Indirect compensation* refers to the general category of employee benefits, including mandated general category of employee benefits, including mandated protection programmes, health, life, and other insurance, holiday, vacation, and medical leaves; executive perquisites, and so forth. Direct compensation is further divided into two components: (1) The wage and salary programme/basic salay, overtime pay, shift differential, etc., and (2) Pay that is contingent on performance (merit promotion hikes) bonuses, gain sharing pay, commissions, etc.

An effective compensation system typically has the following characteristics:

1. It enables an organisation to attract and retain qualified (and necessary) workers.
2. It complies with government regulations.
3. It motivates employees, fosters a feeling of equity, and provides direction to their efforts.
4. It communicates and reinforces an organisation's culture, values, and competitive strategy.
5. Its cost structure reflects the organisation's ability to pay.

Traditional approaches to compensation, management focus primarily on enabling an organisation to attract and retain qualified workers, while complying with government mandates concerning pay. "Status, not contribution, was the traditional basis for the numbers on people's pay checks ... pay was cemented to hierarchical position, regardless of performance," says Professor Kanter newer pay models attempt to balance the traditional objectives with increased attention to motivating employee performance and aligning pay with key organisational performance objectives.

## Objectives

After studying this chapter, you should be able to:

1. Understand the traditional model for compensation systems.
2. Know the basic approaches to job evaluation.
3. Know the contemporary heads in compensation.
4. Know the role of government in compensation .
5. Understand the various forms of indirect compensation including government-

mandated programmes.

6. Understand the different types of pension plans.
7. Understand the competitive of international compensation

## Direct Compensation: Wage and Salary Administration

The traditional model for structuring wage and salary administration has existed in its relatively unchanged form for a long time. The traditional salary administration model is a product of the same complex web of economic, social and political forces that shaped the structure of the present wage policy. In the 18$^{th}$ Century most business owners knew their employees, their performance, and their financial needs, and pay was established on that basis. With the rapid growth of business organisations, bureaucracies were assigned to provide structure, organisation and direction, professional managers replaced business owners, while rapidly growing hierarchies distanced them from workers, organisational systems and structured approaches replaced firsthand knowledge, as efficiency and effectiveness became the primary objectives.

**The Traditional Approach To Compensation:**

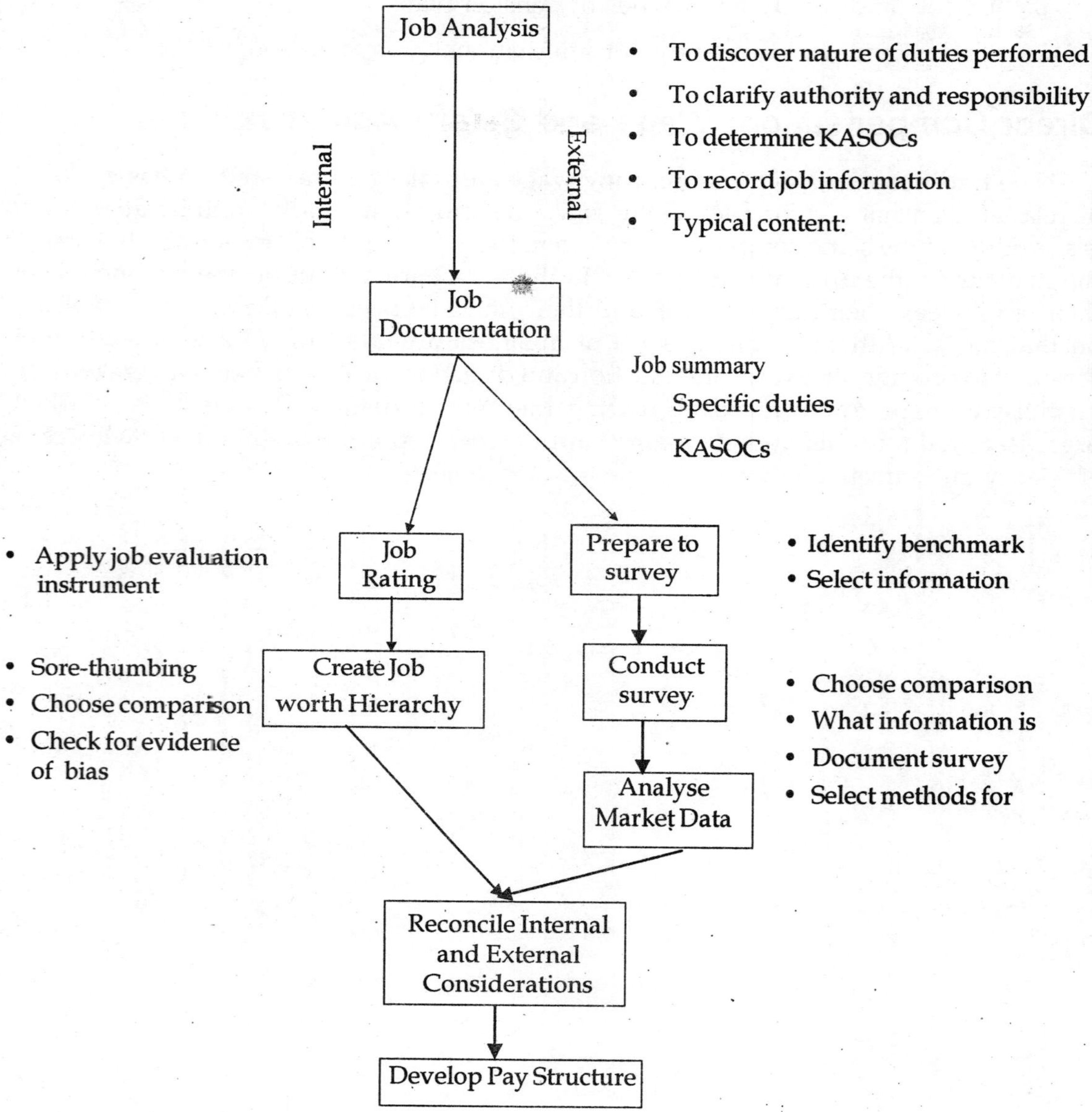


## The Traditional Approach to Compensation: What is Job Evaluation?

Traditional compensation programmes use job evaluation to establish internal equity among jobs. Internal equity means that employees perceive a fair input/output balance relative to others within an organisation (usually but not always people doing the same kind of work). Feelings of inequity, particularly perceptions of underpayment, can lead to job dissatisfaction, lower performance, and higher turnover. Job evaluation is defined as the systematic process of assessing the value of each job in relation to other jobs in an organisation. It is intended to provide a rational, orderly hierarchy of jobs based on their worth to the company by analysing the difficulty of the work performed and the importance of the work to the organisation. The factors used to assess a job's worth are identified, defined, and weighted in the company's job evaluation plan.

The focus of job evaluation is typically on the duties and responsibilities assigned to a job, not on the credentials or characteristics of the person who occupies the job, nor the quality or quantity of the incumbent's performances. This approach assumes that a true sense of job's elements and demands can be ascertained, measured, and valued only through separating jobs from incumbent employees. Traditional job evaluation is described as an objective, fact finding, scientific approach that seeks to measure and quantify the relative complexity, the degree of responsibility, and the degree of effort demanded by the duties assigned to a position. The outcome is a hierarchy of jobs, or a "top-down" list, ranked in order of their assigned responsibilities, or their relative worth. While this is how job evaluation is described, some critics argue that the job evaluation process is discriminatory and at least partially responsible for the differences in pay between male and female dominated jobs.

Job evaluation typically, involves four steps: (1) Job analysis; (2) Job documentation; (3) Job rating using the organisation's job evaluation plan; and (4) creating the job hierarchy.

## Step 1: Job Analysis

Job analysis is the process of collecting and evaluating relevant information about jobs. The data collected should clarify the nature of the work being performed (principal tasks, duties, and responsibilities) as well as the level of the work being performed. Information should include the types and extent of knowledge, skill, mental and physical efforts required, as well as the conditions under which the work is typically performed.

## Step 2: Job Documentation

Job documentation is the process of recording job content information, usually in the form of a written job description, one of the most important products of job analysis. Most job description of the duties, examples of work typically performed, and a statement identifying the knowledge, abilities, skills, and other characteristics (KASOCs) that are required to satisfactorily perform the duties. The ideal job description for compensation reflects not just information concerning "what" a job does, but also the "how" and "why" the duties.

## Step 3: Rating the Job

In the third step, a job's assigned duties are assessed using the job evaluation plan, or instrument selected by the organisation. Discussions about job evaluation approaches focus attention on three basic models: Job ranking, job classification, and point factor plans. Each of these methods is described and explained below. A summary of the approaches is provided in Figure –

| Method | Procedure | Advantages | Disadvantage |
|---|---|---|---|
| Ranking (paired comparison) | Rank order whole jobs for worth or compare pairs of jobs | Simplest method: inexpensive, understandable | Only general rating of "Worth" – not very reliable; doesn't measure differences between jobs |
| Classification | Compare job descriptions to grade descriptions | Simple, easy to use for large number of jobs; one rating scale | Ambiguous, overlapping grade descriptions |
| Point Factor | Reduce general factors to sub factors; give each factor weights and points; use points to determine grades | More specific and larger number of factors; off the shelf plans available (e.g., Hay plan); more precise measurements. | Time-consuming process; more difficult to understand; greater opportunity |

**Fig. 1: Summary of Three Traditional Job Evaluation Methods**

## Job Ranking

The oldest, fastest, and simplest method of job evaluation, job ranking involves ordering jobs from highest to lowest based on some definition of value or contribution. The job that evaluators believe to be the most valuable is placed first, the job that evaluators believe to be the least valuable is placed last and other jobs are ranked in a similar fashion in between, producing a hierarchy. This method typically looks at whole jobs, rather than their component parts, and gives little attention to the particular collection of tasks that comprise any single job. In addition, the basis for comparison is limited to the other jobs in the organisation. No attempt is outside the organisation.

Two approaches to this method are most common: (1) alternation ranking; and (2) paired comparison. Alternation ranking involves ordering the positions alternatively each extreme. For example, beginning with a list of 15 jobs, evaluators try to agree on which the is the most valuable among the collection of jobs, then which job is the least valuable. In the next round, evaluators will try to agree on which of the remaining 13 jobs is the most valuable, then which is the least valuable. This alternating process continues until all jobs have been ranked and a hierarchy of jobs has been developed.

In the paired comparison approach, each job is evaluated by comparing it with every with other job (one at a time). For each two position comparison, the more valuable job is given a score of and when all the possible comparisons have been made, the hierarchy of jobs is developed by counting the number of times that a job was awarded.

Although it is the simplest method, ranking is seldom the recommended approach. The ranking criteria are usually inadequately defined so that the resultant hierarchy is difficult to explain to employers. In addition, since the approach focuses on the total job, often the highest level duty becomes the basis for the evaluation. Finally, the ranking approach yields limited information concerning how much more valuable one job is over another, or how the KASOC of one job relate to those of another. This could be a key drawback for an organisation that is committed to employee development and profitability or to creating cross-training opportunities and career ladders.

## Job Classification

This method was originally developed, and continues to be used by the government. Within this approach, each job is measured against a pre-existing set of job classes that have been designed to cover the full range of possible positions that would be employed by the government. Broad descriptions, or specifications are designed in advance to delineates the characteristics of the jobs that would be placed within that category, within this method, job evaluation involves comparing a position with these generic descriptions and deciding where it fits best ; that is, which job level of responsibility assigned to the job under review. Fig.2 presents the generic descriptions for two job levels within the job classification system.

### Grade Descriptions for Federal Job Classification

#### System Serving as a Yardstick in Job Rating

**Grade – GS-1:** Includes all classes of positions the duties of which are to perform under immediate supervision, with little or no latitude for the exercise of independent judgment, the following: (1) the simplest routine work in office, business, or fiscal operations or (2) elementary work of a subordinate technical character in a professional, scientific, or technical field.

***Grade – GS-18:*** *Includes all classes of positions the duties of which are : (1) To serve as the head of a barrier. This position, considering the kind and extent of the authorities and responsibilities rested in it, and the scope, complexity and the degree of difficulty of the activities carried on, is exceptional and outstanding among the whole group of positions of heads of barriers, (2) to plan and direct, or to plan and execute, new or innovative projects.*

**Fig. 2**

The classification System is relatively inexpensive and easy to administer. But as the number and diversity of position grow, it is increasingly difficult to write level descriptors in advance that will cover the full range of jobs. Without this specificity, the classification method becomes ambiguous and difficult to communicate to workers. In addition, like the ranking method, it is is difficult to know how much difference exists between job levels. Finally, in any whole job rating system, one must be cautious about the same type of rather errors that can creep into performance appraisal. For example, a halo-type error might be one particular component of a position such that he or she assigns the entire job to a grade level that might not be warranted, particularly if the job involves considerable work of a routine nature.

## Point Factor Method

Under a point factor plan, various factors are the basis for determining relative worth. Factors are the specific characteristics of jobs that will be measured. In choosing factors, the organisation decides: "what particular job components do we value? What job characteristics will we pay for?" Mental effort, responsibility, complexity of works physical demands, skill required, and working conditions are the most common factors. Factors chosen by a company for use in a job evaluation plan should be for four characteristics. First, as already suggested, they should represent the job characteristics for which the company is willing to pay. Second, they should be present to varying extent in the jobs to be evaluated. Unless they vary across the population of jobs, there is no point in viewing them as distinguishing features of jobs. Third, they should represent factors that comply with the equal pay act's skill, effort, responsibility, and working conditions framework. Finally, the factors should be business related; that is, they should support the organisation's culture and values, its chosen strategy and direction. Fig. 3 presents a summary of the three major factors within the Hay Plan, which is the most popular point factor plan.

| Knowhow | Problem Solving | Accountability |
|---|---|---|
| Sum total of every kind of skill, however acquired, required for acceptable job performance. Knowhow has three subfactors:<br>(1) Practical procedures, specialised techniques.<br>(2) Ability to integrate and harmonise the diversified functions of management.<br>(3) Interpersonal skills | Original "Self-starting" thinking required by the job or analysing, evaluating creating, reasoning. Problem solving has two subfactors:<br>(1) The thinking environment in which problems are solved<br>(2) The thinking challenge of the problem. | Answerability for action and for the consequences of the action; the measured effect of the job. Accountability has three sub factors: (1) Freedom to act (personal control) (2) The impact of the job on end results (direct, indirect) (3) Magnitude – general dollar size of areas most affected by the job. |

**Fig. 3: Major Factors of the Hay Plan**

Once the factors are identified and described, they should be weighted because all factors are not equally important to an organisation. Typically, factors such as responsibility, decision making, and mental effort are more heavily weighted than physical effort or working conditions. Next, factor scabs must be constructed. Factor scabs are statements of the degree to which the factor is present in any given job. Factor scabs are sometimes referred to as degree statements. Fig. 4 illustrates a typical degree statement for the factor "Physical requirements". Higher degree ratings translate into a greater number of job evaluation points in a point factor.

EXAMPLE OF DEGREE STATEMENTS FOR

THE FACTOR PHYSICAL REQUIREMENTS

## Factor: Physical Requirements

This factor appraises the physical effort required by a job, including its intensity and degree of continuity. Analysis of this factor may be incorrect unless a sufficiently broad view of the work is considered.

## Degree

1. Light work involving a minimum of physical effort. Requires only intermittent sitting, standing, and working.
2. Repetitive work of a mechanical nature. Small amount of lifting and carrying. Occasional difficult working positions. Almost continuous sitting or considerable moving around.
3. *Continuous standing or walking, or difficult working positions. Working with average-weight or heavy materials and supplies. Fast manipulative skill in almost continuous use of machine or office equipment on paced work.*

A higher degree rating for a job translates into a greater number of job evaluation points.

Some organisations that are attempting to develop a more quantitative approach to setting wage rates and to establish internal equity use a statistical method known as policy capturing to derive the weights for the job factors rated in a point factor system. Policy capturing calls for job experts to rate each job on the job factors and then correlate these ratings with the actual pay for these jobs. Through this type of regression analysis, the 'policy "weights that were used in the past to "Capture" pay rates, or the ability of the factor ratings to predict the wages of the jobs understanding, provides the statistical formula that can be used to price jobs in the future. For example, a statistical weight can be desired for each factor such as skill, education level, working conditions, and responsibility. Ratings on these factors can be made and the ratings can be plugged into the regression formula to predict the wage level of the job rated. The approach can also be used to test for any problems in the pay system such as discrimination or wage setting that can not be justified based on actual job context or work performed.

## How does the point factor method differ from ranking or classification?

Unlike job ranking, point factor plans do not rank jobs in an organisation purely based on a comparison of one against another, and they do not rely on a rater's perception of the whole job. Instead, each job is examined concerning the degree to which each factor is present. In this way, the point factor plan is similar to the classification approach in that it uses an external standard, evaluating each job in relation to that standard. Unlike the classification system, however, the point factor approach breaks jobs down into component parts and assigns point values for various characteristics numerical values for each degree within each factor. A job hierarchy is derived by ranking jobs by their total point score

Point factor plans have a number of advantages, the written evaluation enables an organisation to trace, analyse, and document differences among jobs. Such differences can be the foundation for training, development, and career progression initiatives that can benefit the organisation in the long run. The fact that jobs are broken down into parts and evaluated using the same criteria over and over again limits the opportunity for rates explaining job evaluation to employees, point factor plans appear to have a high level of integrity. On the other hand, point factor plans are expensive to design or buy and they are time consuming to install and maintain. Some consultants assert that point factor plans should be administered by an evaluation committee consisting of line operating managers. The time and cost of such commitments must be considered.

In summary, an organisation chooses a job evaluation approach that it believes will best meet its needs and systematically evaluates each job within or against that standard. In addition, many organisations combine elements from each of these approaches to create a hybrid, or combination, approach. Regardless of the method used, job evaluation ratings are typically done by a committee of persons knowledgeable about the jobs under study, with different committees charged with the evaluation of different job families.

### What is a job family?

A job family is a cluster of jobs that fits together as a profession. The clerical family, for examples, clusters various types of secretaries and word processors. The technical family clusters mechanics, electricians, and other skilled trades people.

## Step 4: Creating the Job Hierarchy:

As indicated earlier, the result of a job evaluation plan is a hierarchical ordering of jobs in terms of their relative worth to the organisation. Whether it is created by totalling the points assigned to each position, the resulting top-down list should reflect an ordering of position, that makes sense to and is meaningful for a particular organisation. Before finalising this hierarchical list, it is important that the evaluation be studied carefully in relation to another. Consider this something of a "Sore throbbing" process that looks at the final results of the job evaluation and identifies positions that don't appear to fit best where the job evaluation plan has placed them.

The purpose of a compensation plan is not only to create an internally equitable programme, but also one that is externally competitive. The next step is to consider market place pay practices to that the organisation may effectively complete for workers.

### What is External Equity?

If an organisation expects to recruit and retain workers, it needs to establish a pay strategy that considers pay practices in the market place. This process of pricing jobs is concerned with identifying the market rates or external equity of the jobs under study. When we concern ourselves with external equity, we shift our focus from an administrative value system to an economic one. Thus, one should not expect absolute correspondence between the results of job surveying and the results of job evaluation.

Some small companies, in fact, by pass the time and expense of establishing relative internal worth and go straight ot the market place to find the wage information they need to set pay to just that. This is called a market pricing approach. Some authors say the use of this approach is one of the fastest growing trends in industry today. Others assert that it is not an effective method for two reasons. First, most companies have many jobs that are unique to the organisation and can not be effectively priced using a pure labour market comparison. In these cases, pay information is best obtained for other positions within the job evaluation structure that most closely resemble the position in termes of its relative worth to the company. Second, the importance of a job can differ from organisation to organisation, such that the pure market value may be misleading or irrelevant. A scientist's job is a research and development organisation where he is one of many experts, who enjoys a noteworthy structure of colleagues with whom to collaborate and solve problems, may not be the same as a scientist's role in a manufacturing organisation where she is the one and only expert, serving as the reference point for all technical problems and decision making.

Surveys provide information about the pay trends in the area; but organisations must still make judgements concerning what the information means and how it applies to their own situation. For internal job hierarchy will help surface key differences in the way the market items certain jobs and the importance of a particular job within a single organisational environment.

A well trained HR professional understands the importance of these issues and recognises the need to relate the organisation's pay practices to those that exist in its market place(s). Salary surveying is used for accomplishing this.

## How do you compile Market Data?

Before an organisation compiles labour market salary data, a few decisions must be made. First, the positions that will be surveyed must be choosen. Typically, an organisation surveys lunch mark positions. Benchmarks are well known jobs, with many incumbents, which are structured in such a way that one would expect to find them in the general market place. Typically organisations do not survey unusual or unique positions, not do they survey positions that they use in fundamentally different ways from the rest of the market place.

Next, the organisation should decide what sources it will use to gather market data. There are several options in this regard, each with fundamentally different cost and information quality verifications. Some entrepreneur's, who don't want to spend the time or money conducting or reviewing formal surveys, use the classified ads in the area news paper or speak to employment agency personnel to get an idea of what the market demands in terms of pay. The least expensive and the quickest approach is to obtain data from public sources. A several alternative is to purchase a survey form from a consulting firm. These are more expensive then local or government surveys, but they are usually of better quality both in terms of participants and quality and completeness of information. Third, an organisation can conduct its own survey or can contract with an outside firm to conduct such a survey on its behalf. This is the most expensive of the three options, but it affords the greatest amount of control in terms of the organisations that will be invited to participate, the depth of the information that will be gathered, and the choice of which jobs to include.

**What will be the step, if the organisation goes for conducting its own survey?**

If the organisation chooses to conduct its won survey, it will first need to decide which companies to includes. To do this, the organisation must define the relevant labour, market place based on its current collection of jobs. An organisation may tap different labour markets for different positions, including: (1) Similar organisations in the local market, (2) all employees in the local market; (3) similar organisations in the regional or national markets, (4) all employees in the regional or national markets, or even international markets. Identification of the relevant market is based on the answer to the key question, "with whom do we complete when we want to fire a (job title)?" For example, if the position is a customer service assistant and the organisation typically finds qualified candidates in the local market, regional or national trends are irrelevant.

Sometimes, markets are defined using multiple dimensions, including areas of interest and particular types of employees. When an organisation is interested and particular types of employees. When an organisation is interested in finding research scientists, its market may be the national market for high-technology research and development organisations. In addition, it may seek graduating scientists each year that it will develop over time to fulfil some of its future needs. In this case, depending on the calibre of talent the organisation desires, the market may be masters degree science graduates from the top 25 schools in India. These issues should be given careful consideration during the planning stage. In some cases, the overall effectiveness of the emergent compensation programme fringes on the appropriate identification of comparator organisations.

As we have discussed earlier, the geographical pool expanding for many jobs. Improved technologies, logistics, and communications now make it possible to consider international labour markets to control about costs, even for highly skilled work.

Equally important is ensuring that compensation surveys are performed on the basis of job descriptions rather than job titles. Different organisations title jobs differently. What one company calls a senior accountant may be an accountant elsewhere. A well conducted survey provides a job description for the purpose of job matching. In fact, it might improve the art of surveying considerably if surveying organisations dispensed with the use of job titles and focused solely on job content, labelling the positions under review job 'A', job 'B', job 'C' and so on. A surveying organisation must also decide what information it needs concerning each position. As mentioned above, a well designed survey typically requests information about the elements of direct compensation base salary, additional pay (e.g. overtime earnings, shift differential pay), plus incentive compensation opportunities (e.g. bonuses, gain sharing, incentive profit sharing, commissions, overrides etc.). Most surveys request actual pay averages (the means), medians, and sometimes first and third quartiles, organisations with formal pay structures are asked to report the current salary ranks, job rate, and their current hiring salary. Typically, it is useful to know the member of persons employed in a particular job by a participating company, because large employers have greater capacity to influence the market value of work than small organisations, Additionally, it is good practice to know the general benefits (e.g. membership of professional bodies, company car). Employees do not always value these at this true money value, but a surveying company should consider the types of direct and indirect compensation differences that exist across employers. Finally, a surveying company must also decide how the survey will be conducted. (1) Written questionnaires that mailed/sent; (2) telephone interviews, (3) a meeting of all participating organisations to discuss the survey in general and job markets in particular; (4) personal visit to the companies being surveyed; or (5) some combination of the above. The above options are listed from low to high interms of potential information richness.

## How to Analyse Market Data?

There are almost as many ways to analyse market data as there are ways to conduct labour market surveys. Some organisations look across competitors only very generally, using average salaries, or median starting salaries, or some other indebt that if believes to be meaningful, and make decisions about pay policy. Other organisations spend considerable time and effort with such statistics as least squares regression analysis to aggregate data across jobs and across companies. Certainly different approaches to analysing data will yield different outcomes. An organisation should choose the type and the depth of the analysis based on its own individual needs, the complexity of the market with which it is concerned, the amount of time the organisation can afford to allocate to this project, the professional expertise that is available within the organisation, and the resources that it is able and willing to spend for outside advice and assistance.

Generally, organisations tie their pay practices for most positions to the market average, although there are situations when organisations choose to pay above or below average based on their strategy or goals.

## How to Develop the Final Structure?

How an organisation structures its base salary programme is primarily a matter of organisational philosophy, although market place practices are often important to consider in highly competitive situations. In deciding on the form of the structure, two key questions that must be answered are, "What will be the format of the salary structure"? and "on what basis will actually the employees will be paid?"

Several structural options are available. First, an organisation can use a single rate structure in which all employees performing the same work receive the same pay rate.

Second, an organisation can use a time progression structure in which employees receive pay increases as they reach important tenure milestones. Third, some organisations use a combination of time progression and a merit component. In other words, employees begin at a fixed rate, progress to higher rates solely based on time in job. Then reach a point beyond which they can not proceed except based on merit. Yet a fourth option would be a pay system based on productivity. An individual paid only a sales commission is an example of this. A fifth and increasingly popular option could be some form of base pay with an incentive opportunity, either based on individual, team, unit, or company performance. Finally, many organisations combine various elements of these approaches to create their own. The most common traditional pay structures involves a salary range, with a minimum, midpoint, and maximum pay ranges, as approved to pay rates, provide increased flexibility to allow organisations to consider the particular job-related characteristics of individual employees. Typically, employees move through such ranges based on a combination of experience, tenure, and merit.

In response to the question, "in what basis will we actually pay the employees?" First, an organisation can focus primarily on job content. Under this approach, employees may receive pay increases from time to time, but the principal way of building one's salary is by seeking opportunities to assume greater responsibilities, either through promotions to assume greater responsibilities, either through promotions or other forms of developmental assignments. Second, an organisation can pay for job seniority, or organisational tenure, by advancing the salaries of loyal employees who stay with the company. Third, an organisation can choose to pay primarily for performance. In other words, one employees are fixed, their pay progress to the degree that they contribute directly and in a meaningful way to company performance.

This latter approach typically requires that a formal performance management system be in place to assess contribution. Still a fourth option is to pay primarily for the credentials, or the knowledge's and skills that an individual brings to the particular task. Fifth, it is not unusual for organisations to pay for cost of living particularly when it is on the rise and their employees risk losing economic ground unless their pay keeps pace. Most companies in fact, use some combination of the above factors to determine the pay of an individual.

## Assessing the Traditional Approach

The traditional model of compensation focuses on internal equity (through job evaluation), external equity (through market surveying), and some reconciliation of these to arrive at a final pay structure that is aligned with the organisations philosophy concerning pay and enables the organisation to attract and retain qualified employees. As stated above, this general approach has dominated compensation practice for the past 50 years. Recent developments have triggered a reconsideration of whether their traditional approach continues to the most effective framework for developing pay plans. Several new approaches to pay have developed in the last several years, and many of them represent a break from tradition.

First, the basic nature of work is changing as a result of globalisation, the turbulent business environment, and the shift from a manufacturing to a service economy. TQM thinking has strongly influenced philosophies about where work responsibility, accountability, and control are really housed critics of the traditional approach assort that job evaluation and market surveys are no longer appropriate tools with which to measure and value work. "Job description" types of jobs are no longer the prescribed method for organising work. Typically, they are characteristic of bureaucratic, hierarchical organisational structures in which managers or supervisors decide what authority to retain and what responsibility to delegate. Such thinking assumes that jobs are composed of discreet , describable elements that remain stable for long periods. To day, jobs are more fluid and more broadly defined. Traditional job description talks are being replaced by the concept of worker roles that can for market empowerment, team-based activities, and a coaching style of supervision. Traditional job evaluation plans place value in the size and shape of areas managed, encouraging an empire building mind set that is not aligned with the downsized, leaner, flat organisations of today.

Second, the traditional approach may lose effectiveness as organisations increase their focus on customers and quality. Job evaluation is the product of the scientific management era that valued effectiveness and efficiency above all. Today, successful companies are serving competitive advantage by being fundamentally rely on the assumption that paying competitively is the primary objective. It has been suggested that this concern with what others are doing is not applicable given today's business context.

One strength of the traditional approach was that it conveyed a sense of orderliness, rationality, fairness, and objectivity. Job evaluation plans identify – explicitly an organisation values. Salary surveys are based on the compiling and analysis of specific competitor practices for comparative partners. Despite this systematic foundation, the traditional compensation process provides rumours opportunities for bias, rather errors, and other forms of distortion and controversy. Many have agreed, for example, that traditional compensation programmes have been biased against jobs traditionally held by women.

Referred to as the comparable work dilemma, traditional plans have been criticised for measuring internal job worth and then relying on market survey information to establish wages or salaries within job families. The net result is that some jobs could be rated quite high interms of their job content using a job evaluation plan but paid comparatively low if the market undervalues their contribution. Comparable worth supporters argue that waiting for an economic market adjustment is too slow and that it ignores a basic inequity in our society. They point to countries where women are much closer to equity.

Finally, critics of the traditional compensation approach argue that such programmes do not provide a sense of pay equality among employees. Equity theory is based on a highly subjective determination made at the individual level about his or her perception of inputs and outcomes compared with those of others. They argue that even the fairest, most equitable programme cannot avoid the probability that the perception of many employees may be subjective, personal and incorrect.

In summary, there are a variety of reasons the traditional internal equity/external increase in the number and type of alternative approaches that are being designed and implemented with an eye toward overcoming many of these disadvantages and creating approaches that are more effectively built around today's work and organisational structures.

## Current Trends in Salary Administration

Broad banding is an approach to base pay that is receiving considerable attention in the business organisational Broad banding is the redefinition of an organisation's job hierarchy using less precise concepts and measures than are typically found in traditional job evaluation plans. The result is that the traditional narrow, structured pay grades are replaced by fewer and wider bands. The broad banding approach gives management much greater flexibility in setting and adjusting pay rates. Where a typical pay grade may contain a 50 per cent spread in pay between the minimum and maximum (e.g. 30,000 to 45,000), job band may have a 200 to 300 per cent spread (e.g. 25,000 to 75,000)

| Approach | Description | Advantages | Disadvantages |
|---|---|---|---|
| Broad Banding | Replaces traditional narrow salary ranges (40-60% spread) to fewer bands (200-300% spread) | More consistent with downsized, flatter organisational structures. "Breaks down previous structural pay barriers among jobs to facilitate, empowerment, team work etc. "Greater flexibility; more useful managerial tool." | Traditional Cost control in pay structure is lost. Job pricing more difficult. May be more difficult to communicate to employees. |
| Pay for knowledge | Employees paid on basis of either: (1) Degree of specific knowledge they possesses; or (2) an inventory of skills | Encourages workforce flexibility and expanded competence. Fever supervisors hued as employees improve knowledge and skill. Fosters sense of individual empowerment about pay. | Pay costs may get out of control. Unused skills may get rusty, creating and maintaining skill and competency menus taste time and efforts. Do we pay for inputs or outcomes? |
| Team pay | Any form of compensation contingent in group membership or team results. | Reinforces concepts of teams, empowerment. May better communicate and support organisations culture and goals. | May demotivate top individual performers.Few existing plans; beginning to emerge. |

Insufficient research has been conducted to date to indicate whether broadbanding is a long-term, effective pay model for future pay programmes. Some experts argue that broadlanding could have some noteworthy drawbacks. Traditionally, narrow ranges limited potential earnings. It is not known to what degree an organisation's payroll costs increase without corresponding increases in worker productivity. Some argue that broadbanding is appropriate for higher level positions only.

## Pay for Knowledge Capability or Competence

In these types of plans, employees are paid on the basis of either the degree of specific, technical knowledge they hold or an inventory of knowledge and/or skills, that they possess. These plans are based on the assumption that knowledge, skill, or competence will be translated into improved employee performance and, ultimately, superior organisational effectiveness. Advocates assert that such plans can increase worker productivity and product quality, while decreasing absenteeism turnover, and accident rates. One estimate of the popularity of the approach is that as many as 40 percent of the large organisations use this approach, but only for a very small percentage of their workforce.

Paying for knowledge has long been a viable pay strategy in scientific technical, and professional disciplines in which expertise and innovation were sources of competitive, albeit, intangible, advantage. Business schools, for example typically pay considerably more for an "Assistant Professor" with a Ph.D. than for an instructor with an MBA, these plans are based on the assumption that professional competence increases with longevity in one's profession. Similarly, unionised professions, such as teachers and nurses, have strongly favoured pay based on education and experience. As technology continues to more forward at its rapid pace, such plans are increasing in popularity.

The most modern application of this thinking can be found in organisations designing and implementing skills based pay. Originally found in new, non-union manufacturing organisations, interest in this approach has grown considerably. Although it is not used as widely as its publicity might indicate, its influence has been felt in some industries, such as pharmaceuticals and telecommunications. In a typical skills – based pay plan, the array of knowledges or skills that the organisation values becomes the pay menu. Employee begin at an entry level rate. Incremental pay increases are awarded as employees demonstrate knowledge, or mastery of specific, additional skills. Three types of potentially useful skills enhancements have been identified: (1) Skill depth is increased when employees learn more about specialized areas, moving along a career track to becoming an expert, or master; (2) Skill breadth is improved when employees learn more and more tasks in the organisation; (3) Self management skills – the abilities of employees to schedule work and to perform similar administrative roles – may benefit an organisation in a variety of ways.

Supporters argue its merits: (1) The cross-training and acquisition of knowledge can create a flexible, empowered workforce whose competence extends well beyond the boundaries envisaged in traditional "Job description" jobs; (2) Fewer supervisors are needed, providing support in a downsized, delivered organisation; (3) Programmes foster in employers a sense of power over and responsibility for their own development and their own compensation.

Opponents assert that potentially higher individual pay costs may be uneconomical unless they are offset by higher worker productivity. Second, unless skills are used or knowledges are applied, they become rusty, although the pay may continue indefinitely. Third depending on the growth and direction of the organisation, employees can still reach the top of the pay-scale, resulting in the same frustration that these plans are designed to remedy. Fourth, the process of reviewing, attaching monetary values to, and certifying skills can create the same type of bureaucratic structure and record keeping requirement that these plans are created to eliminate. Finally, one very controversial issue is whether organisations should pay for inputs or outcomes. Skills based pay represents paying for input . In contrast, some organisations believe that the best response to rising costs in uncertain environments is to put increasing amounts of pay at risk, that is paying for outcomes, for the attainment of concrete individual groups or organisational goals. Paying for knowledge, competence, skills, or abilities suggests that these qualities hold potential performance value. But it is up to the organisation to make certain that its culture, work rules, and other control systems ensure that such inputs are transferred into improved work products.

## Team Play Plans

With the wide growth in the use of teams within organisations has come discussion concerning how team members should be compensated. There appears to be a general consensus that a team organisational model requires an alternative compensation approach, but there currently appears to be more questions than answers. One group of experts argues that is it important to distinguish between behaviours that a company values (as in teamwork) versus a true organisational form (as in teams). In addition, at least five types of teams have been identified – management teams, work teams, quality circles, virtual teams, and problem solving teams. In sorting through the types and uses of teams have been identified – Management teams, work teams, quality circles, virtual teams, and problem solving teams. In sorting through the types and uses of teams, theree criteria have been suggested as a basis for determining whether a team is a candidate or some kind of customized form of pay: (1) the team is a dedicated one, that is, the primary work organisational model that is in use; (2) the work is truly interdependent; and (3) the team is empowered to make the majority of decisions concerning its work and such decision making is shared across team members.

Some experts recommend that team organisations use broadbanding in combination with incentive profit sharing plans based on team results. Depending on the environment, a division an/or organisational component may b added to the incentive plan as well some have used pay for knowledge systems, particularly skills based pay, as a compensation approach for teams.

## Government Influence on compensation Issues

The equal opportunity regulations enacted by the government to positively influence social change. The government also provides a legal framework concerning direct compensation within which organisations must operate. These rules ensure that minimum operating standards of fairness and humanity are applied to compensation matters in the employer – employee relationship.

The various methods which the government has adopted to regulate wages in India are as under:

1. Prescribing minimum rates of wages by enacting Minimum Wages Act, 1948.
2. Preventing discrimination in remuneration on the ground of set through Equal Remuneration Act, 1976.
3. Regulating payment of wages through payment of Wages Act and Contract Labour Act, 1936.
4. Protection of workers, claims in the event of insolvency of their employers through sec.529 A of the Companies Act.
5. Compulsory conciliation and arbitration of wage disputes through Industrial Disputes Act, 1947.
6. Setting up of wage Boards, and
7. Setting up of pay commission.

## Indirect Compensation: Employee Benefits

Employee benefits are indirect forms of compensation that are intended to maintain or improve the quality of life for employees. The programmers are federally mandated; unemployment allowance, social security, and workers' compensation. Like direct compensation, the major objective for most organisational indirect compensation programmes is to attract, retain and motivated employers. The rise in the popularity of employee benefits programmes during the past few decades is attributable to a variety of forces. In other words, when an employer offers a health care plan, three things typically occur: (1) The organisation deducts the cost of the plan from its earnings for tax purposes; (2) an employee is not taxed on the cost of the plan that is borne on his behalf by the organisation; (3) an employer is not taxed on the reimbursement he receives under the terms of the plan for covered services under the terms ofl the plan for covered services. Particularly, when individual tax rates are rising significantly, lthese tax advantages make employee benefit programmes attractive alternatives to direct compensation for many employees.

While employee benefit programmes were at one time quite uniform, there is now considerable variance. Benefit programmes vary as a consequence of the organisations human resource philosophy, its size, location, the type of business, and the type of job that an individual holds.

## Five Categories of Employee Benefits

Employee benefits may be classified into five general categories: (1) Government – mandated programmes, including social security, unemployment allowance, workers' compensation, and certain state – mandated disability programmes; (2) employee welfare plans, including all forms of of health care plans, survivor benefits, and disability programmes; (3) pension plans and other long term capital accumulation programmes; (4) time off programmes (whether paid or unpaid), such as paid holidays, vacation saflaticals, and (5) employee services which include education expenses reimbursement plans, child/family care, housing and relocation services, employee assistance programme, and employee recognition programmes.

## Communicating the Benefits Programme

Most employee have little understanding of the costs involved in a benefits programme. According to one expert, employee communication is the "keystone of the programme ..... without effective communication, a benefit programme remains incomplete and the considerable effort and expense consumed in planing, designing, and administering plans becomes largely unproductive while distributing benefit summarises pursuant to the Employee Refinement Income Security Act (ERISA) requirements provides a cursory understanding of major components of the benefit package. The effectiveness of the package is undermined unless employees appreciate the advantages and superiority of the programme relative to compensations. ERISA simply requires that "Summary Plan Descriptions" be "written in a manner calculated to be understood by the average plan participant". Employees must be aware of and understand the benefits that are available to them in order for the employer to fully realise the objectives for which the benefits were established.

The goal in benefit communication should be to present the worth of the benefit package to current and future employees. To that end, many employees now provide counselling for employees to enhance their understanding of the benefit programme. Along the other methods used to explain benefits are pay check inserts, employee publications, posters, and require some employee contribution are not only mere efficient but also tend to enhance employee understanding of the benefit and its cost to the employer. Also, with the growth in cafetaria style plans, employees should be more informed about the costs of the various benefit options.

## Developing an Expatriate Compensation Package:

Although many of the third-counrtry nationals (TCN's) compensation features may vary markedly from those included in a parent-country nationals (PCNS) package, the fact that each is an expatriate compels us to great the TCN as a special case of the PCN in this discussion. The salary and fringe benefits paid to a PCN are intended to ensure that the professionals do not suffer any material loss due to working abroad. By using a balance sheet approach to compensation, most of the companies attempt to keep overseas professionals on at least a financial par with their domestic colleagues. Maintaining such purchase power equality typically proves to be very expensive. The high cost of the compensation package required to induce a professional to mov to, and perform well in a, a foreign country is a function of three factors comprising the assignment profile: (1) the position; (2) the local, and (3) the individual. The primary roles that these factors play in matching a compensation package to an assignment profile are shown in Fig. 4.

## The Major Position Factors

Every position has a unique set of characteristics that occasion a corresponding set of compensation needs. Such position specific compensation needs are summarised below. In general, the length of an overseas assignment is critical for determining a compensation policy. When assignments are for less than a year, major changes are typically not made.

| | | | These Assignment Variables | Occasion these compensation needs |
|---|---|---|---|---|
| Assignment Profile | Position factors | Responsibilities and Duties.Operating performance Assignment duration status and prestige Travel requirements. Remoteness Physical or cultural adversity sanitation Physical Security | Base salary incentive bonus periodic salary adjustments Representation Allowance Official Travel allowance Rest and relation hardship and home leave. Medical Care Hazardous duty or security allowance, ransom insurance. | |
| | Local factors | Housing cost, Housing availability transfer incidentals school availability Economic security, Income Taxes, Purchasing power reluctance to more family income asset exposure, Number of dependents | Housing allowance, Temporary quarters allowance. Reallocation allowance. Education allowance, Refinement allowance, Tax excalisation currency of payment Foreign service Premium. Spousal employment, Home and Auto ProtectionDependent Cost | Compensation Package |
| | Individual factors | | | |

**Fig. 4: Matching a Compensation package to an Assignment Profile**

## Base Salary

A PCN's lease salary must be competitive with the amount that an employee with similar responsibilities and duties would receive at home; it not geared to what a similar job would pay in the host country labour market. TCN salaries are typically priced according to that particular country's going rates.

## Incentive Bonus

Because of variables such as exchange rate changes, transfer prices and inflation over which a PCN manager may have little or no control, a majority of companies base PCN's incentive bonuses on local currency budget compared to actual operating performance.

## Provide Salary Adjustment

Some research suggests the possibility that the longer a PCN remains in an overseas position, the greater is the risk that her job skills will have effected with her eventual return to headquarters. To soften the effect of such an unwelcome contingency, and to compensate for normal serinity based pay increments, periodic salary increases are often included in compensation negotiations.

## Representation Allowance

Managers of medium size organisations working abroad may find that their duties entail dealing with high level individuals such as CEOs of major local organisations in the hoist country. Because authority tends to be more visible in many countries than it is in India. It is often essential that PCN professionals, especially country managers, learn to display the accoutre ments of rank. Such "power signals" may include memberships, chuffeured vehicles, symptoms offices, and prestigious home addresses.

## Travel Allowance

Foreign assignments often require more travel – both local and international than domestic positions. It is common to compensate official travel by reimbursing the transportation component against receipts, and the lodging meals, and incidentals component on a *per diem* basis.

# Summary

Because of the importance that compensation holds for their lifestyle and self-esteem, individuals are very concerned that they be paid a fair and competitive wage, organisations are concerned with pay, not only because for its importance as a cost of doing business but also because it motivates important decisions of employees about laking a job and working on the job.

When designing direct compensation plans, it is important thayt an organisation choose an approach that is in alignment with its organisational philosophy and that supports its organisational goals. In some cases, the traditional approach to pay still provides the best answer. This approach rests on the use of a job evaluation plan (to measure internal job work and foster internal equity), the review of market salary data (to identify externally competitive practices), and the reconciliation of these two in the form of a final pay structure. Due to the basic changes in organisations today and the new global challenges and opportunities, there is a growing search for new direct compensation approaches in the hope that they will better focus employers on achieving organisational goals. Such new approaches to pay include broad banding pay for knowledge (or skills based pay), and team pay plans. To date, however, the relative effectiveness of these new approaches remains to be tested.

Employee benefits programmes continue to grow and expand, although there are considerable differences in the benefits that are offered by different types and sizes of employers. Benefits mainly have been directed at assisting employers in maintaining a particular lifestyle and providing for their long term welfare and security. At the same time, however, the federal government is increasing its security of the existing tax advantages of most indirect compensation plans. The resulting legislation has raised administrative costs of many plans and has chipped away at the ability of some organisations to meet previous benefits commitments.

The government's goal concerning its regulation of pay and benefits is to ensure that discrimination does not exist and that certain minimum levels of fairness are maintained in compensation programmes. A number of central, state and local laws regulate compensation. In addition, regulation is aimed at managing the delicate balance between tax revenue maximisation and maintaining the positive social forces that tax favoured employee benefit plans have contributed to society.

Direct and indirect compensation programmes must be assessed for the extent to which they attract, retain, and motivate the workforce required relative to major competitors. The cost of labour is critical to corporate performance and must be constantly monitored to determine whether costs can be reduced with no loss in the products or services necessary for fulfilling. The organisational strategy. The bottom line is that if the company is not doing it, its competitors may be doing it and a competitive advantage is not for behind. The use of part time employees and outsourcing and the relocation of operations, are all part of a strategy to reduce the cost of labour. By the same token, when required skills for competitive advantage are in great demand, companies that do not respond with competitive pay package will lose out and end up cutting their labour costs or the expense of organisational capability. Regardless of which particular compensation programme is chosen, organisations need the capacity to measure individual or group results so that such performance may be reflected in pay.

***

# 18 Total Quality Management and Human Resources

## Introduction

Total Quality Management (TQM) is more than a fad or a buzzsword. It is even more than a technique for controlling and motivating employees. TQM is a challenge to conventional management techniques and to the theories that underlie them. Therefore, it cannot be simply be grafted onto existing management structures and systems. If its benefits are to be fully realised, then companies need to prepare themselves for organisation wide change – including top management's relinquishing of power. Furthermore, TQM practices cannot be combined with strategic initiatives, such as corporate restructuring, that are based on conventional management theories. The failure of one or both is inevitable.

The success stories of total quality management (TQM) are well known. They include such companies as Teroz, Allen-Bradley, Motorola, Ford, and Hewlett-Packard. These companies committed themselves wholeheartedly to TQM; they made fundamental changes in their management practices and philosophies and improved product quality, but the quality improvement programmes ultimately feel apart. In many of these companies, the TQM programmes lost momentum because disagreements over goals and implementation procedures surfaced, upper-level managers turned their attention to other priorities, and employees became increasingly sceptical about organisational commitment to the programmes.

In other companies, quality programmes elasted resoundingly with other strategic initiatives. TQM will not succeed in a firm unless conventional practices are transformed. The tendency for TQM to create dissension within firms arises not only because TQM conflicts even mere violently with other contemporary trends in management thinking. If TQM is one new management paradigm forcing a rethinking of management concepts and practices, the other is what we call the "economic model of the firm", which is based on the principle of maximising shareholder value. We argue that TQM and the economic model are inherently incompatible, and that companies will need to choose implicitly if not explicitly, between the two. To that end, we explore the differences between TQM and conventional management practices, particularly those influenced by the economic model of the firm.

**Emerging Management Paradigms: TQM and the Economic Model of the Firm**

| | TQM | Economic Model of the Firm |
|---|---|---|
| Organisational goals | Serving customer needs by supplying goods and services of the highest possible quality | Maximising profit line of shareholder wealth |
| Individual goals | Individuals motivated by economic, social, and psychological goals relating to personal fulfilment and social acceptance | Individuals motivated only by economic goals maximisation of income and minimisation of effort |
| Time Orientation | Dynamic innovation and continual improvement | Static optimisation, maximising the present value of net cash flow by maximising revenue and minimising cost |
| Coordination and control | Employees are trustworthy and are experts in their jobs hence emphasis on self management. Employees are capable of coordinating on a voluntary basis | Managers have the expertise to coordinate and direct subordinates. Agony problems necessitates monitoring of subordinate and applying incentives to objectives |
| Role of Information | Open and timely information flows are critical to self-management, horizontal coordination, and quest for continual improvement | Information system matches hierarchial structure : key functions are to support manager's decision making and monitor subordinates |
| Principles of Work Design | System-based optimisation with emphasis on dynamic performance | Productivity maximisation by specialisation on the basis of comparative advantage |
| Firm Boundaries | Issues of supporter customer relations, information flow, common to transactions within and between firms | Clear distinction between markets and firms as governance mechanism. Firm boundaries determined by transaction costs. |

One of the dangers of the economic model is that it has reinforced conventional pre-occupation with sources of static efficiency at a time when some of the most influential ideas relating to the strategy, structure, and competitive performance of firms, including population ecology, and resource-based theory, are concerned with competition as a dynamic process. Recent work on resources and corporate capabilities places special emphasis on dynamic aspects of competitive advantage-investing in irreplaceable, non-transferrable assets and upgrading the basis of competitive advantage through innovation and the development of new skills. These ideas are quite compatible with the dynamic and static optimisation also have different maximisation of productivity and minimisation of cost in the short-term imply the following specialisation; individual incentives linked to quantitative performance in the short-term; parsimony in investment and the use of assets; the imposition of short-term financial targets on divisions and business units, and active management of the asset portfolio and divestment of poorly performing assets. By contrast, managing for innovation involves creating organisational conditions conducive to the creation and diffusion of new knowledge.

## Core Concept of TQM

TQM emphasises on the following core concepts:

### (1) Satisfy the Customer

The focus here is on external customer. Satisfy the customer means to take due care of the customer's overall satisfaction, i.e., quality, cost, service etc. Making the continuous changes to satisfy the customer is an integral part of TQM.

### (2) Management by Fact

The management should know the quality of the product or service that the customer is presently using. This quality level is used as benchmark for further improvement. For this purpose, the management gathers the related facts about the present level and pass on the information to employees of the firm at all levels facilitating take appropriate decisions based on the facts. These facts are an essential aspect of continuous improvement.

### (3) Management based on Human Resources

The management should emphasise their employees understand what to do, how to do the job, get the feedback about their performance. The human resources should be encouraged to take more responsibility for the quality of their work. People can be more committed to make the customers more satisfied and this is possible through their more involvement. The quality is heavily influenced by the continuous involvement of the people rather than by the systems, standards and techniques.

### (4) Total Quality Management is a Continuous Journey

It is a management and continuous long-term journey. It is not a short-term journey based on goals or targets or a project. TQM is a long-term improvement programme based on the incremental change.

### (5) Internal Customers are Vital

Internal customers are more important in comparison to external customers because they are most crucial and complex variable and continuously influence the maintenance of quality. They also influence speed, efficiency, perfectness and value-adition. All work is a business process and is a combination of methods, materials, manpower and machines that taken together produce a product or service

## Measurement of Quality

In-order to determine the future quality level, measurement of present level of quality is more important. Internal quality measurement of product are:

(a) Breach of promise, (b) Performance to standard, (c) Reject level, (d) Accidents, (e) Process in control, (f) Yields scrap, (g) Time cost due to availability of raw materials, (h) Number of changes to work orders, (I) Cost of quality.

### Team Work

People work together in team spirit to accomplish the most difficult goals. People work in teams to maintain and improve the quality. Teamwork enables the people to work from a cross-functional approach.

### People Make Quality

It is a fact that organisational efforts influence to maintain the overall quality. Organisational efforts influence the individuals, as well as teams in the organisation to concentrate on the quality journey.

### Continuous Improvement Cycle

Identifying the present level of quality standards, establishing thed customer needs, establishing the ways and means to produce the product or render service to meet the customer needs, measuring the success and improving the quality continuously are the parts of the continuous improvement cycle.

### Prevention

Preventing the failure to occur is the central system of total quality management. Foreseeing the possible failures and taking steps in advance to prevent them from occurrence. Feeding information forward helps to prevent the failures. This process helps for the creation of the culture for continuous improvement.

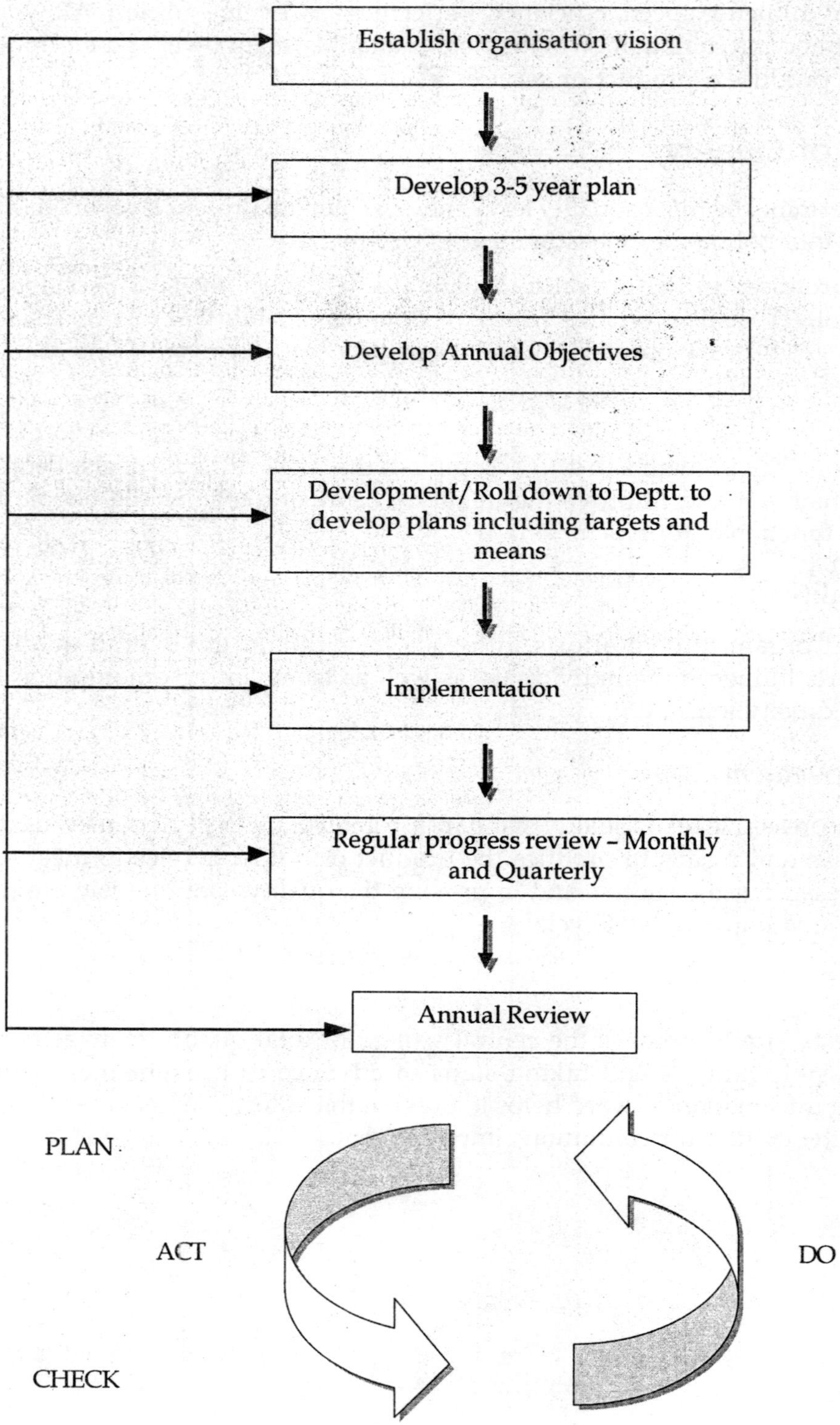


**Fig. TQM Planning Process**

## The Process of Management Control

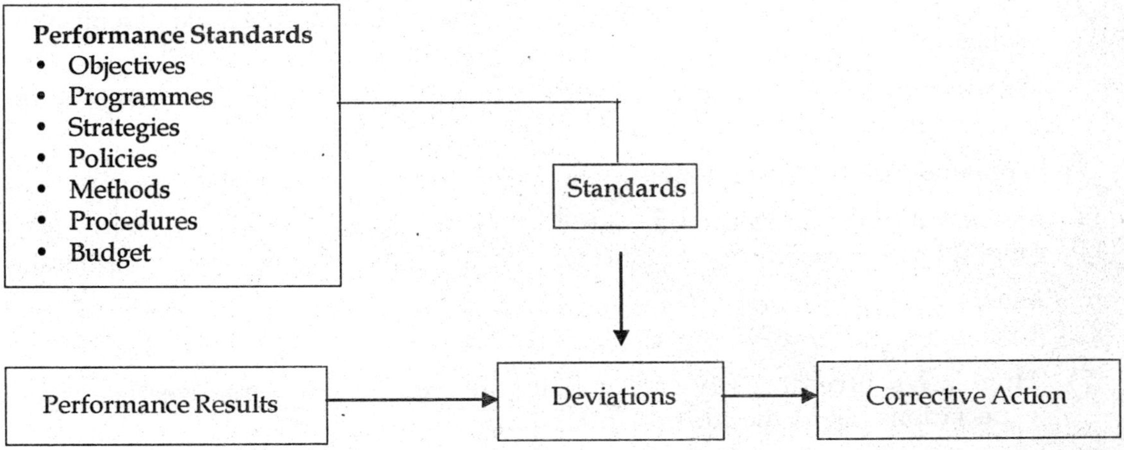


## Management by Objective Process

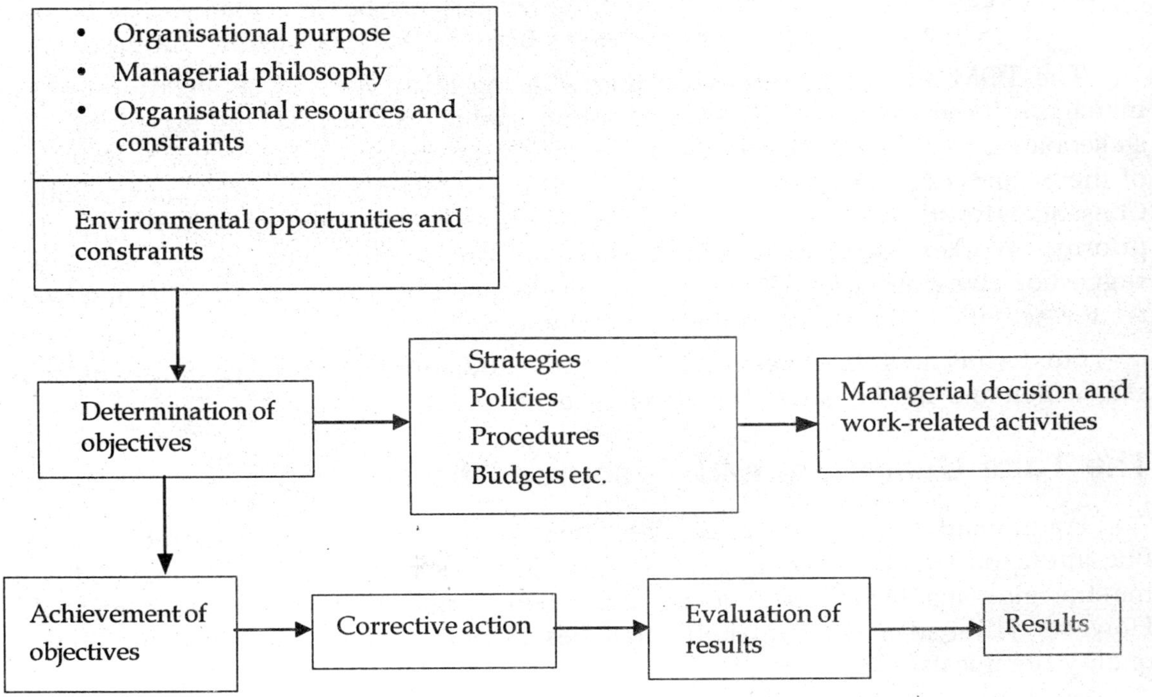


## Human Resource Management and TQM

In any organisation the role of human resources for nurturing total quality management is very crucial. The following forces drive the human resource towards TQM:

(1) Economic liberalisation policy introduced by Government of India in 1991.

(2) Opening the Indian economy to the rest of the globe through the globalisation policy.

(3) Entrusting more priority for private sector to play a positive role in the restructuring and development process of Indian economy.

(4) Tremendous competition among the industries across the globe.

(5) Successful companies accord high priority to productivity and systematically understanding and responding to current and future needs of external customers.

(6) Successful organisations proactively and systematically understand and respond to current and future external customer needs.

(7) Human resource diversity and mobility are creating new employee needs and expectations about the future work culture.

(8) The information technology revolution is reshaping the core competencies needed in a knowledge economy.

(9) Organisational and human resource leaders are being challenged to become effective strategic partners in the creation of world-class work cultures.

The TQM approach initiated changes in the attitudes and expectations of the managers about the roles of human resource managers. Further, the expectations of stakeholders about the HRM profession have also been changing. Traditionally, objectives of the business organisations were restricted to productivity and profit maximisation. Consequently, stakeholders, particularly, the customers and employees were given low priority. Workers' participation in management programmes were limited to offering suggestions by employees. Training and development programmes were limited to job related activities rather than extending to employee capacities.

But the business objectives and total quality HRM approach are to maximise customer satisfaction and market share through improved quality.

## The Total Quality Human Resource Strategy

Traditionally, human resource plans were not integrated with the strategic plans. But, in the total quality organisations, human resources plans should be integrated with the strategic plans. In fact, HR strategies are given top priority in total quality organisations. However, HR managers feel that HR strategies are not yet given due importance in total quality organisations.

The human resource role can be of four types:

(1) Strategic – high profile, i.e., change agent

(2) Strategic – low profile, i.e., hidden persuader

(3) Operation – high profile i.e., internal contractor

(4) Operation – low profile i.e., facilitator

There are several strategies of human resources related to profile total quality human resources grand strategies. Total quality human resource strategic management is also reciprocally interdependent with business strategic management. This is the most important contribution to the total quality orientation of human resources. Total quality human resource approach requires organisation around process (instead of tasks), flatten hierarchies, use teams to manage everything, let customer satisfaction drive output, reward team results, maximise supplier and customer contact and inform and train all employees.

Total quality HR strategy managers must shape, introduce, maintain, and review the total quality initiatives. The TQ human resource managers are actively involved in the following activities in order to shape the TQM:

1. Preparing and synthesizing reports from other organisations that have experience in TQM in conjunction with the management team.
2. Assisting with choices about which TQM approach to adopt.
3. Identifying any internal sources of expertise.
4. Utilising the expertise of practitioners from other organisations.
5. Ensuring that an appropriate infrastructure for TQM is put into place and takes sufficient account of both customer feedback and human resource management.
6. Reviewing current practices, behaviour, and attitudes in the organisation and assuring their degree of fit with TQM.
7. Shaping the type of organisational structure, culture, and ethical climate appropriate for introducing and sustaining TQM.

## Exhibit – 18.1

**Comparison of Traditional and Total Quality Human Resource Management Approaches**

| | Traditional HRM Approach | Total Quality HRM |
|---|---|---|
| Philosophy | A fair day's work for a fair day's pay | Shared responsibility commitment, rewards |
| Business Objectives | Increased productivity, profiability, quality is secondary, focus on labour | Increased quality, productivity, customer satisfaction, employee satisfaction, and loyality. |
| Quality – Objectives | Adequate quality to remain in business, staff – driven approaches to quality improvement | Total quality management and continuous improvement at and across every level. |
| Business – Information – Sharing | Limited to information on an as needed basic for job performance | Open books, share board informantion on profits, productivity, quality, costs, captial spending plans. |

| | | |
|---|---|---|
| Major constituenius | Managers, stockholders, customers, employees | Customers, all employees, stockholders. |
| Employee – Involvement | Programmes : Suggestions, plans, individual employee rewards, usually no formal system | Customers all employees, stockholders. |
| Education and Training | On – the – job training, feedback on job performance | Quality and economic education, multiple – skill training, problem solving and group process. |
| Reward Structure | Management designed and administratered | Designed and adjusted by management – employee committee, formal, early union involvement. |
| Job Security | Labour as variable cost; lay-offs common during business downturns | Formal commitment a key consideration in all decisions. |

***Source:*** Adapted from O'Dell, Carla, *Sharing the Productivity, Pay-off,* reprinted from Production Brief 24 with permission of the American Productivity and Quality Centre, Houston, in Wehther Wiliam B. *et. al.*, 11980). Productivity through people St. Paul, Minn: West Publisher to 336.

## Exhibit – 18.2

**Total Quality Human Resource Grand and Selected Tactical Strategies**

| **Total Quality HR Grand Strategic** | **Selected Total Quality HR Tactical Strategies** |
|---|---|
| Exparision | • Aggressive hiring, training , and promotion.<br>• Promotion of successful experienced personnel.<br>• R & D recruitment.<br>• Expansion advisory teams.<br>• Rapidly rising wage ranges .<br>• Job creation.<br>• OD interventions for expansion.<br>• Communication of tactical strategy throughout organisation. |
| Development | • Job redesign and job combinations.<br>• Retraining.<br>• Job Creation.<br>• Acculturation training.<br>• Expand training and development.<br>• External growth teams.<br>• OD interventions for development.<br>• R & D Recrutment.<br>• Selective lay-offs, if required.<br>• Communication of tactical strategy throughout organisation. |

| | |
|---|---|
| Productivity | • Productivity increases.<br>• Acculturation training.<br>• Easly retirement.<br>• OD interventions for productivity.<br>• Continuous training and development.<br>• Managed turnover.<br>• Efficiency improvement teams.<br>• Communication of tactical strategy throughout organisation. |
| Redirection | • Retraining.¨ Job redesingn.<br>• Reassignments.<br>• Restructuring.<br>• Redirection teams.<br>• VRS/CRS.<br>• Outsourcing.<br>• Reengineering.<br>• OD interventions for redirection.<br>• Renegotiated labour agreements.<br>• Transition training and services.<br>• Layoffs and terminations, when required.<br>• Communication of tactical strategy throughtout organisation. |

## Exhibit – 18.3

**Organisation Design and Human Resource Strategy Implementation**

| Organisation Structure | Strategic Priorities | HR Stretegy Implementation |
|---|---|---|
| Pyramid | Command and control | • Hierarchial, specified career paths<br>• Specific, detailed job descriptions<br>• Pay supports, merit promotions, and commitment<br>• Training is job specific<br>• Information in hands of job managers |
| Delayed Restructured Pyramid | Remove layers<br>Enrich jobs<br>Team Focus<br>Empower Employees | • Limited career paths, horizontal promotions<br>• Share career responsibility with employee<br>• Generic job descriptions<br>• Pay Emphasis individual and team performance<br>• Training emphasises generalist and flexibility<br>• Information shared with teams on need-to-know basis<br>• Careers primarily individual responsibility |
| Networks/ Alliances | • Recreate boundaries to suppliers and customers | • Generic job descriptions |

| | | |
|---|---|---|
| | • De-emphasise functional specialists. Emphasise customers<br>• Team as basic building block | • Training options at individual direction<br>• Pay emphasises individual knowledge and team performance<br>• Information is widely accessible |

***Source***: Milkovich, George T. and Boudreau, John W. (1994) *Human Resource Management*, 7th ed., Burr Ridge.III: Irwin, p.122.

8. Designing and delivering senior management development courses that set the proper tone for TQM.
9. Developing a TQM directory of internal resources and expertise.

TQM by being actively involved in the following activities:

1. Encouraging and facilitating a total quality partnership between company and union leadership in order to establish collaboration to benefit all stockholders.
2. Training all formal leaders (including union officers) in the principles of TQM, advising them of the best means of developing a process of continuous improvement within their areas of influence, encouraging them to persuade everyone to take personal responsibility for their own quality assurance, and being prepared to seek improvements.
3. Identifying the conditions necessary for the successful use of quality management tools and techniques.
4. Providing guidance on what is necessary for the successful employment of teams that focus on quality improvement and how they fit into the organisational structure.
5. Training and coaching facilitators, mentors, and team members in inter-personal skills and how to manage the improvement process.
6. Designing communication events and vehicles to publicise the launch of TQM and early successes.
7. Consulting with employees about the introduction and development of TQM.
8. Institutionalising organisational ethics development programme.
9. Proactively contributing to vision and mission statements and preparing quality objectives for dissomination to staff, customers, and suppliers.

Next, total quality HR strategy managers maintain and reinforce TQM within the organisation by being actively involved in the following activities:

1. Adopting selection processes that target and screen for conceptual, technical, ethical, and social skills that support a TQM environment.
2. Introducing or upgrading the quality awareness and TQM component within orientation courses.

3. Identifying the most appropriate mechanisms for recognising and rewarding achievements, in particular looking at non-traditional reward systems.
4. Ensuring that training in quality management tools, techniques, and processes continues to be provided within the organisation and that the knowledge imparted in such training is being used in the workplace.
5. Redesigning appraisal procedures so that they contain criteria related to specific TQM objectives, appropriate social relations, skills and support personal responsibility, self-assessment, and 360 degree performance feedback.
6. Preparing and overseeing special newsletters or team briefs on TQM and improvement initiatives and the outcome of quality improvement team projects.
7. Assisting continuous improvement and project teams to work effectively and innovate.

Finally, the total quality HR strategy manager review TQM implementation progress by being actively involved in the following activities:

1. Contributing to or leading the preparation of an annual TQM report.
2. Assessing the effectiveness of the TQM infrastructure, including steering committees, quality councils, quality improvement teams, improvement facilitations, project teams, and individual performance.
3. Preparing and administering employee attitude and ethical climate surveys and disseminating their results.
4. Co-ordinating customer comments on the organisation's progress.
5. Benchmarking the effectiveness of the organisation's TQM with that of competitors and best global practices.
6. Facilitating the operation of internal reviews using criteria such as ISO 9000, Six Sigma, Kaizan, the Malcolm Baldridge National Quality Award, or the Doming Prize.
7. Identifying the barriers to continuous quality improvement.
8. Conducting HR, quality, and ethics audits.

Total quality HR strategic management would not be complete if HR practitioners did not review their own activities as they do all other areas. Some of the more typical self–review total quality activities include.

1. Undertaking a department mission analysis of the functional contribution of human resources to the organisation, which could include the following:
   (a) Identifying internal customers and suppliers.
   (b) Agreeing to performance measures as part of service–level agreement.
   (c) Tracking such measurements.

(d) Identifying non–value–added activities.

(e) Taking part in cross–functional project teams to resolve interface problems with customers and suppliers.

2. Selecting new HR employees only with peer and customer involvement.
3. Appraising and rewarding HR staff for teamwork, ethical integrity, and customer satisfaction.
4. Training and developing HR employees on a regular basis.
5. Surveying and distributing the results of HR staff satisfaction and ethical climate survey.
6. Providing advice on ethical problem analysis and conflict resolution within a specified and agreed upon time period.
7. Benchmarking HR policies and processes with world–class models.

***

# 19 Knowledge Management

## Understanding the Importance of Knowledge Management

The world is changing fast and the world of business is changing faster. In the new millennium, business corporations will have to deal with entirely new challenges to meet customer demands, move from competition to collaborative reconfiguration, dovetail supplier and subcontractor processes for the corporate goals and empower employees to be able to meet and surpass customer expectations. Let us understand the term "**Knowledge**" itself in an organisational context. Knowledge management is about storing and sharing the wisdom, understanding and expertise accumulated in an organisation about its processes, techniques and operations. It treats knowledge as a key resource. This knowledge has often been confused with information and sometimes with wisdom because of the somewhat blurred boundaries that exist between the three. The application of knowledge and the practice of knowledge management as a precise science can create wonderful results in any organisational context.

Managing knowledge is becoming a business imperative for those corporations who want to protect their present market share, build future opportunity share and stay ahead of competition. Knowledge management will also be the key driver for those firms who are keen to innovate and change the rules of the game. Knowledge management is as much if not more concerned with people and how they acquire, exchange and disseminate knowledge as it is about information technology. That is why it has become an important area of HR practitioners, who are in a strong position to exert influence in this aspect of people management. The concept of knowledge management is closely associated with intellectual capital. It is also linked to the concepts of organisational learning and the learning organisations. A distinction was made by Ryle (1949) between 'knowing how' and 'knowing What'. Knowing how is the ability of a person to perform tasks, and knowing what is holding pieces of knowledge in one's mind.

## Definition of Knowledge Management

Knowledge management is 'any process or practice of creating, acquiring, capturing, sharing and using knowledge, wherever it resides, to enhance learning and performance in organisations'. Knowledge management is concerned with both stocks and flows of knowledge. Stocks included expertise and encoded knowledge in computer systems. Flows represent the ways in which knowledge is transferred from people to people to a knowledge database. Knowledge management involves transferring knowledge resources by identifying relevant information and then disseminating it so that learning can take place. Knowledge management strategies promote the sharing of knowledge by linking people with people, and by linking them to information so that they learn from documented experiences.

Knowledge can be stored in data banks and found in presentations, reports, libraries, policy documents and manuals. It can be moved around the organisation through information systems and by traditional methods such as meetings, workshops, courses, master classes, written publications, videos and tapes. The internet provides an additional and very effective medium for communicating knowledge. A knowledge management initiative is best taken up if an organisation finds value in building an institutional memory or a comprehensive knowledge base for the firm to enable better application, sharing and managing of knowledge across the various entities within and outside the organisation. Knowledge management has enabled many organisations of worldwide repute to comprehensively change their approach and service delivery capability, both towards their internal employee community and towards external stakeholders. Many large European and American banks these days are focusing on the task of building and institutionalising organisational memory. Also we can see that Indian companies are not lagging behind in this process, starting from medium to big corporate are trying to create a knowledge center. Even we can see that Dr. Manmohan Singh, the Prime Minister has recently constituted a committee to work out on this issue. Models are being developed to describe tasks, processes and customer relationship functions that employees are engaged in with obtained objectives and best practices that are oriented towards achieving them.

## The D, I, K, W Quartet

Let us attempt to understand some fundamental issues on what has come to be known as the D, I, K, W Quartet.

**Data** as we know, is discrete content and does not make much sense by itself.

**Information** is processed and collected data.

**Knowledge** is highly contextualised information enriched with individual interpretation and expertise. In the organisational context, knowledge can also be looked at as information that is tested against the business rules of the organisation, and found to be valid by knowledgeable individuals and is therefore elevated to a level of validated information or knowledge.

**Wisdom** is in a different realm altogether with profundity born out of intuition and deep insight being the key prerequisites. Clearly, it would be sacrilege to even suggest that this is something that one can 'manage'. So while people can talk with great verve about data and information management and now about knowledge management, wisdom one would feel is best left in its pristine state, untouched by automated efforts to manage it. At best, it can be shared.

**Data** is the entity with the least amount of confusion. Everyone understands it and is comfortable dealing with it. The information and knowledge entities are often misunderstood, interchangeably used and have been the topic of a lot of debate and discussions.

Most organisations attempting a knowledge management solution often find it difficult to differentiate information from knowledge. How does an organisation delineate an information requirement from a knowledge need? The unarticulated concern always remains whether, at the end of it all, one has not come up with a slightly modified IS solution. Two simple thumb rules are:

(a) Information can be person independent. Knowledge is highly person-specific.

(b) Knowledge is always contextual. It can never ever be interpreted or used without understanding its context.

This is also why there cannot be any unilateral classification of an entity as either information for person **A,** could in a different context and circumstance transform itself into knowledge for person **B**. Take, for instance, a satellite imagery from NASA which has recorded troop movements in a sensitive area. To a layman, this could be as abstruse as Picasso's art and therefore not of any earth-shattering relevance.

A useful differentiator as described by John Seely Brown is that while "information is fundamentally disembeddable and therefore transportable and reembeddable, knowledge is not. Knowledge lives in its context". Therefore, it is possible to disembed information from one place and use it elsewhere; however, it would not be possible to disembed a piece of knowledge unless it is lifted with its entire context intact.

## The Concept of Knowledge

A distinction was made by Ryle (1949) between 'knowing how' and 'knowing What'. Knowing how is the ability of a person to perform tasks, and knowing what is holding pieces of knowledge in one's mind.

Blackler (1995) notes that 'knowledge is multifaceted and complex, being both situated and abstract, implicit and explicit, distributed and individual, physical and mental, developing and static, verbal and encoded. He distinguishes forms of knowledge as:

- embedded in technologies, rules and organisational procedures;
- encultured as collective understandings, stories, values and beliefs;

- embodied into the practical activity-based competencies and skills of key members of the organisation (i.e., practical knowledge or 'know-how');
- embraced as the conceptual understanding and cognitive skills of key members (i.e., conceptual knowledge or know-how);
- Nonaka (1991) suggests that knowledge is held either by individuals or collectively. In Backler's terms, embodied or embraced knowledge is individual and embedded, and cultural knowledge is collective.

It can be argued (Scarborough and Carter, 2000) that knowledge emerges from the collective experience of work and is shared between members of a particular group or community.

It is useful to distinguish between data, information, and knowledge:

- data consists of the basic facts – the building blocks for information and knowledge;
- information is data that have been processed in a way which is meaningful to individuals, it is available to anyone entitled to gain access to it; as Drucker (1988) wrote, 'information is data endowed with meaning and purpose'.
- knowledge is information put to productive use; it is personal and often intangible and it can be elusive – the task of tying it down, encoding it and distributing it is tricky.

### Explicit and Tacit Knowledge

Nonaka (1991) and Takeuchi (1995) stated that knowledge is either explicit or tacit. Explicit knowledge can be codified; it is recorded and available, and is held in databases, in corporate intranets and intellectual property portfolios. Tacit knowledge exists in people's minds. It is difficult to articulate in writing and is acquired through personal experience. As suggested by Hansen, Nohria and Tierney (1999), it includes scientific or technological expertise, operational know-how, insights about an industry, and business judgment. The main challenge in knowledge management is how to turn tacit knowledge into explicit knowledge.

## The Purpose and Significance of Knowledge Management

As explained by Blake (1998), the purpose of knowledge management is to capture a company's collective expertise and distribute it to 'wherever it can achieve the biggest payoff'. This is in accordance with the resource-based view of the firm which, as argued by Grant (1991), suggests that the source of competitive advantage lies within the firm (i.e., in its people and their knowledge), not in how it positions itself in the market. Trussler (1998) comments that 'the capability to gather, lever, and use knowledge effectively will become a major source of competitive advantage in many businesses over the next few years'. A successful company is a knowledge-creating company.

Knowledge management is about getting knowledge from those who have it to those who need it in order to improve organisational effectiveness. In the information age, knowledge rather than physical assets or financial resources is the key to competitiveness. In essence, as pointed out by Mecklenberg, Deering and Sharp (1999), 'knowledge management allows companies to capture, apply and generate value from their employees' creativity and expertise.

## Approaches to Knowledge Management

### The Codification and Personalisation Approach

Two approaches to knowledge management have been identified by Hansen, Nohria, and Tierney (1999):

1. **The Codification Strategy** – knowledge is carefully codified and stored in databases where it can be accessed and used easily by anyone in the organisation. Knowledge is explicit and is codified using a 'people-to-document' approach. This strategy is therefore document-driven. Knowledge is extracted from the person who developed it, made independent of that person and reused for various purposes. It will be stored in some form of electronic repository for people to use. This allows many people to search for and retrieve codified knowledge without having to contact the person who originally developed it. This strategy relies largely on information technology to manage databases and also on the use of the intranet.
2. **The Personalisation Strategy** – knowledge is closely tied to the person who has developed it and is shared mainly through direct person-to-person contacts. This is a 'person-to-person' approach which involves sharing tacit knowledge. The exchange is achieved by creating networks and encouraging face-to-face communication between individuals and teams by means of informal conferences, workshops, brainstorming, and one-to-one sessions.

### The Knowledge-creating Company

In the opinion of Nonaka and Takeuchi (1995), a core competitive activity of organisations is knowledge creation — 'an organic, fluid and socially constructed process in which different knowledge are blended to produce innovative outcomes that are predicted or unpredictable'. Fundamental to knowledge creation is the blending of tacit and explicit knowledge through processes of socialisation (tacit to tacit), externalisation (tacit to explicit), internalisation (explicit to tacit) and combination (explicit to explicit).

### The Resource-based Approach

Scarborough and Carter (2000) described knowledge management as 'the attempt by management to actively create, communicate and exploit knowledge as a resource for the organisation'. They suggested that this attempt has technical, social and economic components:

- In technical terms, knowledge management involves centralising knowledge that is currently scattered across the organisation and codifying tacit forms of knowledge.
- In social and political terms, knowledge management involves collectivising knowledge so that it is no longer the exclusive property of individuals or groups.
- In economic terms, knowledge management is a response by organisations to the need to identifying their creation and exploitation of knowledge.

## Knowledge Management Issues

The various approaches referred to above do not provide easy answers. The issues that need to be addressed in developing knowledge management processes are as under:

### The Pace of Change

One of the main issues in knowledge management is how to keep up with the pace of change and identify what knowledge needs to be captured and shared.

### Relating Knowledge Management Strategy to Business Strategy

As Hansen, Nohria and Tierney (1999) show, it is not knowledge *per se* but the way it is applied to strategic objectives that is the critical ingredient in competitiveness. They point out that 'competitive strategy must derive knowledge strategy', and that managements have to answer the question: 'How does knowledge that resides in the company and value for customers?' Mecklenberg, Deering and Sharp (1999) argued that organisations should 'start with the business value of what they gather. If it does not generate value, drop it'.

## Technology and People

Technology may be central to companies adopting a codification strategy but for those following a personalisation strategy, IT is best used in a supportive role. As Hansen, Nohria and Tierney (1999) commented:

In the codification model, managers need to implement a system that is much like a traditional library – it must contain a large cache of documents and include search engines that allow people to find and use the documents they need. In the personalisation model, it is more important to have a system that allows people to find other people.

Scarborough, Swan and Preston (1999) suggest that 'technology should viewed more as a means of communication and less as a means of storing knowledge'. Knowledge management is more about people than technology. As research by Davenport (1996) established, managers get two-thirds of their information from face-to-face or telephone conversations. There is a limit to how much tacit knowledge can be codified. In organisations relying more on tacit than explicit knowledge, a person-to-person approach works best, and IT can only support this process, it cannot replace it.

## The Significance of Process and Social Capital and Culture

A preoccupation with technology may mean that too little attention is paid to the processes (social, technological and organisational) through which knowledge combines and interacts in different ways (Blackler, 1995, cited by Scarborough, Swan and Preston, 1999). The key process is the interactions between people. This constitutes the social capital of an organisation, i.e., the 'network for the conduct of social affairs' (Naphiet and Ghoshal, 1998). Social networks can be particularly important in ensuring that knowledge is shared. What is also required is another aspect of social capital: trust. People will not be willing to share knowledge with those whom they do not trust. The culture of the company may inhibit knowledge sharing. The norm may be for people to keep knowledge to themselves as much as they can because 'knowledge is power'. An open culture will encourage people to share their ideas and knowledge.

## Knowledge Workers

Knowledge workers as defined by Drucker (1993) are individuals who have high levels of education and specialist skills combined with the ability to apply these skills to identify and solve problems. As Argyris (1991) points out: 'The nuts and bolts of management .... increasingly consists of guiding and integrating the autonomous but interconnected work of highly skilled people'. Knowledge management is about the management and motivation of knowledge workers who create knowledge and will be the key players in sharing it.

## The Contribution of HR to Knowledge Management

HR can make an important contribution to knowledge management simply because knowledge is shared between people; it is not just a matter of capturing explicit knowledge through the use of information technology. The role of HR is to ensure that the organisation has the intellectual capital it needs. The resource-based view of the firm emphasises, in the words of Capelli and Crocker-Hefter (1996), that 'distinctive human resource practices help to create unique competencies that differentiate products and services and, in turn, drive competitiveness'.

### Ten Ways in which HR can Contribute

The ten ways in which HR can contribute to knowledge management are as under:

1. Help to develop an open culture in which the values and norms emphasise the importance of sharing knowledge.
2. Promote a climate of commitment and trust.
3. Advise on the design and development of organisations which facilitate knowledge sharing through networks and communities of practice (groups of people who share common concerns about aspects of their work), and teamwork.

4. Advise on resourcing policies and provide resourcing services which ensure that valued employees who can contribute to knowledge creation and sharing are attracted and retained.
5. Advise on methods of motivating people to share knowledge and rewarding those who do so.
6. Help in the development of performance management processes which focuses on the development and sharing of knowledge.
7. Develop processes of organisational and individual learning which will generate and assist in disseminating knowledge.
8. Set up and organise workshops, conferences, seminars, and symposia which enable knowledge to be shared on a person-to-person basis.
9. In conjunction with IT, develop systems for capturing and, as far as possible, codifying explicit and tacit knowledge.
10. Generally, promote the cause of knowledge management with senior managers to encourage them to exert leadership and support knowledge management initiatives.

## Integrating Knowledge Management into the Millennium Enterprise

**Some Imperatives and Challenges:** Knowledge management presents an opportunity to integrate all the people and processes that exist within an organisation towards stated corporate objectives. These objectives have already been defined and range from employees to suppliers to subcontractors and to the customers. And today's tools range from the array of information technology solutions – Business Intelligence, Groupware, ERP, SCM, Intranets, the Internet – to every possible form of these are disparate and independent optional initiatives or whether knowledge management can provide a thread of continuity to integrate and align all these initiatives towards the common goals of the millennium enterprise.

All corporations today are faced with enormous challenges that threaten their supremacy even in relatively unchallenged domains. This fiercely competitive environment has been created by a combination of competitive pull factors like globalisation and privatisation, and technology pushes, primarily caused by the rapid proliferation of the internet. The case of the crumbling of the Berlin Wall was brought down by many erstwhile entry barriers. In an environment where product superiority is transient and brand loyalty is becoming an anachronism, the only differentiator will be the quality of the organisation's processes and its ability to attain and sustain 'customer intimacy'. Once the customer intimacy objective has been translated into specific consumer to business electronic interfaces and customer service and response mechanisms, the next stage is to ensure that the enterprise's business processes are all oriented to the needs of the customer. A true market-facing enterprise ensures that customer needs flow quickly down to the last level of response in the organisation and the needs and actions are captured in the legacy systems or ERP bedrock of the organisation. The quick capture, storage, dissemination and use of data, information and knowledge is essential to ensure that quick actions and responses are facilitated by information technology at all levels. This 'process energy' needs to be supplemented by the third imperative – that of people empowerment.

This is where a knowledge-centric approach can really enable a corporation to succeed beyond the expectations of its customers and the capabilities of its competitors. A true knowledge corporation will be one where the principles of knowledge management are applied as an underlying philosophy for all strategic initiatives, ranging from customer interfaces to internal integration of systems to business-to-business interfaces. Included, of course, is the full continuum of the learning organisation from learning systems to performance support to knowledge management.

An analysis of the potential of knowledge management tools and techniques to transform the implementation of each of the initiatives will put the real potential of knowledge management in perspective. Customer-to- business and business-to-consumer transactions can range all the way from simple customer queries and feedback through a web storefront to comprehensive Customer Relationship Management (CRM) tools.

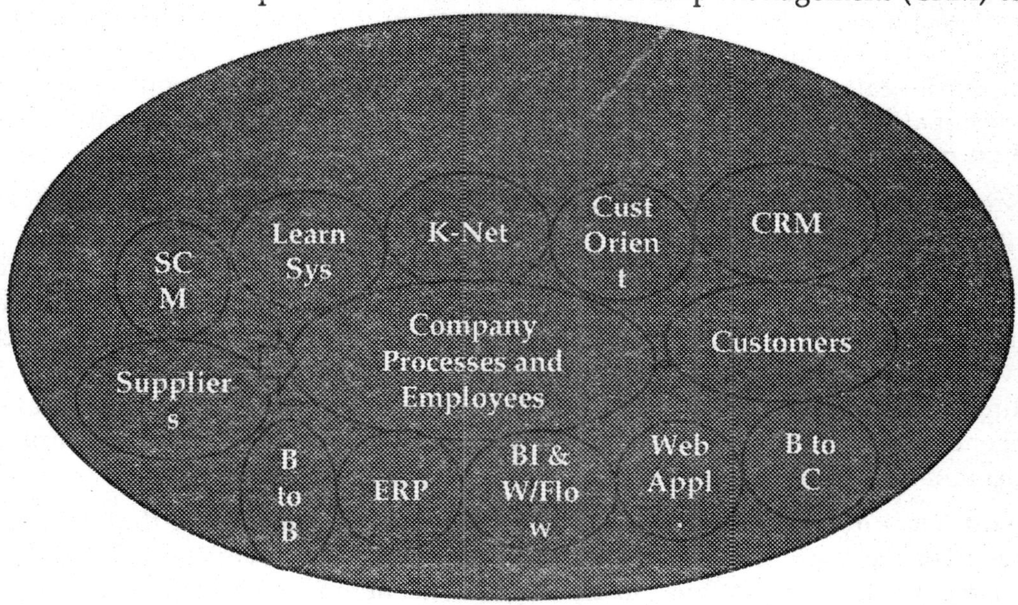


**Fig. The Knowledge Corporation**

The trends in Business-to-Customer (B2C) E-Commerce point towards more and more self-help for the customer to enable customers to access deep down into the innards of the organisation and conduct secure transactions with very little interaction with the employees of the firm. Thinking through the knowledge interventions required to facilitate these self-help environments will call for a deeper understanding of customer buying patterns and psychology to that all the intelligence derived from significant customer interactions can become part of the institutional memory of the enterprise. This will ensure that every future interaction of the customer with the firm becomes richer and will enable the concept of customer intimacy to really come alive.

Consumer-to-Business transactions would be meaningless if the organisation did not build processes to quickly enable the flow of expressed and implied customer needs through the enterprise. Collaborative computing involves the implementation of Groupware and messaging solutions and tools like Lotus Notes have become synonymous with knowledge management. The ability to build 'communities of best practices' and shared ideas is one of the key capabilities of any significant knowledge management initiative and will catalyse the development of a Quick Response and Reflective Organisation. Added to this are collaborative knowledge capture and usage capabilities provided by business intelligence tools which again ensure that processes respond more creatively to customer issues and a true Market-facing Enterprise is built.

Legacy systems and enterprise resource planning applications are typically complete in themselves. The role of knowledge management in the integration of Groupware or business intelligence tools with these larger segments of applications would be to ensure seamless interfacing. This ensures that the results of discussions and intelligence built over a period of time are able to enrich the data or context-specific information stored and also enable customers to get better responses. In the Insurance Company, the real cutting edge to customer response comes when the Call Centre employees interface is able to give in real time not just the data about policies or information about the customer's queries, but also tacit guidance on the best behavioural stance to adopt with the customer based on previous interactions.

Knowledge management also needs to be integrated with the data integration strategy of the enterprise. When this is achieved, it will also enable the business to business transactions from the firm to its virtual enterprise partners — suppliers, subcontractors, distributors and agents — to be energised through knowledge-based interactions. Imagine an extended ERP solution where a comprehensive customer contract has to be executed, involving significant outsourcing and subcontracting and delivery to be made in installments. Synchronisation of all business processes across the supply chain and intelligence and knowledge sharing across the virtual organisation will ensure minimum hiccups and maximum customer and partner satisfaction.

**And the knowledge continuum itself?:** There is no doubt that knowledge management tools, are the best way of making Peter Senge's concept of the Learning Organisation come true. While purists argue that there is a lot more to learning and knowledge than just technology, there is no doubt that the availability of learning, electronic performance support and knowledge bases on tap for ready access are the great potential areas for improving corporate knowledge capabilities. As we move deeper into the new millennium and knowledge processes, tools and technologies get internalised at every stage of business interactions. Knowledge management will provide the visionary organisations with a capability level that will prove a major source of competitive advantage in the Information Society.

***

# 20 Knowledge Processing Outsourcing

## Introduction

In general terms, Knowledge Processing Outsourcing is popularly known as KPO. Business Processing Outsourcing or BPO industry turning into Knowledge Process Outsourcing. KPO Industry handling more high skilled work than the existing BPO Industry.

In today's information driven knowledge economy, KPO is a step-forward in creating new business opportunities for companies. Knowledge process outsourcing or KPO will bring huge job opportunities in the coming days.

Knowledge is power and Information is Knowledge. As we all know, today's economy is Knowledge economy. Knowledge processing is a continuous process of creation and dissemination of information by bringing together the information and facilitate the industry leaders to create knowledge and the meaning is transformed to valuable information. This Information driven Knowledge outsourcing is known as Knowledge Processing Outsourcing or KPO.

Generally, it is believed that KPO is the high intellect "cousin" of BPO (Business Process Outsourcing). In KPO, the emphasis is on higher complexity processes which require the talent of professionals with extensive education and experience credentials. The types of work performed require specific and advanced knowledge of a particular domain, technology, industry, or specialty.

KPO firms provide their professional services from offshore locations – with highly skilled teams typically located in India, China, Philippines, South America, or Eastern Europe.

Examples of the types of tasks KPO firms address include the following:

- Equity, Financial, and Insurance Research
- Data Search, Integration, and Management

- SPO – Sales Process Outsourcing (Sales Collateral Production, Presentation and Proposal Development,
- Lead Generation, Market Segment Studies, Competitive Intelligence, Client Profiling, Client Satisfaction Studies, Sales Analytics & Reporting, Sales Hiring Assistance, CRM Support, etc.)
- Analytics (Data Analytics, Financial Analytics, Risk Analytics) and Data Mining Services
- Business Research/Business Intelligence (Market Segment Studies, Market Sizing, Competitive Intelligence, Business Plan Drafting, New Innovation Identification, etc.)
- Market Research (Phone Surveys, Web Surveys, Client Satisfaction Studies, Branding Studies, Customer Preference Studies, Consumer Surveys, etc.)
- Financial Research (Fundamental Research, Quantitative Research, Modeling, Organisation Research, Deal Research, etc.)
- LPO – Legal Process Outsourcing (Paralegal Content & Services)
- Engineering and Design Services
- Design, Animation, and Simulation Services
- Human Resource Research & Support
- Medical Content Services
- Remote Education & Publishing
- Pharmaceutical & Biotechnology Services
- Research and Development (IT & Non-IT Areas)
- Network Management
- Decision Support Systems (DSS)

## What is KPO?

The maturity and evolution of outsourcing strategies is leading businesses to shift towards the off shoring of high-end processes to low-wage destinations, a trend referred to as KPO. This involves offshoring of knowledge-intensive business processes that require significant domain expertise.

In comparison to BPO, KPO delivers higher value to organisations that offshore their domain-based processes, thereby enhancing BPO's traditional cost-quality paradigm. The central theme of KPO is to create value for the client by providing business expertise rather than process expertise. Hence, KPO entails the shifting from simple execution of 'standardized processes' to carrying out processes that demand advanced analytical and technical skills as well as decisive judgment. **Figure** provides two examples – one

**Figure 1: Examples of two industries – Gradual Migration from Low-end (BPO) to High-end (KPO) Offshoring**

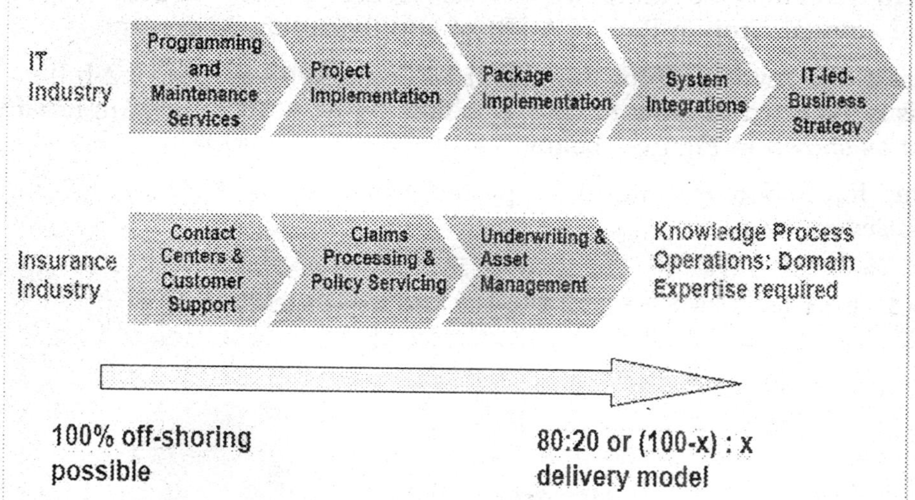


With global businesses becoming more competitive, the cycle time for introducing products and services has become smaller, and customers are more demanding with respect to the quality of services provided. This has forced enterprises to adopt systems and business models that will not only provide operational efficiency, but also add strategic value to their products and services.

KPO services can enable enterprises to reduce design-to-market lead times; manage critical hardware efficiently; provide research on markets, competition, products and services; enhance organisational effectiveness in business administration; and help in dealing with rapidly evolving business scenarios. Finally, the outsourcing solutions for high-end processes, unlike traditional BPO solutions that are commoditized fixed-price solutions, are usually customized and value based. It is often this customization that enhances

Introduction The success in offshoring Business Process operations with respect to reducing costs and often improving quality has encouraged many firms to start offshoring their high-end knowledge work as well. Their underlying expectation is that offshoring high-end processes will result in additional cost savings and operational efficiencies, coupled with access to very good talent in the low-wage offshore countries. We will refer to this offshoring of higher-end services as Knowledge Process Offshoring (KPO).

Attempts has been made to focus on the evolving KPO market, the opportunities it offers, the associated challenges, and the key drivers associated with the move from BPO to KPO.

## KPO – The Challenges and Opportunities

The recent trend indicates that low-end outsourcing services will grow globally with a Cumulative Annual Growth Rate (CAGR) of approximately 26 percent.

In contrast, the revenue from the global KPO market was USD 1.2 billion in FY 2003 and this is expected to grow to USD 17 billion by FY 2010, which implies a CAGR of 46 percent as shown in Figure-2 below.

Following figure demonstrates the expected growth in the BPO and KPO markets over the next seven years.

**Figure 2: Expected Growth in Global BPO and KPO Markets (2003-2010)**

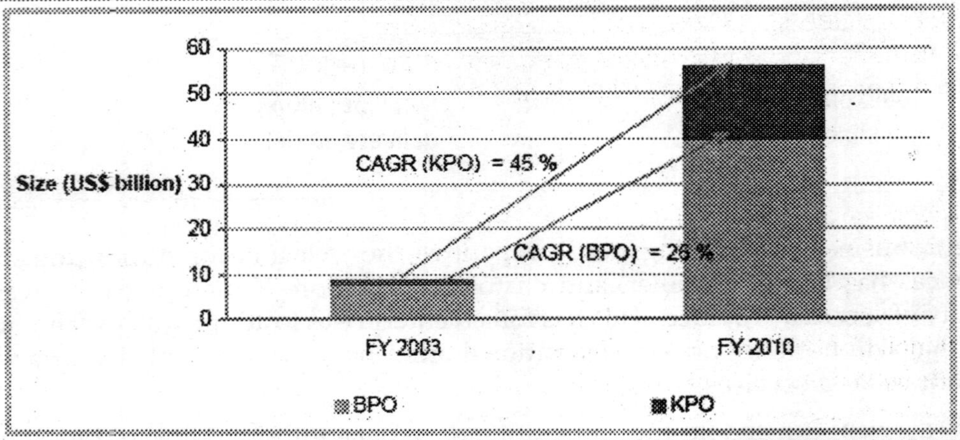


*Source: Evalueserve Analysis*

**Table 1: Comparative Opportunities in the KPO Market (2003 – 2010)**

| KPO Sectors | FY 2003 | SY 2010 | CAGR |
|---|---|---|---|
| Equity, Financial, Insurance Research | 0 | 0.4 | N/A |
| Data Search, Integration and Management | 0.3 | 5.0 | 50% |
| Research and Information Services in HR | 0 | 0.2 | - |
| Market Research and Competitive Intelligence | 0.01 | 0.4 | 70% |
| Engineering and Design | 0.4 | 2.0 | 29% |
| Animation and Simulation Services | 0.1 | 1.4 | 46% |
| Paralegal Content and Services | 0 | 0.3 | N/A |
| Medical Content and Services | 0 | 0.3 | N/A |
| Remote Education and Publishing | 0 | 2.0 | N/A |

| | | | |
|---|---|---|---|
| Biotech and Pharmaceuticals (CRO, lead optimization, and manufacturing processes) | 0.28 | 3.0 | 40% |
| Research and Development | 0.2 | 2.0 | 39% |
| Total (USD Billion) | 1.29 | 17.0 | 46% |

**Source:** Evalueserve Analysis.

## High-end KPO Opportunities – Some Examples

The following are some examples of high-end KPO:

### Intellectual Property Research (IPR)

- An Intellectual Property (IP) specialist in an offshore location can produce a preliminary draft of a patent application, which is then reviewed and modified by a registered patent attorney in the respective geographical locations, before it is filed with the concerned authority.
- Off shoring even a small portion of the patent-drafting process can save up to 50 percent of the total cost (for the end client).
- IP asset management, IP landscaping of technology domains, IP licensing, IP docketing, and IP commercialization services are some other services that can be off shored in a similar manner. These services can be provided not only for patents but also for trademarks, copyrights, and other Intellectual Property.
- Some law firms in different places have already set up their back-end centers in India, and others are joining hands with Indian companies for this purpose.

### Offshoring R&D in Pharmaceuticals and Biotechnology

- Contract research organisations are being widely used by pharmaceutical companies. Other emerging areas within this sector include lead optimization and improvement of manufacturing processes.
- Destinations such as India offer significant cost advantages – often as much as 40-60 per cent – in the areas of contract research and clinical trials.
- Recently, companies such as AstraZeneca and Glaxo-Smith-Kline have set up drug discovery centers at low-cost destinations thereby off-shoring their R&D.

### Analytics and Data Mining Services

- Companies can save significantly – as much as 60-70 percent – by offshoring data mining, analytics, and inventory management work to low-wage countries.
- Demand and channel planning, manufacturing scheduling, and transport planning are examples of some supply-chain management solutions that require the use of mathematical programming, statistical analysis, and computer-aided simulations.

- Destinations such as Russia and India are ideal for these services because they provide a large pool of engineers and even PhDs at substantially low costs. The cost differential between a PhD in the Sciences and Engineering in the US and in India (or between the US and Russia) can range between USD 60,000 and USD 80,000, respectively.

## Challenges in KPO

KPO definitely presents substantial opportunities for players in the outsourcing business. Still, there are some formidable challenges , which include the following:

- Processes executed within the KPO domain require higher quality standards because the stakes for the clients are high. Furthermore, the clients are likely to be apprehensive about the quality of services delivered (especially in view of the fact that these services are being provided by low-cost destinations) and these may be difficult to alleviate.
- In some cases, investment in KPO infrastructure is expected to be higher than that in traditional BPO. For example, a company involved in Simulation and Finite Element Analysis will require high-end workstations, whereas one involved in simple data collection, sorting, and analysis may require moderate capital. Similarly, contract research organisations are likely to require higher amounts of capital.
- The lack of a good talent pool for the execution of projects may often prove to be a hindrance in many countries.
- KPO projects require a higher level of control, confidentiality and enhanced risk management. Laxity in any of these parameters will not only hamper the KPO services being provided, but may also affect the entire business conducted by the client.
- In comparison to traditional BPO services, scaling up of KPO operations will be difficult, primarily owing to difficulty in finding highly trained.

## Problems in Sourcing, Retaining, and Nurturing Talent

KPO companies are faced with the challenge of hiring the best talent and imparting continuous training to these professionals. It is advisable for offshoring companies that venture into the KPO industry to focus on initial training and continuous development modules.

Another key challenge in the management of KPO is the identification of 'performance criteria'. This involves setting the right expectations with the end client, as well as its professionals; continuous assessment and monitoring, constructive feedback, appropriate coaching and mentoring, and identification of the right career path for the company's professionals. For example, any organisation decides the KPA/KRA, and other performance evaluation metrics based on the organisational policies, but here in KPO, the agency has to decide.

## Drivers Behind the BPO to KPO Shift

The gradual shift from BPO to KPO in some offshore countries is expected to change the dynamics of job migration. It can be assumed that more low-end jobs will migrate to emerging low-cost countries (from a percentage perspective and not as an absolute number) such as Ukraine, the Czech Republic, Belarus, Romania, China, the Philippines, and Malaysia. At the same time, KPO jobs are likely to be created in India, Russia, Ireland, Israel, and Canada. Even though some emerging countries, especially those in the Central and Eastern European Region (e.g., Ukraine and the Czech Republic), can provide KPO services, the 'brand equity' of these countries is quite low. Therefore, it is predicted that these emerging offshore locations will not attract KPO services, at least for the time being.

### Buyers of Off- shoring Services Save More at the Higher End

Buyers of offshoring services save more at the high end of the value chain, compared to the low end. Therefore, many of the current low-cost destinations will become a logical choice for companies for offshoring their high-end processes.

### Scarcity of Highly Trained Specialized Talent Pool in the Developed Countries

Developed economies such as the US, the UK, and Western European countries are already facing a shortage of highly trained and specialized professionals in some knowledge-intensive high-skill sectors, such as R&D in VLSI, engineering design, IT, financial risk management, etc. One way to mitigate this skill shortage is to source talent from low-wage developing countries, which produce highly educated scientists and professionals. This has been the practice in the US for the past several decades. The US permits emigration of engineers, scientists, and medical doctors from developing countries, such as India and China. With tighter visa regulations (in the developed countries) and cost-reduction pressures on MNCs, global offshoring of high-end services to low-wage countries to tap the existing talent pool in a cost effective manner is a viable and lucrative option.

### Maturity and Evolution of Present Low-end Destinations to the Higher-end of the Value Chain

The evolution of present low-end destinations to the higher end of the value chain, aided by the maturity of the processes, will result in organisations moving up the value chain to provide KPO services. Commoditization of BPO services will further boost this transition and the better margins expected at the higher end of the value chain might act as a deterrent for companies in accepting low-end work. The barriers to entry in the KPO industry are also higher, and therefore, offshoring companies may not have the same competitive pressures as are there in traditional BPO.

### Some of the Present Low-cost Destinations May No Longer Remain Low-cost

Some current low-cost destinations may no longer remain low-cost due to increase in salaries and hence, may not be able to provide cost-arbitrage benefits to companies that want to offshore these services. For example, Indian salaries have increased at an average of 14 percent per year. If this trend continues, they are expected to increase 2.5 times the current salaries (in constant dollars) by FY 2010, thereby reducing the cost-arbitrage benefit from the present 40 to 25 percent.

## Increasing Number of Professionals in the Offshoring Industry

The number of professionals working in the offshoring industry is expected to increase as more and more companies decide to become involved in BPO and KPO. This will further drive the trend towards the migration of low-end services to high-end services, especially as offshore service vendors (as well as the professionals working in this sector) gain substantial experience and capabilities to provide high value services.

During 2000-2003, the US off-shored 238,000 IT service jobs. It is predicted that this is likely to increase to 775,000 jobs by FY 2010. Further, by the end of March 2004, the US had off-shored about 136,000 BPO (non-IT) jobs, mostly in the call centre segment. Forrester predicts that it is likely to offshore 1.314 million BPO (non-IT) jobs by FY 2010.

Different studies have estimated that the UK had off-shored 35,000 IT service jobs by FY 2003, and this is expected to grow to 110,200 jobs by FY 2010. From different survey results, it has been estimated that 30,000 BPO (non-IT) jobs (mainly in call centers) have already been off-shored by the UK by FY 2003, and 201,100 BPO (non-IT) jobs are expected to move from the UK by FY 2010.

**Table 2: Jobs Offshored by the US and the UK in the IT and 'non-IT BPO' Sectors (By FY 2003 and corresponding Estimates for FY 2010)**

| | IT Jobs | Non-IT BPO Jobs | Total Jobs Offshored |
|---|---|---|---|
| United States | | | |
| FY 2003 | 238,000 | 136,000 | 374,000 |
| FY 2010 | 775,000 | 1,314,000 | 2,089,000 |
| United Kingdom | | | |
| FY 2003 | 35,000 | 30,000 | 65,000 |
| FY 2010 | 110'200 | 201,100 | 311,300 |

**Source:** Evalueserve Analysis

## The Big Irony – Protectionist Lobby is in Reality Boosting the Offshoring Trend

Ironically, the protectionist lobby and their anti-BPO drive in the US and the UK are indirectly helping the proliferation of global offshoring by providing free publicity.

Most of this free publicity stemmed from about 1,980 distinct articles, columns, and discussion documents written in newspapers and magazines in the period between June 1, 2002 and May 31, 2004. This publicity was related to:

- Offshoring and outsourcing to low-wage countries
- Anti-BPO
- Anti-IT outsourcing
- Various legislations in individual US states
- Congressional and parliamentary hearings held at the state and the federal levels in the US and the UK
- Discussions by various legislative authorities including John Kerry (presidential candidate for the November 2004 elections in the US), US President George Bush, and their spokes-persons

In addition to the 1,980 or more articles, a simple Google search shows that the Internet web-logs and websites contain over 210,000 distinct references and 'threads' discussing these issues. Furthermore, CNN and one of its flagship programs, 'Money line' has been spending almost three minutes a day, five days a week, on this topic for the last six months, and it has been continuously updating the list of 350-400 companies that are offshoring to India and China.

Hence, the anti-offshoring drive has definitely increased India's brand image because American and the British companies now feel that Indian companies are capable of almost anything, even rocket science! This is indeed an interesting contrast from the situation four years ago, when the same companies were under the impression that Indian companies can only 'provide software coolies' and 'export cheap IT caders to solve the Y2K problem'. Because of this awareness, it has become easier for Indian companies to move from BPO to KPO, especially in the US and the UK.

Because of the anti-offshoring drive in the US and the UK (and to a small extent in other countries like Canada and Australia), not only India and China but also other low-wage countries including the Philippines, Russia, and Mexico, have gained in publicity. Hence, with the passage of time, this anti-offshoring movement is likely to help even these low-cost countries in improving their brand image and thereby moving up the value chain.

## Key Low-wage Offshore Locations: A Comparative Study

This section attempts to analyze key offshore destinations that are likely to emerge as the hubs of the BPO and KPO sectors. A comparative assessment of key low wage Low-Wage-BPO-KPO-Locations destinations, with respect to some critical parameters, is provided in Table 3.

**Table 3: Comparison of Key Low-wage Offshore BPO/KPO Locations**

| | China | India | Philippines | Ireland | Israel | Russia |
|---|---|---|---|---|---|---|
| Cost of manpower | IT salaries USD 6360 | IT salaries USD 5,375 | IT salaries – USD 4,250 | IT salaries – USD 25,500 | IT salaries are approximately | IT salaries USD 6,120 to |

| | | | | | | |
|---|---|---|---|---|---|---|
| (Case of IT Services) | to 9,540 per annum | to USD 8,960 per annum | to USD 6,800 per annum | to USD 37,500per annum | USD 25,000 per annum | USD 9,180 per annum |
| Geographic Location | 24 X 7 support as China spans 5 different time zones | 24 X7 support | 24 X 7 support | Close proximity to Europe makes it a good near-shore destination | Close proximity to Europe makes it a good near-shore destination | Close proximity to Europe makes it an ideal near-shore destination |
| Demographic Factors | Low proficiency in English | High degree of proficiency in English | Compatibility with the Western corporate culture | Compatability and proximity with the Western culture and proficiency in English | Compatability and proximity with the Western culture and proficiency in English | Compability and proximity with the Western culture |
| Government Policies | Favourable Special Economic Zones (SEZs) | Friendly government policies for IT exports; creation of Software Technology Parks (STPs) | SEZs; license fee exemption; no export tax; supports the IT exports industry | Technology education fund, favourable tax laws and incentives | Strong policies with respect to IP rights, including copyright, trademark and patents | Old laws and tax structure |
| Other Advantages | Uniquely positioned to tap Japanese and Korean markets due to language compatability | Large labour pool with high quality IT training and good project managerial skills | 380,000 graduates proficient in English | Advanced telecom infrastructure | Strong presence in niche software products and services | Moderate labour costs, highly talented labour pool, third-largest pool of engineers and scientists |
| Disadvantages | Language and cultural incompatibility; Insufficient project | Unreliable power infrastructure | Scarcity of trained IT personnel, lack of project management skills | Small labour pool; high labour cost | Population less than six million and hence a small labour pool | Poor infrastructure; high bandwidth; weak telecom structure; |

| | | | | | | |
|---|---|---|---|---|---|---|
| | manage-ment skills | | | | | cultural problems due to its past isolation from other western countries |

**Source:** Evalueserve Analysis.

Low-wage countries. By FY 2010, we expect the following scenario:

- Commoditization of low-end services is likely to occur because the potential barriers to entry are minimal.
- New business models will be created and older ones will cease to exist. The next level of productivity improvements may emanate from this 'creative destruction' of the current 'supply chain of services'.
- Many new business models will rely on re-arranging the supply chain of a given 'process' and on using IT to enhance productivity. One such interesting new model of conducting research has been provided in the Appendix.
- By FY 2010, India and other such destinations might become too costly to provide low-end services at competitive costs. Therefore, low-end work may move to relatively cheaper countries such as Ukraine, Belarus, the Czech Republic, and Malaysia.

## Offshoring is Likely to Restructure the Global Workforce

With the proliferation of global offshoring and distributed delivery models, the emergence of a strictly onshore services workforce (as part of Tertiary-A) and a global information and services workforce (as part of Tertiary-B) is expected, as depicted in this chapter.

The above-mentioned destinations offer both IT and non-IT BPO services. Among them, India offers the widest range of IT and non-IT BPO services; the Philippines currently offers mainly BPO services; and Israel and Russia offer niche services especially in the IT offshoring domain. The maximum benefits of offshoring are currently being realized in the Philippines and India. Moreover, China and India are geographically best located to provide 24x7 support although the Philippines is a close contender in this aspect. From the perspective of cultural compatibility and with respect to proficiency in written and spoken English, Canada, Ireland and the Philippines seem to score over other countries.

Investment and labor policies have been made 'offshoring friendly' by most governments in these countries. Countries such as India, Russia, and Israel have the requisite talent pool to move up the value chain and provide KPO services.

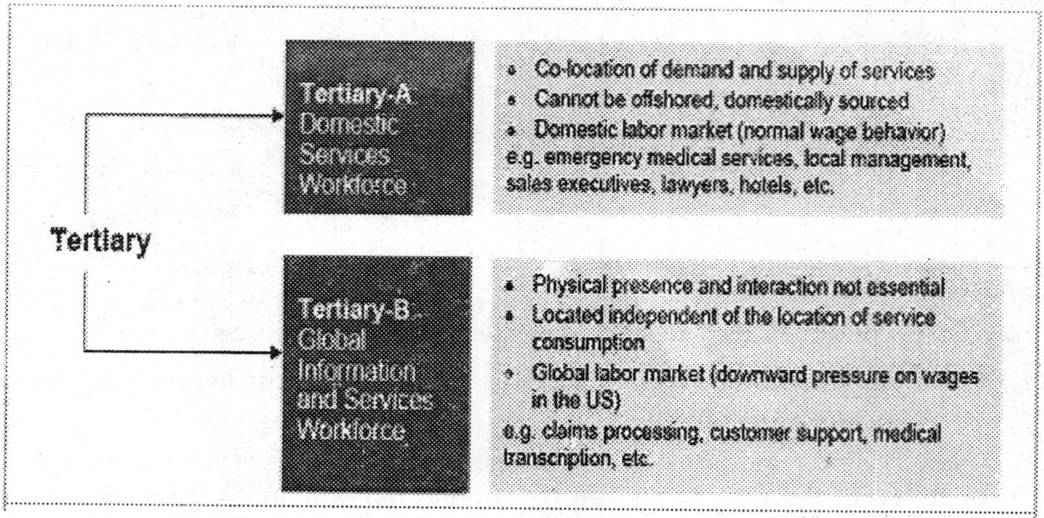


**Fig. 3: Likely Struvture of Global Workforce in the Near Future**

**Source: Evalueserve Analysis**

The major impediments faced by offshore destinations taken up in this study are their small talent pools (e.g., the Philippines, Ireland and Israel) and non-English speaking population (e.g., China and Russia).

### Future Outlook

Globalization of services is in its nascent stage. In fact, even in the IT services sector, only 1.9 percent of the total jobs are being carried out.

## Increase in M&A and IPO Activities Predicted for Indian BPO and KPO Industries

### Top players will dominate the industry with a significant reduction in the numbers of BPO vendors and captives by 2010

**New Delhi – 29 July 2005:** According to a recent study, the Indian outsourcing industry is expected to witness an increase in mergers & acquisitions (M&A) as well as IPO activities, with the total value of deals estimated to be as high as USD 3-5 billion during 2006-10. This will lead to a significant consolidation in the BPO industry, especially amongst the small and medium-size players. Very large BPOs are likely to go the IPO way, capitalising on favourable multiples currently being offered by the industry, while the small to medium-size players will either continue to exist as niche players or be acquired by larger BPOs or western companies. Further, it is expected that there will be an increase in spin-offs and the eventual acquisitions/IPOs of captives. These activities will be driven primarily by the need for expansion, both in terms of geography as well as lines of business, developing multi-location delivery capability, gaining access to a lower cost base, the acquisition of complementary skills, the easy availability of capital through Private Equity firms and capital markets, and the pressure on private equity firms for exit of investments.

The key findings of the study, which maps the M&A trend in the BPO and KPO industries in India, include:

- 7-10 large BPOs are expected to use the IPO route between 2005-10
- 5-10 spin-offs of captives of foreign companies during the same period, which are further expected to be acquired by large BPOs or take the IPO route
- A large number of deals involving large BPOs acquiring small and medium-size niche BPOs and KPOs

The study identifies several trends and drivers for M&A and IPO activities in the Indian BPO and KPO industries:

- MNCs providing outsourced services acquiring established large or mid-size BPO players or small niche BPO and KPO players: To quickly establish an India operation, thereby gaining access to the low cost base in India
- Large BPOs acquiring stake in speciality BPO and KPO firms having expertise in a niche areas: To increase their service offerings (one-stop shop concept) and strengthen their existing line of business
- Large IT companies acquiring BPO/KPO: To leverage their existing customer base in IT for BPO and KPO activities
- Indian BPOs acquiring western companies: To have better client touch-points and spread their business across geographies.
- Private Equity-funded BPO firms taking the IPO or trade sale route: As an exit option for the private equity firms.
- Independent BPOs taking the IPO route: As a means to raise capital for expansion and growth plans.
- Western companies spinning-off their captives: To reduce the complexity of operations after having realised the limitations of captives, which are non-core to their focus areas

However, the study also reveals that ensuring the success of these transactions will be a major challenge for companies. These challenges would be in the form of the cultural mis-match between the players' post-merger (e.g., turning spun-off captives into successful vendors in the open market, foreign companies acquiring Indian BPOs or KPOs), valuation hurdles and key main risks, which may be major barriers for the acquisition of smaller BPOs/KPOs. Finally, IPOs conducted only for financial reasons without strategic rationale may become very costly in terms of actual cost and opportunity cost. "Many Acquiring firms find it difficult to counter post-merger challenges, when they start facing difficulties in integrating various processes, different functions such as Sales and Marketing, Administration and HR, and ensuring that the merged entity has a common culture. Hence, much more important than identifying an M&A opportunity is the process of managing the same, and integrating the two entities."

## India to Account for 71% of Global KPO Revenues by FY 2010

New Delhi, India – 4 May 2005: According to a research finding, the Indian KPO sector will account for 71 percent of global KPO revenues by FY 2010. The global KPO market will grow by 45 percent per annum, from USD 1.29 billion in FY 2003 to USD 17 billion by FY 2010 This high growth in the KPO sector presents a huge opportunity for India in terms of employment generation and wealth creation, which will result in an increase in the number of jobs, from 25,000 in 2003 to 2, 50,000 by 2010. The average annual salary in the Indian KPO sector is currently around USD 8,800 per annum, as compared to USD 6,000 per annum in BPO. This is the outcome of higher revenue per unit and enhanced billing rates. The report also highlights the fact that revenues in the Indian service sector are expected to rise by 12 percent per annum (from USD 306 billion in FY 2003 to USD 675 billion in FY 2010), contributing 57 percent to India's GDP by FY 2010. KPO will contribute around 1.8 percent to the Indian service sector by FY 2010, up from 0.24 percent in FY 2003. The report also explains how outsourcing high-end jobs is a win-win proposition for clients as well as KPO vendors. The chart on the following page indicates the positive change in the cost structure of clients outsourcing high-end jobs to destinations such as India:

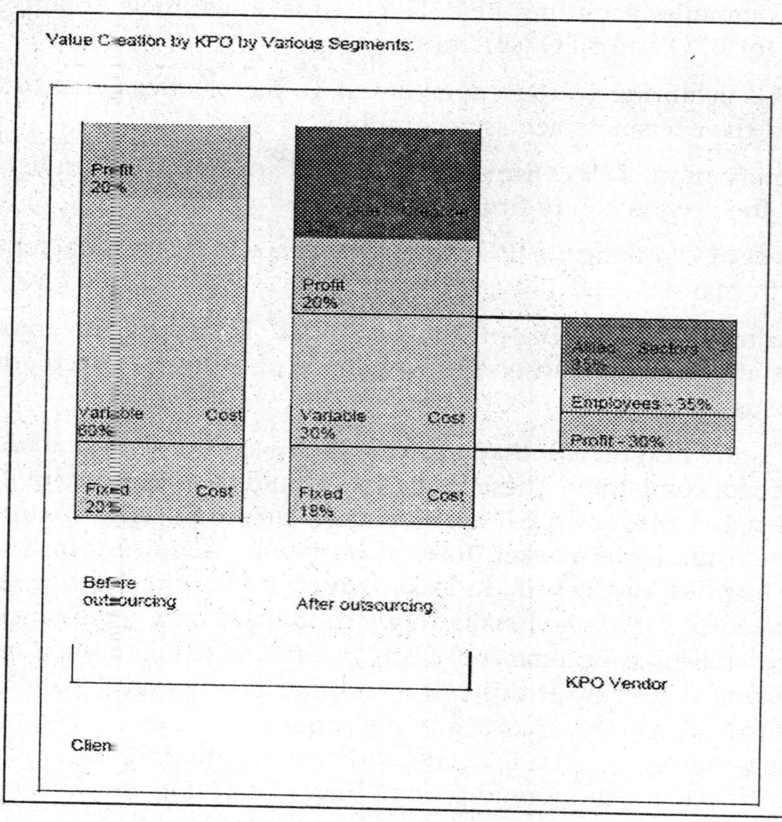

The maximum share of value creation goes to clients outsourcing high-end jobs, thereby cutting costs by 40 to 70 percent and improving quality exponentially. On the other hand, 30 percent of the revenue of a typical KPO vendor is retained in the form of profits (before taxes) and 35 percent goes towards employee costs. The balance, i.e., 35 percent of the revenue, represents overhead costs. This translates into income for the allied sectors, and has a multiplier effect on profit and employment generation. "This multiplier effect could result in two to three jobs being created in other sectors for every job created in the off-shore financial (KPO) sector directly," The report provides an in-depth analysis of the various drivers, value proposition, and imperatives of the KPO sector.

Offshore IT Enabled Services:

- Dedicated Staffing, Offshore hiring of IT professionals
- Outsourcing Software Development.
- Dot Net Programming.
- Custom Application Development
- Web Design and Web Development
- Web Marketing and Web Promotions.
- Data Entry and Data management.
- Web Support, Web Research Services.

"Today time cycle of product and services are becoming smaller, It increased global competitions. We thrive ourselves to provide you High Quality Services, **Improved ROI, Reduced Business Risk and Time Bound Delivery.**"

"Dedicated Staffing is an revolutionary Offshore outsourcing model which helps business to hire a talented, efficient team that **significantly reduce the ongoing operational cost upto 70%, Resulting More Business Gains.**"

**IT Outsourcing is our Domain.** Knowledge Process Outsourcing is highly a value added process in which the achievement of goals is **highly dependent on the skills, knowledge and experience of the people carrying them out.** It may be difficult to manage if outsourcing goes wrong as a well-controlled project require, setting up and running large-scale data acquisition and producing high quality output.

## IT Outsourcing in India

If you are running a process that require extensive labor and IT skill, India will be your destination source. India has exceptional resources and availability of highly Skilled IT professionals that turn out a talented, efficient and a low cost work force. We can help you managing your entire outsourcing venture and provide you efficient deployment of critical resources designed to leverage your outsourcing investments.

Today Indian outsourcing is one of the best ways for CIOs to cut application development and maintenance costs. The key is hiring people who can manage effectively and provide 24/7 support. **A company with superior management skills can reduce your cost to 70% by managing its workforce.**

**Enhanced Value Propositions:**

- Low transition period, higher efficiency.
- Execution of projects through Business Expertise.
- Advance analysis of your requirements.
- Setting up your outsourcing strategy.
- Hiring of professionals with domain expertise.
- Standardizing project specific knowledge process.
- Flawless performance commitment.
- Time bound delivery management
- Business level project management
- 24/7 days support
- Superior communications
- Ensure easy business services.

## India - A Leading Hub for KPO

This evolution needs to be understood from the perspective of the strengths of India as a destination—and driver—of the KPO phenomenon. Analysts put cost advantage, incidentally one of the most significant drivers of KPO, from a KPO assignment at 50 percent. Another critical driver is the deficit of skilled human capital in developed countries like the USA and UK. It is expected that, by 2010, there will be a shortfall of 5.6 million skilled professionals in USA, and 700,000 in UK. This, coupled with the cost advantage, has resulted in high annualized growth in the KPO business.

India is one of the most preferred destinations for KPO because of its competitive edge in terms of a large English speaking labor pool, inherent domain expertise due to a large and developed domestic services industry, knowledge and application of internationally accepted quality standards and processes; in addition to it having the first mover advantage with a well-established vendor base. But other geographies like Brazil, Israel, Ireland, Philippines and China are fast gearing up their education delivery mechanisms to eat a share of this $12 billion market by 2010.

But, on a positive note, India is adding more than three million graduates and professional degree and diploma holders annually. Home to the world's second largest reservoir of engineers and scientists, and the second largest pool of IT manpower, India does possess a distinct competitive edge. To further catalyze the growth in KPO, India should focus on developing a talent pool to manage this expected growth. The future of KPO in India depends not only on how India moves up the value chain in terms of services and offerings but also on how India can retain its competitive advantage of cost arbitrage, pool of knowledge professionals, and quality of deliverables. India is a proven success story in ITO and BPO; KPO is one in the making.

**Source:** Equinox Corporation

## The future of KPO

According to a report by Global Sourcing Now the Global Knowledge Process Outsourcing industry (KPO) is expected to reach USD 17 billion by 2010, of which USD 12 billion would be outsourced to India . In addition, the Indian KPO sector is also expected to employ more than 250,000 KPO professionals by 2010, compared with the current figure of 25,000 employees. A report predicts that India will capture more than 70 percent of the KPO sector by 2010. Apart from India, countries such as Russia, China, the Czech Republic, Ireland, and Israel are also expected to join the KPO industry.

## Comparison of Opportunity in BPO and KPO markets

Low-end outsourcing services have an expected Cumulative Annual Growth Rate (CAGR) of 26% by 2010. In contrast, the global KPO market is poised for an expected CAGR of 46% by 2010. The following figure demonstrates the expected growth in the BPO and KPO markets over the next seven years.

Expected Growth in Global BPO and KPO Markets (2003-2010)

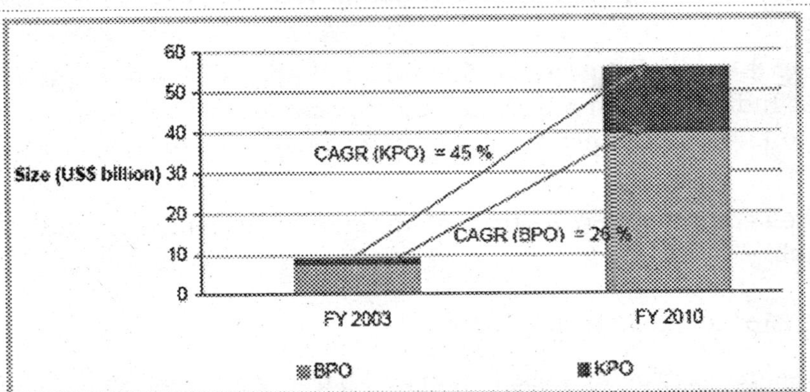


*Source: Evalueserve Analysis*

## What high-end services can be outsourced to the Indian KPO sector?

Here are some KPO services that can be outsourced to India :

- Research and Development
- Business and Technical Analysis
- Learning Solution

- Animation and Design
- Business and Market Research
- Pharmaceuticals and Biotechnology
- Medical Services
- Writing and Content Development
- Legal Services
- Intellectual Property (IP) Research
- Data Analytics
- Network Management
- Training and Consultancy

## The challenges in KPO

KPO delivers high value to organisations by providing domain-based processes and business expertise rather than just process expertise. These processes demand advanced analytical and specialized skill of knowledge workers that have domain experience to their credit. Therefore outsourcing of knowledge processes face more challenges than BPO (Business Process Outsourcing). Some of the challenges involved in KPO will be maintaining higher quality standards, investment in KPO infrastructure, the lack of talent pool, requirement of higher level of control, confidentiality and enhanced risk management.

Comparing these challenges with the Indian IT and ITES service providers, it is not surprising that India has been ranked the most preferred KPO destination owing to the country's large talent pool, quality IT training, friendly government policies and low labor costs.

India is well equipped to meet this emerging sector's challenges and all set to be the global KPO hub!

## Outsourcing Market Research to India

Market research is proving to be an integral part of any business process. It is critical to comprehend one's area of work thoroughly and this can be done by collecting and analyzing information that contributes to a more holistic understanding of consumers, market niches, and marketing programs. Market research aids in providing important information and in guiding business strategy.

### Key Industries that Need Market Research Data Analysis:

1. **BSFI** – Increasing regulatory control and implementation of BASEL II requirements and the requirement of predictive customer analytics and efficient fraud detection systems necessitate data analytics. This would help banks reduce

customer acquisition costs and derive more mileage from existing customers. Also, the formation of statistical score cards for appraisal of credit risk ensures quick response time in the evaluation process as well as total uniformity and removal of bias.

2. **Retail Industry** – Market Research Data Analysis helps retailers to focus on core strategy implementation such as analyses of merchandise, suppliers, operations, inventories, sales and customers thereby ensuring better supply chain management.

3. **Market Research Data Analytics in the Manufacturing Sector** – Optimizing inventory and stocking levels and logistics right from raw materials to finished goods. Demand Forecasting, Optimization and Reporting as well as yield analysis, waste control, operator/shift performance, and quality control metrics.

4. **Pharmaceutical Industry** – Interpretation of analytical data in order to facilitate the security of drug systems and drug discovery process, such as claims analysis or clinical trials. Added to this detailed practitioner and hospital drug prescription data analysis for development of effective marketing strategies to hospitals and doctors.

5. **Healthcare Analytics** – Involves medical cost and utilization analyses, Reimbursement modeling, provider profiling, Quality measurement, medical literature research and HIPAA and IT security.

6. **Insurance Data Analytics** – Objective claims assessments, customer analytic profiles, Risk and fraud assessment, evaluation of medical procedures, tests, and drugs. Insurance data analytics also included loss reserving and subrogation solutions.

7. **Telecommunications Analytics** – Customer and campaign analysis to optimize customer linkage with appropriate product delivery strategy. Market Research Data Analytics can be applied to telecommunications management and retention, taking into account data protection and privacy acts.

Global companies such as GE Capital, American Express, Citibank, Prudential Insurance, Accenture and Honeywell, are already benefiting by outsourcing their market research data analysis work to their captive centers in India.

## Outsourcing SWOT Analysis to India

Everyday your business is faced with new challenges, strengths, weaknesses, opportunities and threats. The good thing is, what happens to be a threat for your competitor could turn into a golden opportunity for you. All you need to do is keep your eyes open and take the right action!

SWOT Analysis (Strengths, Weaknesses, Opportunities, Threats) is also known as TOWS analysis. SWOT Analysis is a powerful technique to throw light on your business possibilities. SWOT Analysis helps you chisel out your strategies in a more streamlined manner and create a niche in the market.

### Strengths

- What do people in your market see as your strengths?
- What advantages does your company have?
- What do you do better than your competitors?
- What unique or lowest-cost resources do you have access to?

Look at your strengths in the context of the competition. If you are comparing your product with a competitor who has a large share of the market, your own large share of the market is not a strength but a necessity.

### Weaknesses

- What should you avoid?
- What could you improve?
- What are people in your market likely to see as weaknesses?

You might need to get into your customers' or competitors' shoes to check if there are weaknesses that they perceive but you overlooked. It is more an internal versus an external view.

### Opportunities

- Where are the good opportunities your company could leverage?
- What are the interesting and promising trends you are aware of?

Opportunities could come your way through:

- Changes in the technology you use
- Changes in the market
- Changes in government policies that are relevant to your business
- Changes in your target audience such as lifestyle
- Events in your industry

You can discover new opportunities by analyzing your strengths. You could also look at your weaknesses and think about the potential opportunities opening up if you eliminate your weaknesses.

### Threats

- What obstacles do you face?
- What is your competition doing?
- Is changing technology threatening your position?
- Do you have bad debt or cash-flow problems?

- Could any of your weaknesses seriously threaten your business?
- Are the required specifications for your job, products or services changing?

Such analysis will often throw light on the future course of action, both in terms of putting problems into perspective and pointing out what needs to be done.

Strengths and Weaknesses are internal and Opportunities and Threats relate to external factors.

## Conclusion

The KPO Industry is comprised of a variety of skills. It is this, with a combination of services that delivers an end-to-end solution. No customer says they want a little bit of BPO and a little bit of the KPO. They say they want a complete package. The market for KPO will be huge, but it will always be a subset of BPO. If it does, what can break out of the business process outsourcing structure may be something like legal process outsourcing. This however will always cater to a very niche market. There is room for separate KPOs, but again, it is very niche. There are specific processes that can stand separately, like legal process outsourcing (LPO), architectural design process outsourcing, portfolio analysis and database analysis. The market hasn't even been scratched yet even though these services are nothing new. Some of these services have been around for 10 years, like analytics.

A lot of people seem to think that the KPO industry is merely a fancy name for higher-end call centers. When you look at KPO as an end-to-end process, then there is far more potential. BPOs evolved past call centers five years ago. Generally, it is discussed that talent is a problem that could impede the growth of the industry. It is not only the industry that should be attempting to tackle this. We as a country need to take this up. May be as a public-private partnership with the government. We do invest a lot on training and it still is not enough. No industry can handle the quality of people that are walking in for an interview. For that attention needs to be paid at the high school and college levels. We need to expand the number of colleges and schools in our country. The difference between the qualities of colleges is massive. The gap between the best and the worst colleges is huge-considering the facilities, the level of pay for the faculty. KPOs are very comfortable with Nasscom and does not need a separate body. It was the IT services that set all this up and it was the BPO Industry that jumped onto the bandwagon. However, over time, special needs will emerge for the knowledge process outsourcing industry and these will need to be highlighted and given special attention.

## References

1. www.outsource2india.com/why_india/articles/KPO.asp - 23k -
2. en.wikipedia.org/wiki/**Knowledge_process_outsourcing** - 26k
3. http://consilience.economictimes.com

4. www.evalueserve.com/ – 26k
5. 021's KPO Services
6. www.cyfuture.com/**knowledge-process-outsourcing**.htm - 29k
7. www.rediff.com/cms/print.jsp?docpath=/money/2005/dec/26bpo1.htm - 8k
8. www.indiadaily.com/editorial/4649.asp - 21k -
9. www.b2kcorp.com/services.html - 38k
10. www.iflexsolutions.com/iflex/solutions/KPO.aspx - 44k
11. www.offshoringtimes.com/Pages/2007/BPO_news1616.html
12. www.tcs.com/Services/BPO_KPO.html - 20k
13. www.evalueserve.com/About-Us/KPO.aspx - 35k


***

# 21 Mergers and Acquisitions

## The Overview

Merger is a tool used by companies for the purpose of expanding their operations often aiming at an increase of their long term profitability. Evidence on the success of M&A however is mixed: 50-75% of all M&A deals are found to fail in their aim of adding value.

Usually mergers occur in a consensual (occurring by mutual consent) setting where executives from the target company help those from the purchaser in a due diligence process to ensure that the deal is beneficial to both parties. Acquisitions can also happen through a hostile takeover by purchasing the majority of outstanding shares of a company in the open market against the wishes of the target's board. In the United States, business laws vary from state to state whereby some companies have limited protection against hostile takeovers. One form of protection against a hostile takeover is the shareholder rights plan, otherwise known as the "poison pill".

Historically, mergers have often failed to add significantly to the value of the acquiring firm's shares (King, *et. al.*, 2004). Corporate mergers may be aimed at reducing market competition, cutting costs (for example, laying off employees), reducing taxes, removing management, "empire building" by the acquiring managers, or other purposes which may not be consistent with public policy or public welfare. Thus they can be heavily regulated, for example, in the U.S. requiring approval by both the Federal Trade Commission and the Department of Justice.

## Aquisition

An acquisition can take the form of a purchase of the stock or other equity interests of the target entity, or the acquisition of all or a substantial amount of its assets.

## Types of acquisition

- Jennifer Russell purchases - in a share purchase the buyer buys the shares of the target company from the shareholders of the target company. The buyer will take on the company with all its assets and liabilities.
- Asset purchases - in an asset purchase the buyer buys the assets of the target company from the target company. In simplest form this leaves the target company as an empty shell, and the cash it receives from the acquisition is then paid back to its shareholders by dividend or through liquidation. However, one of the advantages of an asset purchase for the buyer is that it can "cherry-pick" the assets that it wants and leave the assets, and liabilities, that it does not. This leaves the target in a different position after the purchase, but liquidation is nevertheless usually the end result.

The terms "demerger", "spin-off" or "spin-out" are sometimes used to indicate the effective opposite of a merger, where one company splits into two, the 2nd often being a separately listed stock company if the parent was a stock company.

## Classifications of mergers

- *Horizontal mergers* take place where the two merging companies produce similar product in the same industry.
- *Vertical mergers* occur when two firms, each working at different stages in the production of the same good, combine.
- *Conglomerate mergers* take place when the two firms operate in different industries.

A unique type of merger called a reverse merger is used as a way of going public without the expense and time required by an IPO.

The contract vehicle for achieving a merger is a "merger sub".

The occurrence of a merger often raises concerns in antitrust circles. Devices such as the Herfindahl index can analyze the impact of a merger on a market and what, if any, action could prevent it. Regulatory bodies such as the European Commission and the United States Department of Justice may investigate anti-trust cases for monopolies dangers, and have the power to block mergers.

Accretive mergers are those in which an acquiring company's earnings per share (EPS) increase. An alternative way of calculating this is if a company with a high price to earnings ratio (P/E) acquires one with a low P/E.

Dilutive mergers are the opposite of above, whereby a company's EPS decreases. The company will be one with a low P/E acquiring one with a high P/E.

The completion of a merger does not ensure the success of the resulting organisation; indeed, many mergers (in some industries, the majority) result in a net loss of value due to problems. Correcting problems caused by incompatibility—whether of technology, equipment, or corporate culture— diverts resources away from new investment, and these problems may be exacerbated by inadequate research or by concealment of losses or liabilities at one of the partners. Overlapping subsidiaries or redundant staff may be allowed to continue, creating inefficiency, and conversely the new management may cut too many operations or personnel, losing expertise and disrupting employee culture. These problems are similar to those encountered in takeovers. For the merger not to be considered a failure, it must increase shareholder value faster than if the companies were separate, or prevent the deterioration of shareholder value more than if the companies were separate.

## Financing M&A

Mergers are generally differentiated from acquisitions partly by the way in which they are financed and partly by the relative size of the companies. Various methods of financing an M&A deal exist:

### Cash

Payment by cash. Such transactions are usually termed acquisitions rather than mergers because the shareholders of the target company are removed from the picture and the target comes under the (indirect) control of the bidder's shareholders alone.

Financing cash can be borrowed from a bank, or raised by an issue of bonds. Acquisitions financed through debt are known as leveraged buyouts, and the debt will often be moved down onto the balance sheet of the acquired company.

A cash deal would make more sense during a downward trend in the interest rates. Another advantage of using cash for an acquisition is that there tends to lesser chances of EPS dilution for the acquiring company. But a *caveat* in using cash is that it places constraints on the cash flow of the company Hybrids.

An acquisition can involve a combination of cash and debt, or a combination of cash and stock of the purchasing entity.

## Motives Behind M&A

These motives are considered to add shareholder value:

- **Economies of scale:** This refers to the fact that the combined company can often reduce duplicate departments or operations, lowering the costs of the company relative to the same revenue stream, thus increasing profit.
- **Increased revenue/Increased Market Share:** This motive assumes that the company will be absorbing a major competitor and thus increase its power (by capturing increased market share) to set prices.
- **Cross selling:** For example, a bank buying a stock broker could then sell its banking products to the stock broker's customers, while the broker can sign up

the bank's customers for brokerage accounts. Or, a manufacturer can acquire and sell complementary products.

- **Synergy:** Better use of complementary resources.
- **Taxes:** A profitable company can buy a loss maker to use the target's tax write-offs. In the United States and many other countries, rules are in place to limit the ability of profitable companies to "shop" for loss making companies, limiting the tax motive of an acquiring company.
- **Geographical or other diversification:** This is designed to smooth the earnings results of a company, which over the long term smoothens the stock price of a company, giving conservative investors more confidence in investing in the company. However, this does not always deliver value to shareholders (see below).
- **Resource transfer:** resources are unevenly distributed across firms (Barney, 1991) and the interaction of target and acquiring firm resources can create value through either overcoming information asymmetry or by combining scarce resources.
- **Vertical integration:** Companies acquire part of a supply chain and benefit from the resources.
- **Increased Market share, which can increase Market power:** In an oligopoly market, increased market share generally allows companies to raise prices. Note that while this may be in the shareholders' interest, it often raises antitrust concerns, and may not be in the public interest.

These motives are considered to not add shareholder value:

- **Diversification:** While this may hedge a company against a downturn in an individual industry it fails to deliver value, since it is possible for individual shareholders to achieve the same hedge by diversifying their portfolios at a much lower cost than those associated with a merger.
- **Overextension:** Tend to make the organisation fuzzy and unmanageable.
- **Manager's hubris**: Manager's overconfidence about expected synergies from M&A which results in overpayment for the target company.
- **Empire building:** Managers have larger companies to manage and hence more power.
- **Manager's Compensation:** In the past, certain executive management teams had their payout based on the total amount of profit of the company, instead of the profit per share, which would give the team a perverse incentive to buy companies to increase the total profit while decreasing the profit per share (which hurts the owners of the company, the shareholders); although some empirical studies show that compensation is rather linked to profitability and not mere profits of the company.
- **Bootstrapping:** Example: how ITT executed its merger.

## M&A Marketplace Difficulties

No marketplace currently exists for the mergers and acquisitions of privately owned small to mid-sized companies. Market participants often wish to maintain a level of secrecy about their efforts to buy or sell such companies. Their concern for secrecy usually arises from the possible negative reactions a company's employees, bankers, suppliers, customers and others might have if the effort or interest to seek a transaction were to become known. This need for secrecy has thus far thwarted the emergence of a public forum or marketplace to serve as a clearinghouse for this large volume of business.

At present, the process by which a company is bought or sold can prove difficult, slow and expensive. A transaction typically requires six to nine months and involves many steps. Locating parties with whom to conduct a transaction forms one step in the overall process and perhaps the most difficult one. Qualified and interested buyers of multimillion dollar corporations are hard to find. Even more difficulties attend bringing a number of potential buyers forward simultaneously during negotiations. Potential acquirers in industry simply cannot effectively "monitor" the economy at large for acquisition opportunities even though some may fit well within their company's operations or plans.

An industry of professional "middlemen" (known variously as intermediaries, business brokers, and investment bankers) exists to facilitate M&A transactions. These professionals do not provide their services cheaply and generally resort to previously-established personal contacts, direct-calling campaigns, and placing advertisements in various media. In servicing their clients they attempt to create a one-time market for a one-time transaction. Many but not all transactions use intermediaries on one or both sides. Despite best intentions, intermediaries can operate inefficiently because of the slow and limiting nature of having to rely heavily on telephone communications. Many phone calls fail to contact with the intended party. Busy executives tend to be impatient when dealing with sales calls concerning opportunities in which they have no interest. These marketing problems typify any private negotiated markets.

The market inefficiencies can prove detrimental for this important sector of the economy. Beyond the intermediaries' high fees, the current process for mergers and acquisitions has the effect of causing private companies to initially sell their shares at a significant discount relative to what the same company might sell for were it already publicly traded. An important and large sector of the entire economy is held back by the difficulty in conducting corporate M&A (and also in raising equity or debt capital). Furthermore, it is likely that since privately held companies are so difficult to sell they are not sold as often as they might or should be.

Previous attempts to streamline the M&A process through computers have failed to succeed on a large scale because they have provided mere "bulletin boards" – static information that advertises one firm's opportunities. Users must still seek other sources for opportunities just as if the bulletin board were not electronic. A multiple listings service concept has not been applicable to M&A due to the need for confidentiality. Consequently, there is a need for a method and apparatus for efficiently executing M&A

transactions without compromising the confidentiality of parties involved and without the unauthorized release of information. One part of the M&A process which can be improved significantly using networked computers is the improved access to "data rooms" during the due diligence process.

## The Great Merger Movement

The Great Merger Movement happened from 1895 to 1905. During this time, small firms with little market share consolidated with similar firms to form large, powerful institutions that became even market dominating. The vehicles used were so-called Trusts. To truly understand how large this movement was - in 1900 the value of firms acquired in mergers was 20% of GDP. In 1990 the value was only 3% and from 1998-2000 is was around 10-11% of GDP. Organisations that commanded the greatest share of the market in 1905 saw that command disintegrate by 1929 as smaller competitors joined forces with each other.

## Short Run Factors

One of the major short run factors that sparked The Great Merger Movement was the desire to keep prices high. That is, with many firms in a market, supply of the product remains high. During the panic of 1893, the demand declined. When demand for the good falls, as illustrated by the classic supply and demand model, prices are driven down. To avoid this decline in prices, firms found it profitable to collude and manipulate supply to counter any changes in demand for the good. This type of cooperation led to widespread horizontal integration amongst firms of the era. Horizontal integration is when multiple firms responsible for the same service or production process join together. As a result of merging, this involved mass production of cheap homogeneous output that exploited efficiencies of volume production to earn profits on volume. Focusing on mass production allowed firms to reduce unit costs at a much lower rate. These firms usually were capital-intensive and had high fixed costs. Due to the fact of new machines were mostly financed through bonds, interest payments on bonds were high followed by the panic of 1893, yet no firm was willing to accept quantity reduction during this period.

## Long Run Factors

In the long run, due to the desire to keep costs low, it was advantageous for firms to merge and reduce their transportation costs thus producing and transporting from one location rather than various sites of different companies as in the past. This resulted in shipment directly to market from this one location. In addition, technological changes prior to the merger movement within companies increased the efficient size of plants with capital intensive assembly lines allowing for economies of scale. Thus improved technology and transportation were forerunners to the Great Merger Movement. In part due to competitors as mentioned above, and in part due to the government, however, many of these initially successful mergers were eventually dismantled. The government over time grew weary of big businesses merging and created the Sherman Act in 1890, setting rules against price fixing (Section I) and monopolies(Section II). In the modern era, everyone knows of the controversy over Microsoft, but starting in the 1890s with such cases as *U.S. versus Addyston Pipe and Steel Co.* the courts attacked such companies for strategizing with others or within their own companies to maximize profits. Ironically, such acts against price fixing with competitors created a greater incentive for companies to unite and merge under one name so that they were not competitors anymore and technically not price fixing. The Sherman Act is still under debate to this day, ranging from broad to strict to mixed interpretations. There are many varied opinions on whether it is acceptable to dominate a market based on size and resources, and we must wait and see what the courts of the future will conclusively decide.

### Impact of cross-border M&A

In a study conducted in 2000 by Lehman Brothers, it was found that, on average, large M&A deals cause the domestic currency of the target corporation to appreciate by 1% relative to the acquirer's. For every $1-billion deal, the currency of the target corporation increased in value by 0.5%. More specifically, the report found that in the period immediately after the deal is announced, there is generally a strong upward movement in the target corporation's domestic currency (relative to the acquirer's currency). Fifty days after the announcement, the target currency is then, on average, 1% stronger.

## Why Do Mergers and Acquisitions Fail?

Historically, mergers and acquisitions have been considered to be the exclusive domain of economists, market strategists and financial experts. Thus the financial and strategic aspects of merger and acquisition activity have been extensively addressed. However, the human aspects of these transactions have received relatively little attention. Around the world, retention of key talent, integration of cultures and communication were most often rated as critical activities in the integration plan. Yet, only 10 percent of the respondents stated that human resource management received the top priority during integration. And, just five percent of respondents said communication was a priority. Even the most confident employee can feel insecure in a shifting work environment.

## Why M&A Fails?

Studies shows that those responsible for effecting mergers and acquisitions, usually cite a host of economic, strategic or financial reasons when their efforts prove to be unsuccessful. These reasons include the non-achievement of the intended economies of scale anticipated, poor or ill-matched strategic fit or unexpected changes in market conditions, among others. However, research has proved that these rational economic explanations are not sufficient.

Deliberate initiatives have been taken by the researchers to understand and identify the major reasons of failures in M&A as it is a matter of concern. Typical reasons for failure as quoted by Schuler & Jackson (2001) include:

- Expectations are unrealistic
- Hastily constructed strategy, poor planning, unskilled execution
- Failure/inability to unify behind a single macro message
- Talent is lost or mismanaged.
- Power and politics are the driving forces, rather than productive objectives
- Requires an impossible degree of synergy
- Culture clashes between the two entities go unchecked
- Transition management fails
- The underestimation of transition costs
- Financial drain
- Defensive motivation
- Focus of executives is distracted from the core business
- Cultural differences
- Ill-conceived human resource integration strategy.

Out of these reasons, the most important reasons are cultural clashes, gaps or incompatibility and loss of key talents. Generally, it is believed that cultures of two companies could simply be put in a blender and poured out as a new synergistic company. Cultural issues are overlooked and these companies did not realise the implications of cultural differences. Culture concerns the internationalization of a set of values, feelings, attitudes, expectations and the mindsets of the people within an organisation. This culture provides meaning, order and stability to the employees' lives and influences their behavior. The merger of two culturally different organisations could result in conflict during the period immediately following the merger or acquisition. This often results in a decrease in employee morale, anger, anxiety, communication problem and a feeling of uncertainty about the future leading to separation.

Normally, when there is a merger, the decision is taken at the top, primarily by the financial personnel, mostly on the basis of financial parameters which invariably overlook the soft issues like individual difference and cultural mismatch. The matching at the top expects the synergy at the bottom also which in reality does not happen. Instead of synergy there is a culture clash. Even when there is no direct clash, it is most likely that the cultures of the two firms will differ. If not managed properly these differences can grow easily in aversive diversity, causing productivity problems like low levels of trust and co-operation between groups of employees coming from different firms. Each of the former nuclear firms bears its own cultural values, beliefs and assumptions distinguishing it from others, including the new partner, providing employees with a feeling of collective competence, identity and pride. Somehow, it is being experienced that the integration of both the culture hardly takes place, which leads to a 'they' current than 'we' feeling. The pride in the cultural solutions of the old firm, that kept people together, is now partly a function of the distinction towards other firm's solutions to the same problems. These them-and us feelings do not disappear without proper management. In fact, when left alone, they tend to grow into aversive feelings giving rise to a situation of direct confrontation, sometimes triggering a vicious cycle to develop that affects the performance of the new organisation in a negative way. This mechanism, that is highly probable in mergers and acquisitions, is a second way of accounting for the high percentage of failure in these transactions. It is increasingly being realized by progressive organisations that the employees affected by mergers and acquisitions, and the cultures of the combining organisations, are an integral part of the ultimate success or failure of a merger.

The brightest example of cultural clash in Indian set-up is the clash between Proctor & Gamble, Godrej, and BALCO. Godrej being a traditional value based organisation has a strong culture which demands strong values of paying respect to seniors and adopting line of command which is different in P&G and BALCO. As these are multinational organisations, having highly informal work culture. This results in negative thinking and emotions, coupled with employees experiencing difficulty with reconciling their beliefs with the changes brought about by the merger process. This culture shock compels many talents to quit.

Mergers and acquisitions should, thus, be actively managed and integrated on an ongoing basis. Although the HR professional will generally be responsible for managing the HR issues associated with a merger or acquisition, it is prudent for organisations to create a special position for managing the process of merger for fixing responsibility and accountability for the successful management and integration of the process. His/her responsibility should include the management of people processes and integration of the merger or acquisition process. Many organisations, however, still do not view human resources as critical to their M&A strategy, particularly in the early stages. This is ironic, since cultural incompatibility, poor communication and loss of key employees are the main factors that have proved to be the biggest stumbling blocks to a successful M&A transition.

It is turning out to be a case study in the case of Zuari Maroe Phosphates Private Limited ( a joint venture of K.K. Birla's Zuari Industrties and Maroe Phosphates S.A., Morocco) taking over of Paradeep Phosphates Limited (PPL). The company's initiatives in managing the acquisition process have turned out to be a positive one. In eight month's time, PPL's losses were pruned to an average of Rs.3 crores per month. This success was because of changing people's mindset and practices as claimed by the Managing Director of the Company. He also highlighted that the changing operational practices, fine tuning badly maintained plants, balancing equipment, importing efficient technology are not too difficult. It is changing people's thinking and habits that is difficult and makes the difference. The following steps was taken by the company in the post-acquisition phase to manage the apprehensions of the employees:

1. A clear communication from the new management to the employees regarding their commitment to the organisation in-terms of giving their best performance.

2. Management's commitment not to retrench the people of the acquired company and reach an agreement for redeployment.

## Stages of Merger and Acquisition

The experience of several companies in merger and acquisition activities suggest a model of M&A activity that has three stages:

1. Pre-union
2. In-process union
3. Post-union

In these three stages, all the business functions such as business strategy, finance, marketing, IT and operations are important but the most important function is the management of human resource which only can get rest of the functions integrated. The detail HR initiatives to be undertaken in each of the stages are discussed below.

### 1. Pre-union

This is the stage prior to merger and acquisition, during which it is extremely important to understand both the organisations and their people processes.

The first step towards any union is to identify the reasons for which the organisation is interested for merger and acquisition. Once the reasons and priorities are known, a team can be formed to work dedicatedly on due diligence of all areas of M&A. Most companies exercise the diligence in the financial side of things, but fall short when it comes to human capital issues. M&A should expect significant differences in the human resources function, including its position and key strategic objectives and roles, as well as in approaches to human capital-related programmes and processes. The due diligence process must catalogue all risks and differences and then eliminate the difficulty and expense of rationalizing and aligning these practices to successfully motivate the new workforce. Based on the objectives, potential partners should be selected.

Transition teams are used to study and recommend options for combining the two companies in a merger. To discourage decision-making based on personal agenda or policies, human resource professionals who facilitate transition teams should work with team leaders to run effective meetings. This will give all team members an opportunity to contribute their viewpoints.

As the cultural mismatch is the most important factor of failure in any merger and acquisition deal, it is essential to carry out a thorough cultural assessment exercise of both the organisations in terms of philosophies, values and practices. Moreover, a thorough assessment of the human resources issues within the company, including recruitment and manpower planning, employee relations, labour relations, government compliance, compensation and benefit programmes, human resource information systems, training and development, and safety and environmental issues should be undertaken. This audit address areas of potential exposure with recommended action plans once the deal closes.

## 2. In-process union

This is the second stage of M&A activities, which should normally follow just after the completion of the activities of the first stage. In this phase, the basic objective is to have a smooth integration of managing all transitions to address the apprehensions of the people at work. The most critical issue is to select the integration manager who will lead the whole process of implementation. The various roles of the integration manager include serving as a project manager, communicator, advisor, advocate, relationship builder, facilitator, team leader, ombudsman and negotiator.

A new organisational structure must be created considering the business objectives, elimination of redundancy, parallel systems vs merged systems, geographic locations, commitment to the former organisation and market and PR considerations. Once the boxes are drawn, a talent assessment is essential. Candidates for each position should be identified, selections made and offer extended, recognizing that all will not be accepted. The whole restructuring process should be much faster to manage the transition psychology of people. Here the role of the leader is extremely important to place the structure and strategy, managing the change process, retaining and motivating talents, communication with all the stakeholders of the organisation. A lesson learnt by the folks at GE Capital, that greatly aided successful integration was : decisions about management structure, key roles, reporting relationships, layoffs, restructuring and other career affecting aspects of the integration should be made, announced and implemented as soon as possible after the deal is signed ideally within few days. Creeping changes, uncertainty and anxiety that last for months are debilitating and immediately start to drain value from an acquisition (Ashkenas *et. al.*, 2000). This experience of GE has thrown important light towards quick and successful implementation to achieve success. This also invloves changing people at large in a desired direction through drawing a schedule as per the priorities identified and frozen. Kay & Shelton (2000) have identified the people problem in mergers, which were reported in Mckinsey Quarterly. The findings show the percentage of respondents who believe people activity is critical. 76% believe in retention of key talents, 71% in communication, 67% in retention of key managers and 51% in integration of corporate cultures.

Once the organisational chart is in place, there will be vacant positions to fill, either because people have not accepted a position or because there is noty a qualified internal candidate. The company must create a severance plan and retention-bonus programme to manage through the transitional period. These plans should be fair and equitable enough to do what they are designed to do – retain employees. Likewise, the outplacement strategy should take into account the types of employees being affected and how long it m ay take them to find a suitable position.

Once the structure is in place, communication is the key. It is the first step in assimilating employees into a new organisation and the best chance of making them feel good about it. Both individual and group meetings are appropriate to communicate individual employment status as well as the impact on the new organisation. There should also be extensive planning around logistics for those leaving the organisation on the day of the deal. To minimize stress and uncertainty in the organisation during the merger process, it is essential to develop and deliver educational seminars to help employees and managers manage stress, low morale and productivity issues in work groups. These seminars should focus on specific issues affecting employees rather than on change management in general.

## 3. Post-union

Most of the M&A initiatives are failed because of the lack of seriousness during in-process union stage. Faulty action plans, absence of committed HR professionals, lack of involvement of senior management people lead to mismanagement of change process in the organisation. In the post-union phase, the structure and staffing pattern need to be tested in action in terms of value creation in the organisation. The culture, which is emerged out of the combination of both the organisations, should be monitored in line with the objectives set in for the new organisation. When teo companies with vastly different cultures merge, they help management preserve the best aspects of the old company and carry them into the new company. It requires understanding of what cultural characteristics and values should be preserved from the respective companies and what new characteristics need to be added in the new organisation. In this activity, the senior management people should involve themselves seriously. Moreover, continuous assessment and reassessment are required to evolve the right kind of culture to make the people comfortable as well as achieve the ultimate business goal of the organisation.

After the merger is implemented, problems may arise as and when new teams are formed. These teams may experience interpersonal conflict, undefined roles and responsibilities and confusing procedures as leaders move ahead on operational tasks. Thus, a process requires to be created for developing newly formed teams. HR professionals should review this process; and offer to help launch new teams by providing consultation.

Another important issue is the stake holder's concern regarding the performance of the new entity wherein their stake is involved. The HR department needs to develop a transparent communication channel in order to disseminate the information to the stakeholders related to the developments and achievements after the M&A activity. Proper assessment of the concern will give input to devise a better intervention strategy to manage the stakeholders' concerns. The basic principle in this process to be followed is to make all the stakeholders satisfied with the performance of the organisation. Even the feedback of the stakeholders can be taken for interim alterations wherever required. A solid communication plan can make the difference between instability and ndependability for the employees who are the important stakeholders.

The new entity should learn from the entire process to build up the strength to avail the competitive advantage. The new company must emerge with a unified approach to human resource issues. Policies should be reviewed, created, implemented and communicated companywide to ensure understanding. Compensation and benefit packages must be reviewed, merged, shopped and communicated. Staffing and